OF THE SUBLIME:
PRESENCE IN QUESTION

SUNY Series, Intersections: Philosophy and Critical Theory
Rodolphe Gasché and Mark C. Taylor, editors

OF THE SUBLIME:
PRESENCE IN QUESTION

❀

Essays by

Jean-François Courtine
Michel Deguy
Éliane Escoubas
Philippe Lacoue-Labarthe
Jean-François Lyotard
Louis Marin
Jean-Luc Nancy
Jacob Rogozinski

❀

translated and with an Afterword by
Jeffrey S. Librett

STATE UNIVERSITY OF NEW YORK PRESS

1993

originally published in French as *Du Sublime*
Par Jean-François Courtine, Michel Deguy, Éliane Escoubas, Philippe Lacoue-Labarthe,
Jean-François Lyotard, Louis Marin, Jean-Luc Nancy, Jacob Rogozinski
© Editions Belin, Paris 1988

Published by
State University of New York Press, Albany

© 1993   State University of New York

For information, address State University of New York
Press, State University Plaza, Albany, NY 12246

Production by Christine Lynch
Marketing by Dana E. Yanulavich

Library of Congress Cataloging-in-Publication Data

Du sublime. English.
    Of the Sublime: Presence in Question: essays / by Jean
 -François Courtine ... [et al.] : translated and with an afterword
 by Jeffrey S. Librett.
        p. cm. — (SUNY series, Interactions)
    Translation of: Du sublime.
    Includes bibliographical references.
    ISBN 0–7914–1379–9 (alk. paper). — ISBN 0–7914–1380–2 (pbk. :
 alk. paper)
    1. Sublime, The.   I. Courtine, Jean-François. II. Title.
 III. `Series: Interactions (Albany, N.Y.)
 BH301.S7D813   1993
 111'.85—dc20
                                                          91–9447
                                                             CIP

10 9 8 7 6 5 4 3 2

CONTENTS

❀

NOTE ON THE TRANSLATION

❀

I have attempted in the translations below to find some middle ground between an excessive proximity to the French and an excessive proximity to idiomatic American English. If I have erred, as is my own impression, in the direction of preserving to excess the syntactical letter of the originals, I can only hope that the effect of estrangement thereby generated is in some non-trivial way related to the kind of disorientation characteristic of the sublime.

With respect to quotations from German texts in general, I have checked the French translations against the German originals and existing English translations, referring to the English editions in the notes, but frequently providing my own translations of these passages in the attempt to find some reasonable compromise between readability, fidelity to the German, and fidelity to the French editions quoted by the authors of these essays.

In the case of Kant, where applicable and unless otherwise indicated, the references given parenthetically in the text provide the section number (§), followed by the page number of the French edition, and then by the page number of the English edition. The German edition consulted was the *Werkausgabe*, ed. Wilhelm Weischedel (Frankfurt am Main: Suhrkamp Verlag, 1975). The French editions cited, unless otherwise indicated, are: *Critique de la raison pure*, trans. A. Tremesaygues and B. Pacaud (Paris: Presses universitaires de France, 1986); *Critique de la raison pratique*, trans. J. Gibelin (Paris: Vrin, 1983); *Critique de la faculté de juger*, trans. A. Philonenko (Paris: Vrin, 1986); and *Première introduction à la Critique de la faculté de juger*, trans. Guillernit (Paris: Vrin, 1975). The English editions cited are: *Critique of Pure Reason* (abbreviated CPR), trans. Norman Kemp Smith (New York: St. Martin's Press, 1965); *Critique of Practical Reason* (CPrR), trans. Lewis White Beck (Chicago: University of Chicago Press, 1949); and *Critique of Judgment* (CJ), trans. J. H. Bernard (New York: Collier Macmillan Publishers, 1951). In the case of references to the first version of the introduction to the *Critique of Judgment*, the English edition referred to is the translation by Werner S. Pluhar (Indianapolis: Hackett Publishing Co., 1987) and is abbreviated CJI. These abbreviations are omitted when it is clear from the context which work is being cited.

In the case of Heideggerian vocabulary, I have generally translated "l'être" (German: "das Sein") as "Being" and "l'étant" (German: "das Seiende") as "the being."

The few translator's notes I have added are in each case formulated in such a way that they are obviously my own. I have therefore dispensed with any further indication that they are not the original authors' notes.

I am grateful to the authors of the essays translated here for the time they took to discuss their essays with me in the summer of 1989. I am grateful also to Loyola University Chicago for a Summer Research Award in 1989 which helped finance this work. I am indebted further to David Williams for his assistance in the preparation of the references, to Geert Van Cleemput for his assistance with the quotations from the Greek, and to the patience of Carola Sautter of SUNY Press and the editors of this series. The translations are dedicated to Paula Librett and to the memory of Irving Librett.

PREFACE TO THE FRENCH EDITION

❀

Jean-Luc Nancy

A Being beyond all beauty...the sublime.

—Benjamin

One may be tempted to imagine that our epoch is rediscovering the *sublime*, its name, concept, or questions. But clearly, this is by no means the case, for one never returns to any prior moment in history. The sublime is not so much what we're going back to as where we're coming from. Ever since Boileau's translation of and commentary upon Longinus, aesthetics, or the thought of art—but also thought insofar as it is provoked by art—has not ceased to pursue, either explicitly or implicitly, the question of the sublime. One could demonstrate this without difficulty throughout the entire modern and contemporary history of art, aesthetics, and philosophy. The sublime properly constitutes our *tradition* (in aesthetics at the very least, but then this restriction already entangles us in some of the questions which are today tied to the sublime). The tradition passes on [*La tradition* transmet]. What it passes on to us in the name of the sublime is not *an* aesthetics. It is above all not an aesthetics of the grandiose, the monumental, or the ecstatic, with which the sublime is often confused—admittedly not without certain historical reasons, which must be handled with discretion, even as this all-too-heavy word *sublime* must perhaps gradually be effaced. The tradition passes on the aesthetic as question. Which means nothing other than: sensible presentation as question.

   Sensible presentation is a question (and it requires this phrase, "sensible presentation," the unperceived tautology of which already contains, in a sense, the whole problem) to the extent that thought is organized around the motif of *representation*, which is by definition nonsensible (at least as long as it is still necessary to speak in these terms). Representation constitutes the instance of the "object" for that thought which is fundamentally the thought of the "subject"—that is, for philosophy conceived as the dominant structure and matrix through which the West, as such, understands itself.

1

Representation is articulated in terms of conformity and signification. But presentation puts into play the event and the explosion of an appearing and disappearing which, considered in themselves, cannot conform to or signify anything. This explosive event is what the tradition passes on to us in the names of beauty and/or sublimity. From the moment when representation comes to know itself to be such and comes *to present itself* as such (that is, also to criticize, distance, deconstruct, or destroy itself), a moment which constitutes the history of modern art and thought, it takes up at unknown cost a question—at once traditional and unheard of—of presentation.

The question of the sublime is passed on and down to us as the question of *presentation*. In this collection, the reader will encounter diverse states or orders of presentation (discourse, the summons of appearance, offering, truth, limit, communication, feeling, world, thunder-bolt, etc.). I shall not attempt to (re)establish their unity. They are not diverse figures or denominations of a single essence. It will no doubt become clear that the question of presentation is the question of what is at play at the limit of the essence: thus, at the limit of what is more "essential" to art than its essence as "art" itself, just as the sublime is more "essential" to beauty than the very essence of the beautiful. It is also therefore a matter of something that overflows art in art itself, or of something that overflows from out of art, and puts into communication or contact all instances of presentation (for example, history, community, sense, politics, thought, and even representation, which is itself also one of these instances).

We have no intention of gradually aestheticizing all of existence. Quite the contrary. If the essays in this collection have one common trait, it is that they concede nothing to aestheticism. But the question of presentation is, in fact, nothing other than the question of existence (should one say: sensible existence?) as such. If you like: the question of *being-in-the-world*.

Is it this question that we pursue through considerations on the "sublime"? Not unlikely. At least it is worth putting such a question to the test—by attempting today, some thoughts of the sublime.

This collection arises out of the series "Analytic of the Sublime" published in the journal, *Po&sie* between 1984 and 1986, to which four other essays have been added.

The order adopted here attempts to correspond to a certain thematic distribution of the texts: first, Michel Deguy's study of Longinus (*Poétique*, vol. 58); then the essays that take as their object sublime presentation itself (Jean-Luc Nancy, Éliane Escoubas, Philippe Lacoue-Labarthe—*Po&sie*, vol. 30, 32, and 38). Next, the texts that specify the sublime in accordance with an object or end: those of Jean-François Lyotard (here different from his article in *Po&sie*, vol. 34) and Jacob Rogozinski (also a previously unpublished article), which expressly links up with Lyotard's; Jean-François Courtine's study (which appeared not as part of the original series in *Po&sie*, vol. 37) of the place of the sublime at the heart of German Idealism; and Louis Marin's (*Po&sie*, vol. 33), which no longer concerns a discourse of the sublime, but a "sublime figuration."

March 1987

Chapter 1

❀

THE DISCOURSE OF EXALTATION (Μεγαληγορειν): CONTRIBUTION TO A REREADING OF PSEUDO-LONGINUS

Michel Deguy

Gush, pond, —Foam, roll over the bridge and over the
woods; —black sheets and organs, —lightning flashes
and thunder, —mount and roll; —waters and sadnesses,
mount and raise the floods anew.

—Arthur Rimbaud, "Après le déluge"[1]

In the epilogue, which is perhaps dissimulated by being placed nearly at the center of his great book,[2] Ernst Robert Curtius suddenly raises a plaintive cry over the fortune Longinus has suffered. He emphasizes what one is tempted to call the "absolute" singularity of that work of unknown authorship—for "Longinus" is a kind of pseudonym—Περὶ Ὕψους, which we know in its badly translated title as *Of the Sublime*.[3] To be sure, what Curtius quotes from this work consists in stereotypical formulae on *elevation* and *grandeur*, and expresses nothing other than the pure enigma of grandeur insofar as it remains a mystery. And yet, it is as if Curtius—after all those years of erudition, of the endless quotation of quotations—were to negate his life's work with a strangely hasty gesture of dismissal: "Across two millenniums we breathe [in Pseudo-Longinus] the breath of life, not the mold of schools and libraries. The appearance of this unknown Greek in the first century of our era has something miraculous about it" (399). However, the anonymous author's book has remained as good as lost and unread, always in reserve: it "has never found a congenial spirit" (400)—except perhaps in Curtius himself, although he does not explicitly develop his own reading in any detail. The great reconstructive genealogist of the tradition rather incredibly goes on to say: "'Longinus' was strangled by that unbreakable chain, the tradition of mediocrity. Is that tradition perhaps the strongest support of literary continuity?" (400)— and to hell with Boileau! Curtius says next to nothing further of this lost book and this unpaid debt. I evoke them here through him as the memory of what is more than simply antiparody but rather the very paradigm of nonparody, a thought in search of *the high*, a thought attempting to draw all thought toward *the high*. But what is *the high*?

The intact originality of a missing or forgotten work such as Περὶ Ὕψους (Curtius speaks of the "conspiracy of silence") is due to the fact that this work has managed to avoid being appropriated and capitalized on, that it has managed to get lost, that it has maintained itself and still maintains itself on the brink of disappearance. Chance and precariousness do not cease to mark its history. Thus, the values of fragility, contingency, and perishability—not the inverse—are present side by side here with a singular species of originality.

Is the antithesis between the base fortune of misrecognition, the hidden life of the book of the *sublime*, and its high purpose, its discourse, which is the "discourse of exaltation" (μεγαληγορειν) is this antithesis merely the effect of a contrary chance, a misadventure, or is it a sign intimately related to the very nature of the sublime "thing" itself, a "thing" that would necessarily defy interpretation as the most elevated peak discourages and defies ascent? Obscurity does not simply befall exalted language by chance. Rather, its diverted course, its caricatural deformation, *grandiloquence*, mocking its semblance with a mask, dissimulates it fatally, even more successfully than simple ignorance or forgetfulness, leaving the enigma of its elevation to be resolved, according to Curtius, by *us*.

Of the High

So the author of Περὶ Ὕψους is not the familiar friend of Zenobia, Queen of Palmyra, who was put to death. He has become the anonymous: Pseudo-Longinus. Although we know almost nothing of his life, we do know from his book that he lived in the first century, in the de-paganized Roman Empire—Pan was dead and buried—and at a distance of centuries from the Homeric world where, as he nostalgically recounts, there had still been intercourse between gods and men. He was deprived of gods, then, but on familiar terms with Homer. And the question of the *sublime* was doubtless first of all an attempt to measure the decline of the Orient, to measure the author's distance from the time of gods and heroes when nature had still been a temple of living heroic pillars. The *sublime* was the word and the thought with which to evaluate the greatness of Homer, his speech of grandeur or exalted discourse (μεγαληγορευειν) which had been the first song of humanity. Given that Homer is *the sublime*, what can we modern latecomers do to rival in a mimetic struggle the

Elevated Model, where we will always be worsted, but where our relative greatness will be measurable by the honorability of our defeat?[4]

The sublime measures our failure. If it is a *sacred* relation to the *divine* that constitutes the sublime,[5] then our failure will be equivalent to our distance from the sacred, or to our unbelief, our incapacity to navigate through the straits of the difference (κρίσις) between immortal and mortal.

Is the *sublime*, then, an *aesthetic* category motivated by mere nostalgia? Does it express the wistful longing to remain at least capable of gauging the elevation of the source, of thinking the unity of the measure and the measure of the unity that would permit us to judge the utterances and written works of the ancients and the moderns? Is it a category our extreme distance of twenty centuries ought to make us regard with suspicion, although we admire a belief we nonetheless no longer want and which functions a bit like an alibi?

Perhaps, then, the fascinated relation of Curtius to Pseudo-Longinus (and this was, in my case, the motivation for the reading) is the aggravated repetition (as "homology") of Pseudo's relation to Homer. Are we so far from the high origin that we can no longer even read the book *Of the High,* which measured its own distance from the source? How forgetful we have become, derivative, and dispersed!?

We have no choice but to respond in some way to ancient beliefs, to transpose them for ourselves. Pseudo-Longinus is not so much an author who enviously respects the gods of Homer while dissimulating his disbelief, as rather one who looks at the past in order to reestablish through his own discourse some hope of a truly exalted discourse, precisely *for* the generation that follows him: the Treatise *Of the High* is a letter to young Terentianus. The others are not merely those who have preceded us.

In a certain sense, his interest is the "phenomenological" interest in a return to the things themselves, in this case, insofar as they are those things that had a meaning for one's ancestors, a return which inclines toward what has been and a return which is carried out for the sake of a tradition or a culture by means of a reading of past utterances. Reading him, we pose ourselves the same question he poses himself when he quotes Homer: what is "divine transport"? In doing so, it would be inappropriate for us to despair and to reduce the parameters of our world under the pretext that we no longer believe as they did. Rather, we must simply attempt to translate, through the exertions of our discourse, what can be comprehended of their experience in order to transmit our own.

Homer

Thus, we are confronted with "Homer." In the beginning, as at the end, Homer is there, the master as well as the meter of the sublime.

One of the definitions of the sublime tells us (Κεῖται τὸ μὲν ὕψος ἐν διάρματι [XII, 1; 75]) that it consists in the διαίρειν: the ravishment that makes one pass on; a movement of being carried away, traversal, uplifting, transport (of which the Greek word μεταφορά expresses one of the modes). But in the case of Homer, the measure is given by the gods: τὴν ὁρμὴν αὐτῶν κοσμικῷ διαστήματι καταμετρεῖ (IX, 5; 55). The divine is the transport that measures the cosmic diasteme. The cosmos and the impetuous gods measure each other reciprocally. And Homer, chiasmically crossing gods and men, has given to the latter their primordial measure. "When he recounts the wounds of the gods, their quarrels, their vengeance, their tears, their imprisonment in bonds of relation, their passions of all sorts, Homer seems to me to have made, as well as he could, the men who were at the seige of Troy into gods, and to have made the gods into men" (IX, 5; 55–56).

The End

The conclusion of the book furnishes us, as always, with what we ought not to forget in rereading it. It offers us the commencement of our reading.

We ought not to ignore the fact that it is a letter to a precise addressee. The end of this letter is an ethicopolitical end, at the center of whose nostalgic teaching is this: that it is such a shame "when mortal man wonders utterly at his own bloated parts and neglects to develop what is deathless" (XLIV, 8; 230).[6] What does ὑπεραίρω mean: to "exceed," to overhang all things human (ἀνθρώπινα)? It is a matter of life and death, the gods are "immortals," and the exhortation to the sublime commits us to establishing a relation with what exceeds all perishing, with what is not mortal.

The place where the most powerful insistence of this thought makes itself felt is in one of those passages where the author reiterates what one must understand by our *nature:*

> she [nature] implants into our souls an invincible erotic passion for all that is great [τοῦ μεγάλου] and more demonic [δαιμονιωτέρου] than we. For just this reason not even the entire cosmos taken together can cope with the thrust of human theorizing and percep- tiveness, but man's intentness on perceiving often everywhere goes out beyond the limits of what holds him in, and if anyone gaze around at life in its cycle, he will swiftly understand for what pur- pose we were born, by seeing how much what is "too much" and great and fine holds more advantage in all things…what is contrary to opinion is over and over again wonderful. (XXXV, 2–3; 174–78)

The *critical*, ultimate pinnacle of the *high* is the pinnacle on which the partition between mortal and immortal is made anew. A "life" that does not revolt against its mortality, seeking instead the figure and flourishing of the nonmortal, is not "worthy of being lived."

The pinnacle of sublimity to which one must raise oneself in order to get a view (a view "of the whole," i.e. a symbolic view) is named, among other ways, thus: "Those who are capable of it, are all above the mortal....The high lifts these men almost to the greatness of mind of divinities" (XXXVI, 1; 181).

To elevate oneself to this *high* which was translated by sublime is to carry oneself to the place from which one can get a view of the "mortal condition," to this perspective that is *like* the divine. From this light ledge, the *height* of the high, which is *like* a beyond, one can attain a totalizing and "symbolic" view of living-and-dying and find the equivalent of its enigma in a *word*, the *word of the end*, the word for us, the survivors of the arrival of the death that neither hides itself nor shows itself but gives sense (σημαίνει) and *ciphers rhythm* in *numbers* and *formulae*. *Hyperbole* is the movement by which thought ravishes itself to attain all at once this elevated point. Hyperbole is a flight of discourse, as distinct from *amplificatio*, which is the movement of thought dilating itself in order to reunite and to succeed by abundance. A view, a perspective, is always *like* a view, always a quasi view of what is not visible and has only the visible in which to appear (or has only appearance in which to exist). What is sensible (to the view, to the naked eye) is the medium of transport or translation, the place where what is not visible transposes itself. Metaphor is what originally brings to visibility the figure of what is not visible.

The Theme, the Thesis: Death and the Sublime

What do Pseudo-Longinus's examples talk about? On what, on which themes do they posit their thesis?

In the majority of cases,[7] it is a question of death. The mortal condition and the moment of perishing are always at stake when the *sublime* appears. The sublime is the concentration, the start of the startling that weighs in speech against death. The genre of this speech could be multiplied by a typology: benedictions or maledictions that fall back on the living as they echo off the walls of tombs, hyperboles of the improvised epitaph, defiances, supplications, greetings, oaths, enigmas, execrations, sarcasms, or what the Latins call *de-votio*.

The sublime is the ephemeral immortality of the point gained, adverse speech snatched from death[8] where the totality of becoming-and-passing-away concentrates itself. Sublimity at once belongs to the mortal curve and surmounts it, overhangs it tangentially like a remarkable "turning point" [*point de rebroussement*], a pineal apex where the body is united with and suspends itself in the soul, a utopia of infinitesimal weightlessness as at the labile peak of the highest leap. Nothing remains "in the air," and the fall away from the sublime is fatal.[9] The dead man inters himself and descends—lost—"from the other side."

Perhaps the only *present* is at this moment, "snatched from the order of time," as Proust will say, the present of salvation. In the *Inferno*, all the punished whom Dante visits are rendered contemporaries by virtue of these "sublime" utterances they repeat forever beyond the tomb, fixed in the moment when they chose their damnation. The poet is the witness who passes on the legacy of their eternal final word. The witness—poet, historian, novelist—has heard the supplication at the implacable knees of death. He inscribes its trace on the gravestone of the page.

"Too Heavy," Porthos cried. "Up to the two of us now..." "*Mehr Licht...*" The moment becomes the final moment by means of the speech of the end as received legacy.

There is always, then, a relation between the sublime and the testamentary. Sublime words are words of the end. And the examples of the anonymous one speak incessantly of death.

The *ultimate* is what is at once failure and promise, abandonment and salvation—salvation, that is, for the others. The dying one who says the word of the end carries it away, into the too-late. He is vanquished, but in passing down a speech that can be taken up again. And so—death, where is your victory?—this is the password, the schema of the sublime. One does battle with a disproportion (Pascal) which is ruinous but nonetheless defeated in being musically transfigured. That which levels us in any case is equalled by a speech which constitutes a work. Under certain conditions, defeat with no tomorrow is not defeat. The "ruinous" relation is reversed, something surmounts the "end" by making it pass on and serve as a recommencement: a sublime point of time of double value. The definitive becomes transmissible. The event requires a witness. The addressee is the witness, and speech is the element in which transmissibility can be transmitted. The witness hears, receives, entrusts to language; he takes up speech "on the lips of the dying," in order to promise to "realize" it. He will fail to "realize" it and will transmit in his turn to the survivor the transmutation of his failure.

Interlude

I ask myself what one might learn from music about the sublime, what one might learn from the sublime rendered audible.

What does one mean today when one makes use of the category of the sublime? In what consists for example the sublimity of Schumann's Quintet opus 44?[10] From music one learns yet another sense of the sublime.

It is a *funeral march* with a warmth and a reascending momentum which seem to promise an esape from death; as if these tones led to some way out in the direction of their ascent, although we know well-enough that the summit is a dead end. And so we seek the way out while ascending toward a dead end "summit." We *act as if* the direction of the summit revealed some way out. The elevated point is that from which I get a glimpse of the *land as promised land*, in complete knowledge of the *as if*. He glimpses the promised land as that into which one does not enter; he experiences "in passing on" the revelation of a liberty that will not come to pass in the form of a possession but rather in the being-"liberated" into the possibility of relating to what there is *as* to the promised land. In their turn, they will understand only by passing this music on in their passing on. "Sublime" music provides a movement, the schema of a movement of revelation. This revelation is not a trap, for it is merely the revelation of the *as*, of relating to what is by means of the as. What is is that which appears on behalf of what is.

The sublime work is an *ark* crossing the flood for those—the images of those—who will come after.

A beautiful disorder is an effect of art, Boileau once said, summarizing what he thought he had learned from "Longinus" about the *sublime*. The tradition justified the "disordered" character of the *treatise* on the Sublime by means of the homology—itself a theoretical criterion of the sublime—between the thing in question (the sublime) and the question of the thing (the treatise).

The "sublime" has the character of the *same* transgressing *difference*, carrying away the differences, and par excellence *the* difference par excellence, that is, the difference which divides saying from what it says (the difference between λέγειν and τι, to take up the terms of the Aristotelian definition of speech: λέγειν τι κατά τινος); the "sublime" has the character of the sameness of the Same, extending resemblance on both sides of the dividing bar[11] now surmounted and floating one more instant adrift. The deluge, the sublime, simulates the origin in reproducing it and reproduces it in simulating the origin, the simplicity of the origin, dissimulating still, reserving the diversity of multiplicity, turning itself "inside out" as it hides and "makes one forget" the division one of whose names is the division between φύσις and τέχνη. The reascension to the postulated sameness can only be accomplished in the *re* (reproduction, repetition), in the knowledge of the difference and the awareness of the *mechanisms* (ruses, turns of phrase and pen: "technique") for feigning forgetfulness of difference and its differentiations.

How does one repair and heal? How does one render forgotten the unforgettable division, separation, and abstraction of things, things which have "fallen apart" (*auseinandergefallen sind*), as a Hegelian might say, such as—among others—"nature" (φύσις) and art (τέχνη)? In order to pursue this problematic, one would have to develop its homology with the theological (and then moral) schema of the loss of innocence.

The complex, intricate, and digressive aspect of Pseudo-Longinus's text—permeated by differences between the announced plan and the actual composition of these pages in a document that has been ignored by history, and a document the contingent lacunae of which increase *for us* the difficulty of reading—has to do with the obscurity of the matter in question, the matter of σύνθεσις "itself." Ἐν δὲ τοῖς μάλιστα μεγεθοποιεῖ τὰ λεγόμενα, καθάπερ τὰ σώματα, ἡ τῶν μελῶν σύνθεσις: "above all of that which renders great speech as well as bodies, it is the episynthesis of the members." (XL,5). Is it possible to reconstitute, describe, and understand this force which, as unification, cuts across multiplicity, fits together the *figural* diversifications of discourse in its individual instances, this force from which proceeds its tropological swarming? Does the sublime summarize this point where a spring (πηγή) is allegorized, the source of the five sources of the ὑψηγορία? (Ἐπεὶ δε πέντε, ὡς ἂν εἴποι τις, πηγαί τινές εἰσιν αἱ τῆς ὑψηγορίας γονιμώ-ταται...) (VIII, 1; 45ff).

In order to summarize the course of the treatise—before insisting on certain points—and to intrigue today's reader, I will adopt the manner of an *exhaustive* list of a chapter's contents from a book out of the eighteenth-century:

Trope *by means of which our natures are given a dose of grandeur. Not persuasion, but ecstasy; the thunderbolt. But is this not innate, without* τέχνε? *Like Socrates, rather, the Author believes that this comes from a* τέχνε, *which can be taught. Only art can reveal* nature *as foundation. It is a matter of avoiding mistakes; speech of the great is not grandiloquence—swollen diction, etc., to be avoided. Diagnosis of the true sublime. Enumeration of sublime things; just as what can be regarded from on high* (ὑπεροράω) *is not sufficient (a dominating perspective provides the criterion), so for works; psyche can by its nature elevate itself; what elevates it, what its nature waits upon, is* τω ὕψος; *it appropriates for itself what it receives. The sublime is what produces unanimity; thus it is objectivity. There are five sources of the sublime:* νόησις, πάθος, πλάσις *of the schemas, genuine* φράσις, σύνθεσις; *the first two are of nature, the three others are of* τέχνη. *The measure of divine things is in Homer: a reciprocal measure of divine force and the cosmic diasteme—example—*αὔξησις *(amplification) is not elevation* (διαρμα). *Of imitation—We are the last of the series that leads from the divine inspiration of the Pythian and Homer to the ancients and the moderns—Of images,* φαντασίαι, εἰδωλοποιίαι *which render visible; their relation to* πάθος; *the difference between prose and poetry—schemas or figures that supplement the imagination on the oblique path of orators—Reciprocal support of the sublime and figures: a matter of* λήθη; *examples of intonation as grammatical figure—Of figures: parataxis, apposition, asyndeton, symmory of figures; conjunctions, hyperboles, polyptotes; hypallages; metathesis; periphrases; metaphors. Distinction between quantity* (ἀριθμός) *and greatness* (μέγεθος). *Redefinition of the nature of the soul in terms of its love for what is more demoniacal than we; it surpasses the* κόσμος. *Example of Vulcan. To elevate oneself above the mortal* *condition—metaphor, repetition, hyperboles, ἀντίδοσις—the fifth part or σύν-θεσις; rhythm or harmony, music of words, melopoeia. Attention to abjection; of political liberty, of the debasement of morals, conclusion.*

Pseudo-Longinus treats not the relation between rhetoric and persuasion but the relation between the "stupefying" (θαυμάσιον) and "ecstasy" (ἔκστασις). There is a power of discursive abduction that overcomes all obstacles,[12] all ἐφ᾽ ἡμῖν (I, 4; 9), all that "which depends on us." The question is whether there is an art of teaching this access to the dimension of βάθος and of ὕψος (of the profound and the elevated), a τέχνη, a μέθοδος (II, 2; 12). Thus, Pseudo-Longinus interweaves two main threads: (1) he reminds his reader that the sublime exists, that there is this *high* in things to the level of which the λόγος of a Being who is "by nature *logical*" ought to elevate itself, and (2) he teaches his reader how this *can* be done.

The sublime is what provokes unanimity—and Paul Valéry is faithful to the spirit of Pseudo-Longinus when he has M. Teste say: "the sublime simplifies them." Power in speech (τῷ λέγειν δύναμις) (VIII, 1; 45), poorly translated in Lebègue's French as "oratorical talent") is that which is capable of harmonizing speech with sublime things, of raising the psyche up to its natural place, which is at once the high and the profound, traversing and surmounting differences and diversity. The relation of the sublime to the "Whole" (δια παντὸς καὶ πᾶσιν), which our classics will subsequently call the uni-versal and which characterizes our "innate disposition" or our "nature," is realized through and in the λόγος, and it is teachable. The text remarks the connection between the constitutive passivity of a nature (γενναῖον πάθος) and the megalegorical, the "great-in-discourse" (μεγαλήγορος). Πάθος, our affectable nature, our "sensible intuition," can achieve the *great* in its speech, provided that τέχνη, categorical activity, ally itself synthetically with this pathos, (re)producing elevated discourse through the *schematism* of figures: the sublime thing attains to speech and takes place in the "poem."

The order of figures or the figural is a *schematism*: it lends figure to that which would otherwise have no figure; it con-figures speech with that which is spoken. To speak of *schematism* is to speak of a principle of *unification* of the manifold, a mode of unfolding of unity, but of a unity that cannot be thematized apart from the play of contrasted manifoldness in which it unfolds. To speak of schematism is to speak of a *constitutive* activity: not of an easy classification after the fact, but of what makes both speech and the thing to be spoken attain speech—in *dia-llel*; it is with this highest possibility of gathered-gathering speech, as rare as it is, that the norm—i.e., excellence—manifests itself, and it is the "inferior" rest which is the exception, not the inverse.

The high (ὕψος) is a question of (re)ascent. That to which thought (re)ascends is indivisibly the origin, unity, the elevated. The problematic of (re)ascension is a problematic of *logic* or, as one will later say, reason (which always asks itself how it got where it is, that is, always begins in an experience of disappointment, deception, profusion, and the will to understand the inextricable through that which has "caused" it). This problematic overvalues what comes before it, longs for it nostalgically, wants to relate itself to it, both in order to understand and in order to reproduce by "imitation" its inimitable eventuation. The passage from the multiple to the one—gathering—is analogous to the passage from the low to the elevated. The view from on high (μετεωρολογία) is synoptic. The problematic of *(re)ascension* or "the origin" schematizes or figures itself in accordance with the image of the *high*, the return to the source, the (re)unification of the manifold. The *high* is what dominates by gathering, holds gathered from above and "behind." Images of the source of the river or of the fire above (volcano). Unity, anteriority, and height—or synthesis, a priority, and elevation—are held together, maintained as co-conceivable, by the configuration which compares them reciprocally: schematization by images. Unification, ascension, and palingenesis *say* one another (not in parallel but) in *dia-llel* metaphors.

The main difficulty of the text resides in the question of the articulation or σύνθεσις ("synthesis," a recurrent term, bears the burden of this theme) of the "autogenous" with the artificial (τέχνη). The modulation of the schemas (τῶν σχημάτων πλάσις), or the plastic schematism, is this technical supplement, this leavening of the innate disposition which makes speech rise to the ecstatic (ἔκστασις) heights of the sublime. The difficulty of the text has to do with this: that at each subordinate level of the analysis, there is a local synthesis which is always already implicated in a more radical or "general" synthesis. For example, the "schematism" includes the original utterance (γενναία φράσις), which can be analyzed into the choice of nouns and tropical lexis, of which, in turn, there must therefore also be a synthesis (VIII, 1; 45–50).

Synthesis

Let us start again.

There is multiplicity or manifoldness; hence, there are ingredients, components, compositions of parts for and in a whole. And yet no part, none of the components, ought to be valid or to validate itself for itself. One must indeed speak of each separately, analyze it in order to understand and reconstitute it, but—and this is the paradox—the (necessary) part is not sufficient if it is "self-sufficient," if it believes itself to suffice (to itself).

The whole: the relation of the sublime to the whole characteristic of our innate disposition or *nature* accomplishes itself in the λόγος, and as we have seen, this is teachable. However, it is *transport* which, "carrying the whole away," somehow grants being to *the whole*. The sublime in discourse, the discourse of exaltation, will have the form of the carried away, of rapture. The goal (the excellence to be attained) is in general *to resolve* all the parts through a movement, a carrying away that renders their unity heard and understood anew—through a τέχνη, therefore, that gathers together φύσις and τέχνη. The "whole," which exists only through its composition, is at play in each of its parts, in each of its levels. The whole is at stake in each part, the part includes the whole.[13] For the anonymous author, then, it is a matter of contriving a (re)unification of complementary opposites in each "moment."

There are five sources of ὑψηγορία, chapter VIII instructs, and the fifth, which encloses all the others within itself, not being a part like the others, is synthesis: ἡ ἐν ἀξιώματι καὶ διάρσει σύνθεσις (Lebègue translates this as "organization in view of the dignity and elevation of style"; one could translate it: synthesis in judgment and elevation). Forty pages further on, in chapter XXXIX, we read: the fifth of the parts which are "syn-telic for the High" is ἡ διὰ τῶν λόγων αὐτῶν ποιὰ σύνθεσις: synthesis across the λόγοι. Here it will be a question of harmony and rhythm, of what Ezra Pound will call μελοποιία (XXXIX, 3; 196–98).

Locally, that is, as "fifth part," synthesis will be characterized as a question of rhythm, but at the same time, synthesis is *in general* the unification of all parts, including the fifth. Fatally, the author appeals here to the organic comparison: what makes for greatness (μεγεθοποιεῖ) in verbal matters is, as with bodies, "the episynthesis of the members." Unity is unity of proportion, "the completion in a system of each by the others" (πάντα δὲ μετ᾽ ἀλλήλων ἐκπληροῖ τέλειον σύστημα, XI, 1; 73)—and not at all, of course, in the sense of quantitative extension but rather of *proper measure*. This is why *rhythm too* should not be heard "on its own"; it ought not to uncover itself, or more precisely, it ought not to tap out a cadence without concern for the matter at hand or, as we would say, for the "sense."

The general construction can be divided into two levels: the level of the five ingredients (one of which is the synthesis that is immanent to this level) and the level of their synthetic ordering as union of φύσις and τέχνη.

synthesis of syntheses

φύσις		τέχνη		
1. thought	2. passion	3. figures (schemas)	4. phrasis (choice of words and tropical lexis)	5. synthesis (rhythm)

There is always a φύσις-τέχνη synthesis to operate. On the subordinate level, at the level of each component and its articulation—for example, in No. 3 the synthesis of νοῦς and σχῆμα, or in 5 the synthesis of ῥυθμός and πρᾶγμα—there is the danger of a scission, a fall back into disunion. On the other hand, it may be that unity, or the totalization of the whole, is as effectively made manifest by the tearing asunder of synthesis as by junction and rapprochement.

The sublime is the movement that transposes the cohesion of all the constituents into a mimesis of the model unity which is "Nature." And just *as* Nature (XLIII, 5; 217) has hidden that which is low or base (excretion), suggesting thus that one ought not to allow abjection to show itself, so the *natural* in the speech of the great consists in hiding the technique of the high (I return to this in speaking of λήθη below).

Φύσις *and* Τέχνη

It is a matter of acquiring the innate. The innate is to be educated. Sublimation (elevation to the sublime) is education itself. The author asks himself if there is a τέχνη of the high-and-deep. One cannot just *let* nature *do what it will.* Rather, there is a method, spur and restraint for making the fullness of culture (the sublime) proceed to the accomplishment of *its* nature, that is, to the "psychic" nature which is also *logical* and made for the *beyond* (ὑπέρ). To procure a "discernment" (διάγνωσις) capable of purifying the "logic" of the sublime of its flaws is a preliminary part of the task.

The elevation to the sublime is a strange operation. It is a matter of reattaining the ground, of raising up and carrying away—what? Culture (τέχνη: διδακτικός) leads back to nature (φυσικός: γενναῖος) on condition that nature—for example, the gift of innate eloquence (a person is by nature a being of logos)—is conceived as a movement of self-surmounting.

Nature is attained as ground only if upheaval (ἔκστασις) makes it (re)ascend. "Persuasion" cannot accomplish this, but only the sublime, which is a transport.

An important passage says:

> what one admires in art (ἐπι⁴…τέχνης) is the most painstaking (τὸ ἀκριβέστατον), and in works of nature (τῶν φυσικῶν ἔργων), greatness (μέγεθος). But by nature (φύσει) man is of-the-logical (λογικόν)…in discourse one seeks that which surpasses human things (XXXVI, 3; 182–83).

Technique, then, applied to the natural, contrives painstakingly, cunningly, *in the smallest detail,* what is fit to transport nature to the point of recognizing itself in its "logical" grandeur: i.e., in the discourse of exaltation. The two errors to avoid are, on the one hand, forgetting "the exalted," in the sense of the trans-human, and on the other, neglecting attention to minute details in the preparation of the artefact.

The sublime in speech—speech in harmony with things "which sur-pass" the human in elevation—exploits all resources, all artifices (among which are the figures, or σχήματα), and grounds them (synthesis) in a "solar" unity which *dissimulates*[14] them.

Images, Rhythms, Figures

Did Pound take his famous distinction between *phanopoeia, melopoeia,* and *logopoeia* from Pseudo-Longinus? Perhaps.

Pseudo-Longinus speaks similarly of images (εἰδωλοποιία), rhythm (ἁρμονία), and schematic tropology.

In chapter XV (1; 87), he speaks of images (φαντασίαι) in relation to μεγαληγορία and calls them εἰδωλοποιίαι, which Lebègue translates as "men-tal figuration," apparently in intimate proximity to what Pound translated into pseudo-Greek as *phanopoeia:* "something in the mind" (ἐννόημα παρισ-τάμενον) capable of "engendering" (γεννητικόν) "discourse" (λόγου). A topology which refers to two different "intentions" (βούλεται), that of the poet and that of the orator, differentiates two types of images, and this distinction seems sufficiently radical to separate the poetry of the poets from the rhetoric of the orators.

The former seek ἔκπλησις, "terror" or the striking, and tend to "trans-mythologize" (μυθικωτέραν) to exceed the credible (XV, 8; 93). But the lat-ter, the orators, seek ἐνάργεια, clarity and evidence of exposition.

Pseudo-Longinus passes from images to λογοποεια by means of this difference of will or intent characteristic of poetry and prose (eloquence), respectively. Fantasy shows, makes one see—too much; its images eclipse *evi-dence.* The imagination must therefore be relayed and restrained by figures that are schemas of logos and not "projections of view on the mental screen," as Pound had said. No longer εἰδωλοποιία ("you've got crazy ideas; you're liv-ing in a movie" [*tu te fais des idées; tu fais du cinéma*] as one might say in [French] slang today) but λογοποιία, tropology. Demosthenes is the example here: *he does not make us see* directly, the author tells us, but *suggests* in accor-dance with a figural schema of the imagination, which we could call grammat-ical and which is, in this case, *apostrophe.*[15]

What we would call in our schools *grammatical analysis* represents lan-guage as if it were purely objective, without discourse, subject, "orator," or rhetoric: *schemas* are forgotten. (I mean that a student of the lycée practicing grammatical analysis is not supposed to remark the "figures of rhetoric" because the objectified statement is not referred to the intention of the speaker.) But "back in those days," the grammatical structure (an interroga-tion, an exclamation) was understood as a rhetorical figure, as the schematic disposition of the sentence with respect to its intended message. Further, far from being reserved for orators, this tropology, even more than "images," is for Pseudo-Longinus the site of the poet's true genius. A crucial passage (X, 6; 68) shows that Homer's sublimity consists in his poems' conjunctive force. The author glorifies Homer for having known how to force and forge in the ἔπος of λόγος a turn by which the poem "imitates" in *its* way the pathos of which it speaks: grammatical "representation." Specifically, he solders together separate prepositions (the Greek says: *asynthetic prostheses*). Compressing ὑπό and ἐκ into one (ὑπὲκ θανάτοιο), his versified speech itself *performs* at this moment (like) what it speaks about. By constructing portmanteau words (τῇ δὲ τοῦ ἔπους συνθλίψει), Homer has fashioned (ἀπεπλάσατο) fear in this passage where he is describing a shipwreck; he has "represented" it, that is, he has imprinted on his locution the proper character (ἰδίωμα) of "danger." *The poem does what it says,* as modern poeticians will insist thousands of years later.

But none of these constituents should be there "for its own sake," to serve itself and to be self-sufficient. Not even logos in its tropical λογοποιία, which is in the service of things to be said, "exalted things." The constituent should render itself forgotten in order to enter into σύνθεσις: λήθη and the auxiliary character of λανθάνεσθαι are conceived here as the condition of the possibility of synthesis. In order to understand this, let us make a detour by way of rhythm, the third element which, as I remarked above, Ezra Pound translated by μελοποιία.

Of Rhythm

φθόγγοι κιθάρα,ς οὐδὲν ἁπλῶς σημαίνοντες... "The guitar, taken in itself, signifies nothing at all (XXXIX, 2; 196).

If it is taken alone—on its own, asynthetically (not asyndetically for asyndeton augments the fusional temperature of the sublime mixture), bereft of all alliance or grounding in the reunification the ingredients of which Pseudo-Longinus treats exhaustively as the catalysts of the whole—rhythm— this corybantic rhythm that "constrain[s] the listener to move rhythmically" (XXXIX, 2; 196)—runs away with itself, lets fall its sense, communicates only the trepidations of trance, traceless of sense. As opposed to those votaries of the frenetic, the "crazy" rockers of today, Pseudo-Longinus takes the risk of risk itself. Sense too comprises the tie and medium. Hence, the comparison with the organic: unity *of* the body and of the body with what is not itself, soul or sense; "gathering" which is supposed—indeed, herein consists its sense—to transport the whole to the border of non-sense, hovering above the abyss of the question why. Thus, the gathering is at once oriented toward an end (the unity of which is conceived in terms of affinity), and endless. The *sublime* as reunification (πάθος, νόησις, schemas, rhythm) is the name of the unity that renders forgotten its constitutive elements, the operators *of* the unity. This unity is related not simply to humans, to artifice (work, "production"), but also to that of which human work is an ἀνάλογον, to that of which one of the names is "nature" (φύσις). And the god is one "creator" among others; he too is caught up in the world (κόσμος) of which he is one of the tensors or extensors (see the section on Homer above).

Figures (Resumed)

At the center of the question of "discourse of the high" (ὑψηγορία), there is a relation of reciprocal complementarity, of mutual assistance (of *dia-llel*, or βοήθεια) between the sublime (ὕψος) and figures (σχήματα): "that by nature in a certain sense the schemas struggle with the high and in return they receive from it marvellous competition" (XVII, 1; 104–5) (συμμαχεῖται; the *high* allied with figures in a single combat). Secret alliance: the figure, that "puerile" artifice, should hide itself in the sublime which is its best hideout. For figures, Pseudo-Longinus tells us, are "first of all" suspect like ruses—like Ulysses. Ulysses πολύμητις is the allegory of the schematism. The high does not raise itself without the support of the low, of what is underneath; height can only hold by rising in a pile from the low, which renders itself forgotten in the service that is "naturally" its own, specifically, to support like a slave that in which it consists and into which it disappears: the high. Figures comprise the ladder—or the flight machine, if one prefers—up which "we" (that is, ψυχή) can climb to this natural site, this *elevated site*, from which one no longer sees them, because they permit the one who has flown or fled (ὑπερβολή, for example) to see something else: specifically, exalted things. As we have already read, the most high is in fact the point closest (ἐγγύτερον) to our nature, by which it comes into contact with the superhuman, the nonmortal. Τέχνη transports the soul in raising it up to its nature (φύσις), which is "logical" (λογικόν); logos measures the "high-deep" (μέγα-βαθύ)—as Homer's "divine horses" measured the entire span of the cosmos.

But the diversity of figures is considerable. And it is not my intention here to comment on them or even to restate the list Pseudo-Longinus treats. One might imagine that the tradition up to our own times had collected the names of these schemas and fixed their definitions. Curiously, this is not at all the case. And one observes with surprise, by simply confronting the "Longinian" onomastics with today's "dictionaries of poetics and rhetoric" (for example, the Morier or the Gradus—but of course, not the Lausberg, which lets nothing escape), that such and such a fundamental "schema" in the text, *symmoria* (the schema of schemas), or *polyptoton* or *antimetathesis*, does not even appear by name in our taxonomies, or that certain others (*hyperbaton* or *enallage*) don't have the same definitions, as if the lists had no memory of their origins.

For example, if Henri Lebègue profits from it—on page 32 of his edition, in a specious note—when he (re)introduces the traditional (if not very clear) distinction between *figures of thought* and *figures of style*, he does so because *this distinction does not appear in Pseudo-Longinus's text*. But Lebègue nonetheless claims that the enormous lacuna of the "archetypal" manuscript—four pages—contains—"perhaps"—the famous distinction which has been "announced by the anonymous author in chapter VII." This is not sufficient reason for us to introduce it. Rather, if in chapter XXX (1; 147) the text informs us that we are leaving the νόησις τοῦ λόγου in order to enter into the consideration of φράσις, which is the *fourth part* announced by the enumeration of chapter VIII (1; 45-50), it is because we were in the third, which is called both τῶν σχημάτων πλάσις, "the announcement of the plan" (VIII, 1; 47) and νόησις τοῦ λόγου, "the recapitulation" (XXX, 1; 147). It is not the suspect parenthesis of page 10 of the Budé edition (διοσα δέ που ταῦτα, τὰ μὲν νοήσεω,ς θάτερα δὲ λέξεως, which Lebègue translates as: "there are two sorts of figures, those of thought and those of words") which will arrest our attention: the fashions of schemas (πλάσιςτῶν σχημάτων) cannot be divided—there are only figures of thought.

Logopoeia, too, will induce its own oblivion. For example, just like the other figures, hyperbole (XXXVIII, 3; 189–90) is supposed, under the pressure of pathos (ὑπὸ ἐκπαθείας), to refer in consonance (συνεκφωνῶνται) to some greatness of circumstance (μεγέθει τινί…περιστάσεως). The figures render themselves forgotten if something other than saying-for-its-own-sake mobilizes them. Hence, hyperbole ought to issue from the matter at hand through the mediation of pathos, not the inverse. What "surpasses the human" and takes it beyond itself ought to cut back across it and make it begin anew. The same thing goes, if you will, for names (ὀνόματα): they are the light of the spirit (Φῶ…τοῦ νοῦ) as long as they do not relate to trivial concerns (μικροῖς πραγματίοις) (XXX, 1; 148). The νοῦς would be what adjusts words to things within the occasion (καιρός) (XXXII, 1; 152), that is, within the relation to others.

The force which contains everything always makes in a certain way (τρόπος) "the whole" be, in the form of rapture, and here we are as in the deluge, in re-fusion, in the συνενθουσιᾶν.

The "syn"

The play of the sublime as a whole is itself a gathering; a unification; a seal of πάθος, λέξις, and νόησις, and the reference or circumstance of the great: in the imminence of *mortal* danger, the power of pathos and the lexis which is of sufficient stature to mobilize all resources (τέχνη), that is, in general the antagonism of conjunction and disjunction in order to *express*—as will be repeated across the centuries—the ordeal of this danger. The synthesis of the multiple can either take the "weak" form of hyperbaton, a ruse of disorder which *renders* in a certain way the power of conjunction which is at work, or it can bring the entire charge of speech to bear on one point of the discourse: and this is the *symmory* (or synody) of the figures which makes the asyndetons, anophoras, diatyposes, and so on play into one another (XX). Pseudo-Longinus's example on this point is that of a counsel's plea in the matter of a brawl: as if the advocate's discourse could report what could not be reported by the injured party. In the heat of the action (or passion), the subject submerged by what he is suffering cannot bear witness. But the (descriptive) *plaidoyer* permits one to see in the place of the offended party and to understand him. The speech which replays the events has the power to reveal their truth, by acting on the judges "like the aggressor."

Mimesis

If the "natural" is the instance and event of pathos-laden, disordered discourse *this* side of the "rhetorical" situation—that is, in action or real dialogue —, then correspondingly, art as μίμησις consists in the controlled reproduction of this situation, a retelling which reflexively places into figures (hyperbaton) themselves set apart from the vividness or naturalness of the "real" situation.

Mimesis is a representation of what has come before by means of a special effort of retrospective preparation, *as* "at the beginning." For to be sure, it is the great and the pathos-laden which are at the beginning. One of the insistent key terms of Περὶ Ὕψους is *rapprochement*. For example:

> Therefore...the passions and the heights of discourse, which lie nearest to our minds [ἐγγυτέρω] through a sort of natural kinship and through their light, glitter of their own radiance before the figures, whose art they throw into the shade and as it were keep in concealment. (XVII, 3; 105–6)

Figures favor a general rapprochement of the before and after, of natural and artificial. In short, the reorganization and reunification of all that is separate. The condition of this rapprochement is that figures themselves—having become "abstract" (detached, distant, etc.) through historical, cultivated abuse as through the lie of their cunning polyvalence—be refinalized, reunited, raised up and justified anew in "the sublime"—in the transport of the utterance that serves exalted matters. Thus, the illumination their light favors covers figures over again with the very shadow of their "brightness" (κατακαλύψει) (XVII, 3; 106).

There is *literature* (for Pseudo-Longinus: tragedy, epic, lyric poem, oratorical discourse) which, by means of a special *situation* (reading, recitation, representation, tribunal, agora), becomes *in* life *as* life: i.e., *imitates.* Such literature is a part of the whole which represents the whole and without which the whole would not be *represented* or "reflected." Metonymy works for the symbol; a situation which "imitates" what is coming to pass...when it does not take place. *Imitation* speaks of this relation of inclusion-exclusion from the λόγος, which adds (τέχνη) to what exists (φύσις) its representation.

The λανθάνεσθαι

The hypothesis is that *artifice* does not reign "*at the beginning.*"

But that something like a *crisis* has—always already?—taken place, constituting a second beginning, or rather a beginning after "the origin." A separation takes place, or has taken place, in such a way that rhetorical reflexion can "now" distinguish, on the one hand, the strictly indescribable "norm" of speech-without-figure and, on the other hand, artifice, procedure, and excess, the threat which discursive procedures bring to bear upon speech. Finally, reflexion, or synthesis (yes, already here, there is "synthetic sublation"), miming in a way the origin, separates art from the cunning of figures in order *to render itself forgotten*: this is indeed a lethal event (λήθη), the simulation of a primordial, exalted state of language, *the rhetorical operation of which would render itself forgotten in the exaltation it—lethargically—procures.*

Myth of the origin of speech: at the beginning there is an exchange, an anti-dosis, between these two: the high and figures. Pathos, that which affects and troubles, transports and unbridles, must take part in the struggle, but as integrated, controlled, enlisted, and mastered; it must be brought back into the picture as excess. But how does one make the a-logos enter into the logos? By the *secret* action of artificial figures, as chapter XVII (1; 105) spells out: "Further, the best of figures dissimulates that it is a figure." But how does one hide the figure; how does the orator (ῥήτωρ) bury away (ἀπέκρυψε) the figure (τὸ σχῆμα)? Δῆλον ὅτι τῷ φωτὶ αὐτῷ. Manifestly by its brilliance, its light itself. Figures support (and in gathering enable) speech in the light of the "sublime and pathos" which consumes, subsumes, and assumes them: for the *rapprochement* of our *psyches.* Psyche desires to be brought closer to what is natural to her, to height and light: figures aid[16] her in this rapprochement by lending scintillation to the *sublime* that lives on their "technique." The "Sun" they have helped cause to glow can thus, by illuminating, keep them in the shadows. (Is this the way royalty works in general?)

The height of art consists in dissimulating one's artifices, in covering up one's twists and turns, in rendering nonapparent one's figures, one's unacknowledgeable ruses: the fire of the sublime, founding all of its components, transports the listeners (readers) into ἔκστασις, to the point where they see nothing but fire. Let us hear in this that their disdain with regard to the procedures and turns of rhetoric is transported, submerged, and deafened by the elevation to the sublime, as if the thing itself appeared each time in its brilliance thanks to the light of speech, of discourse, eclipsing, suppressing, and absorbing the conditions of its apparition, the undergirdings and supports, the multiplicity below, the "inferior" diversity....There must be a *swooning syncopation* in the listener—in all listeners, including the speaker—or a loss of knowledge, in order for the rhetorical moment to be *identified* with the moment of natural perfection; a λανθάνεσθαι, or "over-looking," a λήθη, as the condition of the utterance of the "truth" (ἀλήθεια): ἀλήθεια in λήθη and thanks to λήθη, which *renders forgotten* (unremarkable) the contradictory conditions, the *paradox* of the striking utterance of an "exalted truth."

What happens when, in *Britannicus*, Burrhus tells us that he will speak with the frankness "of a soldier who knows ill / How to disguise the truth"? He uses the figure of the *captatio benevolentiae*, the *excusatio*, the emphatic humility of the "nonorator" who is incapable of all…but truth! As simple as that—or rather at the point of confusion of the greatest presumption and "naïveté." And he says this in verse, Alexandrines no less, that is, as nobody in the world actually, "naturally," speaks: the height of *disguise* which makes the naked truth *appear*.

The proper is a figure, the denegated figure, the figure of the denegation of figure.

The figural—rhetoric, which is what one is always dealing with, the place within which all lexis takes on form—deforms the straight path "denuded of artifice," which itself does not exist, but by whose phantom all of our "expressions" are haunted. The road is and is not the road.

It remains to comprehend what is at stake in the difference stubbornly maintained between, on the one hand, the "naïve ones" (*naturalists*) who believe in the simple—*dual* and natural—difference between the proper (direct) and the figural (tortuous) as a situable, controllable difference[17] and, on the other hand, the twisted ones, the "Ulysseans," who—from Pseudo-Longinus to, say, Paulhan—want to reveal the lethargic syncopation, want to make us understand the turns of figuration, the *paradox* of the cunning utterance of the "undisguised" statement, to insist on machination, to reject the *proper* and *natural* as impossible and treat it as a figure. What must the incessantly desired and invoked *natural* be in order for figural language—distorted beyond distorsion, "polymetic," anti-economical with respect to a "more proper" mode of speech—to be constantly suspected, accused, in need of "dissimulating" itself? One must dissimulate simulation, feign ignorance of figuration. Once the turn is unveiled, known as such, one exposes oneself to the accusations of treachery and trickery, of the *original sin* of lexis—but against the background of what postulated radical innocence?[18]

In general and radically, it is, as "people" say, "words," speech, or discourse, that are suspect; and they will always be suspect because the same is the milieu of the truth and the lie (*verum index sui*). What the audience grumbles about is "being duped by pretty words." An insurmountable fear, and the swindler is the one who spices his own discourses with the grumblings of this fear itself, in order to cleanse them of the suspicion of being nothing but words. It is a paradox that has been definitively reflected upon at least since Gorgias's *Encomium of Helen*: words are forever ruses, and it is only in and through words that what one desires will appear, the (in)credible salvation, which is other than words, the other of words, and which one calls *silence*. Discourses are for making silence, and Pseudo-Longinus himself does not escape from the topos of silence where words abolish themselves.[19]

It is thus in words insofar as they *render themselves forgotten,* insofar as they appear as wordless! What I am telling you is not (a) telling. Do not think that what I am telling you, which consists only of words, is only an expression of my intentions. Is *denegation* inscribed in the very heart of speech? As a kind of "performative" constitutive of eloquence? This negativity of a *work against oneself:* a sort of self-destruction at work in the heart of "words" and of the poem? Poetry annuls the poem which annuls itself in poetry (consumes itself there in favor of what surpasses it and which is itself?).

Chapter 2

❀

THE SUBLIME OFFERING

Jean-Luc Nancy

The sublime is in fashion.[1] All fashions, in spite of or thanks to their futility, are means to the presentation of something other than fashion: they are also of the order of necessity or destiny. For destinies, indeed, fashions are perhaps only a particularly secret and discreet way of offering themselves. What then offers itself or what is offered in this recent fashion of the sublime? I will attempt to answer: the offering itself, as the destiny of art.

But the fashion of the sublime has the supplementary privilege of being extremely old. It is at least as old as Boileau's translation of Longinus and the distinction Boileau drew between "the sublime style" and the sublime taken in the absolute sense. From that point on, what had once been, under the names of *hypsos* or *sublimitas*, a category of rhetoric[2]—the discourse that specialized in subjects of great elevation—become a concern, a demand, an adoration, or a torment, more or less avowed but always present, for aesthetics and philosophy, for philosophy *of* aesthetics and philosophy *in* the aesthetic, for the thought of art and for art as thought. In this sense, the sublime forms a fashion that has persisted uninterruptedly into our own time from the beginnings of modernity, a fashion at once continuous and discontinuous, monotonous and spasmodic. The "sublime" has not always taken this name, but it has always been present. It has always been a fashion because it has always concerned a break within or from aesthetics (whether "aesthetics" designates taste or theory). And this break has been willed, intended, evoked, or demanded more than it has been truly revealed or demonstrated: it has been a kind of defiance with which aesthetics provokes itself—"enough beauty already, we must be sublime!" But at the same time, it has not been a matter of mere fashion, as I said, but necessity itself.

The motif of the sublime (the name and category of which are perhaps not even up to the standards of what they indicate, being too used up, already

or still too aesthetic, too ethical, too virtuous, too elevated, in short, too sublime, and I will return to this below)—the motif of the sublime, then,
announces the necessity of what happens to art in or as its modern destiny. Art
itself is doubtless that which is happening par excellence to us (to us others, the
Occidentals), that which is offering us our destiny or deranging our history.
But in the sublime, art itself is deranged, offered to yet another destiny; it has
its own destiny in a certain sense outside of itself. The sublime is tied in an
essential way to the *end* of art in all its senses: that for which art is there, its destination or *telos*, and the cessation, overcoming, or suspension of art.

There is no contemporary thought of art and its end which does not, in
one manner or another, pay tribute to the thought of the sublime, whether or
not it explicitly refers to this thought. One could research and retrace the
genealogies, filiations, and transmissions, from Walter Benjamin—whose role
is certainly decisive—to ourselves. But necessity is always deeper than
genealogies, beginning with the necessity that related Benjamin himself to
Kant, or with the necessity that related Kant, and all of the others with him, to
the destiny or task of art in thought.[3]

I will not explore this history or network. I will content myself with
placing here, by way of opening, several fragments that ought to speak for
themselves:

> For the sake of the unity which the veil and that which is veiled
> comprise in it, the Idea can be essentially valid only where the
> duality of nakedness and veiling does not yet obtain: in art and in
> the appearances of mere nature. On the other hand, the more dis-
> tinctly this duality expresses itself, in order finally in man to reach
> its greatest force, the more this becomes clear: in veil-less naked-
> ness the essentially beautiful has withdrawn and in the naked
> body of the human being a Being beyond all beauty is attained—
> the sublime, and a work beyond all images *[Gebilden]*—the work
> of the creator. (Benjamin[4])

> In the work, truth is at work and therefore not merely something
> true....The appearance arranged in the work is the beautiful.
> Beauty is a mode of being and of presence of truth qua unveiling.
> (Heidegger[5])

> The Kantian theory of the sublime describes... an art which shud-
> ders within itself: it suspends itself in the name of the content of
> truth deprived of appearance, but without, qua art, renouncing its
> character as appearance. (Adorno[6])

> Just as prose is not separated from poetry by any threshold, art
> expressive of anguish is not truly separated from that expressive of

joy...it is no longer a matter of dilettantism: sovereign art accedes to the extremity of the possible. (Bataille[7])

It would still be necessary to investigate whether this placing-in-question of art, which the most illustrious part of the art of the past thirty years represents, does not presuppose the sliding, the displacement of a force at work in [*puissance au travail dans*] the secrecy of works and refusing to step into the light of day. (Blanchot[8])

What is at stake in the sublime is a suspension of art, a placing in question of art within art itself as work or as task. In the name of the sublime, or under the pressure of something that often (but not exclusively) has carried this name, art is interrogated or provoked in view of something other than art. More precisely, it is a matter of a double suspense or a double placement in question. On the one hand, it is aesthetics as a regional philosophical discipline that is refused in the thought of art seized by the sublime. Kant is the first to do justice to the aesthetic at the heart of what one can call a "first philosophy": but he is also, and for this very reason, the first to suppress aesthetics as a part or domain of philosophy. As is well known, there is no Kantian aesthetics. And there is not, after Kant, any thought of art (or of the beautiful) that does not refuse aesthetics and interrogate in art something other than art: let us say, truth, or experience, the experience of truth or the experience of thought. On the other hand, it is art that suspends itself and shudders, as Adorno says, art that trembles on the border of art, giving itself as its task something other than art, something other than the world of the fine arts or than beautiful works of art: something "sublime."

It is as if "aesthetics" as object, as well as the aesthetic object, had dissolved upon the touch of philosophy (and it makes no difference whether they have offered themselves to philosophy or whether philosophy has attempted to conquer them by violence), to leave room for something else (nothing less, in Kant, than the sublime destination of reason itself: freedom). But it is also as if, at the same time, the capture and flight of these objects had required philosophy to think of both art and itself otherwise. In the suspension of art, the task of thought is in question.

But it is in question in such a manner that it does not take over the relay where art leaves off, where art would be both suppressed and conserved in the "true" presentation of truth. Such a thought of the relay, or of the sublation [*relève, Aufhebung*] of art by philosophy forms the most visible part of Hegel's thought of the end of art. But the essential point is precisely that the claim of the sublime forms the exact reverse of the sublation of art.[9]

The thought of the end of art as its sublation and, consequently, as its completion or achievement—which suppresses art as art and consecrates it as philosophy, which suppresses philosophy as discourse and conserves it as art, as the pure art of pure thought—, such thought reverses the sublime. This does not mean that there are two symmetrically opposed ways of thinking art. It means rather that there is one type of thought that reabsorbs art and another that thinks it in its destination. The latter is the thought of the sublime. The former thought, that of Hegel—philosophy as such—does not in fact think art as destiny or as destination but rather the reverse, the *end* of art, its goal, reason, and accomplishment. It puts an end to what it thinks: it thus does not think it at all, but only its end. It puts an end to art by preserving art in and as philosophy. It puts an end to art in the presentation of truth. To be sure, such thought views art as having heretofore comprised this presentation—as a representation and perhaps as presentation in general, always sensible, always aesthetic—but it views art as no longer adequate to this task of representative presentation now that truth has become capable of presenting itself on its own. Thus the end of art is attained, and art is properly *sublated* as presentation, in the presentation of the true. It is suppressed as art and preserved as pure presentation.

What is the case then with art *as* art? What remains of it and where? *Art as such*—as all that is designated as "art" in Hegel or elsewhere and, for example, as figuration or expression, as literature or painting, as form or beauty, as work or value—art as such can remain nowhere but in the element of representation, the end of which was presentation itself. The art that remains there (if such an "art" exists, or if it still merits this name), the art that conceives itself as representation or as expression is in fact a finite art—finished, dead. But the thought that finished it off suppressed itself as the thought of art. For it never thought that which it brought to completion.

It never thought what it brought to completion because art, in truth, was already no longer dwelling in the element of (re)presentation. Perhaps art never served to (re)present except in the philosophical representation of art. Art was elsewhere: Hegel (at least a certain Hegel) wasn't aware of it, but as for Kant, he had begun to recognize that what was at stake in art was not the representation of the truth, but—to put it briefly—*the presentation of liberty*. It was this recognition that was engaged in and by the thought of the sublime. Not only was art not completed by philosophy in this thought, but art began to tremble there, suspended over itself, unachieved, perhaps unachievable, on the border of philosophy—which art thus made shudder or interrupt itself in its turn.

For Kant, the beautiful and the sublime have in common that they have to do with presentation and only with presentation (*CJ*, §23, 84; 82).[10] In both nothing plays itself out but the play of presentation itself, without any represented *object*. (There ought therefore to be a concept, or an experience, of presentation that would not be submitted to the general logic of (re)presentation, that is, of the presentation by a subject and for a subject: basically, the entire question is there). On the occasion of an object of the senses, the imagination—which is the faculty of presentation—plays at finding a form in accord with its free play. It presents (to itself) this: that there is a free accord between the sensible (which is essentially multiple or manifold) and a unity (which is not a concept, but rather free indeterminate unity). The imagination thus presents the image, or rather that there is (such a thing as) "image" (*Bild*). The image here is not the representative image, and it is not the object. It is not the placing-in-form of something else but form forming itself, for itself, without object: fundamentally, art, according to Kant represents nothing in either the beautiful or the sublime. The "imagination" does not signify the subject who makes an image of something but rather the image imaging itself, not as a figure of something else but as form forming itself, unity happening upon manifoldness, coming out of a manifoldness, in the manifold of sensibility, simply as unity without object and without subject—and thus without end. It is on the basis of this general situation of free aesthetic presentation that one must attempt to appreciate the respective stakes of the beautiful and the sublime.

Kant calls the free *Bild* that precedes all images, all representations, and all figurations (one is tempted to say the nonfigurative *Bild*) a *schema* in the first *Critique*. He says in the third *Critique* that aesthetic judgment is nothing other than the reflexive play of the imagination when it "schematizes without concepts": that is, when the world that forms itself, that manifests itself, is not a universe of objects but merely a schema (*skema*, "form," or "figure"), merely a *Bild* that makes a "world" on its own, because it forms itself, because it designs itself. The *schema* is the figure—but the imagination that figures without concepts figures nothing: the schematism of aesthetic judgment is intransitive. It is merely the figure that figures itself. It is not a world nor the world that takes on figure, but the figure that makes world. It is perhaps indissociable from the fake, the fiction, and the dream of a Narcissus: but all of that comes only after the fact. In order that there should be these figures and this scene of representations, there must first be the throw, the surging and beating, of a design, a form, which *figures itself* in giving itself figure, in conferring upon itself a free unity. It confers this unity upon itself, or it receives this unity—for at first it does not have any unity at its disposal. Such is the essential characteristic of imagination, of *Einbildung* operating without a concept: imagination is unity that precedes itself, anticipates itself, and manifests itself, free figure prior to any further determination.

From this starting point—that is, barely having entered into the first modern philosophical assignation of the aesthetic—one can finish very quickly if one likes. By pursuing the logic of this initial constellation of the aesthetic schematism, one can very quickly arrive at the end of art. Indeed, in a sense one must pursue it if only in order to discover that it can function only by ignoring the sublime, which nothing I have said thus far has distinguished as such.

In the first *Critique*, the schematism was said to be a "technique hidden in the depths of the soul." Does the secret of this technique unveil itself in the aesthetic schematism, which presents essentially the pure form of the schematism? It is tempting to think so. The schematism would then be aesthetic. The technique of the schema would be an art. After all, it is the same word, *ars* or *die Kunst*. Reason would be an artist, the world of objects a work—and art would be the first or supreme technique, the creative or self-creative technique, the technique of the unity of subject and object, unity positing itself in the work. One can believe this and proceed to draw the consequences.

One will very quickly obtain two versions of a thereby completed thought of the schematism: either the version of an originary and infinite art, a poetry never ceasing to give itself form in giving form to the world as to thought—and this is the romantic version—or else the version of a technique of originary judgment, which divides judgment in order to relate it to itself as unity and so to give it its absolute figure—and this is the Hegelian version. Either aesthetics sublates philosophy or the converse. In both cases, the schematism is understood (its secret revealed) and accomplished: art or technique—and doubtless, according to the play of complicitous exchange between the two versions, art *and* technique, technique of art and art of technique—the schema is the originary figure *of figuration itself.* That which figures (or that which presents, for here, figuring is presenting), the faculty of figuration or of presentation has itself already a figure, and has already presented itself. It is reason as artist or technician, which comes down to the same thing: *Deus artifex.*

Thus, the imagination that schematizes without a concept would schematize itself of itself in aesthetic judgment. And this is certainly, in one sense, what it does: it presents itself as unity and it presents its unity to itself, presenting nothing other than itself, presenting the faculty of presentation in its free play, that is, again, presenting the one presenting, or *representing,* absolutely. Here, the presenting one—the subject—is the presented. In the beautiful and in the sublime—which are neither things nor qualities of objects but judgments, and more precisely, aesthetic judgments, i.e., the proper judgments of sensibility when it is determined neither by concepts nor by empirical sensation (which constitutes the agreeable, not the beautiful)—the unity of spirit, the spirit as unity, and the accord of the faculties operated in the imagination or, more precisely, *as* imagination presents itself to itself.

It is not so much that art comes to find its reason or reasons here but rather that Reason takes possession of art in order to make of it the technique of its self-presentation. This self-presentation is thus the presentation of the very technique of reason, of a technique conceived as the primary or ultimate nature of reason, in accordance with which reason produces, operates, figures, and presents itself on its own. The schematism is on this account the anticipation of the unity of presentation (or of that which presents) in presentation itself (or in the presented), an anticipation which doubtless constitutes the only possible technique (the only *Handgriff,* "sleight of hand," as the first *Cri-*

tique puts it) by means of which a presentation, in this strict philosophic sense, could ever take place. How would I trace any figure at all, if I did not anticipate its unity, or more precisely, if I did not anticipate myself, the one who presents this figure, as its unity? There is a kind of fore-sight or providence at the heart of reason. The schema is reason which fore-sees and pre-figures itself. It is thus of the nature of the schematism, this artistic *coup de main* of reason, to be "hidden in the depths of the soul": the prefiguration escapes in its anticipation. And it is even basically the hidden, secret character of the schematism that unveils it for what it is: the technique, already dissimulated behind all visible figures, of figurative or presentational anticipation.

In this "schematism without concepts," in this "free legality" or in this "sketch" of the world[11] for the free subject, the cosmetic is the anticipation of the cosmic. The beautiful is not here a quality, intrinsic or extrinsic, subjective or objective, it is more than a quality. Indeed, it constitutes the status and the very being of the subject which forms itself and which presents itself in order to be able to (re)present for itself a world of phenomena. The aesthetic is itself the anticipation of knowledge, art is the anticipation of technical reason, and taste is the schema of experience—the schema or the pleasure, for precisely here *the two are confounded*. Did not Kant write that a primitive pleasure must have presided over the very first knowledge, "a remarkable pleasure, without which the most common experience would not have been possible"? (*CJ*, VI, 34; 24). There is a pure, painless pleasure, then, at the philosophical origin of knowledge and world domination. (That there is no admixture of pain in this pleasure implies that the sublime is not yet involved, a point to which I will return below.) This pleasure consists in the satisfaction provided by unity in general, by (re)discovering (re)union of the manifold, the heterogeneous, under a principle or law. Anticipation arises out of or resides within this enjoyment [*jouissance*] of unity which is necessary to reason. Without unity, the manifold is nothing but chaos and vertiginous danger. United with its unity—a unity which one must therefore have anticipated in order to be able to rediscover and (re)present it, and a unity thus technically and artistically produced—the manifold becomes enjoyment: at once pleasure and appropriation.

Enjoyment, according to Kant, belongs to the *agreeable*, which must be carefully distinguished from the beautiful. The agreeable is attached to an interest, whereas the beautiful is not. The beautiful is not linked to any interest, for in aesthetic judgment I do not depend at all on the existence of the object, and what is important is merely "what I discover in myself" on the occasion of this object (*CJ*, §2, 50; 39).

But does not self-enjoyment arise out of a supreme and secret interest of reason? The disinterestedness of the judgment of beauty, caught in the logic of the *ratio artifex*, is a profound interestedness: one has an interest in the being-anticipated of unity, in the (pre)formation of the figure, in the avoidance of chaos.

Here, the category of the beautiful begins to reveal itself in its extreme fragility. The beautiful and the agreeable already have in common that they "please immediately," in distinction to the good, on the one hand, and the sublime, on the other. If one must also establish a rapport between them in terms of interest—interest in the object in the case of the agreeable and interest in oneself in the case of the beautiful (and are these two things really so different?)—, then one will have to say that the beautiful too involves enjoyment, the enjoyment of anticipation and self-presentation. The beautiful in Kant, and perhaps all simple *beauty* since Kant, arises from the enjoyment of the subject, and indeed constitutes the subject as enjoying itself, its unity and its free legality, as that artist-reason which insures itself against the chaos of sensible experience and clandestinely re-appropriates for itself—thanks to its "hidden art"—the satisfactions that it had lost with God. Unless—even more brutally—it was the subject-artist (the subject of art, philosophy, and technique) who ravished God of His enjoyment.

When it presents itself in philosophy, or rather when it anticipates itself in philosophy (anticipating, in Kant's time, the essentially technical and artificial character of modern reason), aesthetics is suppressed twice in a single instant: once in the end of art and once in the enjoyment of imaginative reason. The two are the same, as one can clearly see: art meets its end, for it consists in the enjoyment in which it achieves itself. Kant is not in this the other of Hegel: in both, what is at stake in the aesthetic is presentation. The presentation of truth rests on the truth of presentation, which is the enjoyment of prefigured unity. The Hegelian spirit does not enjoy itself in any other way: the Kantian imagination is what it enjoys. Or again, the Hegelian spirit is itself the *final* self-appropriating enjoyment of the Kantian imagination. And philosophy gets off on art, makes of art and the beautiful its own enjoyment, suppresses them as simple pleasures, one could say, and preserves them as the pure self-enjoyment of Reason. The *Aufhebung* of art in philosophy has the structure of enjoyment—and in this infinite structure, art in its turn enjoys itself: it can become, as philosophic art, as art or technique of philosophical presentation (for example, dialectical, scientific, or poetic presentation), the orgiastic self-enjoyment of Spirit itself.

Once upon a time, the beautiful was "the splendor of the true": by a singular perversion, which it is difficult to consider without unease, the splendor of the true has become the self-enjoyment of reason.

This is perhaps the philosophic fate of the aesthetic as well as the aesthetic fate of philosophy. Art and beauty: presentations of the true, which uses them for its own enjoyment, anticipates itself in them, and finishes them off.

But far from finishing, we have hardly begun by proceeding thus. We have not even begun to deal with the sublime, and art, in Kant, does not offer itself to analysis before one has passed by way of the analysis of the sublime, which in several respects feeds into the examination of art, in particular by way of the decisive motif of genius. (This is not the place to dwell on it, but let me at least mention here that one can only thoroughly comprehend the Kantian theory of the arts, regardless of Kant's intentions, if one understands its dependence upon the theory of the sublime. This dependence is manifested, for example, by the ordering of his apparently poorly justified table of contents, which places the theory of art within the "Analytic of the Sublime," whereas the latter was supposed to be "a mere appendix" to the "Analytic of Aesthetic Judgments.")

One can gain access to the sublime by passing argumentatively through the insufficiencies of the beautiful. We have just seen beauty thicken suddenly, if I dare put it this way, into the pleasure or satisfaction of reason. This signifies nothing other than that the beautiful is an unstable category, insufficiently contained or retained in the order that was to be properly its own (the pure presentation of presentation). The beautiful is perhaps not quite as autonomous as it appears and as Kant would like. Taken literally as the pure pleasure of pure presentation, the beautiful reveals itself to be responsive to the interest of reason which is all the more interested because it is hidden: it satisfies itself with and is satisfied by its power to present and to present itself. It admires itself on the occasion of its objects, and it tends, according to what is for Kant the law of all pleasure, to preserve its current condition, to preserve the enjoyment of its proper *Bild* and *Ein-bildung*. Doubtless the beautiful, rigorously considered, *is* not in this state of enjoyment, but it is always about to slide into it, to become confused with it: and this ever imminent sliding is not accidental but belongs to the very structure of the beautiful. (In the same manner, one can apply to the judgment of taste the rule applied to moral judgment: one can never say for certain that an action has been accomplished by pure morality; likewise, one can never say that a judgment of taste is a pure judgment of beauty: it is always possible that some interest—empirical or not—has intruded itself. Even more radically or rigorously, it is possible that there is no such thing as a pure judgment of taste and that its disinterest is always interested in the profound self-enjoyment of the imagination.)

However, the same instability, the same constitutive lability that makes the beautiful slide into the agreeable can also carry it off into the sublime. Indeed, the beautiful is perhaps only an intermediate, ungraspable formation, impossible to fix except as a limit, a border, a place of equivocation (but perhaps also of exchange) between the agreeable and the sublime, that is, between enjoyment and joy [*la jouissance et la joie*], to which I will return below.

If a transport of the beautiful into the sublime is indeed the counterpart or reversal of its sliding into the agreeable—and this is what we shall verify— and if in the agreeable the beautiful ultimately loses its quality of beauty (for in enjoyment, in the beautiful as satisfied or satisfying, the beautiful is finished— and art along with it), then one must expect the beautiful truly to attain its "proper" quality only in another sort of departure from itself—into the sublime. That is, the beautiful becomes the beautiful only beyond itself, or else it slides into the space this side of itself. By itself, it has no position. Either it achieves itself—in satisfaction, or philosophy—or it suspends itself, unachieved, in the sublime (and in art, or at least in art that has not been sublated by philosophy).

The sublime forms neither a second wing of aesthetics nor another kind of aesthetic. After all, it is rather unaesthetic and unartistic for an aesthetic. And in the final analysis, it would seem more like an ethics, if one holds to the declared intentions of Kant. But Kant does not seem to see quite what is at stake when he introduces the sublime. He treats the sublime as a mere "appendix" to the analysis of aesthetic judgment (*CJ*, §23, 86; 85), but in reality, the sublime represents in the *Critique* nothing less than that without which the beautiful could not be the beautiful or without which the beautiful could be nothing but the beautiful (which paradoxically comes down to the same thing). Far from being a subordinate kind of aesthetic, the sublime constitutes a decisive moment in the thought of the beautiful and of art as such. It does not merely add itself to the beautiful but transforms or transfigures the beautiful. Consequently—and this is what I am attempting to show—the sublime does not constitute in the general field of (re)presentation just one more instance or problematic: it transforms or redirects the entire motif of presentation. (And this transformation continues to be at work in our own day.)

There is nothing new about the idea that the sublime represents that without which beauty itself would *not* be beautiful, or would be *merely* beautiful, that is, enjoyment and preservation of the *Bild*. It dates from the modern (re)naissance of the sublime. Boileau spoke of "this *je-ne-sais-quoi* which charms us and without which beauty itself would have neither grace nor beauty." Beauty without beauty is beauty which is merely beautiful, that is, merely pleasing (and not "charming"). Fénelon writes: "The beautiful which is only beautiful, that is, brilliant, is only half-beautiful." In a sense, all of modern aesthetics, that is, all "aesthetics," has its origin and raison d'être in the impossibility of attributing beauty merely to beauty and in the consequent skidding or overflowing of the beautiful beyond itself. What is mere beauty? Mere beauty, or beauty alone and isolated for itself, is form in its pure self-adequation, in its pure accord with the imagination, the faculty of presentation (or formation). Mere beauty, without interest, concept, or idea, is the simple accord—which is by itself a pleasure—of the thing presented with the presentation. At least, this is what modern beauty has been or attempted to be: a presentation that is successful and without remainder in accord with itself. (At bottom, this is subjectivity qua beauty.) In short, it is a matter of the schema in the pure state of a schematism without concepts, considered in its free accord with itself, where freedom is confused with the simple necessity that form should be adequate to its proper form, should present just the form that it is, or should be just the form that it presents. The beautiful is the figure that figures itself in accord with itself, the strict accord of its contour with its design.

Form or contour is limitation, which is the concern of the beautiful: the *unlimited*, to the contrary, is the concern of the sublime.

The unlimited maintains doubtless the closest, the most intimate relations with the infinite. The concept of the infinite (or its different possible concepts) gives us in a sense the internal structure of the unlimited. But the infinite does not exhaust the being of the unlimited, it does not offer the true moment of the unlimited. If the analysis of the sublime ought to begin, as it does in Kant, with the unlimited, and if it ought to transport into itself and replay the analysis of beauty (and thus of limitation), it must above all not proceed simply as the analysis of a particular kind of presentation, the presentation of the infinite. Nearly imperceptible at the outset, this frequently committed error can considerably distort the final results of the analysis. In the sublime, it is not a matter of the presentation or nonpresentation of the infinite, placed beside the presentation of the finite and construed in accordance with an analogous model. Rather, it is a matter—and this is something completely different—of the movement of the unlimited, or more exactly, of "the unlimitation" (*die Unbegrenztheit*) *that takes place on the border of the limit, and thus on the border of presentation.*

The unlimited as such is that which sets itself off on the border of the limit, that which detaches itself and subtracts itself from limitation (and hence from beauty) by an unlimitation that is coextensive with the external border of limitation. In one sense, *nothing* sets itself off thus. But if it is permissible to speak of the "unlimited" as of "something" that sets itself off "somewhere," it is because in the judgment or the feeling of the sublime we are offered a seizure, an apprehension of this unlimitation that comes to raise itself up like a figure against a ground, although strictly speaking, it is always simply the limit that raises a figure up against a nondelimited ground. In the sublime, it is a question of the figure of the ground, of the figure that the ground cuts, but precisely insofar as the ground cannot constitute a figure and yet remains a "raising that razes" [*un "enlèvement"*], an unlimiting outline, along the limited figure.

The unlimited begins on the external border of the limit: and it does nothing but begin, never to finish. In addition, its infinity is neither that of a simple potential progression to infinity nor that of a simple actual infinity (or of "infinity collected into a whole," as Kant puts it, and he in fact uses both of these figures or concepts of the infinite). Rather, *it is the infinity of a beginning* (and this is much more than the contrary of a completion, much more than the inversion of a presentation). It is not simply the infinite sprawl of a pure absence of figure. Rather, the unlimited engenders and engages itself in the very tracing of the limit: it retraces and carries off, so to speak, "unto the ground" what this tracing cuts on the edge of the figure as its contour. It retraces "unto the ground" the operation of *Ein-bildung*: but this does not constitute a replication, even a negative replication, of this operation. It does not constitute an infinite figure or image but the movement of a cutting, delineation, and seizure. The sublime will always invoke—that is, if it is anything at all and if it can constitute an aesthetics—an aesthetics of movement as opposed to an aesthetics of the static or the state. But this movement is neither an animation nor an agitation, as opposed to an immobility. (One could doubtless easily be misled, but it is not a version of the ordinary—if not Nietzschean—doctrine of the couple Dionysos/Apollo.) It is perhaps not a movement in any of the available senses of this word. It is the unlimited beginning of the delimitation of a form and, consequently, of the state of a form and of the form of a state. The unlimited gets carried away with delimiting. It does not consist by itself in a delimitation, even if negative, for the latter would still be, precisely, a delimitation, and the unlimited would end up having its proper form—say, the form of an infinite.

But the infinite, Kant declares, cannot be thought "as completely given." This does not mean that Kant, contrary to what I indicated above, has in mind exclusively a potential infinity, the bad infinity, as Hegel would say, of a progression without end. It means, once again, that in the unlimitation involved in the feeling of the sublime it is not exactly a matter of the infinite. The infinite would be merely the "numerical concept," to speak like Kant, of the unlimited, the "presentation" of which is at stake in the sublime. One would have to say that the unlimited is not the *number* but the *gesture* of the infinite (*CJ*, §27, 98; 98).[12] That is, the gesture by which all (finite) form gets carried away into the absence of form. It is the gesture of formation, of figuration itself (of *Ein-bildung*), but only insofar as the formless too stands out—without itself taking on any form—along the form that traces itself, joins itself to itself, and presents itself.

Because unlimitation is not the number but the gesture, or if one prefers, the motion, of the infinite, there can be no presentation of the unlimited. The expressions that Kant does not cease to attempt throughout the paragraphs dedicated to the sublime, those of "negative presentation," or "indirect presentation," as well as all the "so to speaks" and the "in a certain sense" strewn throughout the text, indicate merely his difficulty with the contradiction of a presentation *without* presentation. A presentation, even if it is negative or indirect, is always a presentation, and to this extent it is always in the final analysis direct and positive. But the deep logic of Kant's text is not a logic of presentation and does not pursue the thread of these clumsy expressions. It is not a matter of indirect presentation by means of some analogy or symbol—it is hence not a matter of figuring the nonfigurable[13]—and it is not a matter of negative presentation in the sense of the designation of a pure absence or of a pure lack or in any sense of the positivity of a "nothingness." To this (double) extent, one could say that the logic of the sublime is not to be confused with either a logic of fiction or a logic of desire, that is, again, with either a logic of representation (something in the place of something else) or a logic of absence (of the thing that is lacking in its place). Fiction and desire, at least in these classical functions, perhaps always frame and determine aesthetics as such, all aesthetics. And the aesthetics of mere beauty, of the pure self-adequation of presentation, with its incessant sliding into the enjoyment of the self, indeed, arises out of fiction and desire.

But it is precisely no longer a matter of the adequation of presentation. It is also not a matter of its inadequation. Nor is it a matter of pure presentation, whether this presentation be that of adequation or of inadequation, nor is it even a matter of the presentation of the fact that there is such a thing as the nonpresentable.[14] In the sublime—or perhaps more precisely at a certain extreme point to which the sublime leads us—it is no longer a matter of (re)presentation in general.

It is a matter of something else, which takes place, happens, or occurs *in* presentation itself and in sum *through* it but which is not presentation: this motion through which, incessantly, the unlimited raises and razes itself, unlimits itself, along the limit that delimits and presents itself. This motion would trace in a certain way the *external* border of the limit. But this external border is precisely not an outline: it is not a second outline homologous to the internal border and stuck to it. In one sense, it is the same as the (re)presentational outline. In another sense, and simultaneously, it is an unlimitation, a dissipation of the border on the border itself—an unbordering or overbordering, or overboarding, an "effusion" (*Ergießung*), Kant says. What takes place in this going overboard of the border, what happens in this effusion? As I have indicated above, I call it the offering, but we need time to get there.

In the sublime, then, presentation itself is at stake: neither something to be presented or represented nor something that is nonpresentable (nor the nonpresentability of the thing in general), nor even the fact that it [*ça*] presents itself to a subject and through a subject (representation), but the fact *that* it presents itself and *as* it presents itself: it presents itself in unlimitation, it presents itself always *at the limit*.

This limit, in Kantian terms, is that of the imagination. For there is an absolute limit to the imagination, a maximum of *Bild* and *Bildung*. We receive an analogical indication of this maximum in the greatness of certain objects both natural and artificial, for example, in oceans or pyramids. But these objective grandeurs, these very great figures, are precisely nothing but analogical occasions for thinking the sublime. In the sublime, it is not a matter of great figures but of absolute greatness. Absolute greatness is not greater than the greatest greatness: it designates rather that there is, absolutely, greatness. It is a

matter of *magnitudo*, Kant says, and not of *quantitas*. *Quantitas* can be measured whereas *magnitudo* presides over the possibility of measure in general: it
is the fact in itself of greatness, the fact that, in order for there to be forms of figures which are more or less large, there must be, on the edge of all form or figure, greatness as *such*. Greatness is not, in this sense, a quantity, but a quality,
or more precisely, it is quantity *qua* quality. It is in this way that for Kant the
beautiful concerns quality, the sublime quantity. The beautiful resides in form
as such, in the form of form, if one can put it this way, or in the figure that it
makes. The sublime resides in the tracing-out, the setting-off and seizure of
form, independently of the figure this form delimits, and hence in its quantity
taken absolutely, as *magnitudo*. The beautiful is the proper of such and such an
image, the pleasure of its (re)presentation. The sublime is: *that* there is an
image, hence a limit, along whose edge unlimitation makes itself felt.

Thus, the beautiful and the sublime, if they are not identical—and
indeed, quite the contrary—take place *on the same site*, and in a certain sense
the one upon the other, the one along the edge of the other, and perhaps—I
will come back to this—the one through the other. The beautiful and the sublime *are* presentation but in such a manner that the beautiful is the presented
in its presentation, whereas the sublime is the presentation *in its movement*—
which is the absolute re-moval of the unlimited along the edge of any limit.
The sublime is not "greater than" the beautiful, it is not more elevated [*élevé*],
but in turn, it is, if I dare put it this way, more removed [*enlevé*], in the sense
that it is itself the unlimited removal of the beautiful.

What gets removed and carried away is all form as such. In the manifestation of a world or in the composition of a work, form carries itself away
or removes itself, that is, at once traces itself and unborders itself, limits itself
and unlimits itself (which is nothing other than the most strict logic of the
limit). All form as such, all figure is small with regard to the unlimitedness
against which it sets itself off and which carries it away. "That is sublime,"
writes Kant, "in comparison with which all the rest is small." The sublime is
hence not a greatness that would be "less small" and would still take place
along, even if at the summit of, a scale of comparison: for in this case, certain
parts of the rest would not be "small," but simply less great. The sublime is
incomparable, it is of a greatness with relation to which all the others are
"small," that is, are not of the same order whatsoever, and are therefore no
longer properly comparable.

The sublime *magnitudo* resides—or rather befalls and surprises—at the
limit, and in the ravishment and removal of the limit. Sublime greatness is:
that there is such a thing as measurable, presentable greatness, such a thing as
limitation, hence such a thing as form and figure. A limit raises itself or is
raised, a contour traces itself, and thus a multiplicity, a dispersed manifold
comes to be presented as a unity. Unity comes to it from its limit—say,
through its internal border, but *that* there is this unity, absolutely, or again

that this outline should make up *a whole*, comes—to put it still in the same manner—from the external border, from the unlimited raising and razing of the limit. The sublime concerns the totality (the general concept of which is the concept of unified multiplicity). The totality of a form, of a presentation, is neither its completeness nor the exhaustive summation of its parts. Rather, this totality is what takes place where the form has no parts, and consequently (re)presents nothing, but presents itself. The sublime takes place, Kant says, in a "representation of the unlimited to which is added nonetheless the thought of its totality" (and this is why, as he specifies, the sublime can be found in a formless object as well as in a form). A presentation takes place only if *all* the rest, *all* the unlimitedness from which it detaches itself, sets itself off along its border—and at once, in its own way, presents itself or rather sets itself off and upsets itself all along the presentation.

The sublime totality is not at all the totality of the infinite conceived as something other than finite and beautiful forms (and which by virtue of this otherness would give way to a second, special aesthetics which would be that of the sublime), nor is it the totality of an infinite that would be the summation of all forms (and would make of the aesthetics of the sublime a "superior" or "total"[15] aesthetics). The sublime totality is rather the totality of the unlimited, insofar as the unlimited is beyond (or this side of) all form and all sum, insofar as the unlimited is, in general, on the far side of the limit, that is, *beyond the maximum.*

The sublime totality is beyond the maximum, which is to say that it is *beyond everything.* Everything is small in the face of the sublime, all form, all figure is small, but also, each form, each figure is or can be the *maximum.* The *maximum* (or *magnitudo,* which is its external border) is there whenever the imagination has (re)presented the thing to itself, big or small. The imagination can do no more: it is defined by the *Bildung* of the *Bild.*

However, the imagination can do more—or at least, if it is no longer at this point properly a "power" (*Kraft*), it receives more—there where it can do no more. And it is there that the sublime is decided: the imagination can still feel its limit, its powerlessness, its incommensurability with relation to the totality of the unlimited. This totality is not an object, it is nothing (re)presented, neither positively nor negatively, but corresponds to this: that presentation takes place. It is not presentation itself—neither the exhibition of what is presented nor the presence of what presents—but rather it is *that presentation takes place.* This is the formless form or the form of the formless, the setting-off of the limit's external border from the limit itself, the motion of the unlimited.

This totality is not, in fact, exactly the unity of the manifold: the unlimited offers properly neither a manifold nor the number of a unity. But what Kant calls "the Idea of a whole" is the *union* through which the unity of a whole is possible in general. The sublime is concerned with union, as the beautiful is concerned with unity. But union is the work of the imagination (as unity is its product): it unites concept and intuition, sensibility and understanding, the manifold and the identical. In the sublime, the imagination no longer has to do with its products but with its operation—and thus with its limit.

For there are two ways of conceiving of union. There is the Hegelian, dialectical way, which considers union as a process of reunion, as a purposiveness or finality of unification, and as its result, which is supposed to be a unity. Thus, for example, the truth of the union of the sexes for Hegel is to be found in the unity of the child. The Kantian concept of union is different. Thus, in the *Anthropology* the union of the sexes remains an abyss for reason, just as the schematizing union remains an "art" that has forever escaped our grasp. This means that Kant takes into account union *as such*, precisely in its difference from unity, precisely insofar as it is not or does not constitute by itself a unity (neither an object nor a subject). Union is more than the sum of the parts and less than their unity: like *magnitudo*, it escapes all calculation. As "Idea of the whole," union is neither the one nor the many: it is beyond everything, it is the "totality" on the far or near side of the formal unity of the whole, elsewhere, nonlocalizable, but nonetheless it takes place. Or more precisely, it is the *taking place* of all or the whole in general (thus, it is the contrary of a totalization or of a completion and instead a completing or dawning). That this should take place, that it should present itself, that it should take on form and figure, this "that" is union, is the totality beyond the whole—in relation to which all presentation is small and all greatness remains a little *maximum* where the imagination reaches its limit.

Because it reaches this limit, it exceeds this limit. It overflows itself, in reaching the overflowing of the unlimited, where unity gets carried away into union. The sublime is the self-overflowing of the imagination. Not that the imagination imagines beyond its *maximum* (and still less that it imagines *itself*: we have to do here with exactly the reverse of its self-presentation). It imagines no longer and there is no longer anything to imagine, there is no *Bild* beyond *Einbildung*—and no negative *Bild* either, nor the *Bild* of the absence of the *Bild*. The faculty of presentation (i.e., the imagination) presents nothing beyond the limit, for presentation is delimitation itself. However, it gains access to something, reaches or touches upon something (or it is reached or touched by something): union, precisely, the "Idea" of the union of the unlimited, which borders upon and unborders the limit.

What operates this union? The imagination itself. At the limit, it gains access to itself as in its speculative self-presentation. But here, the reverse is the case: that "part" of itself that it touches is its limit, or it touches itself as limit. "The imagination," Kant writes, "attains to its maximum, and in the effort to go beyond this limit it sinks back into itself, and in so doing is displaced into a moving satisfaction" (§26, 174; 91). (The question arises immediately, since there is satisfaction or enjoyment here, why is this not a mere repetition of self-presentation? Nothing is pure here, nothing made up of simple opposi-tions, everything happens as the reversal of itself, and the sublime transport is the exact reverse of the dialectical sublation.)

At the limit, there is no longer either figure or figuration or form. Nor is there the ground as something to which one could proceed or in which one could exceed oneself, as in the Hegelian infinite, that is, as in a nonfigurable instance which, infinite in its way, would not cease to cut a figure. (Such is, in general, it seems to me, the concept with which one ends up as soon as one names something like "the nonfigurable" or "the nonpresentable": one (re)presents its nonpresentability, and one has thus aligned it, however nega-tively, with the order of presentable things.) At the limit, one does not *pass* on. But it is there that *everything* comes to pass, it is there that the totality of the unlimited plays itself out, as *that which throws into mutual relief the two bor-ders, external and internal, of all figures, adjoining them and separating them, delimiting and unlimiting the limit thus in a single gesture.*

It is at once an infinitely subtle, infinitely complex operation, and the most simple movement in the world, the strict beating of the line against itself in the motion of its outline. Two borders in one, union "itself," nothing less is required by all figures, as every painter, writer, and dancer knows. It is presen-tation itself, but no longer presentation as the operation of a (re)presenter producing or exhibiting a (re)presented. It is presentation *itself* at the point where it can no longer be said to be "itself," at the point where one can no longer say *the* presentation, and where it is consequently no longer a question of saying either that it presents itself or that it is nonpresentable. Presentation "itself" is the instantaneous division of and by the limit, between figure and elimination, the one against the other, the one upon the other, the one at the other, coupled and uncoupled in a single movement, in the same incision, the same beating.

What comes to pass here, at the limit—and which never gets definitively past the limit—is union, imagination, presentation. It is neither the produc-tion of the homogeneous (which is in principle the ordinary task of the schema) nor the simple and free accord of self-recognition in which beauty consists, for it is this side of or beyond the accord of beauty. But it is also not the union of heterogeneous elements, which would be already too romantic and too dialectical for the strict limit in question here. The union with which one has to do in the sublime does not consist in coupling absolute greatness with finite limits: for *there is nothing beyond the limit*, nothing either pre-sentable or nonpresentable. It is indeed this affirmation, "there is nothing beyond the limit," that properly and absolutely distinguishes the thought of the sublime (and art) from dialectical thought (and the end of art as its com-pletion). Union does not take place between an outside and an inside in order to engender the unity of a limit where unity would present itself (according to this logic, the limit itself becomes infinite, and the only art is that which traces the Hegelian "circle of circles.") But there is only the limit, united with unlimitation insofar as the latter sets itself off, sets itself up, and upsets itself incessantly on its border, and consequently insofar as the limit, unity, divides itself infinitely in its own presentation.

For dialectical thought, the contour of a design, the frame of a picture, the trace of writing point beyond themselves to the teleological absolute of a (positive or negative) total presentation. For the thought of the sublime, the contour, the frame, and the trace point to nothing but themselves—and even this is saying too much: they do not point at all, but present (themselves), and their presentation presents its own interruption, the contour, frame, or trace. The union from which the presented or figured unity arises presents itself as this interruption, as this suspension of imagination (or figuration) in which the limit traces and effaces itself. The *whole* here—the totality to which every presentation, every work, cannot but lay claim—is nowhere but in this suspension itself. In truth, the whole, on the limit, divides itself just as much as it unites itself, and the whole is nothing but that: the sublime totality does not respond, despite certain appearances, to the supreme schema of a "total presentation," even in the sense of a negative presentation or a presentation of the impossibility of presentation (for that always presupposes a complement, an object of presentation, and the entire logic of re-presentation: here there is nothing to present but merely that it [*ça*] presents itself.) The sublime totality does not respond to a schema of the Whole, but rather, if one can put it this way, to the whole of the schematism: that is, to the incessant beating with which the trace of the *skema* affects itself, the carrying away of the figure against which the carrying away of unlimitedness does not cease to do battle, this tiny, infinite pulsation, this tiny, infinite, rhythmic burst that produces itself continuously in the trace of the least contour and through which the limit itself presents itself, and on the limit, the *magnitudo*, the absolute of greatness *in which* all greatness (or quantity) is traced, in which all imagination both imagines and—on the same limit, in the same beating—fails to imagine. That which indefinitely trembles at the border of the sketch, the suspended whiteness of the page or the canvas: the experience of the sublime demands no more than this.

In sum, from the beautiful to the sublime one more step is taken in the "hidden art" of the schematism: in beauty the schema is the unity of the presentation; in the sublime, the schema is the pulsation of the unity. That is, at once its absolute value (*magnitudo*) and its absolute distension, union that takes place in and as suspension. In beauty, it is a matter of accord; in the sublime, it is a matter of the syncopated rhythm of the trace of the accord, spasmodic vanishing of the limit all along itself, into unlimitedness, that is, into nothing. The sublime schematism of the totality is made up of a syncopation at the heart of the schematism itself: simultaneous reunion and distension of the limit of presentation—or more exactly, and more inexorably: reunion and distension, positing and vanishing *of* simultaneity (and thus of presentation) itself. Instantaneous flight and presence of the instantaneous, grouping and strewn division of a present. (I will not insist further on this here, but it is doubtless in terms of time that one ought finally to interpret the aesthetics of the sublime. This presupposes perhaps the thought of a time of the limit, of a time of the fainting of the figure, which would be the proper time of art?)

That the imagination—that is, presentation in the active sense—attains the limit, that it faints and vanishes there, "sinks back into itself," and thus comes to present itself, in the foundering of a syncopation or rather as this syncopation "itself," this exposes the imagination to its destiny. The "proper destiny of the subject" is definitively the "absolute greatness" of the sublime. What the imagination, in failing, avows to be unimaginable, is its proper greatness. The imagination is thus destined for the beyond of the image. This beyond is not a primordial (or ultimate) presence (or absence) which images would represent or of which images would present the fact that it is not (re)presentable. Rather, the beyond of the image, which is not "beyond," but on the limit, is in the *Bildung* of the *Bild* itself, and thus at or on the edge of the *Bild*, the outline of the figure, the tracing, the separating-uniting incision, the beating of the schema: the syncopation, which is in truth the other name of the schema, its sublime name, if there be such things as sublime names.

The imagination (or the subject) is destined for, sent toward, dedicated and addressed to this syncopation. That is, presentation is dedicated, addressed to the presentation *of presentation* itself: this is the general destiny of aesthetics, of reason in aesthetics, as I said at the outset. But in the sublime, it turns out that this destiny implies an unbordering or a going overboard of the beautiful, for the presentation of presentation itself, far from being the imagination of the imagination and the schema of the schema, far from being the figuration of the self-figuration of the subject, takes place in and as syncopation, and thus does not take *place*, does not have at its disposal the unified space of a figure, but rather is given in the schematic spacing and throbbing of the trace of figures, and thus only comes to pass in the syncopated time of the passage of the limit to the limit.

However, syncopated imagination is still imagination. It is still the faculty of presentation, and like the beautiful the sublime is still tied "to mere presentation." (In this sense, it is not beyond the beautiful: it is merely the beautiful's unbordering, on the border itself, not going beyond the border—and this is also why, as I will consider further below, the entire affair of the sublime occurs on the edges of works of "fine art," on their borders, frames, or contours: on the border of art, but not beyond art.)

How, then, does the imagination (re)present the limit, or rather—for this is perhaps the same question—how does it present itself at the limit?

The mode of presentation of a limit in general cannot be the image properly speaking. The image properly speaking presupposes the limit which presents it or within which it presents itself. But the singular mode of the presentation of a limit is that this limit must be reached, must come to be *touched*. This is, in fact, the sense of the word *sublimitas*: what stays just below the limit, what touches the limit (limit being conceived, in terms of height, as absolute height). Sublime imagination touches the limit, and this touch lets it feel "its own powerlessness." If presentation takes place above all in the realm of the sensible—to present is to render sensible—sublime imagination is always involved in presentation insofar as this imagination is sensible. But here sensibility no longer comprises the perception of a figure but rather the arrival at the limit. More precisely, sensibility is here to be situated in the imagination's *sentiment* of itself when it touches its limit. The imagination feels itself passing to the limit. It feels itself, and it has the feeling of the sublime in its "effort" (*Bestrebung*), impulse, or tension, which makes itself felt as such at the moment when the limit is touched, in the suspension of the impulse, the broken tension, the fainting or fading of a syncopation.

The sublime is a feeling, and yet, more than a feeling in the banal sense, it is the emotion of the subject at the limit. The subject of the sublime, if there is one, is a subject who is moved. In the thought of the sublime, it is a question of the emotion of the subject, of that emotion which neither the philosophy of subjectivity and beauty nor the aesthetics of fiction and desire is capable of thinking through, for they think necessarily and solely within the horizon of the enjoyment of the subject (and of the subject as enjoyment). And enjoyment qua satisfacton of an appropriate presentation cuts emotion short.

Thus it is a question here of this emotion without which, to be sure, there would be no beauty, artwork, or thought—but which the concepts of beauty, the work, and philosophy, by themselves and in principle, cannot touch. The problem is not that they are too "cold" (they can be quite lively and warm) but that they (and their system—beauty/work/philosophy) are constructed according to the logic I have designated above as the logic of the self-enjoyment of Reason, the logic of the self-presentation of imagination. It is the aesthetic logic of philosophy and the philosophical logic of aesthetics. The feeling of the sublime, in its emotion, makes this logic vacillate, because it substitutes for this logic what forms, again, its exact reverse, or rather (which comes down to the same thing) a sort of logical exasperation, a passage to the limit: touching presentation on its limit, or rather, being touched, attained by it. This emotion does not consist in the sweetly proprietary pathos of what one can call "aesthetic emotion." To this extent, it would be better to say that the feeling of the sublime is hardly an emotion at all but rather the mere motion of presentation—at the limit and syncopated. This (e)motion is without complacency and without satisfaction: it is not a pleasure without being at the same time a pain, which constitutes the affective characteristic of the Kantian sublime. But its ambivalence does not make it any less sensible, does not render it less effectively or less precisely sensible: *it is the sensibility of the fading of the sensible.*

Kant characterizes this sensibility in terms of striving and transport [*élan*]. Striving, transport, and tension make themselves felt (and perhaps this is their general logic or "pathetics") insofar as they are suspended, at the limit (there is no striving or tension except at the limit), in the instant and the beating of their suspension.[16] It is a matter, Kant writes, of the "feeling of an arrest of the vital forces" (*Hemmung*, "inhibition," "impinging upon," or "blockage"). Suspended life, breath cut off—the beating heart.

It is here that sublime presentation properly takes place. It takes place in effort and feeling:

> Reason…as faculty of the independence of the absolute totality…sustains the effort, admittedly sterile, of the spirit to harmonize the representation of the senses with Totality. This effort and the feeling that the Idea is inaccessible to imagination constitute in and of themselves a presentation of the subjective purposiveness of our spirit in the use of the imagination concerning its super-sensible destiny. (*CJ*, §29, 105; 128)[17]

"Striving," *Bestreben*, is not to be understood here in the sense of a project, an envisioned undertaking that one could evaluate either in terms of its intention or in terms of its result. This striving cannot be conceived in terms of either a logic of desire and potentiality or a logic of the transition to action and the work or a logic of the will and energy (even if all of that is doubtless also present and is not to be neglected if one wishes to provide an account of Kant's thought, which is not my intention here). Rather, striving is to be understood on its own terms, insofar as it obeys in itself only a logic (as well as a "pathetics" and an ethics) of the limit. Striving or transport is by definition a matter of the limit. It consists in a relation to the limit: a continuous effort is the continuous displacement of a limit. The effort ceases where the limit cedes its place. Striving and exertion transport the limit into themselves: it becomes their structure. In striving as such—and not in its success or failure—it is less a question of a tendency toward something, of the direction or project of a struggling subject, than of the tension of the limit itself. What tends, and what tends here toward or in the extreme, is the limit. The schema of the image, of any image—or the schema of totality, the schematism of total union—is extended toward and tensed in the extreme: it is the limit at the limit of its (ex)tension, the tracing—which is no longer quantifiable or hence traceable—of *magnitudo*. Stretched to the limit, the limit (the contour of the figure) is stretched to the breaking point, as one says, and it in fact does break, dividing itself in the instant between two borders, the border of the figure and its unlimited unbordering. Sublime presentation is the feeling of this striving at the instant of rupture, the imagination still for an instant sensible to itself although no longer itself, in extreme tension and distension ("overflowing" or "abyss").

(Or again, the striving is a striving to reach and touch the limit. The limit is the striving itself and the touching. Touching is the limit of itself: the limit of images and words, contact—and with this, paradoxically, the impossibility of *touching* inscribed in touching, since touching is the limit. Thus, touching is striving, because it is not a state of affairs but a limit. It is not one sensory state among others, it is neither as active nor as passive as the others. If all of the senses sense themselves sensing, as Aristotle would have it (who, moreover, established already that there can be no true contact, either in the water or in the air), touching more than the other senses takes place only in touching itself. But more than the others also, it thus touches its limit, itself as limit: it does not attain itself, for one touches only in general (at) the limit. Touching does not touch itself, at least not as seeing sees itself.)

The sublime presentation is a presentation because it gives itself to be sensed. But this sentiment, this feeling is singular. As a sentiment of the limit, it is the sentiment of an insensibility, a nonsensible sentiment (*apatheia, phlegma in significatu bono*, Kant says), a syncopation of sentiment. But it is absolute sentiment as well, not determined as pleasure or as pain but touching the one through the other, touched by the one in the other. The alliance of pleasure with pain ought not to be understood in terms of ease and unease, of comfort and discomfort combined in one subject by a perverse contradiction. For this singular ambivalence has to do first of all with the fact that the subject vanished into it. It is also not the case that the subject gains pleasure by means of pain (as Kant tends to put it); it does not pay the price of the one in order to have the other: rather, the pain here is the pleasure, that is, once again, the limit touched, life suspended, the beating heart.

If feeling properly so-called is always subjective, if it is indeed the core of subjectivity in a primordial "feeling oneself" of which all the great philosophies of the subject could provide evidence, including the most "intellectualist" among them, then the feeling of the sublime sets itself off—or affects itself—precisely as the reversal of both feeling and subjectivity. The sublime affection, Kant affirms, goes as far as the suspension of affection, the pathos of apathy. This feeling is not a feeling-oneself, and in this sense, it is not a feeling at all. One could say that it is what remains of feeling at the limit, when feeling no longer feels itself, or when there is no longer anything to feel. Of the beating heart, one can say with equal justification either that it feels only its beating or that it no longer feels anything at all.

On the border of the syncopation, feeling, for a moment, still feels, without any longer being able to relate (itself) to its feeling. It loses feeling: it feels its loss, but this feeling no longer belongs to it: although this feeling is quite singularly its own, this feeling is nonetheless also taken up in the loss of which it is the feeling. This is no longer to feel but to be exposed.

Or in other words, one would have to construct a double analytic of feeling: one analytic of the feeling of appropriation, and another analytic of the feeling of exposition: one of a feeling through or by oneself and another of a feeling through or by the other. Can one feel through the other, through the outside, even though feeling seems to depend on the self as its means and even though precisely this dependence conditions aesthetic judgment? This is what the feeling of the sublime forces us to think.[18] The subjectivity of feeling and of the judgment of taste are converted here into the singularity of a feeling and a judgment that remain, to be sure, singular, but where the singular as such is first of all exposed to the unlimited totality of an "outside" rather than related to its proper intimacy. Or in other words, it is the intimacy of the "to feel" and the "to feel oneself" that produces itself here, paradoxically, as exposition to what is beyond the self, passage to the (in)sensible or (un)feeling limit of the self.

Can one still say that the totality is presented in this instant? If it were properly presented, it would be in or to that instance of presentification (or (re)presentation) which is the subjectivity of feeling. But the unlimitedness that affects the exposed feeling of the sublime cannot be presented to it, that is, this unlimitedness cannot become present in and for a subject. In its syncopation, the imagination presents itself, presents itself as unlimited, beyond (its) figure, but this means that it is affected by (its) nonpresentation. When Kant characterizes feeling, in the striving for the limit, as "a representation," one must consider this concept in the absence of the values of presence and the present. One must learn—and this is perhaps the secret of the sublime as well as the secret of the schematism—that presentation does indeed take place but that it does not *present* anything. Pure presentation (presentation of presentation itself) or presentation of the totality presents nothing at all. One could no doubt say, in a certain vocabulary, that it presents nothing or *the* nothing. In another vocabulary, one could say that it presents the nonpresentable. Kant himself writes that the genius (who represents *a parte subjecti* the instance of the sublime in art) "expresses and communicates the unnamable." The without-name is named, the inexpressible is communicated: *all is presented—at the limit.* But in the end, and precisely at this limit itself, where all is achieved and where all begins, it will be necessary to deny presentation its name.

It will be necessary to say that the totality—or the union of the unlimited and the unlimitedness of union, or again presentation itself, its faculty, act, and subject—is *offered* to the feeling of the sublime or is *offered*, in the sublime, to feeling. The offering retains of the "present" implied by presentation only the gesture of presenting. The offering offers, carries, and places before (etymologically, of-fering is not very different from ob-ject), but it does not install in presence. What is offered remains at a limit, suspended on the border of a reception, an acceptance—which cannot in its turn have any form other than that of an offering. To the offered totality, the imagination is offered—that is, also "sacrificed" (*aufgeopfert*), as Kant writes.[19] The sacrificed imagination is the imagination offered to its limit.

The offering is the sublime presentation: it withdraws or suspends the values and powers of the present. What takes place is neither a coming-into-presence nor a gift. It is rather the one or the other, or the one and the other, but as abandoned, given up. The offering is the giving up of the gift and of the present. Offering is not giving—it is suspending or giving up the gift in the face of a liberty that can take it or leave it.

What is offered is offered up—addressed, destined, abandoned—to the possibility of a presentation to come, but it is left to this coming and does not impose or determine it. "In sublime contemplation," Kant writes, "the spirit abandons itself, without paying attention to the form of things, to the imagination and to reason, which only enlarges the imagination." The abandon is the abandon to total extension, unlimited, and thus at the limit. What comes to pass at the limit is the offering.

The offering takes place between presentation and representation, between the thing and the subject, elsewhere. This is not a *place*, you will say. Indeed, it is the offering—it is being offered to the offering.

The offering does not offer the Whole. It does not offer the present totality of the unlimited. Nor, despite certain pompous accents audible in Kant's text (and in every text dedicated to the sublime, in the word *sublime* itself), does it offer the sovereign satisfaction of a spirit capable of the infinite. For if such a capacity, at the limit, is supposed to be attained, it consists in nothing but an offering, or in being-offered. In fact, it is not a matter here of the Whole or the imagination of the Whole. It is a matter of its Idea and of the destiny of reason. The Idea of the Whole is not a supreme image, nor is it a grandiose form—nor deformity—beyond all images, any more than the destiny of reason consists in a triumphant Ideal. The Idea of the whole means rather (finally, neither "Idea" nor "Whole") the possibility of engaging a totality, the possibility of involving oneself in the union of a totality, the possibility of beginning, along the edge of the unlimited, the outline of a figure. If it is a matter of the whole, then as "the fundamentally open" of which Deleuze speaks with respect to the sublime.[20] The opening is offered to the possibility of gesture which "totalizes" figures, or traces. This possibility of a beginning is freedom. Freedom is the sublime idea *kat'exochèn*. This means neither that freedom is the content or the object of the judgment of the sublime nor that it is freedom that makes itself felt in the feeling of the sublime. In all likelihood, that would make no sense whatsoever, for freedom is not a content, if indeed it is any thing at all. Instead, one must understand this: that the sublime offering is the act—or the motion or emotion—of freedom. The sublime offering is the act of freedom in the double sense that freedom is both what offers and what is offered—just as the word *offering* designates now the gesture, now the present offered.

In the sublime, the imagination qua free play of presentation comes into contact with its limit—which is freedom. Or more exactly, freedom itself is a limit, because its Idea not only cannot be an image but also cannot—in spite of Kant's vocabulary—be an Idea (which is always something like a hyper-image, a nonpresentable image). It must be an offering.[21]

The sublime does not escape to a space beyond the limit. It remains at the limit and takes place there. This means, further, that it does not leave aesthetics in order to penetrate ethics. At the limit of the sublime, there is neither aesthetics nor ethics. There is a thought of the offering which defies this distinction.

The aesthetics of the beautiful transports itself into the sublime whenever it does not slide into mere enjoyment. The beautiful by itself is nothing— the mere self-accord of presentation. The spirit can enjoy this accord, or it can carry itself to the limit of this accord. The unlimited border of the limit is the offering. The offering offers something. I said above that it offers liberty. But liberty is also what does the offering here. Something, a sensible thing, is offered in the offering of liberty. It is in this sensible thing, on the edge of this sensible thing that the limit makes itself felt. This sensible thing is the beautiful, the figure presented by schematism without concepts. The condition of the schematism is nothing other than liberty itself. Kant declares this explicitly when he writes: "the imagination itself is, in accordance with the principles of the schematism of the faculty of judgment (consequently, to the extent that it is subordinate to liberty), the instrument of reason and its Ideas" (*CJ*, §29, 106; 109–10). Thus, it is liberty that offers the schematism, or again, it is liberty that schematizes and offers itself in this very gesture, in its "hidden art."

The sublime offering takes place neither in a hidden world withdrawn from our own nor in a world of "Ideas" nor in any world of a "nonpresentable" something or other. The sublime offering is the limit of presentation, and it takes place on and all along this limit, along the contour of form. The thing offered can be a thing of nature, and this is ordinarily, according to Kant, the occasion of the feeling of the sublime. But since this thing, as a thing of liberty, is not merely offered but also offers itself, offers liberty—in the striving of the imagination and in the feeling of this striving—then this thing will be instead a thing of art (moreover, nature itself is always grasped here as a work of art, a work of supreme liberty). Kant places poetry above all the other arts, describing it as follows: "it enlarges the soul by giving liberty to the imagination and by offering[22] within the limits of a given concept, among the limitless diversity of forms which might accord with it, that form which links the presentation of this concept with a plenitude of thoughts, to which no expression of language is perfectly adequate, and which in so doing elevates itself aesthetically to the level of the Ideas."

There is thus in art more than one occasion for experiencing sublimity.

There is—in poetry at least[23]—an *elevation* (that is, a sublime motion: Kant uses the verb, *erheben* here) to the "Ideas" which, even though it is an elevation, remains aesthetic, that is, sensible. Would one have to conclude from this that there could be another form or mode of sublime presentation in art, that of moral feeling, which would be distinct from the first mode? But in truth, it is in art and as art that the sublime offering happens. There is no opposition between an aesthetics of form and an ethical meta-aesthetics of the formless. The aesthetic always concerns form; the totality always concerns the formless. The sublime is their mutual offering. It is neither simply the formation or formalization of the formless nor the infinitization of form (which are both philosophical procedures). It is how the limit offers itself to the border of the unlimited, or how the limit makes itself felt: exactly on the cutting edge of the figure the work of art cuts.

It would not be difficult to demonstrate—and I dispense with doing so here—the systematic engenderment or derivation of art, in Kant, on the basis of both the beautiful and the sublime. Only in this way can one understand both the order of Kant's table of contents in the third *Critique* and the doctrine of genius, as well as the doctrine of the beautiful as "symbol" of the ethically good.

Beginning with Kant, the sublime will constitute the most proper, decisive moment in the thought of art. The sublime will comprise the heart of the thought of the arts, the beautiful merely its rule. This means not only that, as I have said, mere beauty can always slide into the agreeable (and, for example, into the "sublime style") but perhaps, above all, that there is no "pure" sublime purely distinguished from the beautiful. The sublime is that through which the beautiful *touches* us and not that through which it pleases us. It is joy and not enjoyment [*la joie, non la jouissance*]; the two words are originally the same word. The same word, the same limit affected by the beating of joy and enjoyment. To be touched is sublime because it is to be exposed and to be offered. To experience joy is to be exposed in enjoyment, to be offered there. The sublime is in the contact of the work, not in its form. This contact is beyond the work, at its limit, in a sense beyond art: but without art, it would not take place. The sublime is—that art should be [*soit*] exposed and offered.

Since the epoch of Kant—of Diderot, Kant, and Hölderlin—art has been destined for the sublime: it has been destined to touch us, in touching upon our destiny or destination. It is only in this sense that one must comprehend, in the end, *the end of art*.

What art is at stake here? In a sense, one has no choice, neither between particular arts nor between artistic tonalities and registers. Poetry is exemplary—but which poetry? Quite indirectly, Kant has given us an example. When he cites "the most sublime passage of the Book of the Law of the Jews," that which articulates the prohibition of images, the sublime, in fact, is present twice. It is present first in the content of the divine commandment, in the distancing of representation. But a more attentive reading shows that the sublime is present also, and perhaps more essentially, in the "form" of the biblical text. For this passage is quoted in the middle of what properly constitutes the search for the genre or aesthetics of "sublime presentation." This presentation must attempt neither to "agitate" nor to "excite" the imagination but ought always to be concerned with the "domination of reason over sensibility." And this presupposes a "withdrawn or separated presentation" (*abgezogen, abgesondert*) which will be called a bit further on "pure, merely negative." This presentation is the commandment, the law that commands the abstention from images.[24] The commandment, as such, is itself a form, a presentation, a style.

And so sublime poetry would have the style of the commandment? Rather, the commandment, the categorical imperative, is sublime because it commands nothing other than freedom. And if that comprises a style, it cannot be the muscular style of the commandment. It is what Kant calls simplicity: "Simplicity (purposiveness without art) is so to speak the style of nature in the sublime, as of morality which is a second nature."

It is not the commandment that is simple but rather simplicity that commands. The art of which Kant speaks—or of which, at the limit, he does not manage to speak, while speaking of the Bible, poetry, and forms of union in the fine arts—is the art of which the "simplicity" (or the "withdrawal" or the "separation") commands by itself, that is, addresses or exposes to freedom, with the simplicity of the offering: the offering as law of style.

"Purposiveness without art" (without artifice) is the art (the style) of purposiveness without purpose, that is, of the purposiveness of humanity in its free destination: humans are not devoted to the servility of representation but destined to the freedom of presentation and to the presentation of freedom—to their offering, which is a withdrawn or separate presentation (freedom is offered to them, they offer it, they are offered by it). This style is the style of a commandment or proscription because it is the style of a literature that proscribes for itself to be "literature," that withdraws from literary prestige and pleasure (which Kant compares to the massages of the "voluptuous orientals"): the effort by means of which it withdraws is itself a sublime offering. In short, the offering of literature itself, or the offering of all art—in all possible senses of the expression.

But "style" is doubtless here already one concept too many, like "poetry," "literature," and perhaps even "art" itself. They are certainly inappropriate and superfluous here if they remain caught up in a logic of lack and its substitute, presence and its representation (such as this logic still governs, at least in part, the Kantian doctrine of art as a "symbol"). For nothing is lacking in the offering. Nothing is lacking, everything is offered: *the whole* is offered (opened), the totality of freedom. But to receive the offering, or to offer oneself to it (to joy), presupposes precisely the freedom of a gesture—of reception and offering. This gesture traces a limit. It is not the contour of a figure of freedom. But it is a contour, an outline, because it arises in freedom, which is the freedom to begin, to incise, here or there, an outline, an inscription, not merely arbitrarily, but still in a chancy, daring, playful, abandoned manner.

Abandoned but nonetheless regulated: the syncopation does not take place independently of all syntax, but rather imposes one, or better, it is one itself. In its pulsation—which assembles—, in its suspension—which establishes and extends a rhythm—, the syncopation offers its syntax, its sublime grammar, on the edge of the language (or the drawing, or the song). Consequently, this trace is still or again art, this inscription still or again style, poetry: for the gesture of liberty is each time a *singular* manner of abandoning oneself (there is no such thing as general liberty, no such thing as general sublimity). This is not style "in the accoustico-decorative sense of the term" (Borges), but it is also not the pure absence of style of which the philosopher[25] dreams (philosophy as such and without offering, as opposed to or rather differentiated from thought): it is style, and the thought of a "withdrawn, separated presentation." It is not *a* style—there is no sublime style, and there is no simple style—but constitutes a trace, puts the limit into play, touches without delay all extremities—and it is perhaps this that art obeys.

In the final analysis, there is perhaps no sublime art and no sublime work, but the sublime takes place wherever works touch. If they touch, there are sensible pleasure and pain—all pleasure is physical, Kant repeats with Epicurus. There is enjoyment, and there is joy in enjoyment. The sublime is not what would take its distance from enjoyment. Enjoyment is mere enjoyment when it does nothing but please: in the beautiful. But there is the place (or the time) where (or when) enjoyment does not merely please, is not simply pleasure (if there is ever such a thing as simple pleasure): in the sublime, enjoyment touches, moves, that is, also commands. It is not commanded (an obligation to enjoy is absurd, Kant writes, and Lacan remembered this), but commands one to pass beyond it, beyond pathos, into ethos, if you like, but without ceasing to enjoy: touching or emotion qua law—and the law is necessarily a-pathetic. Here, "sovereign art," as Bataille writes, "accedes to the extremity of the possible." This art is indissociably "art expressive of anguish" and "that expressive of joy." The one and the other in an enjoyment, in a disproppriated enjoyment—that is, in tragic joy, or in this animated joy of the "vivacity of the affects" of which Kant speaks (§54) and which extends to the point of laughter and gaiety—they too being syncopated, at the limit of (re)presentation, at the limit of the "body" and the "spirit," at the limit of art itself.

…at the limit of art: which does not mean "beyond" art. There is all the less a beyond as art is always an art of the limit. But at the limit of art there is the gesture of the offering: the gesture that offers art and the gesture through which art itself reaches, touches upon, and interferes with its limit.

As offering, it may be that the sublime surpasses the sublime—passes it by or withdraws from it. To the extent that the sublime still combines pathos and ethos, art and nature, it continues to designate these concepts, and this is why, as such, it belongs still to a space and problematic of (re)presentation. It is for this reason that the word, "sublime," always risks burdening art either with pathos or morality (too much presentation or too much representation). But the offering no longer even arises out of an alliance of pathos and ethos. It comes to pass elsewhere: offering occurs in a simplicity anterior to the distinction between pathos and ethos. Kant speaks of "the simplicity which does not yet know how to dissimulate"; he calls it "naïveté," and the laughter or rather the smile in the face of this naïveté (which one must not confuse, he insists, with the rustic simplicity of the one who doesn't know how to live) possesses something of the sublime. However, "to represent naïveté in a poetic character is certainly a possible and beautiful art, but a rare one."

Would he characterize this extremely rare art as being henceforth a *telos* of art? There is in the offering something of the "naïve" in Kant's sense. There is sometimes, in today's art, something of the offering understood in this way. Let us say: something of a childhood (doubtless nothing new about this but a more strongly marked accent). This childlike art no longer inhabits the heights or the depths as did the sublime but simply touches the limit, without any disarticulating excess, without "sublime" exaltation, but also without puerility or silliness. It is a powerful but delicate vibration, difficult, continuous, acute, offered upon the surfaces of canvasses, screens, music, dance, and writing. Mondrian spoke, apropos of jazz and "neo-plasticism," of "the joy and the seriousness which are simultaneously lacking in the bloodless culture of form." In what offers art today to its future, there is a certain kind of serenity (Mondrian's word). It is neither reconciliation nor immobility nor peaceful beauty, but it is not sublime (self-)laceration either, assuming the sublime is supposed to involve (self-)laceration. The offering renounces (self-)laceration, excessive tension, and sublime spasms and syncopations. But it does not renounce infinite tension and distance, striving and respect, and the always renewed suspension that gives art its rhythm like a sacred inauguration and interruption. It simply lets them be offered to us.

> My painting, I know what it is beneath its
> appearances, its violence, its perpetual play of
> force; it is a fragile thing in the sense of the
> good, the sublime, it is fragile like love.
>
> —Nicolas de Staël

Chapter 3

❀

KANT OR THE SIMPLICITY OF THE SUBLIME[1]

Éliane Escoubas

Preamble

I shall begin by advancing a working hypothesis to be developed in the following pages. This hypothesis will be secured through an analysis of the Kantian sublime.

The working hypothesis is this: despite its architectonic "façade," Kant's text constitutes itself through the operation of the "imagination" (*Einbildungskraft*). The mode of its "constitution," of its textualization, is not that of a *bauen* ("construction"), but of a *bilden*: the *bilden* of the *Einbildungskraft*. It is that of a *bilden* which is a "fictioning or fashioning" as in the Latin *fingere* ("fashioning" or "forming"), of a *bilden* which erects no edifice and makes use of no scaffolding or platform but "fashions" by tracing conceptual curves, producing thematic turns and folds. It is the work of the turn, of returns, detours, and (dis)torsions; a work of the trope or the strophe which, far from letting the text congeal into the topology or topography which the all too apparent "divisions" of concepts (*Einteilungen*) would seem to comprise, produces instead an *involution* of oppositions.

Take the play of dichotomies in the Kantian text. Each time, a third term—a *Mittelglied*—intervenes not to serve as a "passage" between the two previously "exposed" terms but utterly to transform the course of the given conceptual elaboration. For example, the bipartition of the faculties of knowledge, sensibility and understanding, is turned or re-turned by a third "faculty," the imagination. Similarly, the "division" of understanding and reason is turned or re-turned by the "faculty of judgment" (*Urteilskraft*). And it is on the basis of their common status, as the "intermediate member" (*Mittelglied*), that *Einbildungskraft* and aesthetic *Urteilskraft* tend to coincide. This "equivalence" of *Einbildungskraft* and *Urteilskraft* is so strong that, as becomes evident in what follows, it is the *Critique of Judgment*[2] which completes the Kantian theory of imagination.

The Kantian "return" and recommencement of the imagination will give itself to be read here as a "fashioning" inscribed in diverse versions and diversions: those of reflexion, of *Darstellung* or presentation, and of synthesis. These versions will be the *evidence* of the sublime and its *simplicity*.

Imagination-Reflexion

Einbildungskraft and aesthetic *Urteilskraft* are related, if not identical, by virtue of their common nonobjectivity. They coincide in the retreat [*retrait*] of the object. But this retreat of the object does not have the significance of a lack. The transcendental analytic of the *Critique of Pure Reason* closes with the table of the concept of "nothing" (*Nichts*). This table of *nothing* is organized in four directions. Three of them are inscribed in the statement of the "not one" (*kein*): these are the *ens rationis*, the *nihil privativum*, and the *nihil negativum*—suppression, privation, and negation. One of them, to the contrary, proceeds affirmatively, at the very heart of the retreat or evacuation of the object: it is the *ens imaginarium*. The retreat or evacuation of the object is here neither suppression nor privation nor negation, but evidence of *form*, affirmativity of form: "simple [or "mere," *bloße*—J.L.] form..., without substance, is not an object in itself, but the simple formal condition of this object (as phenomenon), like pure space and pure time which, while they have the quality of forms of intuition, are not themselves objects of intuition [*ens imaginarium*]" (*CPR*, 249; 295). The retreat is here properly a re-treatment or re-tracing which can claim to be properly "something" (*etwas*): form. The imagination gives itself out as the faculty of form at the heart of objective nothingness. The chapter on the schematism already exposed this affirmativity of the imagination, for the schema here arose from the procedure of neutralization (neither...nor): neither sensation nor concept. This "neutrality" of the schema did not make of it the site of a lack but the site of play (insofar as the schema is a "general procedure of the imagination for procuring for a concept its image"). Formality and neutrality constitute the imagination in retreat from the object, in retreat from the image. Nonobjectivity qua retreat is the affirmativity of a propriety of the imagination, the "turn" that gives to the imagination its essential property: formality.

The same is the case for the aesthetic judgment in the *Critique of Judgment*. From the start, the beautiful, as expression of aesthetic judgment, is defined in terms of its quality not as the "relation of the representation to its object," but as the "relation of the representation to the entire faculty of representations" (*CJ*, §1, 50; 38). Here too, the retreat of the object occurs; the judgment of taste, the beautiful, as imagination, constitutes a taking of distance from the *other* of representation, a taking of distance from *what stands over against it* (the *Gegen-stand*). The result of this nonobjectivity or nonopposition is that aesthetic judgment cannot be the site where knowledge occurs. Let us now look more closely at this loss of knowledge, this sort of imaginative or aesthetic hysteria. For the aesthetic judgment is stated through the operation of the "pure cut" and the Kantian text is in mourning for beauty.[3] And yet, in spite of everything, the object is *there*; the statement of the beautiful is only possible through a certain presence of the object. A strange presence, indeed, for the statement that it is beautiful provides me with no knowledge of this object, and the nonobjectivity of this presence reads as the flip side of my indifference to the existence of the object. Nonetheless, it is of the object that I state beauty; I act "as if" (*als ob*) the beautiful were a "quality" (*Beschaffenheit*) of the object (§7). The "without" of the retreat of the object is never unaccompanied by the *simulacrum* [*semblant*] of its presence. This simulacrum, this "as if" (*als ob*), this play of simulation, traverses from one end to the other the entire *Critique of Judgment* and constitutes its thematic matrix, but the course of the development of this simulacrum across the *Critique of Judgment* takes various twists and turns which will inflect it in a direction quite different from that of *Täuschung*, of the mere "illusion" or trap. The primary effect of the simulacrum is to prevent the "pure cut" (*Spaltung*) and the determination of beauty—or of art or the imagination—as *absolute* mourning.

If there is simulation, it is because the imaginary, or the aesthetic, is inscribed in an operation of the *simul*, in the articulation of the simulacrum and the similar: in a *mimetics*. How is this mimetics determined, if not as mirror of the subject—since the beautiful is "the relation of the representation to the faculty of representations itself"—as the "returning" of the subject to itself in a pure auto-affection? The purposiveness of aesthetic judgment, which is a formal purposiveness because it is without concept or purpose, is in fact a subjective purposiveness. This is the sense of aesthetic "pleasure" (*Wohlgefallen*), in its dual aspect as the *delectable* (the beautiful as feeling of *taste*) and as *pathos* (the sublime)—*mimicries* or *affects* of the subject. But what is this pantomimic play, this play of the relay or return of the subject to *itself*? As we know, this pantomimic play also provides *no* knowledge of the subject *itself* (*CJ*, §3, 51; 39–40). The statement of the beautiful states nothing, neither of the object nor of the subject: aesthetic judgment is not determinant but reflexive. As retreat of the subject, mirror of mirrors, relay of relays, and reflexion without determination or end, reflexive judgment is declined in the *neuter*: it is not inscribed in any opposition of same and other, inside and outside. The *simul* of the simulacrum will have to take some form other than that of similitude and reproductive *mimesis*. Moreover, we can now get a glimpse of the singular strangeness of aesthetic judgment: qua judgment, it is the site on which an attribution occurs, whereas qua aesthetic, it cannot *attribute* the beautiful to the object of which it *states* the beauty.

Is there not something of the monstrous (*ungeheuer*) and, hence, the sublime in this strange status of the copula, in the "is" of the "it is beautiful"? Through this monstrosity, one of the two modes of aesthetic judgment, the *sublime* mode, comes to be the origin of *all* aesthetic judgment, that is, the origin both of the beautiful and of the sublime itself. Through this monstrosity, there comes to be a sublimity anterior to all aesthetic judgment. Further, it may be that this *ungeheuer* of the "is" of the "it is beautiful" reveals itself to be the site on which a turn of *mimesis* completes itself. This *ungeheuer* of the "is" of "it is beautiful" is an enthusiastic explosion of *mimesis*: confusion of all terms and terminology, production without end of the neuter (neither the *same* nor the *other*) as the production of form.

Neither the *same* nor the *other*, but the middle, *die Mitte, das Mittelglied*: such is the Kantian imagination. As the operation of mediation, the middle term between sensibility and understanding, it secures in the *Critique of Pure Reason* the operation of knowledge, where all begins in the middle. But as the middle term, it also confounds from the start all terminologies, for imagination is, *like* sensibility, the faculty of "presentations or intuitions" (*Darstellungen oder Anschauungen*). And *like* understanding, it is spontaneous, while sensibility is receptive. The judgment too is a *Mittelglied*. It is the middle term between understanding and reason—the faculty of concepts and the faculty of ideas. However, aesthetic judgment is not founded on the concept of the object, but on the subject's "feeling" (*Gefühl*) of pleasure or pain. What is this *Mitte* where reflexion or reflexive judgment is elaborated? What does the judgment of taste, the beautiful, reflect? It reflects the *Stimmung* of the faculties of the subject: their accord, their harmonious agreement. The *Stimmung* is the *Mitte* that renders possible the statement, "it is beautiful." And Kant interminably reiterates the reference to the *Stimmung* of the faculties throughout the *Critique of Judgment* (even when this *Stimmung* is determined as conflict of faculties, which is the case for the sublime). An incessant punctuation of the text of the *Critique of Judgment, Stimmung* might well be the *Mitte* of Kantian critique, of the entire critical enterprise: *Stimmung* might well operate the erasure of the *Einteilung*—a "harmony" (*Stimmung*) or a "play" (*Spiel*) which would double (and distort) in advance all possibility of partition. For two utterly remarkable characteristics of *Stimmung* need to be emphasized. The first is that the *Mittelglied* (i.e., imagination or faculty of judgment), which operates *Stimmung*, itself becomes one of the two terms between which the *Stimmung* operates: for it is said that *Stimmung* interrelates imagination and understanding in the beautiful and imagination and reason in the sublime—and this turn or trope blurs any topology or topography of the faculties. The second characteristic consists in this: that in the beautiful, *Stimmung* manifests itself directly as the accord or harmony of the imagination and the understanding, whereas in the sublime, *Stimmung* does not at first seem to be able to play any role, since there is here a "conflict" (*Streit*) between imagination and reason. One could oppose the conflict of the sublime to the *Stimmung* of the beautiful. But the opposition does not hold up, for the conflict between imagination and reason, in the sublime, occurs as *Stimmung* of pleasure *and* pain, as their conjunction, whereas the *Stimmung* of the beautiful manifested itself in their disjunction: pleasure *or* pain. This is the second blurring of *bauen* by *bilden*.

What is the sense of *Stimmung* in Kant? An accord of the faculties of representation, *Stimmung* is expressed in judgments (as "feelings") of the beautiful and the sublime, which give us no knowledge of either their objects or their subjects but simply manifest their subjects' "pleasure" (*Wohlgefallen*). The *Stimmung* of the beautiful and the sublime effects itself thus in the retreat of the statement [*l'énoncé*]: it is nothing that can be stated, and it itself states nothing but rather coincides with the process itself of *stating* [*l'énonciation*]. It coincides, that is, with the work of saying, which does not say itself in what is said, or which says itself in what is said without saying itself there. And what is this "pleasure" (*Wohlgefallen*) that *Stimmung* manifests? The beautiful (and then the sublime) turns out to be nothing other than the *pleasure of thinking*— "to feel with pleasure the representational state" (*CJ*, §39, 126; 135)—which can accompany the knowledge of an object but is never this knowledge itself. *Pure pleasure of thinking*—this is what Kant will uncover and at the same time cover up when, concerning the sublime, he refers to the super-sensible faculty, which is not the knowledge of an object but is nonetheless attached to a "field" (*Feld*). And through this gesture of territorialization, Kant tilts his text toward the partition of a *topos*, indeed toward a topology.

Is this "play" (*Spiel*) of *Stimmung* a play of "mirroring" (*Spiegelung*)? Clearly, as the process of stating and the pleasure of thinking, what returns in the play of reflexion and *Stimmung* is neither the *simul* of simulation nor the *simul* of similitude (neither simulacrum nor resemblance). We are dealing here with something completely different from a reproductive mimetics: the play of distanciation and proximity that inserts the statement into the hollow of its being-stated and, conversely, inserts the process or event of stating into the hollow of what it states. We are dealing with a difference without opposition, without ob-jectivity. According to Kant, this play of the faculties is nothing other than *contemplative* pleasure (*CJ*, §12), and it consists in "preserving the representational state and the activity of the faculties of knowledge": "we linger over [*verweilen*] the contemplation of the beautiful." What is the meaning of this *Verweilung* of §12 that determines contemplation? Doubtless it is an "activity" of the subject and thus a possibility of the "inner sense" (qua essential property of the subject), that is, a possibility of time as auto-affection of the subject. But through *Verweilung*, time inscribes itself as quite other than the simple form of succession; the *Weile* of *Verweilung* is neither a partition or part of time nor the incessant flight of time but the *suspension* of time—another name for contemplation. The time of the *sojourn*, of the *Aufenthalt*[4]—where the sojourn is not a place, a territory, but a *taking-place*. It is a pure form of time, for in the *Critique of Pure Reason* Kant says that "time itself does not flow away, but rather things flow away in time." Suspension of time,[5] neither regressive memory nor progressive anticipation but the inscription of an *immemoriality*: such is the sense of the Kantian imagination. The reflexion and *Stimmung* of imagination in its play thus coincide, in this first turn, with the "apprehension" (*Auffassung*) of the pure form of time, the pure form of taking-place—which is also, in its adjudicative aspect, the very process of stating in the hollow of the statement,[6] the installation of a *mimesis* which is not reproductive but productive.

Imagination-Darstellung

For the imagination is the faculty of "presentations or intuitions" (*Darstellungen oder Anschauungen*). What is then its *play* with sensibility, which is itself also a faculty of intuitions? Sensibility is receptive, whereas imagination is spontaneous (for it operates in the absence or self-evacuation of the object). But in order that an object should take place, it is necessary for the manifold or the dispersion of the world to be *received* in accordance with the forms of space and time. Because of the receptivity of sensibility, we have to do with mere "ob-jects" (*Gegen-stände*), which face us, in a merciless op-position and from an irreducible and unmasterable di-stance: our understanding is *intuitus derivatus*—whereas for an intuitive understanding (*intuitus originarius*) the object would be "creation" (*Entstand*). For us, the world must be "given" (*gegeben*). In this di-stance, in this drift of the gift or derivation of the donation [*dérive du don*], the imagination enters the "game" (*Spiel*).

One must therefore remark first of all that as "faculty of presentations or intuitions" the imagination is, enigmatically, the *faculty of the real*. How does it intervene, what is its part in the game? In the *Critique of Pure Reason*, the imagination effects the mediation between the understanding and sensibility, by presenting the concept with its intuition. This presentation is called the *schema*. The schema, "monogram of the imagination" (*CPR*, 153; 183), is not a simple image or "copy" (*Nachbild*) but a process, a relation, a placing-into-relation: the schema is the work (of the schematism), the work of the turn, elaborating a tropology of the concept.

The imagination is—and is the *faculty of the real*—in and as this labour. The image of the imagination is a "view" (*Anblick*) and the imagination is the faculty of "apprehension" (*Auffassung*). It is important to insist on this. In Kant, the imaginary is quite entirely in the real. As a faculty of *Darstellung* or *exhibitio*, the imagination is the faculty of the *reality* of the real. In fact,

Versinnlichung, the sensible transposition operated by the schematism, is *hypotyposis*, "*subjectio sub aspectum*" (*CJ*, §59, 173; 197): it subjects to the gaze or exhibits beneath the aspect. The *aspectum* and *Anblick* are the "giving-one-self" of what gives itself.[7] A "faculty of giving" (*Vermögen des Gebens*), a faculty of the appearing of what appears, the imagination "differs" from sensibility in that the latter receives the being in its *this*, in its *quid*, and the imagination gives it in its form, its *aspect*: appearing—the faculty of the *geben*, of the *es gibt*, of ontological difference.

I have said above that the faculty of aesthetic judgment judges in the presence of the object, but in the withdrawal of its ob-jectivity. In the withdrawal of the ob-jectivity of the being [*l'étant*], this presence is neither essence, the *Wesen* of *Anwesenheit*, nor subsistent presence, *Vorhandensein*. It is the pure scintillation of appearing. The "gift" of the "giving" of imagination resides in this scintillation. This is why, further, the imagination is most evidently at play as faculty of the beautiful and sublime in the *exclamation* of the beautiful and sublime (for the "judgment" of the beautiful and the sublime is not an *attribution* but an *exclamation*), where a kind of formulation of the scintillation of appearing takes place.

Let me adduce three indications of this in the text of the *Critique of Judgment*. The first indication, in Section 26 (92; 91): "One ought not to demonstrate the sublime in products of art...nor in the things of nature [*Naturdingen*], the concept of which involves already a determinate purpose [*deren Begriff schon einen bestimmten Zweck bei sich führt*]...but rather in raw nature [*an der rohen Natur*] insofar as it contains greatness." What is the sense of this *rohe Natur*, as opposed to the *Naturdingen* which involve a determinate purpose? At first glance, *rohe Natur* is wild nature, as opposed to natural things that have been transformed by humans toward the realization of their "ends" (*Zwecke*). *Rohe Natur* includes such things as the ocean, storms, the setting of the sun, and the light of the moon in their evident independence of any human manipulation. Through this independence, raw nature is opposed to cultivated fields, vegetable gardens, and groves, but also to rivers and forests, to landscapes, which are always more or less engendered by the passage of humans, even if one doesn't realize it in looking at them. Where then is the line to be drawn between *Naturdingen* and *rohe Natur*? Does it pass between artisanal manipulation and in-tact wildness? Does not the notion of "purpose" (*Zweck*) authorize a more precise, more profound elucidation? To say that these natural things have a purpose, that their concept involves a determinate purpose, is to say that they are themselves *determined*, that their presentation is the presentation of their *quiddity*, that they are "what" they are. If on the other hand, *die rohe Natur* makes us express sublimity, it does so not through *what* it is, not through these ontic determinations, but through its *how* ("it contains greatness"). When *rohe Natur* impels us to astonishment, at times to admiration, to the exclamation of the sublime, it does so not through its *what* but through its appearing, its "showing itself" as such. Its "greatness" is not the measure of the being, the quantity of the being in its *this*; its greatness is not a determination of the being, but measureless, incommensurable, the *appearing* of what appears. The *rohe Natur* of Section 26 thus indicates that the imagination, the faculty of the beautiful and sublime, is thematized as the faculty of ontological difference, as the faculty of the "*is*" in "it is beautiful" or "it is sublime."

A second indication can be found in the "general remark" of Section 29 (107; 110-11):

> If we call the sight [*Anblick*] of the starry heaven sublime, we must not place at the basis of our judgment concepts of worlds inhabited by rational beings and regard the bright points, with which we see the space above us filled, as their suns moving in circles purposively fixed with reference to them; but we must regard it, just as we see it, as a distant, all-embracing vault [*sondern bloß, wie man ihn sieht, als ein weites Gewölbe, das alles befaßt*]. And the same goes for the spectacle of the ocean, which must not be viewed as we think of it,...we must regard it as poets do, merely by what strikes the eye [*sondern bloß, wie die Dichter tun, nach dem, was der Augenschein zeigt*].

What is the sense of this *sehen bloß, wie man ihn sieht*? Is not this *Augenschein* that gives itself to the gaze of the poet the "showing itself" as such that traverses all ontic determinations? The vast vault of the sky would accordingly be not one thing among others, a being in its particularity, but "what contains all" (*das alles befaßt*), not in the sense of a container itself contained in a still larger container, but in the sense of what is contained in nothing but simply makes *all hang together*, the appearing of what appears—close to what the *Critique of Pure Reason* called the *affinity* of the manifold (127; 139). The imagination, faculty of the beautiful and sublime, is the faculty of the pure "giving to be seen" where there is *nothing* to be seen, the faculty of seizing the being in its Being, in accordance with its manner of Being: "appearing" [*Augenschein*], where the function of the imagination's image is not to imitate but to appear. And one must underscore that this turn of the imagination takes place in the "moment" of the *modality* of the sublime.

A third indication, also in the "general remark" of Section 29 (111; 116): "Simplicity (purposiveness without art) is so to speak the style of nature in the sublime [*Einfalt ist gleichsam der Stil der Natur im Erhabenen*], and so also of morality, which is a (super-sensible) second nature." A contradiction appears at once. First the style of nature in the sublime, as of morality, is called "simple" (*Einfalt*). However, this simplicity gives way to a duplicity: a second "nature," a super-sensible nature, through which Kant's text inscribes itself in the system of architectural dichotomies. There would thus seem to be a kind

of second-floor of nature, a level analogous to that of the sensible but constituted by nonsensible determinations. Nonetheless, interfering with this establishment of various levels or this staged division of nature, a difference
inscribes itself, without high or low, between nature and its style. Its style is
simple. Style is not topologically assignable; nature cannot be divided into
itself and its style. Style is the "how" of its presentation. And this "how" of its
presentation is *simple*. If the "division" (*Einteilung*) passes between a sensible
nature and a super-sensible "nature," this division is a lapsus of the difference
that *unites* nature with its style, that unites them in the unity of a style, that is,
of the simple (*Einfalt*).

The simple (*Ein-falt*, the "One-fold") is the mode of presentation of
nature. It is this *Ein-falt* or this *One-fold* that the imagination gives to be
"seen" in the sublime. With the Kantian imagination, the *One-fold* is at stake,
there is *One-foldness*—in the greatest possible proximity to the *One-in-all* of
Heraclitus.[8] This One-fold makes of the imagination not a faculty of the *double*, the redoubling of the sensible being by a super-sensible being, but a faculty of the "fold" (*Falte*) of the being in its Being, a faculty of the ontological
difference.

The Kantian imagination is the *Darstellung* of the *Einfalt*, the One-fold
as ontological difference. The Kantian imagination is not at all the operation
of a "cutting" (*Spaltung*), and the aesthetic *Urteil* is not a *Teilung*, a partition
or regionalization of the being. Also in Section 29, it is a question of the
Absonderung, the abstraction in which the sublime is inaugurated. However, it
is not at all a matter of a *Teilung*, but of the showing of what, at "work" (*Werk*)
in all showing, does not show up at all: Kant speaks thus of "negative presentation," of "presentation of the infinite." That which, though it is at work in
every show and all showing, does not put in a showing (and only in this sense
steals the show), is *form*—another name for *style*. It is form, or space and time
themselves, insofar as there is no intuition of space and time. The imagination
is "simply" (*bloß*) "negative" presentation or the presentation "of the infinitude" of forms—of space and time, which are not the "cutting up" (*Spaltung*)
of things, but the "fold" (*Falte*), the *Faltung* of things. The Kantian imagination is also the faculty of the *reality of the real*.

Note on Style

Kant's text returns a second time to the theme of form, as style, as fashion and
fashioning in the dimension of the *One-fold*. And in a symptomatic way, this
occurs in the return of the text upon itself, in the elucidation of the "textual-
ity" of the text. In Section 49 (148; 162), one reads:

> There exist in fact two fashions (*modus*) of organizing the exposi-
> tion of one's thoughts, of which the one is called a manner (*modus*

aestheticus) and the other a method (*modus logicus*). They differ in that the first has no measure other than the *feeling* [*Gefühl*] of unity in the presentation, whereas the second obeys determinate *principles*; only the first is legitimate for fine art.

And in Section 60 (176; 200), one reads: "there is thus not a method [*Lehrart*] (*methodus*), but only a manner (*modus*) for the fine arts." It is manifest here that the *manner* of thought or art, like the *style* of nature, is what cannot be assimilated to any determination and does not therefore comprise the object of a presentation but constitutes rather the very process of presentation. It is not the pure and simple disposition (organization) of elements, their structure, for the latter is related to method because it needs "determinate principles." The "manner," as opposed to structure and method, can neither be localized nor otherwise accounted for. Escaping every inventory of beings (toward which the *Lehrart* alludes), it is the incalculable trial or ordeal of Being—*Erfindung* as invention (not inventory) or as encounter [*rencontre*]: "the feeling of unity in the presentation"; it is that which uniquely fashions itself in *Bilden*. Thus, with Kant a notion of form is inaugurated which is not structural but ontological. The *inventus*, the "discovery" of the invention—turn or trope (*tropare* means "to find"), "manner" of thought and art, "style" of nature—is nothing other than the "becoming-form" of nature, or the "becoming-form" of the text; it is neither a putting-into-form of content nor a "design" (*Zweck* or *Absicht*) nor a "structure" (*Bau*) but the *phenomenon* as a mode of encounter. The phenomenon and the "manner" are two faces of the same *encounter*, rooted in the double sense of Kantian *aisthesis*—the astonishing conjunction of the "aesthetics" of the sensible and the aesthetics of art, a conjunction the exploration of which is the matrix itself of Kant's text. This conjunction is what, in the *Critique of Judgment*, Kant ceaselessly encounters (or "finds" or "invents") as what always remains to be interrogated, or rather quite simply said. This "to be said," this "saying" of *aisthesis*, in its double scintillation, but always already unified in the "One-fold," (*Einfalt*), articulates itself or is articulated as "manner."

Imagination-Synthesis

This "manner," this "feeling of unity in the presentation," inscribes itself and Kant's text in another turn: the turn of synthesis. The *Critique of Pure Reason*, in fact, installs imagination in the *Mitte*: as *Mittelglied* between sensibility and understanding, between the sensible manifold and the unity of the concept. As the *Mittelglied*, imagination is the faculty of the "composition" (*Zusammensetzung*) of the manifold or the faculty of "connection" (*Verbindung*). Composition and connection are equivalent to synthesis, to the work of gathering. Here, on the architectural edge of the text, Kant will play a double game. On the one hand, the first edition of 1781 determines imagination in the operation of its own overflowing. In fact, three modalities of gathering, three a priori syntheses, are at work in the first edition of the *Critique of Pure Reason,* and the synthesis of imagination can be found to be at once a part and the whole of synthesis.

Synthesis is triply declined. First of all as synthesis of "apprehension" (*Auffassung*), seizure of the sensible manifold, resumption of what is dispersed, in the play of time as form of the successive; the synthesis of apprehension is a serial synthesis, in the form of "one after the other," of "one by one," installing the series as a series of slices of time, a succession of "nows," the gathering of each "now" into the "now" as such. The synthesis of apprehension is the apprehension of the instant, the *Augenblick,* play of the wink of an eye—and thus *Augenblick* is properly a schema. Secondly, there is the the synthesis of reproduction, also for Kant an operation of imagination, a regressive, anamnesic synthesis, in accordance with the schema of "anew," "one more time," for here too the schema is at play but as the schema of *repetition,* reproduction of the *Abbild,* image, imitation, copy, replication, in relation with the principle of the association and affinity of the diverse. Thirdly, there is the synthesis of recognition, the synthesis of the progression toward the unity that constitutes the concept of the object—here the *one,* the *unit,* is the schema.

One can thus see that the imagination is at the same time one of the three syntheses ("there are three sources of our knowledge: sensibility and the synopsis of the manifold, imagination and the synthesis of the manifold, and apperception as unity of this synthesis" [*CPR*, 105–6; 127]) and the operation of synthesis within each of these three moments, for in each a *schema,* the product of *Einbildung* itself, must intervene. Hence, "imagination" (*Einbildung*) exceeds itself as a topologically situable instance and is at work on all of these levels, in each of these moments. The play of the imagination as play of synthesis functions within each faculty, confounding all dichotomies and trichotomies.

But Kant will then proceed to efface this confusion, in the second edition of 1787, where the imagination comes to be placed henceforth in the "service" of the understanding, contained within certain limits, more or less assigned to the tasks of reproduction and "comparison" (*Vergleichung*). It gives way before "the original synthetic unity of apperception," which is another name for the "I think." A bungled revision on Kant's part, for synthesis in general continues to be the operation of imagination: "synthesis in general is the simple [*bloße*] effect of imagination, that is, of a blind function of the soul" (*CPR*, 93; 112). This passage is maintained in the second edition, but in his own copy Kant replaced "soul" (*Seele*) with "understanding" (*Verstand*).

The result is incomprehensible. Either the understanding thus becomes the entire soul, but then one could no longer comprehend how understanding, in its eminent clear-sightedness, could involve a blind function. Or the imagination, as faculty of synthesis, is identical with the "I think" the blind spot of which is the difference that articulates (unites) the stating and the statement. This difference—which is blinding (but not incisive or cutting) in the senses of both "to make blind" and "to be evident, obvious"—is purely coextensive with the deployment of the one and the other (difference between the representation and its "companion," since the "I think must be capable of accompanying all of my representations"). This identity of the imagination and the "I think" will find its echo in the *Critique of Judgment*, where the beautiful, which is imaginative play, coincides, as we have seen, with the pure pleasure of thinking.

The *Critique of Judgment* takes up again the imagination as faculty of *gathering*. The imagination is in fact described here as the faculty of a double operation: "apprehension" (*Auffassung*) and "comprehension" (*Zusammenfassung*) (§26, 91; 90). This description takes place in the analytic of the mathematical sublime. With regard to a quantum, as in the case of the mathematical sublime, comprehension is not, like apprehension, the simple serial act of summation "one by one" or of the passage from term to term but rather "connection" (*Verbindung*) and this is why it can attain its *maximum*:

> As to apprehension there is no difficulty, for it can go on ad infinitum, but comprehension becomes harder the further apprehension advances, and soon attains its maximum, viz. the greatest possible aesthetical fundamental measure for the estimation of magnitude. For when apprehension has gone so far that the partial representations of sensuous intuition at first apprehended begin to vanish in the imagination, while this ever proceeds to the apprehension of others, then it loses as much on the one side as it gains on the other; and in comprehension there is a maximum beyond which it cannot go.

This "failure" of the imagination makes clearly evident that the fundamental determination of the Kantian imagination is not retention, for its capacity for retention has limits. Rather, the fundamental determination of the imagination resides in the production of a *nonsurpassable* point, of a *maximum*—the result of a synthesis which is not an enumeration or summation "one by one," but the accomplishment of a *summum*, and this *summum* is the engenderment of the sublime. The imagination is thus, strangely, the faculty of the production of the *unimaginable*; it is this unimaginable instance, as an effect of imagination, that the sublime[9] designates. The unimaginable, or the sublime, is the effect of a game of "whoever loses wins" played by the imagination; this game is ruled by the "fundamental measure" (*Grundmaß*), which Kant determines by turns as the unit of measurement and as the maximum: it is the operation of *Being-together*.

Comprehension and *summum* secure for the imagination the status of the faculty of the "together" (*zusammen*), of the *in-simul*. Thus the *simul* takes a turn, changes its direction and sense: Kantian imagination is not at all the faculty of the "simulacrum," but the faculty of *Being-together*. This gathering or logos of the sensible world, this *convocation* of beings in the Open, this *phuein* of *physis* or economy of *physis* no longer has anything to do with an economy of *mimesis*.

The Kantian moment of the imagination is thus that which decisively and definitively rejects the mimetic status of the imagination, with which it was confused from Plato to Descartes. The imagination is no longer the place of "imitation" (*Nachahmung*) after the fact, of "aping" (*Nachäffung*). Through this "turn" *(Kehre),* Kant inaugurates a different epoch of thought and of the sense of Being.

Let me mark two further principle traits concerning the Kantian themes of the imagination and the sublime.

1. At first view, the play of Kantian imagination seems to be play of subtraction. The imagination of the *Critique of Judgment* seems to be the faculty of lack, the trope of *-los*. Is not its immediate determination in fact the "without" of the "without relation" to the object, of the "without theme," the "without concept," the "without purpose," the "without charm," the "without interest," the denial of the existence of the object, the denial of perfection? And this goes all the way to the pure form of the beautiful (formal purposiveness or form of purposiveness)—a pure *remainder*. Even more, the beautiful marks a mere arrest in the middle of the chain of "withouts," for the sublime takes the chain up again, and with the sublime even form itself is foreclosed. The sublime is "without form" or "formless" (*formlos*) (§25, 89; 87).

However, the imagination of the *Critique of Judgment*, faculty of the beautiful and sublime, is the vehicle of another "view" (*Anblick*) of the being, inscribed in another logic, the logic of "pleasure" (*Wohlgefallen*) (or as the French translation says, of satisfaction). The logic of *Wohlgefallen* is an additive logic, a logic of the "more," a logic of excess. It is this "more," this excess of *Wohlgefallen* that, ceaselessly echoing itself, amplifying itself in this echo, traverses the entire text of the *Critique of Judgment*—to culminate in the "deduction of the judgments of taste" which is purely and simply the deduction of this "more," this excess of *Wohlgefallen*. In Section 36 (122; 130), one reads: "However, with a perception, a feeling of pleasure (or pain) and satisfaction [*Wohlgefallen*] can be linked immediately, which accompanies the representation of the object and *takes the place* of any predication; and thus an aesthetic judgment, which is not a judgment of knowledge, can be produced." And further on: "It is easy to see that judgments of taste are synthetic judgments, because they *go beyond* the concept and even beyond the intuition of the object, and *add something* to that intuition *as predicate* which is not a cognition, viz. a feeling of pleasure (or pain)" (123; 131). (In these two quotations, emphasis added—E. E.). This work of deduction, which reinscribes aesthetic judgment as a priori synthetic judgment in its proximity to theoretical judgment, is properly the elaboration of a logic of the "more": the "more" of "accompaniment" (*Begleitung*), the compensatory and substitutive "more" (*mehr*) of "taking the place of," the "more" of "adding to" (*etwas als Prädikat hinzutun*). Paragraph 49 takes up again and redoubles this logic of the *mehr*, by installing the notion, as unexpected as it is enigmatic, of *aesthetic Ideas* (the aesthetic Idea is thus posited in a total equivalence with *Wohlgefallen*). Let us read Section 49 (143–44; 157): "And by an aesthetic Idea I understand that representation of the imagination which occasions *much thought*, without however any definite thought, i.e., any concept, being capable of being adequate to it; it consequently cannot be completely compassed and made intelligible by language." And further (144; 158):

> If now we place under a concept a representation of the imagination belonging to its presentation, but which occasions in itself *more thought* than can ever be comprehended in a definite concept and which consequently aesthetically *extends* the concept itself in an *unbounded* fashion, the imagination is here creative, and it brings the faculty of intellectual ideas (the reason) into movement; i.e., by a representation *more* thought (which indeed belongs to the concept of the object) is occasioned than can in it be grasped or made clear.

And also (145; 158):

> [Aesthetic attributes] do not, like logical attributes, represent what lies in our concepts of the sublimity and majesty of creation, but something different, which gives occasion to the imagination to spread itself over a number of kindred representations that arouse *more* thought than can be expressed in a concept determined by words. They furnish an aesthetic Idea, which…enlivens the mind by opening up for it the prospect of an *unforeseeable* field [*ein unabsehliches Feld*] of related representations. (In these quotations, emphasis added—E. E.).

The same logic ties here the theme of the "more" to that of *Erweiterung*—of the extension or enlargement of the concept. The extension is here first of all that of the concept of nature ("This purposiveness [of natural beauty] does not in fact extend our knowledge of the objects of nature, but our concept of nature" [§23, 86; 84]) and resides in the gift of "giving" (*geben*), in the articulation of the *es gibt*. But it is also the extension of the imagination itself in the sublime: "it is not a matter of a satisfaction [*Wohlgefallen*] occasioned by the object [*am Objekte*], as for the beautiful...but of a satisfaction occasioned by the extension of the imagination itself [*an der Erweiterung der Einbildungskraft*]" (§25, 89; 87).

What is this *Erweiterung*? What is this *Unabsehliche*? What are this unlimitation and this unforeseeable? They are the modality itself of the *sublime*. At this point we can confirm that the sublime is another name for the imagination itself: the *unimaginable* as such. *Erweiterung* is nothing other than the "disproportion" (*Unangemessenheit*) of the imagination, which is its very definition. It is in this that the Kantian imagination is the faculty which confounds and interferes with all the other faculties, which confuses the terms of all dichotomies and trichotomies. It is the antifaculty.

2. Unlimitation, "free play" (*freies Spiel*), legality "without law" (*ohne Gesetz*): such is the imagination—*Urheberin* (§22, 80; 77): "faculty" of *beginnings*.

Where does the imagination "begin"? It "begins" in *Wohlgefallen*, in the event of the sensible, in its *announcement*. What is it that in sensation determines "pleasure"? Not *what* it gives, but *that* it gives itself, the *taking-place* of the sensible itself determines "pleasure." *Wohlgefallen* is not any property of the object, but the coming of the world to the gaze (*subjectio sub aspectum*): the *summoned appearing* [*comparaître*], the presence of the present presentation. In this "summoned appearance" an entirely other mode of temporality inscribes itself: a temporality which is no longer the form of the successive, but the mode of *suspension*.

Kantian imagination—the image of which does not complete itself in *imitating* but in *appearing*—is the other name for Being, the Kantian name for Being. For what is *Erweiterung*, as essential operation of imagination, if not the work of "Openness" (*Offenheit*)? The imagination begins in *Offenheit*. The sublime is the mode of human feeling on the edge of *Offenheit*; the sublime is the pure "affect" of *Offenheit*. It is the feeling one has in the face of "raw nature" (*rohe Natur*) and when one gazes at the starry sky, the ocean, or even the human form, simply "as one sees them," according to the *Augenschein*, when the gaze does not install itself, does not enclose itself in the determinations of beings. In the *Augenschein*, the gaze is not arrested by the being in its this-ness, is not immobilized, but "seizes" *physis* in its *phuein*. The resistance by means of which the imagination elaborates the sublime is not the position of the ob-ject, but the very position of *Offenheit*. Not the yawning of the abyss, but the patency of Openness.

Thus, the "affect" of *Offenheit* culminates in the "pathetics" of the sublime. Concerning the dynamic sublime, Kant explains himself in a manner which is at the very least astonishing. He asserts that, before the spectacle of unbound nature, such as storms, tempestuous oceans, volcanoes, we feel the sublime, on the condition however of not being endangered but in "safety"

(*Sicherheit*). Does the sublime consist then in a mere *simulacrum* of fear? What sense does Kant grant to this *Sicherheit*? Is he saying that we play at being afraid, that we act as if we were afraid, thus reinscribing the sublime in the structure of the lure? Is he saying that the feeling of safety makes us rejoice in an egoistical and cowardly manner before a harrowing spectacle? If this were the case, how could Kant affirm that the sublime participates in moral feeling? Can one not decipher in another way this *Sicherheit*, this feeling of safety and security? For if I am safe, I am safe from the effects of the storm or the unchaining of the ocean, I am safe from the threat of drowning in *what* is happening, in *this* or *that* event, but I am not safe before the (*unforeseeably*) *blinding light* of the happening as such, of the coming to be as such, I am not safe before the *Ungeheuer*, the terrible trial of Being-there. It is in this "difference" that *Sicherheit*, as condition of the sublime, is inscribed.

The Kantian sublime, then, is a distant and intermediate glimpse of the ontological difference: an intermediate glimpse of the appearing of what appears. Of appearing itself. Such is the simplicity of the sublime.

Chapter 4

❀

SUBLIME TRUTH

Philippe Lacoue-Labarthe

1.

In the passages of the *Critique of Judgment* where he treats the sublime, Kant twice quotes examples of utterances which nothing could surpass in sublimity, examples of what has been *most sublimely* said and thought—absolutely.

The first quotation occurs in the "General Remark" which closes the "Analytics of the Sublime" proper. Kant is in the process of positing that the sublime "ought always to have a relationship to the mode of thought, that is, to maxims which attempt to procure for what is intellectual and for the Ideas of Reason domination over sensibility." And he adds:

> We need not fear that the feeling of the sublime will lose by so abstract [*abgezogen*] a mode of presentation—which is quite negative in respect of what is sensible—for the imagination, although it finds nothing beyond the sensible to which it can attach itself, yet feels itself unbounded by this removal of its limitations; and thus that very abstraction is a presentation of the Infinite, which can be nothing but a mere negative presentation, but which yet expands the soul. Perhaps there is no sublimer passage in the Jewish law than the command, "Thou shalt not make to thyself any graven image, nor the likeness of anything which is in heaven or in the earth or under the earth," etc. This command alone can explain the enthusiasm that the Jewish people in their moral period felt for their religion, when they compared themselves with other peoples, or explain the pride which Mohammedanism inspires. (§29, 110; 115)

71

The second quotation (the second and last time: nowhere else in the third *Critique* does one find a similarly hyperbolic presentation of an example) occurs in section 49, one of the paragraphs devoted to the genius, that is, to the sublime artist or the artist of the sublime. This time, the quotation takes place in a footnote and the example concerns, as in the first case, the sublime "of thought." Kant writes:

> Perhaps nothing more sublime was ever said and no sublimer thought ever expressed than the famous inscription on the Temple of Isis (Mother Nature): "I am all that is and that was and that shall be, and no mortal hath lifted my veil." Segner [a university Professor and contemporary of Kant] availed himself of this idea in a suggestive vignette prefixed to his *Natural Philosophy*, in order to inspire beforehand the pupil whom he was about to lead into that temple with a holy awe, which should dispose his mind to serious attention. (146; 160)

Before specifying the reasons I have for establishing a relationship between these two examples, it is necessary that I dwell a bit on the context of this note.

Section 49 ("Of the Faculties of the Mind that constitute Genius") is of paramount importance for the determination and hence for the very possibility of a *sublime art*, and not merely, in a reflexive mode, of a sublime affect or emotion. Kant is defining here what he calls the "soul" of a work or the "life principle of spirit": that *supplement* or *surplus* of life—for the logic of the sublime is (almost) always a logic of the supplement—which exceeds what one could call, with Diderot, mere "technique." The soul is of course literally that which animates a poem, a narrative, or a discourse, a conversation. Now, this principle, Kant asserts, "is none other than the faculty of the presentation of *aesthetic Ideas*," that is, of those representations of the imagination which give "much to think" (the expression is, as is well known, purely and simply transcribed from Longinus), "without any determinate thought, i.e., any concept, being capable of being adequate to [them], and which consequently no language could completely express and render intelligible" (143–44; 157). As a kind of inversion of the Ideas of Reason, these aesthetic Ideas are pure intuitions without concept. But like the Ideas of Reason, "they tend at least toward something which is located beyond the limits of experience." Their aim is thus properly *metaphysical* because the imagination is, Kant writes, "(as productive faculty of knowledge)…very powerful in the creation of an *other nature* as it were out of the real matter that *real nature* gives it" emphasis added—P. L.). As one can see, Kant is being faithful to the tradition here: what is at stake in the sublime, since Longinus, will always have been the presentation of the meta-physical as such. And it is moreover this very faithfulness which makes him say that "it is in poetry that the faculty of aesthetic Ideas can manifest itself in its entire strength" (144; 158). Poetry would be then the sublime art par excellence: an old τοπτoσ, which however owes nothing, or very little, to the supposedly "rhetorical" origin of the aforementioned tradition.

Such aesthetic Ideas are clearly "sensible forms." Kant calls them aesthetic attributes, by contrast to logical attributes: they are the attributes "of an object the concept of which, as an Idea of Reason, can never be presented adequately." For example, the eagle of Jupiter, "holding the lightning in its talons," or the peacock of "the superb Queen of the sky," representing the sublimity and majesty of creation. These attributes do not provide any concept of creation, but they "permit one to think much more than what one can express by words in a determinate concept": poetry and eloquence owe to them "the soul that animates their works" and, in another hyperbolic formulation, they "give to the imagination an impulse for thinking...more than one can think" (145; 159).

I insist on this only because here Kant summarizes the classical thought of the sublime.

Kant illustrates his position with respect to this thought with two examples. These examples will come to be completed in a note, by the example—infinitely more sublime—of the inscription on the pediment of the temple of Isis. But it happens that these two examples, and this is what I wanted to get to, as if by a sort of magnetism or constraint which ought indeed to have its reason, are comparisons where each time, it is a sun that appears, either rising or setting.

The first example is well known:[1] it is the poem by Frederic the Great ("Thus the star of day, at the end of its path...") in which the great king, Kant writes, "animates his rational Idea of a cosmopolitan disposition at the end of life by an attribute which the imagination (in remembering all the pleasures of a beautiful summer day that are recalled at its close by a serene evening) associates with that representation" (145; 159). The second example, in which the comparison (the relation between sensible and supersensible) is inverted, is this verse by a certain Withof, professor of morals, eloquence, and medicine at Duisburg: "The sun arose, as calm from virtue springs" (145; 159).

Since the publication of "White Mythology" by Jacques Derrida,[2] we are aware that a certain *heliotropism* is from the start constitutive of the discourse of philosophy upon its object: the meta-physical. That one sees it at work, with respect to the sublime, has therefore nothing very surprising about it. However, I ask myself—and this will be perhaps finally my question—if this heliotropism or, more broadly, this native phototropism of philosophy is as homogeneous and univocal as it appears. And above all as simple. I ask myself if, under certain conditions, in the motif of light, brilliance, refulgence, bedazzlement, and so on, here or there something might intrude or occur which would be completely foreign to the metaphysical assumption of sight and the unbroken coercion of the theoretical. One should perhaps allow another question of light to dawn, and reexamine quite closely the entire "system of lighting" of philosophy. I will not apply myself to that here, except quite allusively, but I would like the reader to keep present to his or her mind this heliotropic context of the second of the examples I am drawing, less arbitrarily than it seems, from Kant's text.

Thus: Moses and Isis. The two utterances which strike Kant certainly do not say the same thing. However, there are certain affinities between them, aside from their remarkable presentation.

In both cases, for example, the sublime utterance is a divine utterance: it is a god who speaks. In both cases, however, this utterance is not really direct, despite grammatical appearances: it is not in his or her own voice that the god speaks; its speech is reported and inscribed (on tables, on the pediment or in the interior of the temple). Finally, in both cases, and in accordance with their common indirection, the utterance has to do with the nonrepresentation of the god (the god calls "itself" nonpresentable): either in the form of the prohibition of the representation of the god, a prohibition which itself entails a prohibition of representation in general, or in the form of a declaration of impossibility (I cannot be unveiled), which is perhaps nothing but a more subtle—if not more menacing—form of prohibition. Obviously, these affinities are not merely formal. Whatever the differences between the enunciations, these affinities arise from the *content* of the utterances, which is in each case that the god is not presentable. We are confronted then, in Kantian terms (but also in pre-Kantian terms, for this has been said in any number of ways since Longinus), with the canonical definition of the sublime: the sublime is the presentation of the nonpresentable or, more rigorously, to take up the formula of Lyotard, the presentation (of this:) that there is the nonpresentable.

But a great difference remains between these two utterances: they do not draw on the same metaphors. The question they pose is indeed that of presentation and of the limit of presentation: not everything presents itself. But in the first case, the presentation is conceived in terms of the figure, the form, the image (or in biblical terms, the "graven image"). If there is a question, it opens and can only open onto a problematic of the cut [*découpe*] and consequently, as Nancy[3] has shown, of delimitation and unlimitation. (That it opens, and in a classical manner, onto a problematic of representation, in the sense of reproduction and thus imitation, is probably only a consequence of this. I will attempt to return to this.) In the second case, the presentation is thought as unveiling. And perhaps that changes everything.

2.

Perhaps that changes everything. At least this is the hypothesis in terms of which I shall regulate my discourse here.

I take my departure in the formation of this hypothesis—to announce it at the outset—from the Heideggerian delimitation of aesthetics. But not, I should immediately add, without a certain reticence, that is, not without questioning this delimitation or without believing in the necessity of testing, at least concerning one point, its rigor or solidity.

When, in 1935–36, Heidegger undertakes the deconstruction of aesthetics, directly ("The Origin of the Work of Art") or indirectly (the first course on Nietzsche: "The Will to Power as Art"), he calls "aesthetics," in the broad sense, the totality of the philosophy of art since Plato and Aristotle. The chapter of *Nietzsche* entitled, "Six Fundamental Facts taken from the History of Aesthetics," is perfectly clear in this regard:

> The term, "aesthetics," applied to the reflexion on art and on the beautiful, is of recent formation and dates from the eighteenth-century. As for the thing itself, which this name fittingly denominates—the manner of questioning concerning art or the beautiful from the point of view of the state of feeling of the one who produces them or the one who enjoys them—it is as old as the reflexion on art and the beautiful in occidental thought. It is already as an aesthetics that philosophy *begins* to reflect on the essence of art and the beautiful.[4]

This delimitation orients the deconstruction toward an interrogation of the *work* itself, in its essence,[5] unless of course it is the other way around. In any case, things could not be more neat.

> High or great [*große*] Greek art remains without any corresponding cognitive-conceptual reflexion [*Besinnung*], which would not necessarily have to be the same thing as an aesthetics....Aesthetics does not begin in Greece until the moment when great art, but also great philosophy, which follows the same course, are approaching their end. It is in this epoch, the age of Plato and Aristotle, that, in connection with the formation of philosophy, the fundamental concepts are forged [*geprägt, frappés,* "imprinted," "coined," "impressed," "typed out"] which will delimit in the future the circumscription of any interrogation concerning art. (95; 80)

"Aesthetics," then, designates for Heidegger the metaphysical (Platonic and post-Platonic, including Nietzsche) apprehension of art and the beautiful.

But exactly how are these fundamental—and, until our own times, determining—concepts "imprinted"?

Here's what Heidegger writes:

First, the conceptual couple ὕλη·μορφή, materia-forma, content-form. This differentiation has its origin in the conceptualization—founded by Plato—of the entity with regard to its appearance: εἶδος·ἰδέα. Where the entity is considered as an entity, and is distinguished from other entities with a view to its appearance, the contour and the constellation of what is comes into view as outer and inner delimitation. What delimits, however, is form and what is delimited is content. Into these determinations that is brought which steps before our eyes as soon as the art work is experienced as the self-showing, in accordance with its εἶδος, φαίνεσθαι. The ἐκφανέστατον, that which authentically shows itself and the most appearing of all, is the beautiful. By way of the idea, the work of art passes into the characterization of the beautiful as ἐκφανέστατον. (95–96; 80)

The operation to which Heidegger commits himself here is, I believe, relatively strange. In any case, it is surprising and provokes a first reservation.

It is self-evident that the conceptual couple form-matter derives from the predetermination of the entity or being (in its Being) as εἶδος. From the moment when the entity is conceived as aspect or figure—that is, in terms of the cut or contour of delimitation—it divides itself necessarily into limiting and limited. But does this mean that the φαίνεσθαι, the self-showing or the appearing of the entity, its Being-luminous and visible, derives in its turn from such a predetermination? That there should be appearing in general does not depend on the eidetic seizure of the entity, even if it does so for Plato himself. It is nonetheless not Plato who "invented" the πηαινεστηαι, that is, the determination of presence as appearing. What Plato did, however, invent, and it is in this that he is reponsible for philosophy (and for aesthetics), is as Heidegger correctly says that the entity should appear "in accordance with its εἶδος." The inaugural gesture of philosophy (of aesthetics) is the eidetic subjugation of the φαίνεσθαι and not—I will risk the word—the "phantic" seizure of presence. Otherwise, what could be at stake, with regard to the destiny of metaphysics, in a phenomenology? It is consequently difficult to support the argument that the Platonic definition of the beautiful in terms of the ἐκφανέστατον is simply Platonic; nor can one say that "by way of the idea, the work of art passes into the characterization of the beautiful as ἐκφανέστατον." All one can say is that with Plato the eidetic overdetermination of the ἐκφανέστατον—no doubt definitively—introduces itself.[6]

This sort of power play would have every chance of passing unperceived if, in the same period, Heidegger's own definition of the beautiful, taking into account the "step back" in (and vis-à-vis) aesthetics in general, could not in its turn be related to the ἐκφανέστατον. Against all expectation.

I shall remove this definition, for the moment, from its context which is in itself, moreover, quite "illuminating":

> In the work, it is the truth which is at work, and not simply something true....That is how self-concealing Being is illuminated [*gelichtet*]. Light of this kind joins its shining [*sein Scheinen*] to and into the work. This shining [*das Scheinen*], joined in the work, is the beautiful. *Beauty is one way in which truth essentially occurs as unconcealedness.* (*The Origin of the Work of Art,* 42; 56)

That makes much (of) light. But it is less the motif of light and of the lighting/clearing itself (*Licht, Lichten, Lichtung,* etc.) that is decisive here than the manner in which the motif restores to "appearing" (*Scheinen*) all of its semantic density, which is, as is well known, the same as that of the Greek φαί-νεσθαι: "to glitter and glow," "to shine," "to show oneself," or "to appear."[7] And Heidegger does not cease to base himself on this semantic density when, apropos of the work of art and the beautiful, he foregrounds the *Scheinen* and treats it, in his way, phenomenologically.

What is the sense, then, and under these conditions, of Heidegger's operation—or power play, as we have called it above?

There is perhaps an indication and the occasion of a conjecture in the fate Heidegger reserves precisely for Kant. In the course of his recapitulation of the history of aesthetics, Heidegger does not mention Kant's name even once. In addition, curiously, he does not make the slightest allusion to the problematic of the sublime: "sublime" is a word which does not belong to the Heideggerian lexicon, even if the concept—and the thing itself—are everywhere present (if only under the name of "greatness"). That Kant doesn't appear in such a history, which after all claims to be simply "indicative," does not mean that he is simply omitted from the unfolding of aesthetics or that one ought to reserve a place for him outside of it: Heidegger will have multiplied traces of allusions to the third *Critique* and clearly marked the insufficiency of Kantian categories with regard to the question of the essence of art.[8] The absence of Kant means simply that he does not make up a *moment* in the history of aesthetics or, if you prefer, that he belongs to the unfolding of aesthetics proper, of modern aesthetics as Hegel completes and closes it, tracing at the same time the closure of aesthetics in general, i.e., the closure of the philosophy of art in its totality.[9]

However, and nearly at the same time, Heidegger excepts Kant from this tradition (and Schiller with him: "the only one who, with relation to the Kantian doctrine of the beautiful and of art, understood the essential"), as if Kant and Schiller, at least when read in a certain manner, had something to say—in the very language of aesthetics which is inevitably their own but in secretly exceeding, and from the interior, the limits of aesthetics—which touches on the essence of the beautiful and of art. This happens two chapters further on in the lectures, where Heidegger undertakes to plead the cause of Kant against the violent and repeated accusations of Nietzsche (126–34; 107–14). Nietzsche's accusations concern the notion of "disinterested pleasure." Heidegger's argument takes the form of the attempt to correct what he sees as a misunderstanding or misinterpretation. Not only is Nietzsche the victim of Schopenhauer's erroneous and extraordinarily weak reading of Kant—which reads disinterest as indifference and therefore as the suspension of willing—but he does not comprehend the essence of interest, i.e., of the appropriative desire which obliges one always to take and represent the object of one's interest "in view of something else." He does not comprehend that disinterest is the letting-be and letting-come-forth of the object, the "letting...the object produce itself of itself, purely as itself, in its proper rank and dignity," which dictates with respect to the beautiful that behavior which Kant calls "free favor" (*die freie Gunst*) by which, says Heidegger, "we must set free what we encounter as such into what it is, leave to it and grant it that which belongs to it and which it brings to us." In short, the misunderstanding concerns this: far from distancing the object in an indifference, disinterest (or free favor) opens rather the possibility of relating oneself to it in an essential manner. This is why Heidegger can say the following—and here the operation becomes truly quite strange, since it is nearly his own definition of the beautiful that he proposes:

> From this misunderstanding of "interest" comes the error of believing that the elimination of interest would suppress any essential relation to the object. However, the contrary is true. For it is precisely by virtue of the lack of interest that the essential relation with the object itself comes into play. One has not seen that it is only from this moment on that the object as pure object makes its appearance [*zum Vorschein kommt*], that this appearance [*dieses in-den-Vorschein-kommen*: Klossowski adds between parentheses to the French translation, in order to render palpable the resonance of *Scheinen*: "this coming to light" (*ce venir au jour*)] constitutes the beautiful. The word, "beautiful," means the showing-up in the sheen of such a shining [*Das Wort "schön" meint das Erscheinen im Schein solchen Vorscheins*]. (130; 110)

Heidegger generally leaves very little to chance. It is necessary therefore to understand: (1) that Kant is as close as can be to the determination of the beautiful in its essence, to a non-aesthetic (non-*eidetic*) determination of the beautiful, and (2) that only the *Scheinen*, thought through consistently (that is, in the manner of the Greeks), permits access to this essence. This recognition of Kant does not, on the other hand, exclude certain reservations. But it is striking to see the extent to which Heidegger's language here is consonant with that of certain major propositions from "The Origin of the Work of Art." Concerning "free favor," for example: "wouldn't this be rather [if one does not misinterpret it in the manner of Schopenhauer] the supreme effort of our essence, the liberation of ourselves in favor of the restitution [*Freigabe*] of that which in itself has its own dignity, in order that it should have this dignity purely?" Or again, concerning the "pleasure of reflexion [*Lust der Reflexion*]:

> The Kantian interpretation of the aesthetic stance as "pleasure of reflexion" penetrates into a fundamental state of being-human in which man first attains the grounded plenitude of his essence. It is that state which Schiller understood as the condition of the possibility of the historical—i.e., of the history-grounding—existence [*Daseins*] of man.

Read in this manner—in other words, with and against Nietzsche (but also with the help of Schiller)—Kant does not properly belong to aesthetics. In his text, a comprehension of the beautiful surfaces that is more archaic (which does not mean more ancient: it is, to the contrary, as *comprehension*, entirely to come) than the philosophical comprehension. And this comprehension is indicated by one word: *Scheinen*.

Heidegger's complex gesture with respect to the ἐκφανέστατον and his equally complex gesture with respect to the Kantian determination of the beautiful find perhaps their explanation in the nearly insurmountable difficulty Heidegger encounters when he attempts to delimit aesthetics. This difficulty, as one knows, has a name: Hegel.

As he expressly states in the epilogue to "The Origin of the Work of Art,"[10] Heidegger doubts that one can free oneself without further ado from the Hegelian verdict concerning the end, death, or agony of art. After having cited the principal propositions from the *Aesthetics* on art as a "thing of the past," he adds:

> One can hardly avoid this thought and all that it implies by objecting to Hegel that, since the final lecture of his Aesthetics— winter 1828–29 at the University of Berlin—, one has seen the birth of many new works of art and artistic movements. Hegel never wanted to deny this possibility. But the question still remains: is art still an essential and necessary manner in which the truth which is decisive for our historical *Dasein* occurs? And if it is this no longer, the question remains still as to why this is the case. The decision on this dictum of Hegel has not yet been made; for behind this dictum stands all of occidental thought since the Greeks. This thought corresponds to a truth of the being which has already occurred. The decision will be made—supposing that

> it should be made—from this truth of the being itself and with
> respect to this truth [Die Entscheidung...fällt...aus dieser
> Wahrheit des Seienden und über sie]. Until then, Hegel's dictum
> remains valid. This is precisely why the question is necessary as to
> whether the truth that this thought utters is definitive, and what
> follows if this is the case. (66; 80)

Thus, Heidegger subscribes to the Hegelian verdict. More precisely, he
recognizes the truth and the necessity of this verdict from the point of view of
the self-accomplishment of metaphysics (he presents the *Lectures on Aesthetics*
as "the most comprehensive meditation—because they are thought on the
basis of metaphysics—that the Occident possesses concerning the essence of
art"). Hegel completes and accomplishes aesthetics as that science which sanc-
tions and pronounces the end of art, on the basis of which death-sentence aesthetics itself as science is rendered possible. But science, in the Hegelian sense
of the term, takes shape against the background of a "truth of the being which
has already occurred." This is why nothing excludes in principle the possibility of saying a word, if not the last or "decisive" word, on the Hegelian closure
"from this truth of the being itself, and with respect to this truth." And it is
moreover such a word that the lectures on "The Origin of the Work of Art"
strive to articulate.

Heidegger's position here is (necessarily) double. Or to put it another
way: Heidegger gives Hegel with one hand what he takes back with the other.

What he takes back—and this is quite clear despite Heidegger's pru-
dence and his awareness of the difficulty—is the definitive character of the
philosophical or metaphysical point of view. I'll come back to it in a moment.

What he gives, however, is utterly surprising. It is nothing less than this:

First, and it is a matter here, no doubt, of a very profound *political* complicity: art ceases to be "great"—and ceases to be itself, if ever it was *itself*—as
soon as it is no longer constitutive or institutive of a fundamental possibility
of existence, i.e., of a Being-a-people. Hegel would have said: as soon as it
ceases to be religion. Heidegger says: as soon as it ceases to have a historical
destiny.

This is how Heidegger translates Hegel in the course on Nietzsche:

> Parallel to this elaboration of aesthetics [it is a question this time
> of aesthetics in the modern sense] and to the efforts to elucidate
> and ground the aesthetic state, another decisive process accom-
> plishes itself in the history of art. In their historical ascent and
> their Being, great art and its works only give evidence of their
> greatness in as far as they accomplish a decisive task in the histor-
> ical existence of men: specifically, to make the essence of the total-
> ity of beings reveal itself in the mode of the work, and to preserve

in the work this revelation. Art and its work are only necessary as a path and sojourn of man, where the truth of the totality of beings, that is, the unconditioned, the absolute, opens itself up to him. Great art is not great solely on the basis or in virtue of the high quality of the created thing, but because of the fact that it constitutes an "absolute need. "...Parallel to the elaboration of the reign of aesthetics and of the aesthetic relation to art, one observes in modern times the decadence [*Verfall*] of great art in the sense indicated. This decadence does not consist in the reduction of "quality" or the debasement of style, but in this: that art loses its essence, the immediate relation to its fundamental task, which is to present [*darstellen*] the absolute and to install it [*stellen*] as such as measure in the domain of historical humanity. (99–100; 83–84)

The philosophico-political complicity is moreover so strong that having remarked that "the Hegelian accomplishment of aesthetics is great in that it recognizes and pronounces this end of great art," Heidegger responds—for Hegel—to the objection by what one can call the "survival" of art:

Hegel never pretended to deny the possibility that afterward, other works of art would still be produced and appreciated. The fact that such isolated works are only valid as works within the sphere of artistic taste proper to some social levels [*Volksschichten*] does not speak at all against Hegel but precisely for him. This fact proves that art has lost the power of the absolute, its absolute power. (101; 85)

Second, and this is a direct consequence, art and reflexion on art are mutually exclusive. As soon as a theory of art appears, a knowledge or a science, "it's all over for great art." This is the fundamental axiom on which rests the entirety of the introduction to the *Lectures on Aesthetics* and which the figure of Schiller emblematizes quite well, all in all, that "man gifted at once with a great artistic sense and with a profound philosophical spirit" who, in sacrificing in part his art to science, "did nothing other than pay tribute to his epoch." It is the same axiom, or perhaps the same naïveté, that subtends the entire Heideggerian meditation: great art is absolutely anterior to all thought or conceptual "reflexion" [*Besinnung*]. Which sounds much like an evocation of the properly philosophical sense of the conceptual. It is obviously not a question of attributing an aesthetics, in the sense of a theory of production and of reception, even to the Greeks of the fifth century. But if I use the word *naïveté* it is because it is difficult to see how one could dissociate art from *some* sort of thought, if not from Thought in its philosophical sense. Moreover, Heidegger is the first, as is well known, to recognize this and to affirm it. Without going into details, however, and in a peremptory manner, even if the allusion to the essence of τέχνη is perfectly transparent:

> The absence of any such conceptual reflexion on this great art which was their contemporary also does not prove that art was only "lived" ["*erlebt*"] in this epoch as the obscure emergence of "lived experiences" ["*Erlebnisse*"], untouched by any concept or knowledge. Fortunately, the Greeks had no lived experiences, but in turn they were so originally endowed by a clear knowledge and by such a passion for knowledge, that in this clarity of knowledge they had no need for any "aesthetics." (95; 80)

In the final analysis, Hegel—affirming that art "is far from being the most elevated expression of the truth," or that "the peoples have deposited in art their highest ideas," but not yet in the "element of thought"—is more coherent. But it is precisely this coherence that Heidegger refuses (otherwise, "The Origin of the Work of Art" and the commentary on Hölderlin would still be aesthetics). And it is such a refusal that comprises the entire difficulty of his operation.

In any case, we can explain in this way the surprising modification Heidegger imprints upon the Hegelian version of the birth of aesthetics (or the end of great art). Because the end of art, its τέλος or destiny, is truth (but what else is it for Hegel?), there are two ends or two "deaths" of art: the one is produced in the declining fifth century that witnesses the birth of philosophy itself (but Hegel still accepted, as great art, the "golden age of the late Middle Ages"[11]); the other is contemporary with the development of aesthetics properly speaking which Hegel deliberately completes. In reality, Hegel is conceived, on the one hand, as the one who possesses the *metaphysical* truth of art and the end of art, thus making it impossible to be taken in by Nietzsche's "reversal" or the laborious attempts of the nineteenth century to reconstruct or reconstitute a great art (Wagner[12]), and on the other hand,` as the one who can be enclosed in turn within the field of aesthetics, the field of the philosophy of art, from the standpoint of a broader and deeper vision of aesthetics, from the standpoint of a more "archaic" end of art and a—totally—other interpretation of truth. The Heideggerian closure of aesthetics exceeds the Hegelian closure because it comprehends the "truth of the being" in terms of which this Hegelian closure had traced itself out.

One has to make a decision then—if one can—about this very truth of the being. But what is this truth? The course on Nietzsche, but also "The Origin of the Work of Art" (including the enormous effort expended upon withdrawing the concept of *Gestalt* from any Hegelian overdetermination[13]), leaves no doubt on this subject: it is the *eidetic* truth of the being, from which proceeds the entire conceptuality of aesthetics, including its modern versions. For from its inception philosophy organizes a complicity between the eidetic apprehension of the being and the conceptualization of art in terms of the creator and the amateur and not of the work itself. And this complicity conditions an impoverished interpretation of τέχνη as mere know-how, activity of fabrication.[14]

Therefore, the entire question is whether or not there is a determination of the being more "archaic" than the eidetic determination. If the response is in *Scheinen* (φαίνεσθαι) and if the debate with Hegel requires more or less secretly a re-evaluation of Kant and Schiller, that means—and this is the result of the entire operation:

1. That Kant is obviously included in the Hegelian closure of aesthetics, less for the reason that the third *Critique* still proposes itself as a theory of taste than because Kant still formulates the problematic of the beautiful and the sublime in terms of eidetic presentation—in this case, in terms of imagination.

2. That Kant, no less obviously, exceeds the limits of such a closure: first of all, because the subjectivism of the third *Critique* can be wrenched, with the help of Schiller, from the terrain of "subjectivity" (the "pleasure of reflexion" points in the direction of the historical essence of man); secondly, and above all, because the comprehension of the beautiful in its essence as pure *Scheinen* translates a complete rupture with the eidetic apprehension of art.[15]

3.

"Complete rupture" is perhaps saying quite a bit.

Finally, however, a certain Kantian relinquishment of aesthetics—but neither in the form of a renunciation nor, indeed still less, in the form of an explicit denunciation—entails that Kant, according to Heidegger, withdraws in part from aesthetics, even though he seems in all respects to inscribe himself within it. Beneath the emphatic and unjust vociferations of Nietzsche, one can hear, with the attentive ear of Schiller, a completely other voice resonating in the third *Critique*: a voice *already* fundamentally incapable of articulating the language of aesthetics or of sustaining its discourse up to the end.[16] And this relinquishment—this manner of letting-go secretly pursued with respect to aesthetics—precedes (and herein lies part of its enigma) the Hegelian closure of aesthetics: within aesthetics, and before it completes itself, the ground of aesthetics itself begins to yawn. Or at least, it is as if a sort of "pocket of resistance" had formed, an invisible enclave, which would have escaped in advance from the imperious and gigantic encirclement of Science. Indeed, the stakes are immensely high: nothing less than the historical possibility of a great art. That is to say, the possibility, still to come, of art *itself.*

Now, it is my hypothesis that such a relinquishment is perhaps precisely what enters into Kant's thought by way of the sublime or to be more accurate: by way of a certain thought of the sublime.

The thought of the sublime, in fact, absolutely does not interest Heidegger. Even in Kant and Schiller. He maintains on this subject a total silence which, as always in Heidegger, means that it is "inessential." We do not know—and this is not by chance—the reasons for this silence. I believe however that, on the model of other Heideggerian operations, it is not too difficult to imagine them.

The thought of the sublime, for example, is a belated thought, born in the womb of the Hellenistic schools, not truly or authentically Greek, but contaminated by Latinity—and even para-Judaic and Christian (τὸ "Υψος, from the first diaspora on Greek soil, designates the God of the Bible: the Most-high). Aside from this, it is a thought that comes from rhetoric: it does not attain to philosophy, after its resurgence in modern times, except by the path of French poetics and English aesthetics. It actually forms a minor tradition. Even as a thought of excess, of unbordering, of beyond-beauty, etc., it attests to an exhaustion of the sense of the beautiful. It is not by chance, therefore, that aesthetics *strictu sensu* lays claim to it. Contrary to appearances, it wants to provide a weak thought, that is, a thought precisely *without* grandeur.

But these are still relatively exterior reasons. Two others seem to me more decisive.

First, since Longinus, and in its very concept, the sublime has been conceived in accordance with the metaphysical distinction par excellence, that is, in accordance with the distinction between the sensible and the supersensible which we inherit from Platonism. Up through Kant, it is simply the translation of this distinction into an ethico-aesthetical, i.e., theologico-aesthetical mode.

Second, insofar as it defines itself negatively in relation to the beautiful, the sublime offers essentially nothing more (motif of excess) and, moreover, nothing less (motif of the nonpresentable) than the concept of the beautiful on which it does not cease to depend. It offers indeed nothing other: it is quite simply a counterconcept of the beautiful.

All of this amounts to the assertion that Heidegger was capable of subscribing to the Hegelian version of the sublime: the sublime is nothing but the first degree of the beautiful. Moreover, he does so, even if indirectly, when, in the course on Nietzsche, he places into relation to Nietzsche's aesthetics—the aesthetics of the reversal of aesthetics, aesthetics as anti-aesthetics—the famous sentence from Rilke's first "Elegy": "For the beautiful is nothing / But the commencement of the terrible," wherein one can decipher without too much trouble the Rilkean definition of the sublime.[17] One could not formulate more aptly the dependence or subordination of the sublime with respect to the beautiful. But this formulation probably already commits one to subscribing still *philosophically* to the point of view of the "most comprehensive meditation...that the Occident possesses concerning the essence of art." Hegel, then, seems to possess the metaphysical truth of the sublime.

The reason for this is quite simple: from the moment when the *Idea* of the beautiful is defined in terms of the figural *adequation* of (spiritual) content to (sensible) form—the Ideal of art—and from the moment when adequation ("reconciliation," as the *Aesthetics* puts it) is posited as the very need of philosophical Spirit, the sublime, that is, the inadequation of form to spiritual content, is inevitably conceived as a moment which precedes the moment of the beautiful or art properly speaking. This is why the sublime, which Hegel situates in symbolic art, is not yet art (it is even, at the limit, in the Jewish moment, the prohibition of art). But it goes without saying that such a definition, in terms of adequation (the ὁμοίωσις) of sensible and super-sensible and of the spiritual conformity of the *Gestalt*, presupposes the eidetic determination of the being. It is indeed explicitly the truth[18] of such a determination. And Hegel in fact conceives of the relation between the beautiful and the sublime only on the basis of this determination. I take this example from the *Lectures on the Philosophy of Religion*:

> Sublimity is the form which expresses the relation between God and the things of nature. One cannot call the infinite subject sublime: it is the absolute in and for itself, it is holy. Sublimity is the phenomenon, the relation between this infinite subject and the world; it is the Idea that manifests itself in exteriority. The world is conceived as the manifestation of this subject, but as a nonaffirmative manifestation, or as a manifestation which, although affirmative, has as its principal characteristic the negation of what belongs to nature and to the world as lacking in conformity; and thus this phenomenal manifestation reveals itself to be superior [*erhaben*] to the phenomenon, to the reality, and the latter is posited at the same time as negated. The phenomenalized Idea shows itself to be superior to that which manifests it, or if one wishes, the phenomenon lacks conformity to the Idea.
>
> In the religion of beauty [Greek art], the signification reconciles itself with the material, sensible element...; the spiritual reveals itself completely in this exteriority; the latter signifies the interior which one knows entirely in its exterior form. Sublimity, on the contrary, makes the matter disappear in which the sublime appears. Matter is expressly conceived as not being in conformity.[19]

Clearly, this is a "dialectical" comprehension of the sublime. But it is by no means merely the "dialectical version" or the "dialectization" of the sublime: it is not the "Hegelian" truth of the sublime but rather the truth *as such* of the sublime—once the sublime is thought, as it always has been, in terms of the beautiful, itself in turn interpreted in terms of the eidetic comprehension of the being. Hegel contents himself basically with *verifying* this, and quite consistently: if the essence of the manifestation or presentation is its form—delimited and finite—and if the sublime is and has always been thought as the manifestation or presentation of the infinite, under whatever name it might be, then in its very structure the sublime is contradictory. The sublime is indeed, from the speculative point of view, the contradiction par excellence, which art, revealed religion, and philosophy (Science) successively attempt to "reconcile." This is why the formula of the *Aesthetics*—the manifestation of the infinite annihilates the manifestation itself—states not merely the metaphysical truth of the sublime, but the sublime truth of metaphysics. It is the original oxymoron, ever since Longinus the figure par excellence of the sublime, which one sees asserting itself everywhere in the Hegelian treatment of the sublime.[20]

The truth of the sublime is thus dialectical, is dialectics itself. It follows that if the sublime is in a certain sense the excess of the beautiful, it is only so *by default*, such that it is effectively the beautiful that is the sublation and truth of the sublime. The sublime is the incompletion of the beautiful, which is, the beautiful seeking to complete itself. And in this reversal of the entire discourse of aesthetics on the subject of the beautiful and the sublime, the thought of the sublime comes to complete itself in its turn. When Hegel says of Moses that he only has, "down there...the value of an organ" (65; 137), he speaks the truth of what Kant attempted to elaborate in the name of "negative" or "restrictive" presentation: he speaks the truth of the Kantian interpretation of the prohibition of (re)presentation. From underneath the metaphysical pathos of excess and overflowing, Hegel will have simply flushed out this naïveté: the definition of the sublime does not remain any the less a *negative* definition. For this reason, the essence of the sublime is nothing other than the beautiful.

One could verify this in practically all the "classical" interpretations of the sublime, Burke's included. But one could verify it above all in an emblematic manner, in what happens to the figure of Moses as soon as it enters into art as a manifest stake of "great art" under the inevitable surveillance of the aesthetic discourse.

When for example—but it is a major example—Freud undertakes to elucidate the "enigma" of Michelangelo's *Moses*, he is forced, despite himself, to submit himself to a dialectics of the sublime, up to the point where he must acquiesce before the contradiction he confronts, and finds himself obliged to restore Moses to its enigma. This text has often been considered weak and disappointing with regard to the analytic problematic. It has often and justly been seen as containing the trace of an unthought or original obstacle of psychoanalysis.[21] What has been less explicitly remarked, however, is the precision and rigour with which Freud's essay inscribes itself into the tradition of the aesthetics of the sublime. It is an absolutely Schillerian text, and the solution of the enigma, if there is a solution, belongs totally to the concept of dignity which is, according to Schiller, the "expression in the phenomenon" of the "mastery of the drives by moral force," that is, of "spiritual freedom."[22] Freud translates this notion into the following terms, in which one can readily recognize the lexical and thematic elements characteristic of the sublime code:

> Michelangelo placed on the tomb of the Pope another Moses, superior to the Moses of history or tradition. He transformed the theme of the broken tables of the law, not permitting the anger of Moses to break them, but the danger that they could be broken appeases this anger or at least restrains it in the moment of the act. In this way, he introduced into the figure of Moses something new, something superhuman, and the strong mass as well as the exuberant musculature of this powerful character are just a concrete expression of the highest psychic exploit of which a man could be capable: to defeat his own passion in the name of an end for which he knows himself to be destined.[23]

This solution, evidently, is none. In order to overcome the obstacle of "negative presentation," Schiller had already proposed the notion of "sensible signs" of the super-sensible, a notion that moreover does not cease to guide Freud in his inquiry. He was nonetheless not quite capable of avoiding a certain dialectization:

> In all rigor, the moral force of man is not susceptible of presentation, since the super-sensible can never be rendered sensible. But mediately it can be represented to the understanding by sensible signs, as is evidently the case in the dignity of the human form. (413; 217)

This does not prevent Schiller from finding, if only by means of Winckelmann, the example of a work of art where the struggle between the sensible and the super-sensible can be deciphered in the very form of the work. As if by chance, the example is a work of monumental statuary, the famous *Laocoön*:[24]

> Suppose that we see the signs of particularly painful affect in a man, in the category of those first completely involuntary movements [which Schiller has discussed above]. However, even as his veins swell, his muscles flex convulsively, his voice falters, his breast heaves, and his stomach contracts, still his voluntary movements remain gentle, the expression on his face remains free, his eye and forehead remain serene. If the man were merely a sensible being, all of these traits, having a common source, would remain in mutual accord, and would therefore in the present case all have

to express indifferently his painful condition. But since he mixes calm traits with those of suffering, and since a single cause could not have opposed effects, this contradiction of traits proves the existence and influence of a force which is independent of the pain and superior to the impressions to which we see the sensible element succomb. And in this manner, calm in suffering—in which dignity properly consists—becomes, although only by the mediation of inferential reason, the presentation of the intelligence in man and the expression of his moral freedom. (414; 218)

But one can readily see where the difficulty lies. Sublimity is legible in the "contradiction of traits" which signifies in a mediated form—but nonetheless *presents*—"calm in suffering" or dignity. But the contradiction, in this case, is perfectly *adequate* to that which it is supposed to present, that is, precisely, a conflict: between sensible and super-sensible, between a "strong interest" of "the faculty of desire" (of which suffering is nothing but one effect among others) and liberty. Thus, Schiller provides here a pure and simple instance of the beautiful.

This is just what bothers Freud when, in the case of the replacement of anger by suffering, he adapts this description to his purposes. To be sure, there remains this aggravating detail: the figure he treats is the representative of the prohibition of representation: Moses is the "graven image" that figures the mastery of an anger aroused by the spectacle of idolatry, i.e., by the cultic worship of the graven image. That Freud preserves his silence on this *paradox* (a key word since Longinus, and perhaps the major concept of the theory of the sublime[25]), that he pretends not to pay any attention to this strange fold that at once joins and divides representation and represented by virtue of the very fact that there is representation here, is the sign, not of a blindness or a "forgetfulness," but of a presentiment: that here what is at stake is the possibility or impossibility of art from the standpoint of aesthetics.

On the one hand, Moses can become angry, thereby obeying his destiny or spiritual mission, in a movement one could be tempted to consider properly sublime. But this anger, as an impulse, is precisely not sublime. And above all—this is the true difficulty Freud confronts—it would be necessary to conceive the project of Michelangelo, what Freud calls his "intention," as an attempt to figure the (sublime) hatred of figuration. But Freud does not choose this alternative.

On the other hand, Moses can master his anger, in conformity with the Schillerian definition of sublimity. But in this case, again, there is quite simply adequation: that which the figure figures is the (sublime) renunciation of all hostility toward figuration. *Moses*, in clear opposition to Judaic (Mosaic) sublimity, is a hommage, grandiose but beautiful, paid to art in its eidetic determination. Or, if you prefer, the tables of the law which Moses retains *in extremis* under his arm signify in a Hegelian manner that the essence of the sublime is the beautiful.

This is why, before the force of such a contradiction, Freud acquiesces and leaves the matter undecided. But this acquiescence is itself subjected to the (aesthetic) logic of adequation, which in this case takes the form of the criterion of success. With Michelangelo, Freud confesses, we are at the limits of art—at least of a certain idea of art:

> Is it fitting to attribute to Michelangelo—the artist in whose works such a plethora of ideas struggles for expression—such naïve indecisiveness concerning these striking and strange traits of the statue of Moses? Finally, one can add in all humility that the artist shares with the critic the responsibility for causing this uncertainty. Michelangelo often approached in his creations the extreme limit of the expressible: perhaps he did not succeed entirely with the Moses, if his intention was to have the beholder divine the storm aroused by violent emotion through the signs that remain behind when, the storm having subsided, calm is restored. (220; 106)

The difficulty at work here (but one can find it elsewhere: it constitutes the essential, necessary incompleteness of Schönberg's *Moses and Aaron*[26]) has to do perhaps finally with this: the prohibition of representation—the iconoclastic prescription, as Goux says—is a meta-sublime statement: it states in a sublime manner—in the absolute simplicity of a negative prescription —sublimity itself, the incommensurability of the sensible to the metaphysical (to the Idea, to God). In thereby ceasing to be the pure "organ" of this utterance, in becoming a figure and thus contradicting the message he carries, *Moses* emblematizes the aporia of the eidetic apprehension of the sublime and also of art, in the sense of "great art." If you like, and even if it is an oversimplification: in the contradiction of which it is the site, the figure of *Moses* reveals two things:

1. Either Hegel is right: the Mosaic law is, in its very negativity, effectively sublime in that it states the essence of sublimity, namely, that negative presentation signifies the negation of the presentation. No art, in a Platonico-Hegelian sense, can escape this situation. A priori and a posteriori, Hegel possesses the truth of the sublime, and from Michelangelo to Schönberg the figure of Moses symbolically marks the impossibility of a great "modern" art (that is, in Hegel's terminology, of a great "romantic" art). And this is moreover probably what condemns art, in its aspiration toward great art, to exhausting itself in the presentation of its proper impossibility and, consequently, to combatting figurality in all its forms.

2. Or else art is not *essentially* a matter of eidetic presentation, and this is perhaps what Schiller attempts with some difficulty to say when he speaks of

"sensible signs" or of "mediate presentation." But if art is nonetheless *presen-tation* (and how could one define it otherwise?), what does it essentially pre-sent other than form or figure? Or in a more general manner, what could a noneidetic presentation of the being be? What could be at play in presentation that would not be of the order of the εἶδος, the aspect or the view?

This question, which concerns presentation (and no longer representa-tion, at least in the sense invoked by the philosophy of art), is doubtless the question which, secretly and in near silence, (re)emerges for the first time since the inception of philosophy with Kant's thought. It is precisely this ques-tion that is rumbling beneath the Transcendental Aesthetic and the disruptive effect of which on philosophical discourse in general makes itself felt also in the problematic of art. I would like to think here that it is emblematized by Kant's second example of absolute sublimity, the mysterious formula inscribed on the temple of Isis: "I am all that is, that was, and that will be, and no mortal has lifted my veil."

4.

In distinction to the utterance of Moses, the utterance of Isis is not a prescrip-tive but a constative. It says mystery itself, and for this reason, as is well known, it has always been taken to be the model of the esoteric utterance as such. In particular, the utterance of Isis circulated widely toward the end of the Enlight-enment, marked as that period was by Masonic mysticism, from Hamann to Hegel and from Schlegel to the Novalis of the *Disciples of Sais*. If one abstracts from the metaphor that carries it, it is, qua constative, an utterance of truth: it says the truth or the essence of divinity, namely, that divinity cannot be unveiled. And that Kant should give it a "rationalist" interpretation, that he should translate it (Isis means Mother Nature) and treat it thus as a sort of prosopopoeia of nature, does not fundamentally alter the truth uttered and does not affect its mystic significance. Inscribed at the threshold of the book by Segner, it is supposed to fill the reader with a "sacred shudder, which should dispose the mind to a solemn attentiveness"; and one divines rather easily that this is what permits its hyperbolic association with the biblical law: the sentence of Isis concerns also the nonpresentability of the meta-physical understood as truth or essence of φύσις. It echoes also the φύσις κρύπτεσθαι φιλεῖ of Hera-clitus. It presents the "fact" that there is the nonpresentable.

However—and I return thus to the question of the metaphor, *if it is a metaphor*—the nonpresentable is conceived here as non-unveilable, and this makes a big difference because the prosopopoeia of nature in its totality, or of the totality of beings (it is the totality itself which is nonunveilable, that is, the unity of all that is: its Being), is also a prosopopoeia of truth. The sentence of Isis is not simply an utterance of truth but an utterance of the truth of the truth,[27] that is, of the play of veiling and unveiling, of presentation and of the non-unveilable. It takes the (well-known) form of: "I, the truth, speak." That is to say, in this case—but isn't it always thus when truth speaks?— "I, the truth, tell the truth of (or about) the truth." And this is no doubt why the sentence is absolutely sublime. For it is a strictly contradictory sentence. The syntactical equivalent, if you will, of an oxymoron.

What does it mean, in effect, "to tell the truth"? By an immemorial constraint—at least as far back as philosophical memory can reach—which does not arise out of any metaphorical decision, telling the truth is unveiling the truth. Truth-telling, in this sense, as we know since Aristotle, and as paragraph 7B of *Being and Time* reminds us, is *apophantic*: it lets us see (or lets appear: φαίνεσθαι) on the basis of (ἀπό) that of which it speaks. It renders manifest or patent, it unveils. Truth-telling is the λόγος ἀληθής. But what is produced in Isis's sentence—and this is probably the reason why it has been so fascinating—is that telling the truth about itself, telling the truth of the truth and unveiling itself as the truth, truth (unveiling) unveils itself as the impossibility of unveiling or the necessity, for finite (mortal) Being, of its veiling. Speaking of itself, unveiling itself, truth says that the essence of truth is nontruth—or that the essence of unveiling is veiling. The truth (the unveiling) unveils itself as veiling itself.

One may recall Hegel's jubilation. This jubilation surfaces in his description of the (symbolic) passage from the symbolic, sublime world (the Orient, Egypt) to the world of the first emergence of Spirit as such, that is, of self-consciousness: Greece. This passage is double. It occurs first of all by means of the response of Oedipus (the one who knows) to the enigma of the Sphinx.[28] But it occurs also, heliotropically, by means of the inscription of the sanctuary of the deity Neïth at Saïs. The sun rises in the Orient. It makes the stone sing (the statues in the temple of Memnon). But the sun or Spirit itself remains, in Egypt, enclosed in the stone, despite the ephemeral apparition of a solar cult which will give Freud much to dream about. Greece, in turn, is the country of the "great midday," the sun at its zenith. Spirit has come out of stone: out of enigmatic inscriptions and tombs. The philosophical Occident begins with this departure from Egypt, this breaking away from the somber, stony empire of the dead. Hegel cites the inscription: "I am all that is, that was, and that will be, etc." But the sentence adds, he says: "The fruit that I bore is Helios (the solar deity)." And he comments:

> This (solar) clarity is the spirit, the son of Neïth, the mysterious nocturnal divinity. In the Egyptian Neïth, truth veils itself still. The solution is the Greek Apollo. This is his proposition: "Man, know yourself."[29]

The truth of truth is pure and simple unveiling, the simple departure from the night, the pure brilliance of the sun. It is the apparition of Spirit in its light as self-consciousness and subject. This is why, deciphering the enigma, Hegel can rejoice.

Inversely, in Isis's sentence, as Kant declares its sublimity, it is not a question of Helios, and still less of Apollo—the "solution." No sun dissipates the veiling of the deity, no self-consciousness dissolves the contradiction of the discourse of truth on itself. The sentence is left to its paradoxical enigma, the enigma which engenders not rejoicing but a "sacred shudder." *The truth, in its essence, is nontruth.*

This proposition that the truth, in its essence, is nontruth figures, as you may recall, in the second of the lectures of Heidegger on "The Origin of the Work of Art" (40; 54). It comes up shortly before Heidegger defines beauty as "this shining [*Scheinen*] joined in the work" and as "a way in which truth occurs as unconcealedness" (42; 56). In this proposition is summarized Heidegger's analysis of the contradictory structure of ἀ-λήθεια, an analysis which is destined to show that "it belongs to the essence of the truth as unconcealedness [*Unver-borgenheit*] not to give itself in the mode of a double concealment [*Verbergen*]." By "concealment," or reserve, Heidegger means the essence of the *Lichtung*, of the brightness or the clearing, of the "empty place" or the Open, "where the being comes to hold itself." "The clearing...is in itself at once concealment" (39; 53), that is, the essence of the ἀλήθεια is the λήθη (the essence of unveiling is veiling); the clearing itself, the unveiling of the being, does not give itself. Or if you prefer: the uncovering [*ouverture*] without which the being cannot appear and present itself as such, this covering [*couverture*] itself—which, "thought on the basis of the being," says Heidegger, is "more being" than the being—does not present itself, that is, *is* not in the mode of what is. The opening-uncover-ing, the clearing, is no being: "This open center is therefore not surrounded by what is; rather, the lighting center itself encircles all that is, like the Nothing which we scarcely know" (39; 53).

This veiling of the unveiling, this reserve of the clearing, says Heidegger, is double. On the one hand, it is a dissimulating "instability" (*Verstellen*): a being "slides in front of the being," veils it, gives it out for what it is not; and here is the origin of appearance and of error. This first reserve affects the being in "*what* it is" (*Washeit*, or *quidditas*). But it is on the other hand, and above all—that is, essentially—"refusal" (*Versagen*), and it affects thus the being in its very Being, in its "*that* it is" [*Daßheit*, or *quodditas*]: "The being refuses itself to us down to that one and seemingly most minimal feature [*Geringste*] that we encounter nowhere better than when, of a being, we can only say: that it is" (39; 53).

This refusal is precisely what Isis says: "No mortal has lifted my veil." If you will, it is finitude itself, but on condition that one understand finitude as "something more than simply the limit of knowledge." For it is, Heidegger adds, "the beginning of the clearing of what is cleared [*der Anfang der Lichtung des Gelichteten*]" (39; 53–54). That is, the condition of possibility itself of unveiling. This is why Heidegger can write—and the "metaphor" of the curtain before a stage does not appear here by mere chance:

> Concealment can be a refusal, or be nothing but dissimulation. We are never fully certain whether it is the one or the other. Concealment conceals and dissimulates itself. This means: the place opened in the middle of that which is, the clearing, is never a rigid stage with its curtain always raised and on which would play itself out the play of that which is. Rather, the clearing never occurs except as this double concealment. (39–40; 54)

If time were not lacking, it would be necessary to show how Heidegger's thought here completely revises the Transcendental Aesthetics from the perspective of the thought of ἀλήθεια. For having argued that the clearing is nothing other than the open, this pure space without ontic localization (this void, he will say later), Heidegger adds immediately: "The disclosed Being of the being is never a state which would already be there, but always an occurrence [*Geschehnis*]" (40; 54).[30] That is, pure temporality and, as will appear, pure historicity.

The question on which one must insist, however, is this: what "occurs" here? Answer, which goes, so to speak, without saying: the clearing itself (ἀλήθεια) as concealment, unveiling itself in its essence. So how does this occurrence signal itself, since it cannot do so by way of any sort of appearing or presentation, and since it exceeds all modes of Being of the being, although it nonetheless happens or, as we say, takes place? It order for this occurrence to signal itself, the being, in its very familiarity, must suddenly become "estranged." The occurrence is the estrangement or becoming-uncanny of the being: the *Un-geheure*, its de-familiarization:

> We believe we are at home in the immediate circle of beings. That which is, is familiar, reliable, ordinary. Nevertheless, the clearing is pervaded by a constant concealment in the double form of refusal and dissembling. At bottom, the ordinary is not ordinary; it is extra-ordinary, uncanny. (40; 54)[31]

One will say that this is still "negative presentation." Not at all. Heidegger, moreover, prevents any misunderstanding: after, several lines further down, having said that "the truth, in its essence, is nontruth," he specifies: this sentence "does not mean that truth is basically falsity. It also does not mean, in a dialectical representation, that truth is never itself but always also its contrary" (40; 55). The estrangement or defamiliarization of the being is not any sort of "negative presentation"—one must not precipitately latch onto either the *Un* of *Ungeheure* or the *Un* of *Un-Wahrheit* for the simple reason that the estrangement affects the *presented*. Starting with *that which is presented*, presentation itself (or the "fact" that there is presence) comes, in an absolutely paradoxical fashion, to "present" itself. Or rather, because the word *presentation* is no longer fitting: happens, occurs. And this is the *Ereignis*.

Now, it is the work of art, essentially, that produces this happening of the clearing as reserve, the happening of the ἀ-λήθεια as the defamiliarization of the Being-familiar (unconcealed) of the being. Such is the "stroke" or "shock" (*Stoß*) that the work provokes. Mysteriously added to the given being, as a supplement or *surfeit*, it has the singular power to show itself as created and to indicate thereby, as the being that it is, *that* there is such a thing as the being:

> In a work...this fact, that it *is* as a work, is just what is unusual [*das Ungewöhnliche*]. The event [*Ereignis*] of its being created does not simply reverberate through the work; rather, the work casts before itself the eventful fact that the work is as this work, and it has constantly this fact about itself. The more essentially the work opens itself, the more luminous [*leuchtend*] becomes the uniqueness of the fact that it is rather than is not. The more essentially this thrust comes into the Open, the stranger [*befremdlicher*] and more solitary the work becomes. In the bringing forth [*Hervorbringen*]of the work there lies this offering [*Darbringen*] "that it be."...
>
> The more solitarily the work, fixed in the figure [*festgestellt in die Gestalt*], stands on its own and the more cleanly it seems to cut all ties to human beings, the more simply does the shock come into the Open that such a work *is*, and the more essentially is the uncanny [*das Ungeheure*] thrust to the surface and the long-familiar thrust down. (52; 65–66)

Heidegger adds immediately that this shock is without violence:

> for the more purely the work is itself transported [*entrückt*, which is one possible translation of the Greek λανθάνειν] into the openness of the being —an openness opened by itself—the more simply does it transport us [*einrücken*] into this openness and, at the same time, beyond the ordinary. To submit to this derangement [*Verrückung*] means: to transform our ordinary relations with the world and the earth, to restrain [*ansichhalten*] our usual doing and evaluating, knowing and observing in order to sojourn within the truth as it happens in the work. (52–53; 66)

De-familiarity, alienation and derangement, shock, simplicity, transport, retreat, and reservation: all of this, as you will have recognized, is the vocabulary of the sublime (as it is patently evident with *das Ungeheure*) or at least its transcription in the Heideggerian idiom. But it is obviously not merely a matter of vocabulary, just as one cannot say that Heidegger is innocent in matters of traditional vocabulary. What this text describes, in its own way and at a depth doubtless unknown before it, is the experience of the sublime itself. That is, it describes precisely what Heidegger elsewhere—notably concerning anxiety or Being-unto-death—ascribes to the *ek-static* comportment of *Dasein* and *ek-sistence*. The shock produced by the work, the estrangement of the being, is such an ecstasy or ravishment. It is the "precipitation beyond oneself," as Burke[32] says, which, from Longinus to Boileau and from Fénelon to Kant, has been described as the properly sublime emotion or affect—on condition, Heidegger would say, that one understand this πάθος in its strictest sense.

But what happens in this experience or trial [*épreuve*]? On the borders of a being that "estranges" the entirety of what is, and in accordance with the proper glow or radiance of this being, it *happens* to become present (or to appear): that there is (such a thing as) the being and not nothing. The work is that absolutely paradoxical being (the "Being-being," as Heidegger writes in the *Introduction to Metaphysics*[33]) which nihilates [*né-antise*] the being in order to make Being itself appear and come to light, glow, and scintillate. The work opens the clearing, the luminous opening in which, as a being, it holds itself, and on the (empty) ground—the groundless ground—of which the being comes to manifest itself. The work presents ἀ-λήθεια, the no-thing, luminous with an "obscure illumination," which "is" the Being of what is. And this is sublimity.

In a certain way, and by a further paradox, Heidegger verifies the Hegelian determination of the sublime: the manifestation of the infinite anni-hilates the manifestation itself. It is exactly this movement that traverses these pages. Or rather, it would be, if Being could be likened to the infinite (which is strictly impossible), but above all, Heidegger thought manifestation as the eidetic presentation of the being, that is, in accordance with an account that was only attentive to the *Washeit* or to the quiddity of the being. What the work de-familiarizes, or what the presentation of presentation nihilates (but precisely does not annihilate), is the presented being, the being such as it is, such as it presents itself ontically, such as it ceaselessly cuts a figure against the background of that which is in general. The presented being, the being in its *Washeit*, is perhaps never thinkable except as εἶδος. The presented being always *figures itself*, installs itself in its stature, makes a *Gestalt*. And it is, more-over, thus that Heidegger in turn thinks the being-ness of the work. But the work—and it shares this singular privilege with *Dasein*—is not merely of the order of the being. It is the opening of this: that there are beings. In other words, once the *Daßheit* of the being is in play, presentation as figuration becomes secondary. Anterior to the cutting of the figure of this or that being, or even to what one could still *imagine* to be the cutting of the figure of the being in general against the background of the void (but the void does not constitute a foundation, a background, and the being *in general* does not cut any figure whatsoever), there is the: "that there are beings." This is what the work, in fact, *offers*, but this offering, this *Darbringen*, as Heidegger says, is that of a pure appearing, *Scheinen* or φαίνεσθαι, the pure epiphany of the being as such. That which is, insofar as it is, does not cut (any figure) but glows and scintillates in the night without night, in the beyond-night of the void, which is the clearing itself.

This is why there is no negativity in the motif of reserve, reservation, and retreat, or in the accent placed upon λήθη. And it is why the "phantic" apprehension of the sublime cannot (immediately or ever) give rise to any dialectization. This apprehension does not posit that the sublime is the presentation of this: that there is the nonpresentable (that is, if I am translating correctly: that there is some negative being). For this apprehension does *not* postulate any "negative presentation"; it posits simply that the *sublime is the presentation of this: that there is presentation*. It is a matter—if you like, and although I regard the term with a certain mistrust—of an "affirmative" comprehension of the sublime, that is, of "great art."

5.

Of course, Heidegger transfers all of this into the account of the beautiful: the path from *was ist* to *daß…ist*, from "what the being is" to "that the being is," means for him the path from the beautiful in its philosophical, eidetico-aesthetic determination to a more original determination of the beautiful. Once again, this (properly sublime) thought of the sublime[34] doesn't want to know anything about the sublime.

And yet, it is in the thought of the sublime—a certain thought of the sublime—that the memory has been maintained, however vague or half-forgetful, of a comprehension of the beautiful which is more original than its Platonic interpretation in terms of the εἶδος-ἰδέα. One ought to ask oneself if the thought of the sublime—a certain thought of the sublime, which might well be, in turn, the original thought of the sublime—is not born (in a rebirth or renaissance) of the concern to (re)discover that which, in the beautiful, is manifestly irreducible to its eidetic apprehension. I am referring to that *je-ne-sais-quoi* without which, as everyone knows, the beautiful would be merely beautiful, and which is perhaps—at least it seems so to me—a refulgence, an extreme of light, the very brilliance of appearing: the ἐκφανέστατον.

This is, I believe, what happens in what remains the initial thought of the sublime, that is, in Pseudo-Longinus' treatise, at least on condition that one read it not as a work of rhetoric or of poetics, that is, as I said, of "criticism" (which it *also*, of course, incontestably is), but rather as a philosophical work, or at least as illegible without the presupposition of a precise philosophical intent beneath each of its fundamental statements, an intent which moreover has nothing to do with the occasional recall of this or that ancient banality from stoicism or anywhere else.[35]

What is this philosophical intent? It is to think the essence of art anew in terms of the sublime, the great, and consequently to ask oneself under what conditions the great is possible in art. One knows moreover that Longinus places himself in a properly modern posture and that he conducts this interrogation with respect to examples of the Greeks' "great art" (the tragedians, Pindar and Sappho, Thucydides, and Plato) considered as forever in the past, "finished" or "finite."

Longinus's initial question—quite classically for a treatise of this type, and in perfect conformity with the inherited τόποι of Socratism—is, in fact, a restricted question. It asks whether or not the sublime comes from a particular τέχνη; whether or not there are "*technical* precepts" (II, 1) of the sublime. In this first question, τέχνη is taken in the narrow, weak sense of "practical know-how" [*savoir-faire*]. And one expects from the very beginning the traditional collection of examples and recipes, which this treatise in part certainly provides, for Longinus immediately announces his thesis: yes, the sublime comes from a τέχνη: I am not of those who say that the sublime is innate and therefore resistant to all didacticism, and I will prove it. However, in this departure, and quite simply because Longinus bases himself at the outset on the opposition between the innate and the acquired, an entirely other sense of τέχνη resonates. The innate is in fact what is φύσει: it is the gift of nature and the work of nature (τὰ φυσικὰ ἔργα); it is consequently all that comes in art (in τέχνη) from φύσις itself. And one is familiar with this problem: it is the problem of genius, of the *ingenium*, such as, through Kant and Nietzsche, it will dominate the thematics of the sublime.

Kant, one may recall, defines genius, that is, the artist of the sublime, as follows:

> *Genius* is the talent (or natural gift) which gives the rule to art. Since talent, as the innate productive faculty of the artist, belongs itself to nature, we may express the matter thus: *Genius* is the innate mental disposition (*ingenium*) *through which* nature gives the rule to art. (§46, 138; 150)

In his own way, Longinus says nothing other than this. Not merely is his definition of the genius the same: he speaks of "great nature" (μεγάλη φύσις, IX, 11; or μεγαλοφυΐα, XXXIII, 4), of extraordinary gifts or presents (δεινα δωρήματα), of gifts of heaven (θεόπεμπτα, XXXIV, 4), and so on. But above all, the relation he establishes between φύσις and τέχνη is of the same sort.

What does Longinus actually say? Or rather, what is the sense of his demonstration? That is, how can he assert of the sublime at once that it arises out of φύσις (out of genius) and that it arises out of a τέχνη, if not from τέχνη as such or in general? How can he, in short, expose himself to the oxymoron inscribed in the very title of the paragraph of the third *Critique* devoted to the notion of genius: "Beautiful Art is the Art of Genius"?

Longinus proceeds in two steps:

> If anyone would look to see for himself that in passages that are emotional and lofty nature often loves to be a rule unto itself [αὐ-τόνομον] and does not love to be random and without an orderly way [ἀμέθοδον] of presenting things; and that it is nature which underlies all things as a kind of first element and archetype of creating, though technique is sufficient to know "how much" to say and the right moment in each case and also to provide a fixed discipline and usage; and that great things are subject to danger when left alone by themselves, apart from knowledge, unsteady like ships without ballast, left to impulse and unlearned audacity; as they ought to have the spur, so ought they to have the bridle. (II, 2; 12–13)

Thus, the argument is at first that φύσις, in the case of the sublime, is "autonomous." This means that φύσις is "a rule unto itself" and that, as Kant will understand and "translate" it, nature gives—of itself and through itself—the law (or rules) to art, since nature is not, as Longinus tells us, "random and without an orderly way" or method. The natural gift is thus rule-governed or methodical, and genius—as such—receives its rules only from "nature." This is why Longinus can say that φύσις (and I am transcribing literally) "has constituted itself in all things as the principle and the archetypal element of all birth [αὕτη...πρῶτόν τι καὶ ἀρχέτυπον γενέσεως στοιχεῖον ἐπὶ πάν-των ὑφέστηκεν]." And it is also why he attributes to "method," as a mode of τέχνη, all that which has to do with the successful accomplishment of the natural gift: measure, a sense of the opportune moment, and practical sure-footedness. All of this can be calculated and can be learned, as Hölderlin would say. And one must know how to calculate, because there is a danger that threatens genius abandoned to itself: the danger of going too far. But one can see that by the same token τέχνη is thought here merely as the regulation of a natural force, a power of control. And it is only within this limit that the art of the sublime arises out of τέχνη.[36]

But what does this mean, more fundamentally? Precisely this, which is the second step of the demonstration:

> Just what Demosthenes used to say about the common life of mankind—that good luck is the greatest of goods, but second, no

less important, is making good plans (and if the second is not present, it will entirely remove the value of good luck)—I would say about speeches and writings: [nature has charge of good luck, technique of good planning. But what is most important is that we can learn from no other source than technique what in speeches and writings depends wholly on nature. If, as I declare, he who looks down on those engaged in useful learning would make for himself a peroration of these things, he would no longer consider theorizing on the subject "too much" and useless]. (II, 3, 13–15)

The editor of the French edition, Lebègue, takes this passage to be questionable: it only appears in one of the manuscripts (of the twelve or so which have been preserved more or less intact). In this manuscript, moreover—a fifteenth-century copy edited for the first time in 1964—Longinus's text is mixed with the text of *Problems of Physics*, attributed to Aristotle. However, not only is the thought developed in this passage absolutely coherent, but it provides what is certainly one of the most precise interpretations ever of the Aristotelian theory of μίμησις such as this theory appears, in its essentials, in book B of the *Physics* (194a).

Demosthenes' adage, one of the "great banalities" of ancient wisdom, which serves as an analogical support of Longinus's argument here, is this: there are two goods: the first, and highest, is happiness (τὸ εὐτυχεῖν) which, as its name indicates, does not depend on us; the second, which however is not less exalted, is wise planning, appropriate judgment of existence: if this latter is lacking, the former is lost. The structure of this relationship is that of a *necessary supplementarity*: all gifts of nature or of the gods, all favorable fates, are as nothing if one does not in addition make good decisions. Now, this same structure, Longinus says, regulates the relation between φύσις and τέχνη. In conformity to Aristotle, Longinus literally conceives τέχνη as the *over-growth* of φύσις, that is, of appearing (φαίνειν), as growth, blossoming, or opening (φύειν) in the light. Within the limits imposed upon him by the genre with which he is involved, a kind of "theory of literature," Longinus says this in the following manner—here again I am transcribing —: "the fact itself that there should be one among the things which one finds in discourses which depends only on φύσις, from no other place than from τέχνη we have to learn it." In other words, only art (τέχνη) is in a position to reveal nature (φύσις). Or again: without τέχνη, φύσις escapes us, because in its essence φύσις κρυ-'πτεσθαι φιλεῖ, it loves to dissimulate itself.

This is not only what *Physics* book B gives us to understand when it says that τέχνη completes φύσις. It is further quite precisely what one must understand when, in chapter 4 of the *Poetics*, concerning poetry or poetic art (ποιητική), Aristotle defines τέχνη as μίμησις: it is representation, if one

understands this term properly as presentification, rendering-present. I draw
here on the translation of Roselyne Dupont-Roc and Jean Lallot:[37]

> Poetic art in its totality seems to owe its birth to two causes, both
> of them natural [φυσικαί]. From their infancy, men have,
> inscribed in their nature [σύμφυτον], at once μιμεῖσθαι—and
> man differentiates himself from other living beings in that he is
> the most mimetic [μιμητικώτατον] and in that he produces
> [ποιεῖται] his first knowledge [μαθήσεις] through mimesis [διὰ
> μιμήσεως]—and the pleasure of works of imitation.

Τέχνη, of which poetry is only one mode but perhaps the highest mode
if one attends well to what Aristotle says here, is the production (ποίησις) of
knowledge (μάθησις). And perhaps one will understand here that Heidegger
does not by chance insist on translating τέχνη as *Wissen*. This knowledge
appears through μίμησις insofar as μίμησις is the faculty of rendering present in general, the faculty of representing, which does *not* mean reproducing
in the conventional sense of reduplicating, and still less copying or aping, for if
this were the case, it would be hard to see what knowledge is doing here.
Rather, it means rendering present that which needs to be rendered present,
that which without this rendering-present would not be present as such and
would remain dissimulated, "encrypted." Μίμησις ("representation"), in
other words, is the condition of the possibility of the knowledge *that* there is
something (and not nothing), a knowledge which is, in turn, the condition of
the possibility of the multiple knowledges of the beings that are. For this reason—and because μίμησις defines the relation of this singular knowledge
with φύσις—μίμησις renders apparent or discloses φύσις as such. Μίμησις
reveals φύσις, and it is due to this proper power of μίμησις that one can
define something like what Martineau is right in calling the "apophantic"
essence of τέχνη.[38] And it is this, I believe, that Longinus echoes when, concerning what arises from φύσις, he says, "from no other place than from
τέχνη we have to learn it [ἐκμαθεῖν]." An ancient knowledge of μίμησις and
of τέχνη, of the essence of art, resists in Longinus as it probably resisted
already in Aristotle. "Resists" ought to be understood here as: resists the Platonic interpretation of μίμησις.

    It is on the basis of such a mimetology that Longinus undertakes to treat
of the sublime. But for this very reason his treatment of the sublime has an
entirely different significance: it is not simply the question of great art that is
posed but, within the question of great art, the question of the possibility and
essence of art.

    This is what explains at first that the fundamental enigma of art is for
Longinus—as it will be also for Kant—the enigma of the transmission of
genius, that is, if you like, the enigma of the history of art. If, on the one hand,

that which in the sublime arises from τέχνη (in the restricted sense) and from didactics is finally relatively little and certainly not the essential, and if, on the other hand, great art and the innate gift of the sublime are nonetheless τέχνη (in the strong sense), τέχνη in the sense of a gift granted by φύσις to humans in order itself to be enabled to appear, then the question arises as to how genius comes about or awakens itself, as to what path (ὁδός) leads to the sublime and how the destination of the great is formed.

The response, here as in Kant, is itself enigmatic: Longinus suggests that this origin of genius is (in)explicable. That is—and one will not be surprised—he explains it in terms of μίμησις (but this time in the agonistic sense) and ζήλωσις, the emulation of the great, "inspired" poets of the past (like the Pythian on her tripod). The genius of these poets exhales as from the fault in Delphi, the effluvia that penetrate the souls of their successors (XIII, 2–4). The transmission and the repetition of genius takes place by means of a sort of (mysterious) mimetic contagion that is not, however, an imitation. As Kant attempts to explain it, one must not use great works of art as models of an "imitation" (*Nachmachung*) but as pieces or elements of a "succession" or "heritage" (*Nachfolge*). But "it is difficult," he adds, "to explain how that is possible. The ideas of the artist arouse in his disciple similar ideas when nature has endowed the latter with a similar proportion of the faculties of the soul" (§47, 140; 152).

This notion seems, of course, to be worth about just as much as the figure of the fault at Delphi. But in fact, Kant explicitates what Longinus means: the rule that the genius gives to art is not (didactically) transmissible by normal paths, for (1) it is not a concept (by definition, concerning the beautiful), and (2) the genius does not know what he or she is doing or, in any case, as distinct from the "head" such as Newton, he is incapable of showing how it is done: "no Homer and no Wieland can show how his ideas rich in poetry and nonetheless at the same time pregnant with thoughts arise and gather themselves in his brain." The rule ought therefore to be "abstracted" from the great works, through contact with which genius can be awakened. And such contact means simply "to draw on the same sources from which an exemplary creator drew and to borrow from one's predecessor simply the manner of proceeding" (§47, 139–40; 152). Which does not exclude, for Kant as for Longinus, an extremely rigorous agonistic, with its historical scenes and instances: what would Homer have said, what would he say, and what will posterity think? (XIV, 1–3; 85).

But this mimetic rivalry involves neither "pillage" nor the least envy or jealousy—no serious artist can seek the enjoyment of this petty game. If there is μίμησις, it is, in a manner quite expected since Plato, in the mode of the "imprint" or "impression" (ἀποτύπωσις) made by a beautiful ἦθος, a beautiful work of plastic or other art (XIII, 4; 83–84). The enigmatic transmission of genius arises out of a typology: he whom great art *impresses* can be a genius.

From there, moreover, and in complete conformity with Longinus, Kant derives the idea of the *classical* in art:

> That one can rightly praise the works of the ancients as models and that one calls their authors classics, as if they formed a certain nobility among writers, which by its example gives laws to the people—this seems to indicate a posteriori sources of taste and to refute the autonomy of taste in each subject. (§32, 118; 124)

This passage says clearly that the ancients are in fact a priori models of art: there is a sort of transcendentality of the ancients. Certain works a priori have been in conformity with the universality of the judgment of taste. It happened once. And this is doubtless why art has once arrived at its limit. If one can hope for an infinite progress from science (it is a matter of the "brain"), one cannot hope for any such thing from art:

> But for genius art stops somewhere, for a limit is imposed upon it beyond which it cannot go, a limit which presumably has been reached long ago and cannot be extended further. Again, artistic skill cannot be communicated; it is imparted to every artist immediately by the hand of nature; and so it dies with him, until nature endows another in the same way, so that he only needs an example in order to put in operation in a similar fashion the talent of which he is conscious. (§47, 140; 152)

But in addition, this limit is by no means an end of art, as distinct from what happens in the Platonico-Hegelian version of art. Genius can—always—produce itself anew. It will not surpass the ancients but it can—always—be as great as they: Wieland, says Kant; Hölderlin, says Heidegger. Or Trakl, or George.

But there is something much more important than this. From the moment when μίμησις, fundamentally, is conceived as "apophantic," there follow two apparently contradictory consequences:

First, insofar as the sublime—great art—arises from τέχνη in the restricted sense, it is indeed necessary, Longinus says, that τέχνη come to the (corrective) aid of φύσις:

> Though of course in reply to the one who wrote that the Colossus, with its mistakes, is not better than the "Spear-bearer" by Polycleitus, it may be said (in addition to many other things) that though what is wondered at in technique is the greatest precision [τὸ ἀκριβέστατον], in the workings of nature it is greatness, and by nature the human being is characterized by eloquence; and while in statues likeness [τὸ ὅμοιον] to a human being is sought,

in speeches and writings, as I said, what transcends the human [το ὑπεραῖρον τὰ ἀνθρώπινα] is sought....Still...though correctness without any slip is more a matter of technique or art, the sublime...is the work of genius, so that technique must everywhere provide support for nature. (XXXVI, 3–4; 182–84)

It is necessary, then, to moderate the excess of the sublime. But this means evidently also that art, τέχνη in the restricted sense, is capable only of assiduousness, the exactitude of perfectionism. In this sense μίμησις is interpreted as ὁμοίωσις, resemblance. In statues, what is sought is resemblance (το ὅμοιον) to the human. And this defines and sums up the beautiful as aspect (εἶδος) in the mode of the resemblance. Inversely, as a consequence, in the sublime (great art), an entirely other μίμησις is at stake. Doubtless this is because great art is first of all, for Longinus, the art of the λόγος and because by nature a person is essentially λογικόν, a speaking-being. What is sought is the superhuman, that which surpasses things human: nothing which, by definition, could be reproduced. Great art has nothing to do with the εἶδος because it has nothing to do, essentially, with the déjà vu, the already-present.

Second, in the sublime as such (in great art), art ought to efface itself. Longinus asserts this with respect to hyperbaton, that figure which "consists in an order which dissociates words or thoughts from their customary sequence and constitutes, so to speak, the most true character of a violent passion" (XXII, 1; 119–20):

In the superior writers, imitation, thanks to hyperbaton, approaches the workings of nature; for art is thus fulfilled, when it is the general opinion that it is nature at work, and...nature comes out luckily whenever she has in her a technique that escapes notice.

If I transcribe: τέχνη accomplishes its purpose when it seems to be φύσις, and φύσις succeeds when it encloses τέχνη in hiding it from the view (λανθάνουσαν). This proposition closes a lengthy development in which Longinus shows that hyperbaton, syntactical dissociation, is appropriate to the expression of a violent πάθος, such as anger, fear, indignation, or jealousy. Disrupted λόγος reveals the affect and makes it appear. In conformity with its apophantic function, μίμησις makes φύσις itself—natural πάθος—emerge. But in this very revelation or this presentification, in the apparition of φύσις, τέχνη effaces itself: it is the same thing as the φύσις it reveals.

In deciphering φύσις, in other words, τέχνη ciphers itself: as Longinus indicates in a word, it is the very play of ἀλήθεια; and this is why, moreover, the sublime λόγος is for Longinus the true λόγος, that is, the unveiling. The paradox of the effacement of τέχνη is evidently inscribed in the oxymoron constitutive of genius: natural art. And it entails this hyperbolic logic that I have attempted to articulate elsewhere:[39] the more τέχνη accomplishes itself, the more it effaces itself. The height of μίμησις is in its veiling and its dissimulation. This is indeed in all probability what prompts Kant to say that the sublime is to be found in simplicity. And it is also perhaps what Hölderlin understood by sobriety.

But how is τέχνη supposed to efface itself? As is well known, Longinus addresses this problem under the heading of the effacement of the figure (σχῆμα) which, he says, always fights on the side of the sublime and comes to its aid. But the use of figures, he adds, is a delicate matter because "the artifice of figures is properly suspect and awakens the suspicion of entrapment" (XVII, 1; 104). This is why "the best figure seems…that figure which hides [διαλανθάνῃ] and which casts into oblivion its own existence." The example Longinus seeks in Demosthenes is of little importance here. What is important is the question he poses: "What hides [ἀπέκρυψε] the figure in this case?" And above all, what is important is the response he provides: "Evidently, its very refulgence [δῆλον ὅτι τῷ φωτὶ αὐτῷ]." For he adds immediately, revealing thereby that this light or refulgence is not there by chance:

> Just as a faint gleam is almost made to disappear when the sun radiates all around it, so rhetorical contrivances grow faint when greatness is poured over them from all sides. And something not different from this occurs in painting: although light and shadow are portrayed in colors on the same surface side by side, the light meets our eyes first, and not only is it more conspicuous, but it also appears [φαίνεσθαι] to be much nearer. Now in speeches and writings, since emotion and sublimity lie nearer to our souls— because of a kind of natural kinship and because of their dazzling effect [διὰ λαμπρότητα]—over and over again they appear to us before the figures, and they cast technique into the shade and keep it hidden (XVII, 2–3; 105–6)

This light is by no means due to the genius of comparison. One must take it literally: it is the sublime light, i.e., the light the sublime is when the sublime is thought in its truth as the unconcealing, the ἀλήθεια of what is (φύσις). Τέχνη—μίμησις—is the illumination of φύσις: this is, literally and in all senses, the truth of great art. And this is of course why great art cannot be seen—the light it throws casts it into shadow. It makes essentially no "form," "figure," or "schema" come into presence. It presents, while im-presenting itself [s'imprésentant], that there is the existent-present [de l'étant-présent]. And it is a bedazzlement.

This same light—the brilliance itself of the ἐκφανέστατον—does not cease gleaming and fulgurating in Longinus's text. Sublimity, "brought out at just the right moment, makes everything different, like lightning" (I, 4; 9). And concerning Demosthenes: "he outthunders, as it were, and outshines orators of all times: one might actually be more capable of opening his eyes toward a thunderbolt bearing in on him than to set his eyes on the emotions of this man as they come one on top of another" (XXXIV, 4; 172).[40] "Pretty expressions are in reality the proper light of thought [φῶς ἴδιον τοῦ" νοῦ]." Or again, Longinus says that the aging Homer, the Homer of the *Odyssey* (the genius par excellence), is comparable to a setting sun (IX, 13; 60).

One could multiply these examples. The sublime says itself through light and glittering. And it says itself so well in this way that, in two notable passages (the tradition has noted them), it finds itself exemplified by light itself.

First, there is the example (celebrated up through Hegel) of the *Fiat lux* of Genesis, the example of that sort of absolute performative whose sole aim is: that it should be. Here God reveals himself to be the principle (ἀρχή), in that he is precisely the λόγος ἀποφαντικός: the speech of the pure appearing or epiphany, for it is light itself which appears as that on the basis of which all visible things present themselves.

The second example occurs when Longinus, in a long apparent digression opened by the praise of Demosthenes as thunder, as cited above, gathers together his theses on the sublime: the superiority of the sublime over the beautiful consists in the fact that it responds to our destiny. Φύσις, Longinus says, does not consider us as a base and vile creature but as a creature destined to greatness: it has introduced us into life and the totality of the world as into some great panegyric to contemplate (θεάομαι) all that takes place within it (XXXV, 2). Humans are there, in other words, in order that the totality of what is should be taken in view. And this is why, Longinus adds, φύσις has given birth (ἐνέφυσεν) in our souls to an invincible ἔρως for all that is eternally great and for all that is more divine (δαιμονιώτερον) than ourselves.

What does Longinus mean to say here? What does this invincible ἔρως bespeak? That the totality of what is suffices neither for the θεωρία nor for the διάνοια of humanity: "Even in its totality, the world [ὁ σύμπας κόσμος] does not suffice for the *élan* [ἐπιβολή] of human theory and thought" (XXXV, 3; 177). A person is a meta-physical being, or more precisely—because Longinus has such a high idea of φύσις (he conceives of it, in effect, as Being)—a meta-cosmic, that is a meta-ontic Being. And ἔρως, here, which moreover is mixed up with ἀγών (with violence, and not merely with emulation), is strictly what Heidegger defines as the transcendence of *Dasein*. As Longinus says, the ἐπίνοιαι of humanity, the thoughts we project before and beyond ourselves, frequently surpass the limits of what surrounds us. And it is in this that we recognize that for which we are born.

It is here that a second light erupts, a fire rather, which is nothing other than the fire of φύσις.

> Therefore we are (heaven knows) somehow driven by nature to wonder not at small streams, even if they are clear and useful, but at the Nile and the Danube and the Rhine, and still more at the Ocean; nor, of course, are we more astounded by that little flame which we kindle, when it preserves a pure gleam, than by the gleam of the heavenly bodies, though they are often gloomed over, nor do we generally consider it more worthy of wonder than the craters of Aetna, whose eruptions carry up rocks and whole mounds from its abyss and sometimes pour forth rivers of that fire born of the earth and which obeys no law but its own. (XXXV, 4; 178–80)

It is this, the ἐκφανέστατον. Of which one can see—I imagine that it is useless to insist on this—that Hölderlin has retained its memory.

Longinus concludes, "If what is useful or even necessary to man is within his range, in turn the astonishing, for him, is always the paradox." Τὸ παράδοξον: normally, this phrase goes untranslated; however, I'll translate it das Unheimliche, thinking obviously of the Heideggerian use of the word but also of this famous definition by Schelling: "One calls unheimlich all that which was supposed to remain secret, veiled, and which manifests itself."

6.

Thus, the ἐκφανέστατον, at least, a certain interpretation of the ἐκφανέστα-τον, will have been at stake in the sublime. And the ἐκφανέστατον will have been able to constitute such a stake because one will have nonetheless known, here or there, perhaps by the effect of a sort of beyond-memory of what had never been properly said or thought, that this beyond-light (a translation for ἐκφανέστατον) is the strange clarity of Being itself, "although obscurity often attains it," its bedazzling night without night—like the lightning which is its sign in Hölderlin (but also what he calls the "sober clarity"). Because thus one will have thought, here or there, that "great art" has regard precisely for that, which presupposes of course that, in one way or another, one endures its view, even if it is never perhaps a matter of mere vision. The Lichtung, the clearing or the opening of appearing, is beyond all light.

A contemporary of Heidegger—apparently a theologico-metaphysical thinker, in his way—expressed this with rare vigour in a text which, for various reasons, Heidegger could not have failed to read and with which in any case "The Origin of the Work of Art" is joined by relationships which I would consider rather troubling. I am referring to Walter Benjamin and his essay on "*The Elective Affinites* of Goethe." I tear from their context several sentences in which all is said. I give them simply to be read or understood. To conclude:

> All that is essentially beautiful is indebted constantly and in its essence, but in infinitely varying degrees, to appearance [*Schein*]. This bond of debt attains its highest intensity in that which is manifestly alive, and precisely here [in Goethe's novel] in a clear polarity of triumphant and extinguishing appearance. For all that lives is lifted out beyond [*enthoben*] the realm of the essentially beautiful, and the higher the life-form the more this is so; accordingly, the essentially beautiful manifests itself in the form [*Gestalt*] of the living most of all as appearance. Beautiful life, the essentially beautiful, and apparent beauty, these three are identical....The beautiful, even if it is itself not appearance, ceases to be essentially beautiful when its appearance disappears. For this appearance belongs to it as its veil, and the law of the essence of beauty thus shows itself to be this: that beauty can only appear as such in the veiled....Beauty is not an appearance [*Schein*], a veil covering something other than itself. Beauty itself is not appearance [*Erscheinung*], but essence, an essence however which remains the same as itself only when veiled. Therefore, even if everywhere else appearance is deception, the appearance of the beautiful is the veil thrown over what is necessarily the most veiled. For neither the veil nor the veiled object is the beautiful, but the object in its veil. Unveiled, it would prove to be infinitely insignificant [*unscheinbar*]....Thus, in the face of the beautiful, the idea of unveiling becomes the idea of the impossibility of unveiling....Because only the beautiful and nothing besides can be essentially veiling and veiled, the divine ground of the Being of beauty lies in the secret. And thus the appearance in beauty is this: not the superfluous veiling of things in themselves, but the necessary veiling of things for us....For the sake of the unity which the veil and that which is veiled comprise in it, the Idea can be essentially valid only where the duality of nakedness and veiling does not yet obtain: in art and in the appearances of mere nature. On the other hand, the more distinctly this duality expresses itself, in order finally in man to reach its greatest force, the more this becomes clear: in veil-less nakedness the essentially beautiful has withdrawn and in the naked body of the human being a Being beyond all beauty is attained—the sublime, and a work beyond all images [*Gebilden*]—the work of the creator....

Only nature is impossible to unveil; it retains a secret for as long as God allows it to subsist. Truth is discovered in the essence of language. The human body strips itself, a sign that the human being itself steps before God.[41]

Chapter 5

❀

THE INTEREST OF THE SUBLIME

Jean-François Lyotard

Use, interest, benefit (profit), and sacrifice: the text of the *Critiques* treats its themes—the true, the good, and the beautiful—with these concepts (but there are also others, for example, the incentive and the motive) borrowed from the domain of economy. For the faculties, too, have their economy. This economy always intervenes on two occasions: wherever Kant elaborates the cooperation of the faculties with one another; and wherever he attempts to comprehend how the faculty in general, which is nothing but a capacity or potential power, can actualize itself in empirical reality, how the capital of the potential powers of thought can invest or "realize" itself in acts.

By focusing on the *interest* of the feeling of the sublime, one touches a raw nerve of the "organism" of the faculties. The analysis of the beautiful still allows one to hope that the subject will ground itself as the unity of the faculties and that the accord between real objects and the authentic destiny of this subject—the Idea of nature—will be legitimated. But even if it is nothing but a "simple appendix" (*CJ*, §23, 86; 85), the "Analytic of the Sublime"—like a meteor careening into the work devoted to this double edification—appears to put an end to these hopes. And it is the interest of the feeling of the sublime that detonates, as it were, this disappointment.

I have left to these notes on the third *Critique* (i.e., the *Critique of Judgment*) the tone and rhythm of the lectures for which they were destined, as I did also for "Sensus Communis."[1] And like the latter, the present text is part of a course on the sublime begun five years ago.

1.

The feeling of the beautiful is a reflexive judgment, singular (although it claimes universality), immediate, and disinterested. It arises only from one

faculty of the soul, that of pleasure and pain, and it takes place on the occasion
of a form. Its fate as disinterested pleasure, indeed, depends on this radical
formality of its occasion. If it arose out of the least attachment to the *matter* of
the given, for example, to color or to tone, it would regress into the sort of
"pleasure" [*agrément*] that results from a fulfilled "inclination." By virtue of
its existence here and now, the object would then have exercised an "attraction" on the mind.

Attraction is one case of interest, the empirical, "pathological" case. The
will's maxim, or the purposiveness of its desire, is oriented toward the enjoyment [*jouissance*] of the object. The mind takes a servile interest in the existence of this empirical object: its pleasure is that of dependence, of "having a
taste for…"

One might expect that it would suffice to discriminate between pure
and impure taste in order to emancipate aesthetic pleasure from the enjoyment of the object. That is, one might expect that it would suffice to distinguish from *Sinnengeschmack* (sensuous taste) a *Reflexionsgeschmack* (a reflexive taste) (*CJ*, §8, 58; 48). Reflexion in general, above all in this exemplary
mode of the immediate judgment of the beautiful (or simply feeling), would
seem to exclude all interest defined by a submission of the will to a determinate object. This is because reflexion consists in judging without determinate
criterion, without rule of judgment, and thus here without being able to anticipate the sort of object or the unique object that could procure pleasure.

However, this distinction in terms of the faculties of knowledge (determinant versus reflexive judgment) hides another distinction in terms of the
faculties of the soul (*CJ*, IX, 42; 34), and more specifically in terms of whether
they are pure or empirically applied. Kant opposes three sorts of satisfaction
(in the broad sense), three sorts of relation to the feelings of pleasure and pain.
An object can "satisfy" (*vergnügen*) properly speaking, it can "please"
(*gefallen*), or it can be "appreciated, esteemed" (*geschätzt, gebilligt werden*) (§5,
54; 44). This object is thus called, respectively, agreeable, beautiful, or good.
On the part of the subject, the motive corresponding to this object is called,
respectively, inclination, favor, or respect. Only favor, granted thus to the
beautiful, is "a disinterested and *free* satisfaction," Kant writes, "a unique, free
satisfaction." Sensuous taste presupposes inclination; it wants satisfaction,
properly speaking, and it is interested in the agreeable. Reflexive taste presupposes favor. "Pleasure" (*Gefallen*) befalls it. And the beautiful is the "object"
that (be)falls. The German word *Gefallen* indicates with sufficient clarity the
extent to which the beautiful befalls it, falls from the clouds, comes utterly
unexpected. One cannot dress for the occasion [*on n'y est pas paré ni préparé*].
The French language has the expression *un bonheur*, which is not at all the
same as *le bonheur*, for this ingenuousness of satisfaction. Disinterest is a condition for *avoir des bonheurs*. But it is not a guarantee.

Two remarks concerning this first distinction. First, in a given case of the empirical application of aesthetic judgment, it can happen that "what has already pleased by itself without the consideration of any interest whatever" arouses subsequently an interest in its existence, in the existence of this thing (§41, 129; 139). Thus, for example the inclination to live in society can come to take over where pure aesthetic pleasure leaves off: sociability turns out to realize itself through taste, in that the latter involves the demand that all participate in it (§41, 129–30; 139). It is necessary, however, to separate this latter demand, inscribed a priori in the transcendental analysis of aesthetic feeling, from all empirical inclinations to communicate this feeling. It is necessary, in short, to admit that the promise of a universal participation in taste, which is analytically attached to taste itself, is not due to any interest in a determinable community (§41, 130–31; 140). Pure "favor" cannot become inclination without the beautiful becoming the agreeable, in which case aesthetic pleasure is lost.

This argument arises from the distinction between the transcendental and the empirical. But it also appeals—and this is my second observation—to the difference between the faculties of the soul. Satisfaction in the narrow sense fulfills an inclination. It functions in terms of an economy of desire which presupposes a lack and the expectation of its suppression, satiation, the "enough"—the *genug* that can be heard in *Vergnügung*. But taste takes place only on condition of the absence of expectation. If it obeys any purposiveness, no one knows—I mean, even transcendental analysis cannot know—how to produce the concept of its purpose, the object that would come to satiate it. It is not determined. This does not mean that it is infinite but rather that the satisfaction in which it consists is independent of any inclination. That there is no desire of beauty. One has either the one or the other, either desire or beauty. That is: either the faculty of desire or the faculty of pleasure and pain. And this is not easy for us to think today, perhaps for us in particular as Occidentals, haunted as we are by the passion of willing, this grantedness or this grace (*Gunst*) which comes unsought. A pleasure takes place "first" as such, which comes to fulfill nothing and can disappoint nothing. Irrelative. A motivation, "favor," which moreover nothing motivates: (a)motivation.

I return to the three satisfactions. There is the third, "appreciation," "esteem" motivated by respect and taking the good as its object. The relations between aesthetics and ethics play themselves out in the situation that Kant attributes to the pleasure of esteem. And with this localization the point is determined at which the sublime will be inserted into Kant's transcendental characterization of affect, his transcendental sentimentality. This object, the good, is placed on a par with the object of any empirical need, at least with regard to the constraint each imposes. Only favor procures a "free satisfaction." Respect, as we have seen, is in itself a free affection. But the law—after the fact, so to speak, and insofar as it prescribes, even if it prescribes nothing but a form for actions to be accomplished—imposes upon the will an interest

in certain specific objects. Since we are now in the practical field, under the
law of "action," these objects are actions, or rather, because the law is formal,
maxims of actions. And they become powerfully interesting through the very
fact of their being prescribed. "When the moral law speaks, there is no longer
objectively any freedom of choice concerning what should be done" (*CJ*, §5,
55; 45). Thus, we see here the return of the constraint of the object, even if,
subjectively and empirically, the "good maxims"—the good objects—remain
to be determined in each case.

   Constraint returns here because the faculty of desire returns. "Esteem,"
in this regard, shares with satiation, *Vergnügung*, the same concern, which is
the proper concern of the faculty of desire: the attainment of "that which is
good" (§4, 52; 41–42). To be sure, within what one can reasonably judge to be
good, one distinguishes the *wozu gut* ("the good-for") from the *an sich gut*
("the good *tout court*"), but both presuppose "the concept of a purpose." And
one ought further to separate from the utilitarian (the good-for...) the agreeable, in which reason plays no part whatsoever (*CPrR*, 71–76; 59–65). But it
remains nonetheless the case that in these two extremes of satisfaction, the
agreeable and the good pure and simple, between which the useful mediates,
despite their diversity with respect to reason, a common trait can be recognized that *distinguishes* both from aesthetic pleasure: interest, "a certain interest relative to their object" (*CJ*, §4, 53; 43). Even the pure moral good differs
from the others only in the degree of interest it arouses: it evokes "the highest
interest," and the reason there is only this quantitative difference is that in
each case the will is involved, as opposed to what happens in aesthetic pleasure. Where there is will, there is interest: "to will something and to take satisfaction in its existence, that is, to take some interest in it—these things are
identical" (§4, 54; 43).

2.

The disjunction between aesthetics and ethics is here apparently beyond
appeal. It obeys the heterogeneity between the two faculties of the soul at play,
the feeling of pleasure and pain and the faculty of desire, respectively. In the
third *Critique*, however, it was a matter of establishing a bridge between the
capacity of knowing and the capacity of willing, and the feeling in question,
aesthetic feeling, was supposed to serve as the central pillar of a bridge with
two arches between these capacities. And yet it seems that the first arch is
missing, the one which was supposed to open the passage from the will to feeling. Indeed, interest forbids us to build it. The hope of a unity of the subject,
of unity between its diverse capacities, seems thereby to have been definitively
shattered. It seems that there will always be a dispute [*un différend*] between
"tasting" and willing or wanting, and thus not one but two heteronomous

subjects: the subject that does not cease to be born to itself—without even taking any interest in its birth, without willing it—in the pure pleasure of the beautiful, and the subject that does not cease to be induced to act in the interest of the realization of the law.

This divorce does not go uncontested. The critical judge proposes a profusion of conciliatory procedures, notably in paragraphs 42 and 59, which have generally been read as if they exposed the Kantian "thesis" on this problem. According to this reading, the feeling of the beautiful in fact contains an interest, an "intellectual interest" (§42, 131; 140–41), to be understood here as nonempirical. This is an interest precisely in realizing what the moral law prescribes, an "intellectual" interest because it is attached to the "object" whose willed realization practical reason prescribes: the good (§42, 131–33; 140–43). And in the other paragraph, this "thesis" is supposedly reaffirmed and rendered more precise. The missing arch of the bridge can again be built, thanks to a certain scaffolding—a scaffolding which is indispensable to the critical strategy insofar as it permits one to cross over the "abysses" opened up by the heteronomy of the faculties—called "hypotyposis," *subjectio sub aspectum* ("submission to the view"), the operation of placing in view—despite everything—something that corresponds (analogically) to an invisible object (§59, 174ff; 197ff). This is the case for the object of an Idea of reason, which is not presentable by itself in intuition but of which one can present an intuitive analogue: a "symbol." Beauty could in this manner be the "symbol of morality" (§59, 173; 196).

Many thinkers—harried by the haste to conclude, whether their motives be good or bad—plunge down the path thus broken and manage in fact to get to the other side, despite all Kant's multiple warnings, in order to reimplant the old head of the bridge, in order to reaffirm the *archaic* argument—archaic for Western thought at least—that one can infer the good from the beautiful, that if one feels well and makes the other feel well, one realizes the good and makes the other realize the good. Or as Lacoue-Labarthe[2] would say, if one fictions or figures the given tastefully, in accordance with beauty, one moralizes individual *ethos* or communal *politikon*. Thus one reopens the road, which had for a moment seemed lost, toward an "aesthetic education." But one does so only by failing to take into account Kant's incessantly and explicitly articulated reservations with respect to any conclusive, inferential use of analogy. He writes, for example: "Two things being heterogeneous, one can assuredly *think* one of them by *analogy* with the other, even from the point of view of their heterogeneity; but one cannot, departing from what renders these things heterogeneous, conclude or *infer* the one from the other by analogy" (§90, 268; 315). Thus, one can maintain: "like the beautiful, so the good," but not: "if beautiful, then good" (nor the converse). An aestheticization of ethics or politics is deauthorized in advance by this reservation. Such an aestheticization is exactly what Kant calls a transcendental "illusion" or "appearance."

I would add that, inversely, one ought not to confuse the aspiration, the call that affects the mind and the debt it consents to incur when it undertakes to realize a beautiful work of writing in the literary, artistic sense, in obedience to the demands of the beautiful—one ought not to confuse this obedience with the attention to the moral law, with the felt obligation to act in accordance with the principle of universalization which the law entails as prescriptive reason or as sole rational prescription. If one made the work a direct testament of the law, one would occult the aesthetic difference, one would obscure a territory—that of beautiful forms—and a condition at stake there, the pure pleasure these forms procure, both of which ought to be protected from all interference. "To write," in this sense, is not a means of attempting—even if in vain—to pay off one's debts to the law. (Or if it is, then the sense of "to write" would have to be displaced—displaced evidently in the direction of the sublime.) In other words, "the antinomy of reason for the *feeling of pleasure and pain*" should not be confused with "the antinomy of reason for *the faculty of desire*" (§57, 168; 190).

The principle of the heterogeneity of the faculties suffices to forbid both this confusion and that other illusion which subordinates the feeling of pleasure and pain to the faculty of knowing and which maintains "that the judgment of taste dissimulates a judgment of reason on the perfection of a thing," the difference between the two judgments being thus nothing more than a matter of "distinction" (§15, 70; 64). Taste would, on this view, be the "confused" appreciation of a purposiveness *with* purpose present in the object which would be in principle accessible to clear cognition. But of course this is the Leibnizian thesis against which the entire third *Critique* militates, according to the general strategy of an autonomization of space-time with respect to the understanding, a strategy already operative in the first *Critique* (i.e., the *Critique of Pure Reason*) but more timidly there than in the third.

And to say just one word more concerning the first of these confusions, the confusion of the good with the beautiful: its dissipation by critique ought to discourage in addition all "philosophy of the will," beginning with the "will to power." For the latter reduces ethics and politics to "values" and thereby grants itself the authority to treat them as mere "forms." "Affirmation" in Nietzsche is conceived as formation, artistic creation. The good and, secondarily, the true maintain themselves only by means of their "beauty." This position is indeed an extreme expression of the obsession with fashioning, which after the *Critique* is no more authorized than the obsession with preestablished harmony. Both violently impose a unity on Being.

Let us return to our bridge. The analogical scaffolding is far from having the foundation of a true bridge. I have just evoked the risks, or at least some of the risks run by any thought that precipitously attempts this fragile passage. But Kant does attempt to consolidate it because it is requisite to the unification of the subject he envisages. I shall now examine the strategy of this con-

10/2

Prof. Westing.

We have ordered

2 additional tables
for Rm 3355 and
will remove the
broken table from 3455,

Luanda

solidation. Its significance will become clear when we then attempt to situate sublime feeling in relation to ethics.

Two series of arguments of two different sorts. The one draws on the transcendental properties common to aesthetic and moral judgment, the traits shared by aesthetic and moral judgment that authorize their analogy. I will call these arguments *logical,* because they limit themselves to comparing the two judgments according to what mere transcendental logic permits. The others draw, to the contrary, on the regulative Idea of a nature finalized in terms of the model of art. They use the "guiding thread" that critical teleology draws out of the concrete texture of existences which comprise the world. Let us call them *teleological,* with all the circumspection that the use of this term in Kant's work, especially in the third *Critique,* makes necessary. They follow or at least accompany the elaboration of the Idea of nature in this book, whereas the logical arguments are foreign—and so to speak anterior—to this elaboration.

Logically, the beautiful and the good share a family resemblance. They please immediately; without or before all interest; in accordance with a free relation of the faculties of which they are respectively the "objects"; they are considered to be necessary, to require universal assent or participation (§59, 175–76; 199–200). These somewhat forced resemblances require corrections even in Kant's view. These corrections are such that the difference between the good and the beautiful opens anew. It is a concept, the concept of the law, that inspires without mediation moral feeling; it is an (inconceivable) imaginative form that occasions taste. (Of course, one is "obliged" *before* knowing why, but the law which obliges is conceivable.) In morality, it is the will that is free, in the sense that it is dependent only on a prescription of rational form (the "type" of legality) (*CPrR,* 85ff; 75ff); whereas in taste, it is the imagination that is free. It produces new forms—quite "beyond" the "agreement with the concept" which limits the schema (*CJ,* §49, 146; 160)—to the point of "creating another nature so to speak on the basis of the matter with which real nature provides it" (§49, 144; 157). This freedom incites or excites the understanding to vie with imaginative creativity for the greatest comprehension or comprehensiveness. Thus arises a "play"—itself "free"—between the two faculties, an "enlivening" (*Beförderung*) (§35, 122; 129). The claim of singular taste for universal assent is not supported by the authority of any concept, whereas the universalization of the maxim is required analytically by the very definition of the concept of the law. And to conclude this term by term comparison, as for interest, the beautiful concedes nothing to it; "it pleases beyond *all interest,*" whereas "the morally good is necessarily linked with our interest" (§59, 175; 199).

Nonetheless, the opposition is not so sharp as I am making it seem here, not even in Kant's logical argumentations. The good is indeed linked with an interest. However, as Kant repeatedly clarifies, this interest "does not precede" moral judgment but rather "results" (§59, 175; 199) from it. Practical judgment is not "founded" on any interest "*but it produces one*" (§42, 132; 142–43). This reversal of the position of interest is essential to the critique of morality. The law *does not result* from the will's interest in the good, it commands this interest. Such is "the paradox of the method": "*The concepts of good and evil should not be determined before the moral law (to which it apparently should serve as foundation), but only (as happens here) after this law and through it*" (*CPrR*, 76; 65). If in morality the will envisaged the good as its object "before" the object was prescribed for it, it would depend on the good object, just as it depends on an empirical object, desirable, agreeable, or useful. There would be in this case no transcendental difference between pure *pathos* and pure *ethos* but merely a different object. In both cases, there would be a conditioned imperative, an imperative conditioned by an object, "interested," hypothetical. If you want this (the good, or some chocolate), do that.

In order to escape from this ruinous consequence, "heteronomy" (*CPrR*, 78; 66), which would destroy all ethical difference and induce scepticism or cynicism (there are some who love the good, others who love chocolate), one must for Kant reverse the order of determination. The law seizes the will—"immediately"—through an obligation "without regard for any object" (*CPrR*, 77; 65–66). It can prescribe to the will only prescription itself. Its *dictum* (its content) is reduced to commandment without object. And by its *modus* (the modality of this prescription), it ought to prescribe prescription necessarily. It is posited as not being able not to be posited. As in the demand for assent implied by taste (one must concede this resemblance mediated by a common *sollen* that would merit a separate treatment), so here we are concerned with a necessity which translates itself practically into the demand that this law should be able to be the law of each moral "subject," of all the "you's." It is universally imposed.

This purloining [*dérobade*] of the object is well known—this rediscovery of the condition of ethics, which is the pure ought "before" any object. (I say rediscovery because this absence of object is already present in the "Hear, O Israel.") Thus, a "disinterested" condition. The feeling of obligation, respect for the law, is not attached to the existence of any object. The law itself is not an object, one does not love the law. However, it prescribes action. It prescribes the realization of what is "good, purely and simply" (*CPrR*, 77; 66). It induces interest for the "objects" judged capable of making this good exist. Obviously, these objects do not exist beforehand, since the goal is to make them exist in practice and not to know them in theory. One must *do* the good, not discover it. These "objects" are actions to be performed, judgments to be carried out. The law induces an interest yet to be determined, an interest in "maxims" which can put the will in a position to do the good.

It is here—precisely, powerfully, and only here—that interest plays a role in the moral domain. It results from or is "produced" by the law. If the good is interesting, this is because first of all the law ought to be realized. The law says:

actualize me and it says only that, without saying *what* the "self" of the law *is*. It adds merely *what could* be a "good" [*bonne*] actualization: universalizable, extensible to all particular wills. This condition, or rather this supposition (*so daß, als ob*), determines the interest in certain modes of actualization.

Compared to aesthetic judgment in terms of this aspect of interest, moral judgment does not seem, in Kant's eyes, so distant from it that one could decide between them by a simple yes or no. Moral judgment is "analogous" to aesthetic judgment in that the former "accords an immediate interest to its object" (§42, 133; 143), and this interest is "equal" to that which can be associated with taste. The sole difference is that the interest of taste is a "free interest, while [ethical interest] is founded on an objective law" (§42, 133; 143). This conciliation is to be taken, as one can see, *cum qrano salis*. On the aesthetic side, "free" interest can only be a disinterested interest ("favor") where "no interest, neither of sense nor of reason, compels assent" (§5, 55; 44). And on the ethical side, how could an interest for "its" object *immediately* seize the will, if it is "founded on an objective law," that is, necessarily *mediated* by the empty categorical imperative from which it has then to derive, with the assistance of the mere clause of universalization, maxims which will finally cause it to be interested in certain actions?

If the two judgments are members of one family, then it is clear that they are presently in family counseling. Their relationship is structured by an improbable analogy. It is necessary that there be some passage from the beautiful to the good. But if one holds strictly to the transcendental logic, this passage begins to pass one by. For there is no interest at all in the felt immediacy of taste, whereas in ethics, there is indeed an interest, secondary to be sure, but secondary precisely because it is deduced from the conception of the law, an interest which could not be more mediated, an implication of interest. Interest is the result, in ethics; in aesthetics, disinterest initiates.

3.

Is the affinity between the beautiful and the good more conclusively demonstrated by the argumentation I have called *teleological*? The reasoning is as follows:

1. The mind has no interest in the law. But the law commands it to do good, and interests it in "acts" capable of actualizing the good. (This demand for actualization is exercised on all the faculties which, by themselves, are nothing but "facultative," that is, possibilities.)

2. The mind has no interest in the beautiful. But that the beautiful takes place provides pure (disinterested) reflexive judgment with an opportunity to exercise itself and to realize itself in the present. What furnishes this oppor-

tunity is apparently art, which produces the beautiful. But only on condition that art itself solicit no interest and hence, also obey none.

3. Beauty's model of disinterested actualization, however, is furnished by "nature." As far as we can know, nature expects no gain from the landscapes and harmonies it offers to the mind. It does not produce the beautiful with any (concept of a) purpose in mind. Art is only pure if it produces like "nature," which is itself, hence, the paradigm of pure art.

4. Thus, in procuring occasions of pure aesthetic pleasure for the mind, "nature"—as artist and/or work of art—demonstrates that a disinterested activity of judgment which is merely possible can actualize itself as such. In this way, it shows itself favorable to the demand for the actualization of the possible—of the facultative—in general, and in particular to the demand for the actualization of that faculty of disinterested action which is the rational will.

5. Practical reason thus finds itself interested in the disinterested pleasure that "natural" beauties arouse (*CJ*, §42, 131–33; 140–44; *CPrR*, 134–36; 124–26).

This then is the backbone of the "teleological" argumentation by means of which critical thought proposes the affinity of the beautiful with the good. One might be tempted to give it the twist of a dialectical logic: an (ethical) interest in (aesthetic) disinterest. But this dialectic would not be critical. Critique has the task of exposing the condition of this pretended dialectic, and this condition is not the concept in the Hegelian sense but the merely regulative Idea of a nature oriented purposively (such as an art can be) toward the actualization of the powers of the mind. According to the principles of critique, far from authorizing a logic of negation, which would homogenize by a movement of "sublation" (*Aufhebung*) the yes (of interest) and the no (of disinterest), this Idea ought rather to ground its own legitimacy (to "deduce" itself in the Kantian sense). The deduction reveals the exercise of a third faculty, that of reflexive judgment which, although it is also in play in both cognition and morals nonetheless does not lack its own "territory," that of art and nature, where it exercises itself "purely," "in accord with itself." This evidently complicates matters of unification, suspended henceforth in the "nondemonstrable" Idea of a naturally artistic teleology, and requires that one include a supplementary faculty in the synthesis of the first two faculties. It is thus as a critical philosopher that one must examine the play of interest and disinterest which in principle permits one to establish an alliance (to "bridge" the gap) between aesthetic favor and ethical respect. Such an examination is all the more "useful" as it reveals the exact point at which the feeling of the sublime will come to disorganize this play, in breaking the fragile alliance between the two "satisfactions." The possible consequences of the localization of this fracture—both for the Idea of "nature" and for the general project of constituting the mind as a subjective unity—draw themselves, so to speak, of themselves. Only the former consequences will be treated here; the latter, concerning unified subjectivity, are only sketchily indicated.

But first, it is necessary to reconsider the demand for the actualization of the faculty. This demand extends to all the powers or faculties of the mind. They are nothing but possibilities. How then do they become acts of the mind? How does it happen that on such and such an occasion (at the "right moment"?), phenomenally given or not, the understanding or taste or the will is exercised? How is the distance crossed between *posse* and *esse*? Precisely—through "interest."

In the second *Critique*, Kant seeks to establish the primacy of pure practical reason over pure speculative reason (*CPrR*, 134; 124). This primacy, he explains, cannot be intrinsic. One cannot maintain that the practical use of reason provides "a more penetrating view" (*CPrR*, 135; 126) than its theoretical use. One can say neither that it is more penetrating "in itself," nor that it has a "better" ontological grasp.

Formulated critically, this primacy is finally not transcendental. The conditions in accordance with which a capacity of the mind *is capable* are simply what they are. It would be absurd to claim that some are more "radical" than others. In turn, when it is a matter of actualizing any *one* of these capacities, it is permissible, even inevitable, to ask under what condition this performance takes place and which of these capacities—or still another, which one would have forgotten about—is in charge of this "use." This term *use*, strange at first sight, returns along with *interest* and *motive* throughout the *Critiques* to circumscribe a sort of political economy of the faculties. The use of a faculty is like the transformation of its transcendental "value" into acts of the mind, like its production and consumption. This transformation or realization, similar to the transformation of money into commodities, is governed by an interest. Interest is "the principle that contains the condition under which this power only [each of the "powers of the mind"] is put into action" (*CPrR*, 134; 124). It does not consist in "the simple harmony [of reason] with itself" in accordance with each of its faculties (which fixes the status of its "a priori conditions") but "only [in] its extension" (*CPrR*, 134; 124). The interest of the use of a faculty is an interest of the faculty itself: in making use of it, the mind effects its potential, "realizes" its credit as much as possible. And thus it "extends" the range of the faculty by manifesting its power *in actu*. The faculty is like a bank of possible judgments. An entrepreneur draws on its interest in order to make use of the given faculty.

But the entrepreneur needs a "motive" (*Triebfeder*), which is the double, *within* experience, of the faculty's own interest, a sort of incentive to invest the facultative power. To the bank's interest in realization must correspond an entrepreneurial interest on the part of reality—the empirical mind—in imprinting on experience the mark of a given facultative power. This interest is not a priori, but must be calculated because the empirical mind runs the risk of loss whenever it actualizes one of its powers. An interest "can never be attributed to a being other than one endowed with reason and signifies a motive for the will, insofar as this motive is *represented by reason*" (*CPrR*, 92; 78). There is a reasonable calculation to be made because the actualization of a power of the mind does not occur without risk—of bankruptcy, or at least of a major loss or deficit—for the empirical mind. And if a closeout sale can thus endanger the actualization of a rational potential, it is because certain obstacles oppose themselves to this actualization.

> These three concepts of a motive, an interest, and a maxim [which, according to the economic metaphor, would be the entrepreneur's strategy] can only be applied to finite beings. For they all pre-suppose a limitation of the nature of a being..., a need to be excited into activity [here is the incentive to invest], because an interior obstacle opposes itself to this activity. (*CPrR*, 92; 80)

When the mind is interested by the actualization of one of its faculties, it is interested *in* this faculty. This is the mind's rational motive, and the mind has to sacrifice some other interest that is itself not reasonable or is rationally impure. This is why rational interest has to be negotiated. The entrepreneur is not a saint.

In the passage on which I am commenting, Kant analyzes the motive and the interest of, for, and in rational morality, the motive that incites one to do the good and the interest this incitation or incentive (the maxim) can have for the spirit. The obstacle is easy to designate: what will have to be placed at a distance in and by the actualization of practical reason, in and by the "use" of the moral law, is the self-enjoyment of the empirical ego [*la jouissance-de-soi du moi empirique*], its preference for itself, its arrogance. "The representation of the law suspends the influence of self-love and the illusion of presumption" (*CPrR*, 89; 78). Kant seems not to have enough words to express all that the spirit will have to "sacrifice" in order to realize the moral law. Still, one would be wrong to place the accent on the calculation of the sacrifices to be made in view of actualizing the good prescribed by the law. One would thereby confuse respect with enthusiasm, ethics with sublime aesthetic. And this is the whole question.

Practical reason is interested in its actualization in a way which differs from that of the other faculties such as the understanding. As specifically *practical* reason, it contains in its intrinsic condition of possibility—in the imperative form of its law—the necessity of its realization. It prescribes to the practical mind (to the empirical will): "Act!" and this signifies nothing other than: "Actualize me!" But in order for this effect to be obtained, this will must possess or be subject to a motive capable of surmounting the internal obstacles represented by preestablished motives, that is, by the will's attachment to the empirical ego.

Practical reason's interests cannot gain a hearing unless it creates in the ego an "interest" which is disentangled from its favorite object, the ego itself. But "disentangling" implies here not merely changing the object of interest or reorienting toward the law an interest formerly fascinated by the ego but rather transforming the nature of interest itself. For what rational law demands is its *own* interest and not that of the ego. But this interest induces, on the empirical side, the paradoxical motive of a "disinterest." The law does not offer the ego a new object in which to invest, and in the appropriation of which it might find some gain. The law itself cannot be such an object. It does not propose to the ego any "content" which would permit the ego to overdetermine (and not even by means of a "sublimation" in the Freudian sense) the interest of the law by the ego's own interest. The law must not authorize the least equivocation in the obedience it requires. The ego as such may not hope for any advantage, for example happiness or pride, from its having listened to the law. Rather, it must give itself to the law without any subjective (empirical) interest. The law must produce in the ego a disinterested motive, without either "pathos" or calculation. The interest *of* the practical rational faculty is such that it must actualize itself without arousing any empirical interest *in* this faculty.

The motive and interest of theoretical reason are less clearly circumscribed in the first *Critique*, and I leave them aside here (*CPR*, 358–65; 422–30). What is certain, in any case, is that they are different from the motive and interest which "put into practice" practical reason. Indeed, this is why their *Verbindung* ("connection") (*CPrR*, 134; 124) presents a problem. According to Kant, the problem is not dramatic, in the sense that the one would have to "cede" its place to the other. This *would* be the case if theoretical and practical interests were initially "contradictory," which is not necessarily the case. The question is only one of hierarchy or "primacy": which is "the higher" of the two, the interest in extending knowledge or the interest in extending morality?

The answer is well known: without impinging upon the internal functioning and interests of knowledge or cognition, practical reason possesses the primacy of interest. But the argument that establishes this priority merits attention. The motif of the hegemony of the practical is not merely due, as one usually maintains, to this: that only the ethical grants the mind necessary access, by way of obligation—i.e., by way of the intimation of the moral law—to the supersensible instance of freedom (the absolute of causality), whereas knowledge can only lead to the supersensible (the absolute of the world) by way of a "maximization" of its concepts (*CPR*, 381–85; 449–54) which, although it is inevitable, is of no cognitive use, since this extension (*CPR*, 260; 307) transforms them into Ideas that are not determinable by intuition, "indemonstrable" (*CPR*, 166; 199). Instead, Kant's argument for the hegemony of the practical takes first of all the form of a tautology. "One can in no way demand that practical reason be subordinated to speculative reason, thus reversing their order, for all interest is definitively practical" (*CPrR*, 136; 126).

All interest is practical. On the one hand, transcendental interest attests to a sort of "need" to actualize the faculty, a pressure on the part of the possible toward its own realization, which is pure *prattein*, a sort of facultative "will to be" (which would merit lengthy examination). On the other hand, on the empirical side, this facultative "will" can only put itself into effect if it manages to gain a hearing by that aspect of the mind which is immersed in the world of empirical interests, conditions, and attractions. This aspect of the mind has to "pay attention" to (*achten*, "respect") or take into account the "pressure" of the faculties; it has to be susceptible of being "motivated," mobilized, or moved by this pressure. This is precisely the condition of the actualization of the facultative power considered from the point of view of a reasonable, practical, and finite being: that he or she should be able to be moved (in both the physical and the affective senses of the term) by this power.

Thus, "even the interest of speculative reason is conditional" (*CPrR*, 136; 126). Science does not thereby become the servant of morality. Rather, what actualizes knowledge, what extends the domain of knowledge, what impels the exertions of scientific research (obviously, according to its own rules and not according to moral law), is itself conditioned by a transcendental interest: by a "will to effect" the understanding's potential, by a will "to make use," by an impatience, as we would say today, to perform cognitive competence, to make knowledge *of* the world exist *in* the world. And in the empirical realm, the realization of knowledge requires that other "interest," corresponding or responding to the speculative interest of reason, a "motive," "the subjective principle of the determination of the will of a being" (*CPrR*, 85; 74). This being is not immediately omniscient (or benevolent, where it is a question of actualizing the good); its reasonable theoretical (and practical) spontaneity is fettered and therefore needs to be "excited." Indeed, humanity is constitutively related to ignorance, evil and perhaps even, concerning the interest of the reflexive faculty, ugliness.

When it is a matter of morality, the chains that must be shed are the chains by which inclinations restrain the exercise of good will. Empirical willing is always already invested in and fixated on these "charms" or "attractions." Preoccupied. The purely reasonable practical motive cannot assert itself except in the company of a "pain" (*CPrR*, 86; 75), a mourning for attractive objects, a withdrawal of previous investments and fixations. This mourning thus has to affect the "object" *par excellence* which poses an obstacle to respect and the good motive: the *ego* (*CPrR*, 89–90; 79) which, however, according to Freud remains after the loss of attractive objects and, indeed, lives off this loss. This dark aspect of respect is the "humiliation" of the "presumption" and "arrogance" of the empirical ego, of its "overestimation" of itself (*CPrR*, 86–87; 76). Narcissism must be thrown down [*jeté à bas*], vanquished. The ego feels itself seized by obligation, affected by respect for the law, and turned toward its realization only to the extent that it feels itself disseized and abandoned, its "pathological" dependency broken—disoccupied. It never quite gets there. This mourning remains a melancholia. This is the dark side, finitude. But it is only the obverse of respect, not its condition.

On its bright side, respect is a "motive" (*CPrR*, 91; 81). It is the empirical attention to pure practical reason. It is "the law itself" as listened to, a law which is "interesting" because "from the concept of a motive flows that of an *interest*" (*CPrR*, 92; 82). This interest is independent of empirical interests, "the mere interest one takes in observing the law" (*CPrR*, 92; 82). It is an interest itself without interest, in the sense that it does not result from a calculation of enjoyment. "Respect for the law is not a motive for morality, but morality itself, considered subjectively as motive" (*CPrR*, 89; 78). Just like the listening to the order to listen: it is the ethical itself. Realized or not, this order is listened to before being heard and understood. Which is what the German word *Achtung* says. Thus, the law makes itself a motive, on its bright side. As a regard [*égard*].

Achtung is above all a regard, a regard one has for something which is not there, is not an object, and does not lead to passionate intrigues either in the sense of the passion to know or in the sense of the passion to desire and love. It is indeed hardly a feeling at all, which would necessarily be "pathological," but instead a "singular feeling," of a "so particular nature" (*CPrR*, 89; 79). The law opens its clearing, its *facies*, in the closed texture of the conditioned. That it is unconditional, "categorical," is what gives it its simplicity, its lightness. The clearing it opens consists in nothing, it exists in this: that regard is due to duty, under all circumstances, including those "inferior and commonly bourgeois" (*CPrR*, 90; 79). The regard is a motive of repose, a state of feeling which is a nearly a-pathetic pathos. And it is perhaps appropriate here to recall that "apathy" (*apatheia* or *Affektlosigkeit*) is to be counted among the sublime feelings, with this advantage over enthusiasm: that it "has for itself…the satisfaction of pure reason" (*CJ*, §29, 109; 113), which enthusiasm, with its excessive *pathos*, lacks. There is an entire range of nuances in disinterested feelings, a scale that runs from pure aesthetic favor to pure ethical regard. And the intermediary "tones" are all sublime.

What then finally is the character, structure, position, or sense of interest in the sublime?

4.

There are many sublime feelings—not just one, but an entire family, or rather an entire generation. Let me weave for a moment the novel of this *genos*. On

the genealogical tree of the "faculties of the soul," the *genetrix*, like the beget-
ter, is a "sensation," a state of feeling of pleasure and pain. But the father is
happy, the mother unhappy. The sublime child will be contradictorily comprised of suffering and satisfaction. This is because, in the genealogy of the
faculties of "knowledge" (in the broad sense, insofar as the powers of the mind
relate to objects), the parents come from widely divergent families. She is "faculty of judgment," he "reason." She is an artist, he a moralist. She "reflects," he
"determines." The (paternal) moral law determines itself and determines the
mind to action. Reason wants good little children, requires the engenderment
of just, moral maxims. But the mother, the reflexive, free imagination, knows
only how to unfold her forms without predetermined rules and without
known or knowable goals.

In her love affair with understanding, "before" her encounter with reason, it may be that this freedom of "forms" found itself in unison with the
power of regulation and that an exemplary happiness [*un bonheur*] was born
of this encounter. But in any case, no children. Beauty is not the fruit of a con-
tract but the flower of a love and, like what has not been conceived by interest,
it passes.

The sublime is the child of an unhappy encounter, the encounter of the
Idea with form. This encounter is unhappy because the Idea reveals itself to be
so unwilling to make concessions, the law (the father) so authoritarian and so
unconditional, the respect that it commands so exclusive, that this father will
undertake nothing to arouse the consent of imagination, not even a delicious
rivalry. He scatters all forms, or forms scatter themselves, tear themselves
asunder, and become unmeasured in his presence. He fertilizes the virginal
devotee of forms with no regard for her favor. He demands that all have
regard only for himself, the law, and its realization. He has no need whatsoever of a beautiful nature. He needs imperatively a violated, exceeded,
exhausted imagination. She will die in giving birth to the sublime, or at least
she will think she is dying.[3]

The sublime thus indeed possesses something of the appearance of
respect, which it has from its father, reason. But the *Erhabene*, the sublime, is
not *Erhebung* (*CPrR*, 93; 83), the pure elation which the law inspires (*CPrR*,
99; 89). Violence, "vigor," is necessary to the sublime; it breaks away, gets carried away. Respect, however, simply raises itself to attention. In the sublime,
the imagination must be subjected to violence, because it is by way of its suffering, the mediation of its violation, that the joy of seeing—or almost seeing—the law can be obtained. The sublime "renders so to speak intuitable the
superiority of the rational destiny of our faculty of knowledge over the greatest
power of sensibility" (*CJ*, §27, 96; 96). And this "joy…is only possible by the
mediation of pain" (*CJ*, §27, 98; 99).

The mourning entailed by respect of the law is but the dark side of
respect, not its means. The ego cries out because its will is not saintly. But that

the ego should cry out is not a necessary condition of respect, but merely a fact of finitude. Respect does not measure itself in sacrifices. The law means you no harm; it "means" you, as it were, nothing at all. The sublime, on the other hand, requires suffering. It is supposed to hurt. It is "counterpurposive" (*zweckwidrig*), "inappropriate" (*unangemessen*), and it is sublime "for this reason" (*CJ*, §23, 85; 83). It needs "presentation," which is the function of imagination, its mother (*CJ*, §17, 73; 69 and §23, 84; 82) and "presumption," this native illness of the servile will, in order to manifest their nullity before the law.

One may smile at this infantile scenario. But in aesthetic matters, it is a permissible "mode" of exposition (*CJ*, §49, 148; 162). Let us take up again the *modus logicus*. Kant is not unaware that the good is more closely related to the sublime than to the beautiful. "Considered aesthetically, the intellectual, moral good, which is purposive in itself, should be represented not so much as beautiful but as sublime" (*CJ*, §29, 108; 112). That's the thesis. What is the effect of this proximity between the good and the sublime on the status of nature from the standpoint of the aesthetics of sublimity? "The concept of the sublime of nature," Kant writes, "is much less important and rich in consequences than the concept of the beautiful in nature," and the sublime "indicates in general nothing purposive in nature itself, but merely in that possible *use* of our intuitions of it by which there is produced in us a feeling of a purposiveness quite independent of nature" (*CJ*, §23, 86; 84).

The word *use* is underlined in the text. To comprehend its import, one has to return to the teleological argument and to the parallel and paradoxical relation exposed there between the interests of aesthetic favor and ethical respect. I have said that practical reason is interested in procuring for itself a disinterested listening: this is respect for the law. Reflexive judgment is also interested in offering the mind occasions for disinterested judging, freed of any pathological inclinations, cognitive motives, or even good intentions: this is the favor of the beautiful. The *use* of these two faculties, which are heterogeneous in the a priori conditions of their respective functioning, requires the same sort of paradoxical *motive* in both instances: disinterested interest. As favor is the less suspect the more natural the beauty of which it is the occasion, so the law is interested in nature as in what spontaneously provides disinterested satisfaction.

The teleological argument adds a different gesture to the logical, strictly analogical argument for the affinity of the beautiful with the good. The mind traces a gesture while it experiences the aesthetic pleasure of a landscape. Let us call natural beauties—deprived, as Kant requires, of all material attraction—*landscapes*. They "speak," or through them nature "speaks" to us "figuratively" (*figürlich*) in "ciphered inscriptions" (*eine Chiffreschrift*) (*CJ*, §42, 133; 143). The cipher remains unknown. Landscapes are indecipherable, insusceptible of conceptual "exposition" (*CJ*, §57, 167; 189). They are accessible "only" through taste, i.e., feeling. But this *only* casts a kind of sidelong glance into the "interior." The mind senses a quasi purposiveness in the silent messages landscapes comprise, a quasi intentionality or quasi regularity. But "as we do not encounter this purpose anywhere out there, we seek it naturally within ourselves and, in truth, in what constitutes the final purpose of our existence, that is, our moral destiny" (*CJ*, §42, 133; 144).

This gesture of turning or returning is surreptitious. Concerning the sublime, Kant speaks of a "subreption" with reference to the "conversion of respect [*Achtung*] for the Idea of humanity in our own subject into respect for the object" (*CJ*, §27, 96; 96). It is this projection, this objectivation that the Analytic of the Sublime criticizes: there are no sublime objects, only sublime feelings (*CJ*, §26, 95; 95). However, a subreption is already implicated in taste, but one that goes the other way, from the object toward the subject. The landscape alludes, through its escape from determination, to the destiny of mind. The favor with which one receives it induces the timidly suspended "turn" or twist of respect. The allusion to the law goes no further than this oblique gaze. It will be necessary to erect the entire "objective" teleology in order to legitimate this turn (*CJ*, §42, 133; 143). This teleology itself will be comprised of nothing but a texture of "guiding threads." But one of these threads is spun out by the light gesture of aesthetic subreption.

The sublime, however, cuts the thread, interrupts the allusion. "It indicates nothing purposive in nature itself, but only in the possible *use* of its intuitions" (*CJ*, §23, 86; 84). It does not know nature, which is *unerklärlich*, inexplicable and undisclosable for the *Aufklärer* who would determine its proper status apart from all metaphysical delirium (as in Leibniz or Hegel) (*CJ*, §74, 210; 243). The sublime does not even heed this sidelong gesture toward the ethical which is permitted by the aesthetics of nature, and which law seems to require for its realization.

Nature sends no signals to the mind, however indirect, which would indicate its proper destiny. Rather, the mind makes "use" of nature. The object, "as formless or without figure," "formless and without purposiveness," is "*utilized* in a subjectively purposive manner, not judged *for itself* and by reason of its form (so to speak *species finalis accepta, non data*)" (*CJ*, §30, 115–16; 121). To be sure, this implies an inversion of the relation to the object, but above all it implies an inversion of interests, and thus a re-placing in question of interesting disinterests. It is possible to make use of natural antipurposiveness or—as we can say for the sake of simplicity—of anti-nature. I will return below to what "anti-nature"—not a Kantian term—might mean in the economy of the subject or of the mind as subjective nature. It suffices for the moment to understand that the word here designates nature insofar as it induces the mind to neglect its beautiful forms. "It is possible that the object, once perceived, contains within itself, for reflexion, not the least purposiveness concerning the determination of its form" (*CJI*, XII, 83; 439). It is not at all a matter of monstrosity, not even of size. Rather, form simply ceases to be of any pertinence to matters of aesthetic perception. The sublime does not receive the object according to its form, according to its subjective, internal purposiveness. Form does not make the soul resonate with the tone of *un bonheur*.

To what "use" does the mind put nature or anti-nature in the experience of the sublime? The "First Introduction" to the third *Critique* answers: "a contingent *use*" (*CJI*, XII, 82; 439). "*The purposiveness of nature from the subject's point of view*" ceases to induce "in" the subject his or her own "natural" purposiveness, experienced as a harmony of diverse capacities. Instead, it is a "purposiveness residing a priori in the subject," "an a priori principle (granted, a merely subjective principle)," which "makes possible a purposive *use* of certain sensible intuitions." The contingency of this use resides in the fact that it "presupposes no particular technique of nature" (*CJI*, XII, 83; 439). Natural art, of which taste was so to speak the reverberation within the subject, the internal "harmonics," is silent.

It is, on the contrary, the mind which, from afar and on high, imposes a purposiveness all its own on what remains of nature when natural form is no longer "given" (*data*) as a work of art, but merely "received," "taken" (*accepta*), and redirected. It is not the work of nature or the "landscape" that points to the (ethical) destiny of which the sublime is the excessively vigorous feeling—not even obliquely as in taste. Rather, it is the mind that actualizes this destiny, arbitrarily, autonomously, in connection with a "contingent" object, by seizing the occasion furnished not by the landscape but by its a-morphosis, its formal neutralization.

Consequently, the part played in sublime presentation by the imagination (or sensibility) as by the stabilization of forms ought to be quite minimal. Which is why in Kant's vocabulary, the sublime is called a "feeling of the spirit," (*Geistesgefühl*) (*CJI*, XII, 84; 440), in opposition to taste. Its actual province is that of a purposiveness proper to the spirit which is indifferent to the purposiveness of forms. What sets sublime feeling in motion and supports it is no longer the "purposiveness of objects in relation to the faculty of reflexive judgment," but "inversely...following the concept of freedom, a purposiveness of the subject in relation to objects concerning their form or even their absence of form" (*CJ*, VII, 38; 28–29). A reversal, if not a conflict, of modes of purposiveness. By the beautiful, the subject is induced to listen to nature, including his or her own. By the sublime, nature is spiritually deforested by that other subject required by the law. For ultimately, *Geistesgefühl* is nothing other than "respect for moral Ideas" (*CJ*, §54, 161; 180). And the satisfaction that can affect it is not a "pleasure" (*Gefallen*) but a "satisfaction of esteem" (*Schätzung*) (*CJ*, §5, 54; 44; §54, 161; 180).

If one pursues the consequences of this reversal of purposiveness, one may finally find it unsettling that a completely "spiritual" feeling, which apparently expects and learns nothing from its object (nature) nor even from the forms of intuition, still deserves to be called "aesthetic." It should "nonetheless" still be called "aesthetic," Kant writes, "because it, too, expresses a subjective purposiveness which does not rest on the concept of an object" (*CJI*, VII, 83; 440). The sublime is, like taste, a reflexive judgment "without the concept of an object, simply with regard to a subjective purposiveness" (*CJI*, VII, 83; 439). That suffices to classify it as aesthetic, because *aisthesis*—sensation—signifies here not "the representation of a thing (in sense, qua receptivity belonging to the faculty of knowledge)," but "a determination of the feeling of pleasure and pain," a representation which "is related only to the subject and serves no knowledge, not even that by which the subject would *know itself*" (*CJ*, §3, 51; 40). That which judges (itself) *by* the state of the subject—by its internal "sensation"—is aesthetic. Such sensation is by no means any sort of information about the object, be it internal or external. In contrast, the sensation that the senses provide is informative and an indispensable component of judgments of knowledge. It arises from logic (*CJ*, §15, 70; 64; *CPR*, 54; 66–67). But as for the "spiritual feeling," it belongs to aesthetics despite its indifference to sensible forms, in that it is, like taste, a noncognitive judgment that the subject passes not on an object but occasioned by an object and in accordance with the mere subjective state of the spirit.

But the occasion of this judging sensation has a completely different status in taste from the status it has in the sublime. And this difference of occasion ought to affect the system of interests at play in each case. The sublime object is no longer the occasion given to a form to transform itself organically, if I can put it this way, into *un bonheur* of the soul, by a sort of transitivism of natural and spiritual modes of purposiveness. Instead, it is through its absence of form, or rather considered independently of its forms even if is not totally formless, that the object, so to speak, despite itself, furnishes an occasion for practical reason to reinforce its influence on the subject, to extend its power, in accordance with its facultative interest. And to be sure, the subject thus constrained by the law turns toward it, exposes itself to that law, without being impelled by any interest, hence in accordance with the sole ethical motive, "respect" (*Achtung*). But can one say as much of the dark side of the sublime, darker than that of respect, since it is here the *condition* of the feeling in question, and not merely its obverse? And will one still want to say that the sublime indifference to form is the sign of a "disinterest"?

In the sense of the transcendental interest that impels the faculties to actualize themselves, the disaster of forms which the sublime requires implies an alteration of the interfacultative hierarchies. The understanding (or reason in its cognitive use) must renounce its actualization, whereas in taste, as one may recall, forms evoke its actualization by defying and exciting it. The prospect of knowledge, to which beauty still allows access, even if aporetically (*CJ*, §§55–57, 162–65; 182–87), is at one stroke effaced by the sublime. In turn, reason—the faculty of pure Ideas—seems to have a strong interest in the disorganization of the given and in the defeat of both the understanding and the imagination. In the lacuna thereby opened, reason can in fact render nearly "intuitable" (*CJ*, §27, 96; 96) to the subject the Idea of his or her true moral destiny.

If it is now a matter of the interest or disinterest felt by the empirical subject affected by sublime emotion, and if one sets aside the "disinterested interest" that it experiences as a result of the moral law within, this subject's indifference to the forms of objects might seem to arise not from any disinterest or interest but rather from a *noninterest* [inintérêt] pure and simple. Imaginative forms have no pertinence whatsoever for the awakening of a "spiritual feeling."

However, if one takes a closer look, one sees that the absence of imaginative forms is itself not without interest for the subject in its discovery of its true destiny. If their nonpertinence is a means, if the suffering their impossibility induces in the mind is a "mediation" which authorizes the "joy" of discovering the true (ethical) destiny of the mind, and thus authorizes respect, this is because the disaster of forms, however "counterpurposive" it may appear for taste and for the purposiveness of nature, is—or at least can become—itself nonetheless purposively oriented toward the Idea of this true destiny (*CJ*, §27, 98; 99). There is in this something of a "logic of the worst" [*logique du pire*] or at least an aesthetics of the worst, which would not put into "play" the ugly, but the amorphic. The more the antilandscape exceeds the realm of forms, the more the power of pure (practical) reason finds itself "extended" and actualized, the more its greatness is confirmed. Pure practical reason wagers on the misery of favor in order to effect the elevation of its law. As I have said, quite differently from what takes place in respect—which has simultaneously two faces, the light and the dark—the sublime mediates (perhaps dialectically) the light through the dark. The clearing opens itself up through deforestation.

This indirect—not to say, perverse—interest, this secondary benefit, drawn on the quasi "disappearance of nature in the face of the Ideas of reason" (*CJ*, §27, 96; 96), is what motivates or accompanies the "use," the "contigent" use the mind *makes* of nature (as anti-nature) in the sublime. Let us reread: "The concept of the sublime in general indicates nothing purposive in nature itself, but only in the possible *use* of its intentions, in order to render sensible [*fühlbar*] in us a purposiveness which is utterly independent of nature" (*CJ*, §23, 86; 84). On the part of the empirical subject, as is confessed in this "in order to render sensible," there is the motive of a powerful interest. The disaster of forms is interesting. And thus, the movement is interested by means of which the imagination is subjugated to a purposiveness which, however, is incompatible with its own, the free production of forms. "Imagination deprives itself of freedom, since it is determined toward a purpose in accordance with a law other than that of empirical use" (*CJ*, §29, 106; 109). What benefit or profit is paid for in advance here? The profit one expects of a sacrifice. And who profits? Nature is sacrificed on the altar of the law. "In doing this, imagination acquires an extension [*Erweiterung*] and a force greater than those it has sacrificed but of which the foundation is hidden and, instead of this foundation, what it feels is sacrifice and destruction, at the same time as the *cause* to which it is submitted" (*CJ*, §29, 106; 109).

The "contingent use" of nature thus arises from a sacrificial economy of the faculties. The regard or respect the sublime has for the law is obtained and signaled by a use of forms that is not the use to which they are destined. We are confronted here with a conversion (or perversion) of destiny, which perhaps always connotes the institution of the sacred. The sacred requires *potlatch*, the destruction or consumption of the given, of present "wealth" (presence, gift) (*CJ*, §49, 146; 160) or natural form, in order to obtain in return the countergift of the nonpresented (of *manna?*). "This power (of the moral law) makes itself properly known in the aesthetic sphere only through sacrifices" (*CJ*, §29, 108; 111). In the aesthetic sphere. Set fire to the beautiful so that the good will come back [*te revienne*] as a ghost out of its ashes. All sacrifice entails this sacrilege. Pardon can be obtained only by the abandonment, the banishment, of a prior gift, which must itself be infinitely precious. Sacrificed nature is sacred. The sublime interest evokes such a sacrilege. One is tempted to say: an ontological sacrilege. In any case, here, a facultative sacrilege. The law of practical reason, the law of the law, bears down with all its weight on the law of productive imagination. It makes use of it. It subjugates the productive imagination right down to its a priori conditions of possibility, its proper autonomy, its heterogeneity with respect to the conditions of morality. But this servitude of the imagination is "voluntary," violently interested. The faculty of free forms "deprives itself of freedom," and this, "in order to render sensible" a law which is not its own (*CJ*, §29, 106; 109). The imagination, in sacrificing itself, sacrifices nature, aesthetically sacred, with a view to exalting the saintly law.

As in any sacrificial mechanism [*dispositif*], a calculation of interests is involved here, a discount on feelings. Annul favor, and you will have respect. It appears easy to make this calculation coincide with the calculation of a dialectic (for example, the master-slave dialectic: renounce enjoyment and you will have recognition). This would indeed be the case if Kant let himself go to the point of becoming Hegel, if he envisaged a law which would be negotiable at the cost of renouncing beauty in the gift-for-gift that organizes dialectical logic and guarantees its profits, its—however eternally deferred—final *Resultat*.

But quite to the contrary, Kant denounces the "blindness" of the "choice" of goal and hopes of "realization" (*CJ*, §29, 108; 112) involved in this sort of economy of the worst [*économie du pire*] or of the more through less, this transport interested in de-naturalization, which he calls "enthusiasm" (although it also has various brothers). Being a "vigorous affect," a violence of feeling, the sublime "cannot in any way serve the satisfaction of reason" (*CJ*,

§29, 109; 113). This "use" thus remains useless, without ethical use. The law does not allow itself to be bent by the consumption of forms. For the law unequivocally demands mere respect, a pure disinterested obedience. It has no need of heroic demonstrations. Respect is not something to be obtained, not even by mortification of the flesh. It is an immediate reverence. It is one thing that this veneration should produce as one of its effects, as I have said, humiliation of *amour-propre*. But it would be quite another if this sacrifice of the ego or of imaginative forms were the *condition* of respect. Respect takes place without condition; it is "morality itself, considered…as motive" in the empirical subject (*CPrR*, 89; 78). It cannot be acquired, even at the cost of all nature. No more than the law, respect cannot be the object of trade, even expiatory trade.

And especially transcendental trade. I mean: above all, if the trade implies that one power of the mind "yields" to another, for example, the faculty of formal presentation to the faculty of being obligated by the law. And "yields" not merely domination over a given field of extension but its very conditions of possibility, its autonomy—in this case, the freedom of its presentational activity and its disinterestedness. This surrender, this rendering of accounts to reason, doesn't merely overthrow the specific functioning of imagination. It disorganizes also the very principle of practical reason, which is precisely the unconditional character of the law and of the respect due it. The general economy of *all* the faculties is thereby dislocated.

The second *Critique* uses the word *Frevel* (*CPrR*, 135; 126) to designate this radical concession, this subjugation of one faculty to another, which entails also the disorganization of the other—in this case, the always threatening subordination of practical to speculative reason, "the reversal of order." *Frevel* signifies a crime of impiety, a sacrilege. There is something *frevelhaft* about the sublime. Or to put it differently, respect, according to its pure ideal, which is the bright side of the law, cannot in any way enter into the calculation of profits and discount sales of an economy of sacrifice. It arises from a noneconomy which would be the régime of saintliness. Its dark side, the loss it entails, is due to the fact that the empirical subject is not saintly but finite. But it remains the case that the sacrifice of this finitude cannot buy saintliness. Practical reason could never be "satisfied" at the cost of this transcendental madness.

In short, enthusiasm is not pious. It is the profane (if not profaning) way—and thus the aporetic way—of gaining access to piety. The internal conflict by which it is shaken pits the motif of the sacred against the motif of the saint. But I said that it has brothers—an entire generation of other sublime individuals. I cannot detail here the whole collection, even those Kant enumerates: "anger," "rebellious despair," self-involvement, "sadness," "chagrin" (*CJ*, §29, 109; 113 and §29, 112; 116–17), "inaccessability [of the soul] to danger" (§28, 100–1; 102), "humility," the upright and free "admiration" of God (§28,

101–2; 103), without forgetting "duty, sublime and great name" (*CPrR*, 98; 89). It would not be impossible to establish a sort of periodic chart of these sublime individuals according to the degree of "sacrifice" each offers. It is nearly zero in respect, obviously, where the humiliation of the ego is a mere shadow cast on a finite will by the light of the law. It would bring the mind to the limits of "madness" (*CJ*, §29, 111; 116), on the other hand, in radically negative affects such as "rebellious despair" or that nearly "misanthropic chagrin" inspired by the evils of life which humans impose upon each other through their "puerility" (§29, 112; 116–17). In the face of such variety, the demon of anthropological taxonomy nearly regains possession of the critical spirit, and indeed, this demon had opened the way to the question of the sublime, if somewhat differently, in the *Observations* of 1764–66. Nonetheless, in the catalogue of sublime children, the specific difference that unites them can be demanded of each: that it should be a "vigorous affect" (§29, 109; 113). Read: sacrificial, some more, some less. None (except respect for the law) is ethically valid. And as "aesthetic," they are all suspect of being interested in the (negative) use they make of natural forms. "The theory of the sublime," of all sublimities, remains thus "a mere appendix to the analysis of the aesthetic judgment of natural purposiveness" (§23, 86; 84–85). One x-rays there the bastards born of a sudden infatuation [*coup de foudre*] of nature with or by the law.

It remains to examine the implications of this disaster for the unity of the subject and for the community of (aesthetic) feeling

Chapter 6

❀

THE GIFT OF THE WORLD

Jacob Rogozinski

Passage

Under what conditions is a thought of the sublime possible? How does the thought of the sublime in Kant's *Critique of Judgment* relate to these conditions?[1] This question cannot be reduced to its "aesthetic" dimension. The third *Critique* is not a philosophy of art arbitrarily attached to a philosophy of life. In seeking to locate a transcendental principle of the faculty of judgment, Kant is in quest of a *passage*. He is in quest of that "bridge over the abyss" which "renders possible the passage (*Übergang*) from pure theoretical reason to pure practical reason," from the domain of nature to the domain of freedom (II, 25; 12). This quest presupposes that nature is itself sufficiently organized, sufficiently purposive to allow the regulation of the supersensible to be inscribed within it. Guided by the principle of a natural purposiveness, the faculty of reflexive judgment orients itself toward the passage in question by discovering the traces of order in the disorder of the world, a quasi legality in the contingency of phenomena. This faculty permits us to think what Kant calls, enigmatically, "the unity of the supersensible substratum" (II, 25; 12). The concept of this unity is a liminal concept, theoretically indeterminate, which designates "the point of union [*den Vereinigungspunkt*] of all of our a priori faculties" (§57, 165; 187), the unknown root of our modes of openness to Being. It resides "within us as well as without" (IX, 42; 33), doubtless because it is situated this side of all demarcation of an inside and an outside, of a "subject" and an "object." And this unitary accord of our "faculties"—of the different capacities or powers of opening—ties the radical knots at once of the world and of the living community which accords in the understanding of this world.[2] In this sense, the third *Critique* is interested in beauty—or more precisely, in the beautiful and the sublime of art and nature—*only* to the extent that aesthetic judgment holds the promise of passage.

133

On first view, nothing could appear more classical than this procedure, including the—in the strict sense, *meta-physical*—privilege it confers upon beauty. For is not beauty according to the *Phaedrus* the only Idea that still glows with its original brightness in the otherwise dark realm of appearances, the only Idea that can amorously transport us beyond the realm of the sensible? On the other hand, it is not certain that the *Critique of Judgment* maintains the beautiful in its ancient priority. Indeed, not the beautiful, but the sublime will lead to the point of passage. Whereas the feeling of the beautiful arises merely out of the play of the understanding and the imagination and concerns only the finite forms of phenomena, in the sublime the imagination struggles with reason itself, the faculty of the unconditioned, which "extends" the imagination and opens it up to the infinitude of the Ideas. Its effort "obliges us to think nature itself in its totality as the presentation of something supersensible" (§29, 105; 108). We have to do here with a presentation "which renders so to speak intuitable [*anschaulich*] the supremacy of our rational destiny" (§27, 96; 96). How is one to understand this quasi intuition of the supersensible? As is well known, the *Critique of Judgment* distinguishes two modes of *Darstellung* ("presentation"), the *schema*, which directly presents a concept in intuition, and the *symbol*, which operates indirectly "by the mediation of an analogy" (§59, 174; 197). According to Kantian doctrine, no sensible intuition can be adequate to the Ideas of reason, which can only be evoked by means of symbols. Beauty in art and nature—the "ciphered language" of beautiful forms—has by virtue of its symbolic significance the value precisely of an *analogy* of morality. The formal structure of analogy is such that it always maintains an irreducible gap between the terms between which it establishes a relation. If beauty is understood—in conformity with the tradition—as allegory or symbol, if it reflects in the sensible the distant glow of the Good, it glitters only with a borrowed brilliance, and the work is beautiful insofar as it signifies at a distance what it is not and cannot attain. By erecting the beautiful into a symbol of the Good, one re-opens the abyss in the very gesture through which one claims to surmount it. The fact that the "Critique of the Faculty of Aesthetic Judgment" culminates in privileging the symbolism of the beautiful as a "passage from sensible attraction to moral interest" (§59, 176; 200) tends to prove the failure of its project.

How could the sublime manifest the super-sensible directly, without recourse to the mediation of the symbol? The schematism is the "direct presentation" of a concept of the understanding, its transposition into sensible intuition with the aid of an intermediary representation of the imagination. However, according to Heidegger, the transcendental imagination is the common root of the understanding and sensibility; the only reason why it can succeed in passing from the one to the other, in unifying them in the schema, is because it already contains within itself their hidden unity. The truth of the passage would be this: that it does not "pass" between two heterogeneous orders while maintaining their separation but rather reduces them to their prior unity, where they join one another like two sides of the same coin, or like the slopes of a single relief. If the sublime provides the site of a passage, it ought to provide this site as schema and not as symbol. And Kant does sometimes describe the sublime in terms of schematism. Thus, poetry is that art, most sublime of all, which in "aesthetically elevating itself to the level of the Ideas," makes us consider nature "so to speak as the schema of the super-sensible" (§53, 154; 171). Such formulations remain, however, both rare and allusive. If the schematization of the sublime is the road that leads to the passage, one can say that Kant took a different road.

Doubtless he did so because the sublime is opposed to the fundamental traits of the transcendental schematism. As the work of imagination, the schema is a *Bilden*, a placing in view and an imposition of form. It is a pure power of figuration, which presents to the view the horizon whereon the visible appears. For the sensible is chaos, a dynamic melee of sensations where no figure traces itself out, no figure demarcates its outline against other possible figures. The schematism, as Nietzsche will remember, is called upon to give form to this chaos, to impose upon it a stable order. The imprint of the schema marks off a field within the profusion of the possible, determining there a unique mode of appearance, and it is only thus that a finite figure can appear and fix itself as it emerges from the infinity of possibilities. What allows the imagination to schematize, to delimit a field and to bind together what is diverse, are the forms it sketches. *Form*, says Kant, is not merely *Gestalt*; it does not designate the arrested contour of a figure but the movement of its figuration, the tracing of its limit, the unification of its diversity. This in-formation of what is formless in finitude is what is most beautiful: it is beauty itself, where the imagination exults in the organization of chaos. The aesthetic schematization of beauty would be then the originary schematism of the imagination: functioning before all conceptualization and all representation of objects, its figurative power here figures itself in the self-affection of a subject, a tiny all-too-human god, whom it pleases to give form to the world. Complacencies of the play of pretty forms: these comprise our cheap thrills [*notre bon plaisir*], the ultimate ideal of a time abandoned by Ideas and gods.

This sovereign exultation of the subject interrupts itself only at the moment of the sublime. Whereas beauty "concerns the form of the object, that is, its limitation," the feeling of the sublime seizes us in the presence of "a formless object to the extent that the unlimited here represents itself" (§23, 84; 82). This is the feeling of unlimitation, or rather of de-limitation, born of the subversion, the *sub-limation* of a limit, as phenomenal forms disfigure themselves and the organization of the sensible undoes itself and it returns to its primal indistinction. And it is "in its chaos or in its disorder [*Unordnung*], in its most wild and unruly devastation [*Verwüstung*] that nature best arouses the Ideas of the sublime" (§23, 86; 84). In liberating the powers of chaos, it de-schematizes the sensible, destroys the work of the imagination. If the harmonious order of beauty and life bear witness to a quasi purposiveness, it is comprehensible that the sublime will in turn "appear to violate purpose [to be *zweckwidrig*] in respect of the faculty of judgment" (§23, 85; 83). In the problematic of the *Critique of Judgment*, the possibility of the passage to the supersensible is grounded precisely in the principle of a purposiveness of nature. The counter-purposiveness of the sublime appears to forbid any accord between nature and the faculty of judgment; it supports the disquieting hypothesis of a "chaotic aggregate" of phenomena, of a "step-mother nature" [*stiefmütterlich*] who would no longer allow herself to be subordinated to the Law of freedom.[3] It thus tends to ruin the chances of passage, the promise of a reconciled community.

At the moment when it is taking us closest to the passage, the sublime violently tears us away. What was supposed to be the center of the third *Critique* will have been nothing but an insignificant appendix. But perhaps this is only an appearance. If the sublime were nothing but disorder and insane devastation, it would provoke only fear or horror and that transcendental pain which is induced by the absence of purposiveness. But "the sublime pleases": the afflicted joy that it awakens is supposed to be the index of a hidden purposiveness. The task of the *analytic of the Sublime* will be to expose this purposiveness of counter-purposiveness, to deliver its latent form at the heart of the formless. Moreover, in order to be judged sublime, a phenomenon must not be absolutely deprived of form: to the nonlimitation that disfigures it must be "added by thought the notion of its totality" (§23, 84; 82). The category of totality designates for Kant "plurality considered as unity" (*CPR*, 97; 116). What could this function of unity be in the case of the sublime? What bonds would be sufficiently powerful to *contain* chaos, to reduce it to the one in the very movement of its unbinding? There must be some such bonds, for if there were not, if the object could not be "comprehended as a whole," the least trace of purposiveness would disappear. The phenomenon would no longer be sublime, but "monstrous" (*ungeheuer*) (§26, 92; 91). A precarious demarcation indeed, for sublimity raises itself "to the limit of the monstrous," just this side of horror, and is always on the point of disappearing into it.[4] The same movement of disfiguration that distinguishes the sublime from beautiful forms always carries the sublime in the direction of the deformed or formless. It must, however, establish a border between itself and monstrosity: what is at stake here is the intention of the *Critique of Judgment*—the possibility of judgment itself—that the sublime should have about it "nothing of the monstrous…or of the hideous" (§26, 92; 91), that it should preserve the outline of a form on the verge of chaos. A strange form, without figure, which gives itself only in deforming itself and which is perhaps the purest of forms, the secret armature of the sensible. The aesthetics of the sublime will thus permit the discovery of an order hidden beneath the appearance of chaos. The savage anarchy of phenomena will be paradoxically the surest index of a super-sensible order. It will have been necessary for the texture of appearances to tear, for the world to be delivered up to devastation, in order that an aesthetics of the sublime should signal the opening of the passage.

But do we know at all what is aesthetically sublime? In positing that "the authentic sublime cannot be contained in any sensible form" (§23, 85; 83–84), Kant forbids us at the outset to search for examples of it in nature or art. It is only by means of a "subreption," a paralogism of aesthetic judgment, that we call works of art and landscapes "sublime," that we consider a mere disposition of our faculty of judgment to be a real quality of the object. Nothing *is* sublime in this world. It does, however, happen that this feeling overtakes us: doubtless because the sublime is precisely what *happens*, the pure occurrence of the event. Despite everything, Kant will not have hesitated, at least once, to perform what he forbids, namely, to designate a "work" as sublime, that is, as the most sublime. Even if it is in the detour of a furtive footnote, supplementarily: "One has perhaps never said anything more sublime or expressed a thought in more sublime fashion than in the inscription on the temple of Isis (mother *Nature*): 'I am all that is, that was, and that will be, and no mortal has lifted my veil'" (§49, 146n; 160n). What is so sublime about this veiled figure? Is it the veil which covers it and its impossible unveiling—the metaphor of a truth which reveals itself only in the concealing movement of a primary opacity, which no mortal would know how to render transparent? An entire epoch, before Kant and after him, allowed itself to be captivated by the enigma of the veiled goddess, desiring to pierce the mystery, to pass beyond the veil, to discover there, according to the different versions, horror (this would be Rousseau's version), death, or the mirror, the pure act of mirroring itself and speculating on itself (this would be, after Novalis, Hegel's version).

As careful as he was to avoid all the mystic "revelation," to respect the reserve of the secret, it seems that Kant will not have been able to prevent himself from lifting the veil in his manner, from exposing what "Isis" means. In the *Critique*, she symbolizes Nature, the totality of phenomena in space and time. She presents herself as the unity of the infinite All in the three dimensions of time—"all that is, that was and that will be"—which escapes the clutches of a "mortal" or finite spirit. The impossible figuration of this All, or its figuration *as* nonfigurable, gives birth to sublime feeling. What could be the relation of the sublime to the infinity of nature? The veiled idol reappears some years later, in the text, *Von einem neuerdings erhobenen vornehmen Ton in der Philosophie*, a polemical text in which Kant takes to task enthusiasts who dream of denuding Isis, or rather, thanks to a "mystical tact," of "intimating" her presence behind the veil. This *Schwärmerei* is the delirium of metaphysics, insofar as, since Plato, it has attempted to know the super-sensible, to embrace the absolute totality in an intuition. However, at the end of this text of 1796, the signification of the sublime figure seems to have changed: "The veiled goddess before which...we go down on our knees is the moral law within us."[5] That which, in the *Critique,* represented Mother Nature, has suddenly become an aesthetic figuration of the Law "in its sublimity and its impenetrable mystery." How have we passed from sensible nature to a law of the super-sensible, from an Idea of speculative reason to a determination of practical reason? Is this a mere inconsistency, the equivocal sense of an allegory, or rather the sign that the sublime is the site of the passage? And that it has to do, in its essential structure, with the veiling of truth and with the truth of the veil? The aesthetic Idea of the veiled Isis would then designate the junction of two worlds, and this bridge across the abyss would be the most sublime thing of all. In what sense does sublimity assure this passage? How can it give us, on the edge of the sensible realm itself, a schema of the super-sensible?

Violences

The feeling of the sublime comes from an "effort of the imagination to treat nature as a schema" for the Ideas. Herein resides "that which is terrible to sensibility and yet is attractive. [It is attractive] because reason violently exercises [*eine Gewalt...ausübt*] its power over the sensibility, to the sole end of extending this sensibility in conformity with its proper realm (which is practical) and of making it look out into the infinite which is for it an abyss" (§29, 102; 104–5). The schematism of the sublime presupposes an "extreme tension" of the imagination, which awakens in us a contradictory emotion where attraction mixes with fright. This double affect reveals the "violence" of reason in its efforts to "extend" sensibility to infinity, to open it onto the abyss of the Ideas. How does this violent opening put us in the presence of the infinite and what does this "practical" infinity signify? Why does the feeling of the sublime imply a sort of oscillation, a "rapid succession of repulsion and attraction by the same object?" (§27, 97; 97).

　　It is a matter of a double movement of which the repercussion resonates along the flesh, of a dynamic alternation between the inhibition of the "vital forces" and their sudden expansion—a "negative pleasure" mixed of joy and pain. Kant makes it quite clear that these two affects are quasi simultaneous: what is frightening is "at the same time" (*zugleich*) attractive, as if the attraction of the super-sensible contained its frightening aspect, as if its frightening abyss did not cease nonetheless to fascinate. Sublimity arises there too at the limit, between the pleasure that beauty inspires and the repulsion of the monstrous, in an ambiguous perspective where the unfolding of the imagination toward the object is complicated by a reflux or a folding back onto itself, in such a manner that this retracing of its steps inscribes itself already in the initial impulse, as the trace of a flexion that arrests it, curves it back, and returns it against itself. Doubtless this gesture does not characterize only the trajectory of the imagination in the sublime event: one might even say that it defines the transcendental imagination in its essential structure.

In fact, Heidegger describes the transcendental synthesis of the imagination—the very movement of transcendence—as an ec-static self-affection, a looking-away which looks back toward itself.[6] It is the opening to the world, the initial orientation that forms the horizon within which the being [*l'étant*] comes to appear, within which it appears to us as object. As a finite—receptive and sensible—transcendence, it requires a sensible transposition of the horizon, the transcendental schematism of the imagination, in order to make objective knowledge possible. But the character of objectivity, this consistent ob-jection which opposes itself, does not come from the being as such: it must be pre-formed within the horizon of transcendence, must offer itself to this transcendence like a resistance this transcendence imposes upon itself. It is this trait of ob-jection that Kant calls the transcendental object = *X*: that which is found or finds itself posed over-there or "over-against" (*Dawider*) (cf. *CPR*, 117; 134)—the across-from, the unknown from beyond, which *is* nothing but permits the constitution of the being in its Being. As the offering of a limit, of a pure form where transcendence inflects itself and links itself freely, *Dawider* is one of the first names of Being. That is to say, it is one of the first names of time, for the objectivating opposition is a self-objectivation, where "the subjective ob-jects itself to the subject as the objective."[7] It is an encounter of its limits with its limits, and time, the form of the inner sense, is "the manner in which the spirit is affected by its own activity" (*CPR*, 72; 87)—the chiasmus of auto-affection. One will thus, it seems, be obliged to conclude with Heidegger that "the transcendental imagination is originary time" and constitutes the essence of finite subjectivity.

As is well known, the Heideggerian interpretation treats only the first *Critique*. This interpretation appears to be confirmed, however, in the *Critique of Judgment*, by the eminent role that the "Analytic of the Beautiful" confers on the productive imagination and also by the structure of reversed intentionality that the "Analytic of the Sublime" attributes to it. But perhaps we are allowing ourselves to be misled by a superficial resemblance. Perhaps the double movement of the aesthetic imagination does not correspond to the auto-affection of transcendental imagination. Or perhaps, if that double movement is rooted in ecstatic transcendence, it raises this transcendence to the highest power, up to the point where this transcendence comes undone.

In the emotion of the sublime, one experiences "the feeling of the impotence of the imagination for representing the Idea of a whole; in this the imagination attains its maximum and, in the effort to exceed it, collapses into the abyss of itself" (§26, 91; 91). In its objectivating intention, the imagination, respecting its limits, folds itself back on itself in the halt that it haltingly imposes on itself. In its sublime excess, it trangresses its maximum, passes to the limit, unlimits itself infinitely. Is what it encounters at infinity, where it breaks and comes undone, still the same *Dawider*, the finite Being or the Being-finite of fundamental ontology? Must not a thought of originary finitude in principle revoke the possibility of an opening onto the infinite?

In the ontological synthesis described by Heidegger, the project of transcendence ob-jects the horizon of the world to itself only in order to return to itself as subject. In fact, the imagination hardly departs from the circle of its auto-affection, receives nothing that it has not already pre-formed: it never truly *exposes* itself. In contrast, sublimity scatters the imagination or sets it to flight; broken and powerless, it recedes into itself and this ebb is a failure and a collapse. Thus, the sublime awakens in us the "feeling of a destiny that exceeds completely the domain of the imagination." How is one to interpret this decline of the imagination? Does the "Analytic of the Sublime" remain caught in the recoil of Kant's thought, the panicked retreat before the abyss of the imagination which Heidegger thought he could read in the late Kant, beginning with the second edition of the *Critique of Pure Reason*? Or could it be that the "Analytic of the Sublime" discovers to us another abyss, unexplored by the first *Critique*, a more radical dimension—that of the un-imaginable?

In the perspective of the "Transcendental Analytic," a failure of the imagination would be inconceivable. The imagination is the faculty of synthesis, which collects the manifold and unifies it; the imagination is that "indispensable function" of the mind "without which we could never and nowhere have any knowledge" (*CPR*, 93; 112). Actually, it is not merely knowledge, but already sensible intuition, the appearing of phenomena, that presupposes a "preliminary synthesis," a unifying composition of the manifold. The element of this synthesis could only be the pure form of time, wherein every sensible figure takes on form. Indeed, Heidegger can go so far as to identify the three ecstases of temporality with the triple synthesis of imagination. If the latter ceased to put itself into effect, the unity of experience would be dislocated, the world of phenomena would become "a blind play of representations, that is, less than a dream" (*CPR*, 126; 139). It would become a chaotic, unstable universe, the pure play of simulacra, the play of the last hypotheses of the *Parmenides* or of the Cartesian evil genius which the famous text on the cinnabar evokes only to dismiss it immediately. It is this danger that the trial of the sublime awakens, this haunting of chaos, of what is disgustingly out of this world [*de l'im-monde*], revived by the spectacle of the ocean unleashed, of the "wild disorders" of nature. The awakening of this danger attests to a failure—at least a provisional failure—of synthesis. And an aesthetics of the sublime would indeed be impossible if the imagination did not break down. We know, however, that on pain of disappearing into monstrosity sublime deformation is never absolutely formless; it preserves the plan of a form at the limit of chaos. The trace of a form maintains itself, then, despite the foundering of imagination. The ontological synthesis is not the ultimate synthesis, the initial bond of the world, and the "Deduction" of the first *Critique* must accordingly be rectified.

What could this radical binding be? If it is more primitive than the temporalizing imagination and survives the ruin of this imagination, what is its relation to time? Is it not called upon to play in the schematism of the sublime the same role as the imagination in the schematism of the categories, which would make of it the faculty of the passage, the bridge over the abyss of the super-sensible? How should one characterize more precisely the schematization of the sublime? Perhaps one has not been sufficiently attentive to a term that returns several times in Kant's text: *violence*. Mediated by the imagination's effort to schematize the Ideas, reason "exercises its violence" on sensibility (§29, 102; 105, and cf. also §29, 108; 112). Kant specifies that "in the aesthetic judgment on the sublime this violence [*Gewalt*] is represented as exercised by the imagination itself as an instrument of reason...according to the principles of the schematism of the faculty of judgment" (§29, 106; 109–110). In this extremely elliptical formulation, the entire enigma of the schematism of the sublime is condensed. It seems that, once defeated and submitted to reason, the imagination puts its own violence at the service of the Ideas. In order that it should be able to exercise "by itself" the violence of reason, it must itself already be violent. This is exactly what Kant has affirmed several pages earlier: the imagination "does violence to the inner sense," and "makes the subject feel its violence" (§27, 97; 98). What does he mean by this? In what way can it exercise a violence on the inner sense, that is, on time, if it is identical to time? Kant had never before described in these terms the operation of imagination, and he would never do so again. These brief notations are nevertheless the barely sketched beginnings of a new thought of imagination and temporality. They indicate the point where Kant came closest to formulating the passage of which he was in search.

When one considers this text more closely, a new difficulty presents itself. Apparently, the violence *of* the imagination does not suffice to incite the feeling of the sublime. In effect, the sublime appears "to do violence *to* the imagination" (§23, 85; 83), as if another violence were required, as if the violent tension of the imagination provoked or evoked in turn a counterviolence of reason, which is "the authentic form of the ethical," (§29, 106; 109) the imperative vocation of its Law. Is one to understand by this that the sublime emotion arises in the confluence of two opposed violences? Or instead, that there is always only one violence, that of the imagination, which can be turned against itself?

It would then be necessary to say that, at the call of the Law, the imagination *does itself violence*: that in imposing its violence on time, the imagination violates itself and only ever has to do with itself. The schematization of the sublime would still obey the logic of auto-affection, and the ethical Law itself would be nothing but a connective modality of the imagination. But is it quite certain that the imagination encounters nothing beyond itself? According to Kant, "a force [*Macht*] is called violence [*Gewalt*] if it is superior to the resistance of that which itself possesses force" (§28, 98; 99). The *dynamic sublime* is this modality of the sublime that "makes [us] discover in ourselves a power of resistance of a completely different kind," capable of "measuring itself against the apparent omnipotence of nature," that is, of the transcendental imagination whose synthesis formally constitutes nature. What is this super-sensuous force the resistance of which breaks the power of the imagination? Is it the moral Law? And how can it counter the violent pressure of the imagination?

Doubtless the imagination could not fracture and collapse into ruin if it were not already divided, at odds or in conflict with itself. As the quasi presentation of an unlimited greatness, the *mathematical sublime* requires a "fundamental measure," an aesthetic evaluation of greatness. This presupposes two synthetic operations of the imagination, apprehension (*Auffassung*) and comprehension (*Zusammenfassung*). "Apprehension causes no difficulty, for it can be pursued to infinity; but comprehension becomes ever more difficult the more apprehension progresses, and it quickly arrives at its maximum" (§26, 91; 90). In the aesthetic evaluation of an object, the imagination seeks to take in the series of apprehensions at a glance, to collect them in the unity of a synthetic comprehension. Normally, it manages to succeed in this, but when it is a matter of an immense object "the eye needs a certain time" to complete the operation, and this time is found to be lacking: "the first perceptions disappear before the imagination can seize the last ones" and its comprehensive seizure thus encounters its limit. It is in attempting to transgress this limit—to sub-limate itself—that it becomes dismembered, torn between the progression to infinity of its apprehensions and the limited, finite character of its comprehension. If the imagination fails to present the infinite, to lift the veil of Isis, this is because it is essentially finite, because it is finitude itself, in its powerless violence. The excessively powerful resistance which surmounts its violence and reveals its finitude is invested in the trace of a limit, of a *Dawider*. And this limitation is imposed on it by the gigantic proportions, the measurelessness of a phenomenon.

At first sight, it is the vastness of space—the colossal massiveness of the pyramid, the limitless extension of the ocean or the starry sky—that restricts the range of imagination. But spatial immensity introduces us to a more radical measurelessness which is temporal. On the point of foundering, the imagination discovers that *it needs time*, and that time is lacking: in its impossible comprehension of space, it experiences its temporal finitude. But how can time escape from the imagination, given that the imagination is temporal through and through? Perhaps the "Analytic of the Sublime" obliges us to place in question anew the Heideggerian interpretation: the imagination would not, then, be identical with originary temporality; the violence the imagination inflicts on time and the temporal failure of its synthesis would be the indices of a dispute or "incompatibility" [*différend*] between time and the imagination, of a primordial discord the sublime event reveals.

To bring this incompatibility to light is a difficult task. It presupposes that we have already elucidated another conflict, where the temporal limit of the imagination discovers itself, its internal staggering, the discord between apprehension and comprehension. This laceration itself has a temporal significance: it puts into question the essential determinations of time. In the sole passage where Kant evokes the violence of the imagination, he signals that this violence has its origin in comprehension. It comes from the radical finitude of imagination. It is the violence of finitude that attempts, ardently and in vain, to hold back time. In fact, the "comprehension of plurality in the unity of the intuition" is a "comprehension in an instant [*in einem Augenblick*] of what has been successively perceived" that "suppresses [*aufhebt*] the temporal condition in the progression of the imagination." It is also a "subjective movement of the imagination that does violence to the inner sense"—a violence which "will be all the more sensible the greater the quantum which the imagination comprehends in an intuition."

The violence of imagination is at work in every effort at comprehension, whatever the extension of the temporal series. When the object is small, the intensity of synthetic violence remains barely perceptible and passes unnoticed. In the case of an immense magnitude, this violence becomes intense in the extreme and becomes perceptible just before it founders. The experience of the sublime thus reveals a latent violence inherent in the synthesis of the imagination, and an aesthetics of the sublime would be impossible if the pure imagination were not violent in its very essence.

The "comprehension" in question here should not be understood in a psychological or conceptual sense. It is the unifying intention of imagination that turns back toward the beginning of the temporal sequence, seizes anew the plurality of the apprehensions which have already floated by, and repeating the trajectory of the entire series, reduces them to the unity of the present instant. It is in these terms that the "Transcendental Deduction" had described the "synthesis of reproduction in imagination." Inseparably tied to the synthesis of apprehension, to the reception of the "now" that forms the horizon of the present, the synthesis of reproduction receives anew the past "nows" and takes them up again, reproduces them. It opens the horizon of the past in the unity that harmonizes this past with the present. This very synthesis, which the first *Critique* designated as the origin of time, is determined in the *Critique of Judgment* as a violence imposed upon time. First of all, because it is *retention*, because it attempts, against time, to retain the temporal flux, to keep present what passes, to connect to the present what does not cease to distance itself from the present, and because it thus does violence to the passage, the *passivity* of time. Secondly, because it is *synthesis*, "comprehension of plurality in unity," because it intends to establish a linear continuity in the discontinuous succession of apprehensions, to occult the essential discontinuity of the time. Time can be said to be discontinuous in two very different senses. In this passage from the third *Critique*, it is only a matter of the series of apprehensions, of the instantaneous seizures of the present now which succeed each other one by one. However, Kant does not always hold to this naïve conception of time. The "Transcendental Deduction" made it possible to think temporal discontinuity in a more radical sense as the ecstatic unity of the triple synthesis, as that unique pressure that divides itself and floods toward the three dimensions of its present, its past, and its future. In its effort to retain the passivity of the past within the horizon of the present, to mask temporal difference beneath the appearance of a homogeneous flux, the violent synthesis of imagination works toward a leveling of time. In reducing time to a continuous and uniform series of now's, this synthesis submits temporality to the reign of presence, to the *maintenance* of time. Presence as such is violence.[8]

The violence of the imagination is supposed to arise from the now. It is supposed to have its roots this side of all reproduction in the pure presentation of the present, the synthesis of apprehension. This first synthesis is already "comprehension of plurality in unity"; it operates a successive unfolding, a "traversal" (*Durchlaufen*) of diversity and the "comprehension" (*Zusammennehmung*) of this deployment (cf. *CPR*, 112; 131). It is already syn-thetic, comprehensive, that is, violence. Each instant contains its charge of violence, which explodes ceaselessly toward its past and its future and projects itself into them in order to gather them into presence. According to Kant, the possibility of experience rests on this synthetic connection of the manifold. If all synthesis is violent, this elementary violence is the condition of the possibility of all objective knowledge, of all experience, of the least perception. Without this *transcendental violence*, which opens the horizon of phenomena, no phenomenon at all could appear and link itself to others in the cohesion of a world. In keeping with the problematic of the first *Critique*, one could even say that this transcendental violence engenders the radically originary forms of space and time. If the synthesis of reproduction ceased to effectuate itself, "if I always let the preceding representations escape from my thought...and if I did not reproduce them as I arrive at the following representations, no complete representation...not even the fundamental representations, the most pure and completely primary ones of space and time could be produced" (*CPR*, 114–15; 133), and the world would come unhinged in a formless confusion. This is what *seems* to happen in the experience of the sublime. Nonetheless, we know that in this experience a trace of form is preserved beneath the appearance of chaos. The form of all forms is time: since the unity of a connective form maintains itself throughout sublime disconnection, one must admit that the failure of the temporalizing imagination does not entail the ruination of time, that this failure does not extend to the ultimate nerve of time.

Our hypothesis is confirmed: originary temporality is not identical to transcendental imagination; it is not reducible to the auto-affection of this imagination and cannot be confused with the representations the imagination gives of it. The violence of presence is the condition of all re-presentation. But time cannot properly be represented: as the "Transcendental Aesthetic" emphasizes, its pure form is not susceptible of figuration, and this is why "we seek to supplement this defect by recourse to analogies and we represent the passage of time by a line which extends to infinity" (*CPR*, 63; 77). This supplementary figuration already presupposes the violence of the imagination: for one must do violence to time to keep it present, to represent the nonpresentable "instance" of originary temporality by means of an external intuition. It is only at the cost of this violence that the synthesis of the imagination can constitute "fundamental representations" of time, notably its spatial representation in the form of a continuous and infinite line of which the *gramm* dominates the ordinary precomprehension of time. Without this spatial representation, time would remain a formless form, a pure nothing (cf. *CPR*, 249; 295), and no phenomenon would be able to find its place in time. The violence inflicted on time belongs to the very movement of temporalization: it forms a spatialized and homogeneous time, the de-temporalized time of phenomena, which can be schematized by the imagination in order to found objective knowledge. The schema of a reality "is precisely this continual and uniform production of reality in time" (*CPR*, 154; 184), and the set of schemas exposed by the "Analytic" "are nothing other than the *a priori* determinations of time according to rules." They are a "transcendental product of the imagination," which captures time, submits it to the categories of the understanding, and imposes on it their rule and measure. Kant remarks that the schemas "restrain" the categories in limiting them to the conditions of sensibility. They limit the forms of sensibility, space and time, as well, imposing upon them the yoke of the categories. The schematism of the categories thus operates a restriction, a contraction, which narrows the horizon of the possible. "The singular has renounced the free disposition over the possible, and thus it can become an example for the identical that rules as such the diversity of what is possible."[9] In schematizing, the imagination does violence to the possible. It engenders that monotonous time, mutilated of its possibilities, where past and future are the mere recidivism of the eternal present. Where the past is never passed by, never delivered or pardoned, but relentlessly reproduced by the synthesis of reproduction which recalls this past to the present as what haunts it. Where the advent of the future is without adventure, already recognized by the synthesis of recognition which identifies it in advance and has been expecting it forever.

If originary temporality were identical to imagination, nothing *other* would be possible, nothing sublime could happen. In fact, this feeling seizes us when the imagination fails to identify time, to comprehend it in the unity of synthesis—when time is radically lacking. In the impossible view of the pyramid, past perceptions disappear before the imagination has been able to grasp the perceptions that follow. The violence of synthesis breaks down in connection with this escape of time, it exhausts itself in the activity of holding time in presence, of retaining the passivity of the past and preventing the adventure of the future's advent. It is thus that it collapses, torn asunder between the already-no-longer and the not-yet. And its ruin reveals a primitive time [*temps sauvage*]—in the sense in which Merleau-Ponty speaks of a brute or primitive Being—which rips apart and flees into the distances of the future and the past. If the sublime is distinct from the beautiful, their difference is first of all of a temporal order. Beautiful form plays off by itself in the grace of a present without presence; it gives itself to the instant, in a singular apprehension where it *makes a present* of its beauty. The sublime is the formless-limitless, which exceeds all presentation and all finite duration. The infinity of the past is sublime, and even more the faceless infinity of the future.[10]

The sublime manages to schematize nonfigurable, prephenomenal time only at the cost of a transcendental disfiguration, of a de-schematization of the world, only by breaking the schemas preformed in the violent synthesis of imagination, the schema of substance as "permanence of the real in time," the schema of causality as succession of the manifold in time, etc. What these schemas forbid us to think, what they absolutely exclude, is a rupture in the temporal series. "The fact of coming to be [*Entstehen*] does not concern substance....There is simply change and not origination [*Ursprung*] out of nothing" (*CPR*, 192; 230). *Transcendental freedom*, as the power to initiate a series of phenomena, cannot be admitted in a universe schematized by the synthesis of the imagination. Its mere possibility would suffice to destroy the necessary unity of experience. But the sublime de-schematization of these schemas reveals the radical discontinuity of time. Inaugural freedom was incompatible only with a mutilated representation of time: in its first manifestation, originary temporality is freedom.

What the sublime revelation discovers, at the limit of the formless and at the risk of chaos, is the event of origination. Even more than Being-untodeath, Being-in-origination is the possibility of the impossible. The feeling of the sublime overtakes us the instant the chain of phenomena breaks apart, when time gives itself another chance, delivering all at once the horizon of possibilities. It is thus that the passion of Law and of Ideas can suddenly seize a nation; that the work of the genius invents itself without a model; that the call of the Law liberates us from a bad repetition, in a change of direction, a *Bekehrung* which is, Kant says, "like a new origination." The sublime schematizes the freedom of the world, the power to commence afresh. It thus makes it possible to think an aesthetics of innovation, an ethics of conversion, a politics of revolution. What is most sublime would be the event in which the totality of the possible is discovered, the infinity of the Maybe, which metaphysics names God.

However, all the weight of everyday experience denounces the "illusion of freedom." In the first *Critique*, whose vocation is to ground objective knowledge, transcendental freedom remains a problematic concept. The disruption of origination makes no sense in the world of phenomena: it would ruin the coherency of their connections, "which is precisely what distinguishes experience from the dream" (cf. *CPR*, 353; 413–14). In phenomenalizing itself, time de-temporalizes itself; it covers over its division and renounces infinite possibility. The schematizing violence of the imagination operates this cover-up, this de-sublimation of time. No text by Kant authorizes us to characterize this phenomenal temporality as "vulgar" or "fallen." Although a "product of the imagination," it is not "imaginary," in the sense of an illusory or fictive representation. Indeed one must see in this temporality the condition of all objective truth. But it is nonetheless dissimulating, and the truth it supports is initiated by means of a transcendental untruth. The time of phenomena masks the phenomenalization of time, the violent de-temporalization of time as form of phenomena. The violence of presence dissimulates itself in that—and in what—it presents. Each phenomenon can appear only by occulting this original violence, in re-covering the ecstatic fracture of time, the temporal tearing of imagination. The totality of phenomena—Nature—is the veil of Isis, the texture of which is woven of the thread of temporality. What weaves the veil is the violence of the imagination, concealed in the apparition of phenomena, in the luminous appearance of the world. The imagination is the violence of the veil, which veils itself and dissimulates itself under an illusory transparence. With respect to this beautiful appearance, the sublime would be the test of truth. Stretched to the extreme, to the breaking point, the hidden violence of the imagination becomes quasi perceptible, at the moment when it comes apart. The violent truth of the world, latent in each phenomenon, discovers itself in its laceration. The sublime reveals the veil.

Does this mean that it lifts or sublates [*relève*] the veil, that it un-veils? The pretention to denuding the goddess, to letting her flesh be "divined" through the thinness of the veil, is according to Kant the exalted revery of the *Schwärmer*, the dream of metaphysics. There is, in the sublime, a degree of "madness" (*Wahnsinn*) which seems quite close to this visionary "insanity" (*Wahnwitz*). Which is why Kant makes an effort to differentiate between them: "It is insanity least of all which can accord with the sublime"; in fact, the latter is a "pure, merely negative presentation which...entails no danger of *Schwärmerei*...precisely because the presentation is merely negative" (§29, 111; 116). This is an essential distinction but a precarious one, as necessary and fragile perhaps as the demarcation between the sublime and the monstrous.

What is at stake here is the truth of the sublime: the determination of the truth implied by the thought of the sublime and, more profoundly, truth *as* sublimity. Far from claiming to lift the veil of Isis, or to *sublate* it in the sense of a dialectical *Aufhebung*, the sublime revelation reveals nothing. Unless it is the veil itself, nonfigurable weave of time. Is the sublime, as the display of the veil in its blind opacity, truth itself, the veiling unveiling of *aletheia?*[11] Metaphysical illusion would be born then in the forgetting of this truth: for it is not the veil as such but the desire for its impossible sublation that sustains the delirium of the *Schwärmer*, the phantasm of Absolute Knowledge. As dissimulating as it may be, the imagination is not what creates this illusion. In Kantian terms, one could say that it is important to distinguish between the *transcendental* violence of imagination, the veiling that constitutes the world of phenomena, and the *transcendent*—i.e., metaphysical—intention of pure reason, the claim to raise itself above phenomena, to grasp things in themselves, and to give us knowledge of the super-sensible.

But this critical demarcation needs to be nuanced further: without being itself illusory, the violence of the imagination is nonetheless the matrix of metaphysical illusion. If the imagination that levels time works in the service of presence, the metaphysical privilege of the present culminates in the intention to abolish time, to sublate it in the eternity of the always-present. The de-temporalizing temporalization of phenomena culminates in the illusion of the atemporal. One can, in fact, show that each of the transcendent Ideas of reason—the subject, the World, and God—is supported by an annulment or a denial of the temporal conditions of intuition. Thus, the appearance of a substantial permanence of the Ego tends to occult its temporal discontinuity, the intermittency of the ego I am. On the basis of the permanent presence of the subject "at different times," metaphysics infers its persistence "at all times," the immortality of the soul.[12] In the very gesture through which they deny it, the Ideas of reason also presuppose the linear time of phenomena, already violated and schematized by imagination. Metaphysics would only intensify this de-temporalizing violence, augment it infinitely—up to the sublime point where it founders. Kant does not analyze this passage-to-the-limit, this un-limitation that constitutes the speculative illusion. He never relates it to the sublime tension of the imagination. However, if metaphysics is the passion of un-limitation—*Trieb zur Erweiterung* (*CPR*, 36; 47)—if it is the desire to unveil, the forgetfulness of finitude, this is perhaps because it has its roots in the (self-)exceeding trance or transport of the imagination, that sudden madness which bears its ruination in its train.

As certain passages in the *Critique of Judgment* suggest, the pure imagination, which unfolds the finite horizon of phenomena, refuses to allow itself to be enclosed within this horizon. In the presentation of aesthetic Ideas, it "strives to rival reason in the realization of a maximum," and raises itself "beyond the limits of experience" (§49, 144; 158). Transported "beyond the sensible" by its impetus toward the Ideas, it "feels itself unlimited," and its sub-limation is a "negative presentation of infinity" (§29, 110; 115). The sentiment of the sublime arises then at the limit of metaphysics: on the undecidable margin where, having attained its maximum, the imagination strives to transgress this maximum—to "extend" (*erweitern*) it—to embrace the infinite. But its comprehension is temporally finite, and thus, on the point of presenting that which cannot be presented, it comes undone and collapses. All of this will have taken place in a single instant: it is "at the same time" that the imagination feels both its extreme tension toward and its powerlessness to attain the infinite (§26, 94; 94) in the instantaneous oscillation of intention and retreat, of attraction and repulsion, of audacity and timorous fall. The violent "rivalry" of imagination and reason then is nothing but a maddened play of the imagination with itself and the source of transcendental illusion. Not—as the tradition teaches from Plato to Malebranche—because the imagination is a "deceptive power," the "enemy of reason," but because it is pure reason itself, as the faculty of delirium. In the sublime failure of the imagination, metaphysical illusion deconstructs itself. The violence of finitude acknowledges its powerlessness to comprehend the infinite.

To Infinity

The event of the sublime befalls us when the metaphysical violence of the imagination encounters the infinite as its trait of ob-jection, as the rampart of a *Dawider*. The sublime is the feeling of the infinite.[13] "Nature is thus sublime in those of its phenomena the intuition of which arouses the Idea of its infinity" (§26, 94; 94). It is a question here of the infinite of *nature*, of its "total infinity as phenomenon." But this is itself a "contradictory concept." For this reason, Kant continues, the "greatness of an object of nature, to which the imagination applies in vain all of its faculty of comprehension, ought to lead [*führen*] the concept of nature to a super-sensible substratum...great beyond all measure of the senses" and "to extend" the spirit in a practical perspective (§26, 94–95; 94). This *Führung*, this movement which guides us from sensible infinity to another infinity, is this not the passage we have been seeking, the bridge over the abyss of the super-sensible? All the questions with which we are confronted—the questions of the schematism of the sublime, of the conflict of time and imagination, of the passage between sensible and super-sensible—lead back in this crucial passage to a single question: what is the role of the infinite here? At first view, the sense of the text is clear. The imagination "demands totality," it "insists on a presentation for all the members of a continually growing series, without excluding even the infinite from this demand" (§26, 93; 93). However, this common notion of the infinite, as "absolute totality of a progress without termination," is naïvely dogmatic. It is this notion that underlies the first antinomy of rational cosmology, the insoluble conflict between a thesis which negates and an antinomy which affirms the infinity of the world in space and time (cf. *CPR*, 338–47; 396–409). From this point of view, the total infinity of nature is a "contradictory concept," while practical infinity is an empty idea, and only a vague analogy enables one to establish a relation between the two. A "vast trench" continues to separate the super-sensible from the world of phenomena. Kant will not have deepened his reflexion on the Idea of the infinite, which seemed to be able to provide a hinge between the two domains. He will have recoiled before the abyss of the infinite.

Is this his final word? Does he see sensible infinity as nothing but a contradictory notion, a simple illusion of reason? As is well known, the "Transcendental Aesthetic" defines space and time as "given infinite quantities" (*CPR*, 57-B; 69). This definition seems to contradict that given in the "Dialectic," which affirms that "a given infinite quantity is impossible" (*CPR*, 340; 400). But the point is that we are dealing here with two different concepts of the infinite. The first antinomy rests on the concept of a quantitative infinity—that of a quantity without end, of indefinite series of juxtaposed or successive phenomena. The infinity of space and time, however, is not a *quantum*, a relative quantity, but the "absolutely large," *magnitude*. It is not situated at the end of a summation without end, but pre-given all at once as the form of intuition. The infinity of the world according to the "Dialectic" is that of an "infinite aggregate of real things," of "infinite series of successive states" (*CPR*, 338; 397), the unachieved recollection of separate elements which are added together or are composed externally. In the "Aesthetic," the infinity of space and time designates, to the contrary, the uncomposed unity of an originary *community*. Finally, if the dialectical infinity is an inconsistent notion, the infinity of space-time has the consistency of a *pure form*, which dwells in a retreat from phenomenal forms and presents itself in the guise of the formless. These three characteristics—magnitude, community, and informal formality—qualify both the infinity of the sensible according to the "Aesthetic" and the "aesthetic" infinity of the third *Critique* which awakens the feeling of the sublime. Even while it rejects the infinity of the world as a contradictory notion, Kant's oeuvre remains silently pervaded by another thought of the infinite, which orients it toward the opening of the passage.

"We call sublime that which is great absolutely" (§25, 87; 86). If the evaluation of quantity or greatness were merely mathematical, an aesthetics of the sublime would be impossible. In the logical comprehension of quantity, the understanding calculates the dimensions of the object with the aid of relative quantities. This arithmetic measurement, however, remains abstract and empty of sense unless it is supported by a "first measure" (§26, 90; 90), an aesthetic evaluation of size and distance, where we take the measure of the world "in a single glance." It is at this pre-logical, pre-objective level, in its naïve embrace of the world, that the finite comprehension of the imagination can encounter its maximum, the sublime limit on which it breaks. Aesthetic evaluation "presents greatness absolutely" (§26, 91; 90); at the foot of the pyramids or before the ocean, it places us in the presence of the absolutely great, and only the infinite is absolutely great (§26, 94; 93). Infinite greatness: not an infinite quantity, not a quantity at all in the mathematical sense. In fact, "to be great [*Groß-sein*] and to be a quantity [*eine Größe sein*], are completely different concepts (*magnitudo* and *quantitas*)" (§25, 87; 86). Magnitude is the Being-great of all quantity or greatness, that which gives it its size, the gesture of a tracing, of a first measure which no finite quantity could measure. If the finite is the quantitative, the measured, the commensurable, magnitude is infinite by its un-measure. It can present itself as an immense quantity, "in comparison with which all the rest is small." But quantitative immensity is not un-measure: magnitude is a "greatness which is equal only to itself," great "beyond all comparison," *infinitely other* than all finite quantity. In this sense, it is neither large nor small, and the colossal is as little sublime as the most extreme smallness. It even happens that, in a time dominated by emphasis on grandeur, the sublime finds refuge in the tiny or the laughable, the grain of a voice, the brilliance of an instant.

No series of phenomena is truly infinite; no sensible figure, however enormous it may be, can be ajudged sublime. And Kant can conclude that "the sublime ought not be sought in the things of nature, but solely in our Ideas" (§23, 85; 83). A hasty conclusion, which precipitates the "Analytic of the Sublime" into an impasse. At the moment when his analysis of infinite magnitude was leading him to the threshold of the passage, Kant holds to the dialectical concept of the infinite, to the illusory infinity *in* space and time, without considering the infinity *of* space and time. Due to its failure to articulate itself with the "Transcendental Aesthetic," the thought of the sublime stops short of its goal. It is this articulation that it is possible to envisage. All the traits of magnitude are, in fact, also found in the pure forms of space and time. Magnitude is the infinitely great that has no quantity but supports each quantum of greatness and gives it its measure, always "equal to itself" in each of its parts. Likewise, space is nowhere in space, although it *gives rise and gives place* to each of its regions, and its least parcel is still space, just as "any part of time is time."[14] The infinity of space and time thus implies a singular relation of the parts to the whole. According to Kant—and this is one of his essential theses—composition is the mark of finitude.[15] Within the horizon of finitude, the parts precede the whole and are aggregated or juxtaposed to compose the whole synthetically. In contrast, in the infinite form of space and time, "the infinite contains the foundation of the part" (*D1770*, 73; 67). It makes its parts arise *in it*, supports them and holds them in its web. Its "co-parts" (*compartes*) are therefore not *parts*—separate portions of space or slices of duration—but internal limits, which ceaselessly de-limit themselves, sub-limate themselves at the heart of the unlimited whole. They are "unthinkable in themselves," co-implicated by the whole and compromised in it, in solidarity at the heart of an originary uncomposed unity, which is the world itself as *universitas, Inbegriff*—community. The feeling of the sublime is awakened by the infinite of the world: it is the feeling of community.

What of this community? The *Dissertation of 1770* designates it as *lex* and *nexus*. The infinite community of the world is form, that is, the connection of a multiplicity, and this "connection which constitutes the essential form of the world" holds the manifold together, assures its affinity, or again, as Kant says, its coalescence (*D1770*, 50–53; 58). Space and time are these originary forms of connection where the sensible unfolds itself in its pure diversity, before all apprehension and all comprehension, before the synthesis of the imagination. One would be wrong to represent them to oneself as a monotonous and void extension, a uniform duration. As a priori forms of intuition, they already contain a "pure manifold," a "manifold of sensibility a priori," unlike the empirical variety of phenomena *in* space and time, which is supposed to arise out of a primitive diversification of space and time. It is possible to interpret in this sense the note of the "Analytic" where Kant remarks that "the form of intuition gives merely the manifold." (*CPR*, 138; 170)[16] The a priori forms of space and time are nothing other than this giving: they don't come to reconnect retroactively, synthetically, an already given empirical diversity but make the manifold of the sensible appear out of the unity of the connective form from which this manifold arises as manifold and which keeps it in community. Pure form is gift, that is, partitioning [*partage*]: power of differentiation, of dispersion to infinity. If the essence of all form implies unification of a multiplicity, the outline of a limitation, transcendental form is only form insofar as it deforms itself or becomes deformed. Disseminating itself, it disjoins or de-limits itself, and its sub-limation draws it into the waters of the formless. But its infinite disjunction is precisely what harmonizes the manifold: what makes a gift of it and adjoins it. Across their diffraction, space and time remain "essentially one" and preserve the essential structure of form throughout the movement of sublime deformation. What thus presents itself as chaos is the ordering of pure forms, from which proceed all empirical order and disorder. By defining space and time as "given infinite quantities," as the donation of an infinite form, the "Transcendental Aesthetic" breaks with a long tradition which identified *Form* and *Gestalt*, which apprehended all form on the basis of *eidos*, the finite figure of phenomena, as the stable limit of a contour. From the point of view of finitude, the infinity of transcendental forms necessarily appears monstrous and formless. In truth, its apparent confusion contains the infinite profusion of possibilities. It opens itself onto the entirety of the Maybe, the ideal of pure reason (cf. *CPR*, 415–21, 487–95), which idolatrous metaphysics personifies and names God. The *Critique* is called upon to deconstruct this hypostasis, to discover beneath the veil of the idol the sublime chaos of the world.

The forms of the sensible can be contained by no sensible form. They are not "figures" in the traditional sense, but rather the opaque ground, *Grund*, against which the explosive brightness of finite figures stands out. Plato called the invisible and formless matrix of all form the *chora*, "brought into movement and cut up into figures" by the types whose imprint it receives "without ever taking on a form similar to those that penetrate it." The *chora* is the form(lessness) of pure space, the transcendental site of the world. Up to now, I have only considered the temporality of the sublime. However, this feeling seizes us always on the ground of space, before a spatial un-measure. The sublime discovers to us the pure form of space, which is irreducible to the abstract spatiality of extension. This form is that of a primitive space prior to phenomena but already differentiated, dissymmetrical, heterogeneous, traversed by fractures and rendered uneven by reliefs. According to Kant, the internal ground of spatial diversity is situated in "the space proper to the body," its primordial *orientation*, structured by the opposition of high and low, front and back, left and right. The carnal matrix of space remains most often hidden: "we cannot perceive what, in the form of a body, has to do solely with its spatial relation except by its symmetrical opposition to other bodies"[17]—such as when hands meet and when flesh touches flesh. The flesh is sublime from the moment of this first contact, of this tactile chiasmus, wherein the carnal spacing of the world is revealed. Clearly, Kant did not follow this path much further. Nonetheless, the third *Critique* does not fail to signal that our feelings are "always corporeal" (§29, 113; 119), that emotion is born of an excitation and an arrest of "vital forces." Emotion is thus rooted in the carnal materiality of life. It participates in what the *Anthropology* calls "the impression of life," which never affects any determinate organ, any part of the organism, but is diffracted across the entire body and overflows its limits. "The frisson that pervades man in the representation of the sublime" is of this type; it "flashes through the body everywhere there is life in it."[18] The feeling of the sublime is the living flesh of Being that feels itself live and incarnate itself. "Chaos is the name of the life that incarnates itself":[19] the veil of Isis is the infinite of the flesh.

Carnal diffraction of space, ecstatic explosion of time: could their differences be the truth of the sublime? But the infinite form of the world is community, that is, connection and unity of the manifold. Space, like time, is "essentially one." Their infinitude is that of a continuous totality, of an intertwining where all conspires and sympathizes. Radical unity on a measure with infinite dispersion. This cannot be the abstract unity of a *quantum*, nor that of a synthesis, but a *transcendental unity*. In the Analytic, Kant compares this qualitative unity to "the unity of theme in a dream, in a discourse, in a fable" (*CPR*, 98; 118). What assures the cohesion of time is the persistence of one temporal *style*, of one gait, a singular manner of precipitating myself at every instant toward my future in order to let it flow away into the past. And each instant gives me anew all of (the) time, like a continuous pressure that divides itself from itself and remains one in and through this very division, held in unity by the maintenance of a unique point-source. In the same way, the divergent dimensions of space cross each other and emanate from a central Here, from the singular pole of a unique, fleshly body. Thus, the originary community is at once dispersion of the One and reception of the Many: gathering of the manifold, which one must not conceive as a gathering of disjointed parts, a synthetic collection of separate elements. Synthetic composition is the concern of imagination: it is the violence of the synthesis that collects and links together a preliminary diversity. But the finite violence of imagination fails to comprehend the infinite, and the sublime is the mark of this failure, the sign that the ultimate link of the world is not the work of imagination. The connective form of space and time connects itself of itself by an immanent auto-synthesis, before all intervention of the imagination or the understanding. It is therefore not a *synthesis*, which always presupposes the thetic operation of a consciousness or of a constituting subject. It corresponds rather to what Kant sometimes characterizes as "synopsis" of the manifold in a pure intuition, and which Heidegger proposes to call *syndosis*:[20] a unifying co-donation, shared offering, which imposes no external link on the diverse and is therefore not, in the strict sense, violence. Nothing is more sublime than this secret community of the world: that which Kant will designate in the *Opus Posthumum* as a "seizure of the One and the All in One," where form is the gift of Being.[21] He will define the passage then, the "physical *Übergang*," as a "general principle of interaction" of phenomena, "linked to all of the universe because space and time are absolute unities."[22] One can judge sublime the aesthetic figurations of this passage, such as that of the veiled Isis who symbolizes the hidden unity of "all that is, was, and will be." Or, closer to us, that of a Book that contains all books, or of the point Aleph "where all the places in the universe viewed from all angles meet without becoming confused."

What is at stake in the *Critique of Judgment* is becoming more clear. The task was to ground a transcendental principle of the faculty of judgment, to justify the reflexive constatation of a coherent order in the contingency of nature. This ordered connection of the empirically manifold translates onto the level of the phenomena the initial connection of the world. It schematizes the syndosis, the uni-diversity of space and time. Kant calls purposiveness the "lawfulness of the contingent," its conformity to the form of a law. The third *Critique* is in quest of a principle of the purposiveness of the forms of nature. It seeks to discover *purposive forms*, "singular things in the form of systems," fragments of order emerging from disorder which bear witness to a super-sensible order. It is possible to distinguish three modes of reflexive judgment, which correspond to three types of formal purposiveness: the beautiful, the sublime, and life are the schemas of the syndosis; they incarnate finitely the infinite form of community. Are they simply equivalents, or is there here some sort of gradation? In what sensible face do the traits of the super-sensible reproduce themselves most faithfully? On a first level, we encounter "objective purposiveness": organic systems of which the parts are only possible by means of their relation to the whole and where the parts mutually engender each other in recreating the unity of this whole (cf. §§64–65). Each living being carries within itself in this manner the living form of the world. In the judgment of beauty—and first of all in this "free" or "vague" beauty which Kant distinguishes from "merely adherent" beauty—another dimension of syndosis unveils itself, the dimension of the free appearance of the manifold in the One. The accent is no longer placed on the internal connection of the parts but on the free play of forms, legality without law and purposiveness without purpose. Transcendental formality schematizes itself here in the "vision of changing figures" (§22, 83; 81) where the manifold is unified without a rule—arabesques and ornamental scrolls, flickering of a flame or waves of a stream, which are as many floating and unstable schemas, the hesitant contours of which reconstitute themselves every instant only in order to efface themselves anew. In its unrule, beauty manifests better than life the structure of syndosis, its immanent giving of the manifold gift, where form ceaselessly deforms itself, partitions and apportions itself, alters itself in remaining one and the same. Its scope remains nonetheless limited by the finitude of the imagination. The most free beauty still restrains the play of this syndosis, restricts form still to the contour of a figure, imposes on form an appearance that fixes it, an outline that freezes it. When beautiful form frees itself of figurative constraints, when it disfigures itself and unlimits itself, only then does it tend to the sublime, to the point of appearing chaotic and formless. But chaos is the supreme order: the finite figures of the phenomena mask the infinity of pure forms and only a radical disfiguration of the world reveals the world's Law. The *limen* of the sublime is the threshold of the passage.

Of a passage which, as we are beginning to understand, does not lead to another world that would be distinct from the world of phenomena. In the ordeal of the sublime, the ancient opposition between sensible and super-sensible is unsettled: the third *Critique* implies another thought of the super-sensible, which does not hide behind the veil of Isis, but weaves the texture of this veil; which does not reside beyond the sensible, but lies this side of it as its substratum or its reverse, as its form-in-retreat which makes a gift of sensible diversity and retires in the movement through which it appears. The unity of the super-sensible substratum is the connective form of the world, its *nexus* or its Law. It is this form of law that presents its profile when the failure of synthesis permits a glimpse—upstream of all phenomena—of the gift of syndosis, its transcendental *Urform*, which is *Gesetz*—positing of the sensible—and *lex* or *logos*, obliging reception of its diversity. The truth of the sublime is that it discloses, in its opacity, the faceless form of the Law. What appears within the horizon of finitude as an additional violence, through which the violent tension of the imagination is broken, is in truth the power of the gift, the sovereign excess of infinitude over the finite. An infinitude which is no longer that of the Cartesian God, and which is not superabundance of bounty and love, but the imperative obligation of a Law.

This Law of the world is the Law of community, as *universitas* or *Inbegriff*, but also as *Urgemeinschaft*: carnal archi-community the agreement of

which supports this world and accords it in its Being. The first vocation of
ethics is to prescribe this accord. This side of the determinations of morality—
- the diverse formulations of "Kantian Morals"—- the Law commands nothing other than this community. In Kant's perspective, and in his language still
marked by the tradition, the community that organizes itself in the name of
the Law is the *reign of purposes*, the highest form of the categorical imperative:
it is the "final purpose [*Endzweck*] of the existence of a world," and the *highest
good* possible in this world (cf. §§84-87). The sublime is the announcement of
this end, the promise of community.[23] One must not consider it then as an
aesthetic illustration of a preestablished moral rule. As the schema of the
super-sensible, the sublime cannot be exterior to what it schematizes: it is the
Law itself, and the sublime community destines itself as always still to come,
still deferred and promised. The infinity of the future is what is most sublime
in time. The infinitude of the sublime, however, cannot be the illusory infinity
of the "Dialectic," the inaccessible end of an indefinite progression. The infinite form of community is supposed to have been always already given to us,
as it is supposed to be offered anew every instant. For it is the gift of the world,
veiled by the appearing of the phenomena, and transparently transpiring in
the tears in the veil. The monotonous time of the schematism covers over the
brilliant explosion of its donation. It may please the subject to figure forth for
itself a world in the assurance of its auto-affection. In the certitude that nothing is happening, that nothing sublime could ever befall it. But what erupts
into the distress of this time, what recalls the subject to its chance and con-
vokes it in its freedom—that is sublime. That is what ought to come, what is
always about to come, what is deferred to infinity and remains in wait. One
can judge to be sublime the story of this indefatigable waiting on the threshold
of the Law.

Chapter 7

❀

TRAGEDY AND SUBLIMITY: THE SPECULATIVE INTERPRETATION OF *OEDIPUS REX* ON THE THRESHOLD OF GERMAN IDEALISM

Jean-François Courtine

In his elegant "Essay on the Tragic,"[1] Peter Szondi noted, with reference to the interpretation of Greek tragedy sketched by Schelling in the last of his *Letters on Dogmatism and Criticism*[2] (an interpretation whose guiding thread is Sophocles' *Oedipus Rex*): "This interpretation of *Oedipus Rex* and of Greek tragedy in general marks the beginning of a period in the history of the theory of tragedy in which the focus of interest is no longer on tragic effect (*to tes tragodias ergon*), but on the phenomenon itself." And after having retraced in broad strokes Schelling's analysis, Szondi notes again by way of conclusion:

> In Schelling's interpretation, the tragic hero does not merely succumb to the 'superior power' of the objective, but he is punished for having succumbed, and even for having engaged in the combat, and thus the positive value of his attitude—that will to freedom which constitutes the 'essence of the Ego'—turns against him. One can call this process, with Hegel, 'dialectical'. (13; 45)

I will not investigate here whether this last characterization is well founded, nor whether it is possible to find evidence of any sort of phenomenology of the tragic in Schelling's work. I would like simply—after having examined more closely what may seem like a mere "digression" in the *Letters*, placing it in the context of its immediate problematic—to pose the question of whether and to what extent Schelling's analysis can be considered as the first speculative theory of the tragic phenomenon and, consequently, as something decidedly epoch-making, marking a true rupture in the "poetic" exegesis of tragedy, that is, indeed as the first resolutely philosophical interpretation since Aristotle's *Poetics*.

I would also like to examine whether and to what extent the theory sketched in the *Letters* anticipates the interpretation proposed in the *Lectures on the Philosophy of Art* (1802–3), and more precisely still in what sense this fleeting sketch constitutes the true germ, the central kernel of the a priori deduction of the poetic genres exposed in the Jena *Lectures*.

Finally, I will ask whether one can view tragedy, in accordance with the triple function Schelling assigns to art at the end of the *System of Transcendental Idealism*,[3] as the supreme accomplishment of art, as the work par excellence, that work which more than any other illuminates the essence of art and its properly philosophical or speculative import.

From the end of the *Letters on Dogmatism and Criticism*, passing by way of the *System* of 1800, and up to the *Lectures* of Jena, Schelling carries out, through his interpretation of Greek tragedy, a preliminary elaboration of the entire philosophy of Identity from his earliest attempts on.

If one would comprehend the sense and importance of the brief analysis of Greek tragedy that opens the tenth *Letter*, one must first of all situate it as precisely as possible in the (harshly discontinuous, sinuous) general economy of the *Letters*. In the *Letters*—whose mode of exposition, the epistolary genre, is particularly well adapted to his design—Schelling pursues several objectives: first of all, he attempts to mark clearly the sharp separation between dogmaticism and dogmatism (or rather, thoroughgoing or consistent dogmatism— read: Spinozism), and to struggle against the risk of dogmatization to which, in his day, criticism is exposed.[4] Further, and above all, he attempts to bring to light the problem with which both dogmatism and criticism are necessarily faced: the problem of the "enigma of the world" (*das Rätsel der Welt*) (I, 3, 78), as Schelling says, or again the problem of the justification of the "domain of experience" (I, 3, 79), that is, of the finite and its relative autonomy. The question concerns thus, if you will, the difficult determination of the finite Ego and its fragile status. In addition, and finally, Schelling attempts to show why the profound antagonism between the two types of possible systems is irreducible, to disengage the underlying practical postulates from each of the given theses and, having thus "changed terrain," chosen a new field on which to maneuvre—that of practical realization—to place the imaginary correspondent, the fictive addressee of the *Letters*, before the true and ultimate alternative: to know *who* he is or *who* he wants to be, *what or whom* he gives himself to be practically—and to decide consequently[5] either for unlimited activity or for absolute passivity—abandon, repose in the arms of the world.

One might ask oneself, however, if the alternative between dogmatism and criticism, posed in these terms, still allows one to do justice to the power of the objective world; if the effort to realize the absolute within oneself by an unlimited activity does not lead one to rob the object of all consistency, to make it lose its essential status of resistance; and if, inversely, the abandonment of oneself to the world, the Empedoclean aspiration to throw oneself "into the arms of the infinite" and to lose oneself in the "young world"[6] does not represent a merely illusory triumph for the power of the objective. For if the objective dominates as a result of the measureless passivity of the subject, it ends up owing its victory to the subject itself insofar the subject abandons and renounces itself in disappropriating itself.

One could show this in detail, it seems to me, by following the analyses of the eighth *Letter* concerning the intellectual intuition and the (quasi necessary) illusion of Spinoza and of all authentic *Schwärmer*. This is why the fictive addressee of the *Letters* legitimately can and even ought—it seems—to introduce *in fine* a third possibility. This possibility necessarily imposes itself on one's thought as soon as one's considerations are no longer limited to the subject-object couple, or the principal antagonism between freedom of the Ego and power of the objective, and as soon as this latter power presents itself, even if only by means of a historicization of these conflictual terms, as an "*excessive* power" (*Übermacht*).

The alternative onto which the ninth *Letter* opens is, if not quite deceptive, at least incomplete. To be sure, it is important *to decide*, that is, to halt or hold up the type of *destiny* that everyone is at every turn in a position to make his or her own, in conformity with the fundamental opposition of dogmatism and criticism:

> In dogmatism, my destiny is to annihilate all free causality in myself, not to act myself, but to let absolute causality act in me, to restrain ever further the limits of my liberty, in order to enlarge to this extent those of the objective world—in short, absolutely unlimited passivity....For criticism, my destiny is this: to struggle to attain to unmovable selfhood, unconditioned liberty, activity without limits. So be it! Such is the supreme requirement of criticism. (I, 3, 104, 106)

But we have to take a third element equally into account; we still have in effect something to learn: "that there exists an objective power which threatens to annihilate our liberty and that, penetrated by this firm conviction, we have to struggle against it and in so doing *perish*" (I, 3, 106). This last possibility not only ought not to be excluded in principle, but ought in a sense to remain always in view, ever present to the spirit. Not as a "real" possibility, but at the very least as an *imaginary* possibility, which as such ought to be entrusted to art (to artistic representation)—and even to the highest art: tragedy.

Why has such a possibility disappeared as a "real possibility" if indeed it ever had a reality other than that precisely of *Darstellung*, "representation and

spectacle"? Schelling limits himself to saying laconically that the eventuality of
the frontal conflict between the Ego in its free "self-affirmation" (*Selbstmacht*)
and some sort of power defined primarily by its excess or its "unmeasure"
(*Übermass*) vanished long ago before the light of reason. Schelling had already
evoked in the preface to *Vom Ich* the necessity of delivering humanity definitively from "the terrors of the objective world" (I, 3, 107).[7] The concrete possibility of envisaging any violent struggle against the excessive power (*Übermacht*) disappeared at the same time as the idea of destiny and its superior
force emptied itself of all true content. Such an idea belongs henceforth to
another age, is characteristic of a bygone period of history conceived in its
totality as "continuous revelation, progressive self-unveiling of the absolute":
the *tragic period*, evoked as if in passing at the end of the *System of Transcendental Idealism.*

It is important, however, to maintain in the sphere of art the vivid representation of this possibility, or more concretely this struggle of freedom against
objective power. For what reason? What is it that justifies the necessity of this
reminder? On what is the permanent value of such a representation based?

Before (indirectly) doing justice to these questions, and on the threshold of his first interpretation of the tragic process, Schelling begins by rejecting
the problematic that underlies both classical and *Aufklärung*[8] exegeses of this
process, a problematic one can put in these terms: "How was Greek reason
able to bear the contradictions of its tragedy?" Or again: "What rendered contradiction bearable in the eyes of the Greeks?" Oedipus Rex is naturally the
heroic figure who illustrates most neatly such a contradiction in its inadmissi-
ble quality. Schelling presents him in these terms: "A mortal, destined by
fatum [*Verhängnis*] to become a criminal, struggling himself against this
fatum, and nonetheless terribly punished for a crime which was the work of
destiny!" (I, 3, 106).

Schelling's gesture, which consists in placing radically in question a
received problematic ("How was Greek reason...?"), interests me here in particular because it repeats in a sense—and I will return to this—his gesture in
the eighth *Letter* with respect to Spinoza. "I ask myself," the fictive addressee
objected, "how a spirit as limpid as his, a spirit the sweet clarity of which illuminates his entire life and work, was able to bear such a destructive principle,
a principle indeed of annihilation?" (I, 3, 86). Schelling is referring here to the
principle of all *Schwärmerei*, which formulates its intractable demand as follows: "Return to the divine original source of all existence, unite with the
absolute, annihilate the self."

But let us return to tragedy. Schelling's response to the received, quasi
obligatory question of the unbearable contradiction consists in showing that
the ultimate ground or foundation of the antinomy consists—beyond mere
"reason"—in the resolute affirmation of that which at first seems utterly scan-
dalous, the supreme injustice. The transmutation of contradiction into a

superior reason and of conflict into reconciliation was mediated precisely by the struggle to the death between human freedom and the power of the objective world. To be sure, once this power had become an excessive power (a *fatum*), freedom had to succumb, and since it did *not* succumb *without a struggle*, freedom had to be punished for and through its very defeat. To punish the "criminal," although he or she succumbed only to the superior power of destiny, was still a way—a paradoxical way, if you like[9]—of recognizing the intangibility of human freedom and of paying it a supreme hommage. Thus, Greek tragedy magnified the freedom of its heros, even if they were condemned in advance, precisely by revealing in all its bitterness the terrifying and rigorous logic of the struggle between freedom and the implacably superior power of destiny. "It was an exalted idea," Schelling notes, "to allow man to accept his torture voluntarily, even for an inevitable crime, and to manifest in this way his freedom through the very loss of his freedom, to have him succumb while declaring the rights of his free will" (I, 3, 107).

To manifest one's freedom even through the loss of this freedom itself, to sacrifice oneself to freedom by voluntarily accepting to be tortured for a crime of which one remains innocent or which one had to commit against one's will, in order to recognize it only *retrospectively* [*après coup*]—in all senses of the expression—this is in Schelling's eyes the grandiose conception on which Greek tragedy rests at its highest point, a conception owing to which freedom and necessity can be finally conjugated and reconciled—*at least within the limits of art.*

What is in fact valid for the mimetic space of representation, for the scenic space properly speaking—the inexpiable struggle of human freedom affirming the irreducible autonomy of its "proper power" (its *Selbstmacht*) in the face of the superior power of destiny—can neither be applied to the ethical sphere (the very sphere which, let us recall, is at the heart of the *Letters* of 1794–95) nor a fortiori serve as a rule for a "system of action." Such a system—the system of the struggle to the death, of the unconditional affirmation of imprescribable rights of freedom in the face of the absolute which is fantasmatically realized or objectivated outside of me—such a system would presuppose nothing less than a "race of Titans."

Having retraced in broad strokes the general perspectives of Schelling's interpretation, we can see clearly Schelling's break with the Aristotelian tradition: his analysis is truly no longer centered on "tragic effect," no longer centered on the cathartic function of representation and the identification with the hero which this function necessarily presupposes on the part of the spectators.[10] The key concepts of Aristotle's definition of tragedy as a specific figure of mimesis (*eleos kai phobos*, but also *hamartia*) apparently no longer play any role whatsoever. To be sure, tragedy remains for Schelling a kind of presentation or representation: it exposes or gives to be seen, it stages in the proper sense (*Darstellung*) the tragic process, that is, the conflictual process at the heart of which—at the end of which—freedom and necessity become identical with one another, in a sudden flash before our eyes, as they have been identical from the beginning in the absolute itself. The ninth *Letter* had, moreover, reaffirmed this identity in principle:

> He who has reflected upon freedom and necessity will have discovered on his own that these principles must necessarily be united in the absolute:—freedom because the absolute acts in function of its unconditional self-empowerment;—necessity because the absolute can act only in conformity with the laws of its essence. In the absolute, there is no room for any will susceptible of straying from a law, but no room either for any law which it wouldn't first have given to itself through its actions, for any law which would retain any reality independent of these actions themselves. Absolute freedom and absolute necessity are identical. (I, 3, 107)

But despite this identity in principle, what justifies the permanence of tragic representation is still the "work" (*ergon*) which this representation properly accomplishes: to make manifest, at the very heart of the most extreme inner conflict, and when all seems definitively lost, the possibility of a superior identification. What made the contradictions of which their tragedies were woven bearable to the Greeks was not principally some "effect" of restored harmony or the purification of certain affects which would permit one to substitute pleasure for painful emotions, but, more fundamentally, the fact that the spectator's catharsis points to this reconciliation which is at work in tragedy itself, a reconciliation of which tragedy constitutes, as it were, the unequalled *event*. One can thus understand better why such an interpretation, centered from the first on tragic *action* (the *drama*), should necessarily and in the same gesture underscore the unsurpassable limits of all presentation of this type: *they are the limits of art*. For the spectacle of tragedy is always *illusory*: it anticipates in effect the absolute—and asymptotic—(re)unification of antagonistic terms, whatever one wishes to call them: freedom-necessity, finitude-infinitude, Ego-absolute object.

This is why one can ask oneself if, in the complex economy of the *Letters*, the interpretation of Greek tragedy does not represent the aesthetico-positive flip side of the Spinozist illusion; if, in other words—this time words taken from Hölderlin—tragedy ought not to be considered as "the metaphor of an intellectual intuition."[11] But let's return for a moment to Spinoza, the eponymous hero of thoroughgoing and fully coherent dogmatism. Spinoza took his departure from an experience the immediacy or originarity of which could not be placed in question, the experience of "self-intuition" (*Selbstanschauung*). It is in this intuition of the self by the self—which by definition can only be an intellectual intuition[12]—that the Ego identifies itself, assures itself of its proper selfhood. "This intellectual intuition produces itself," Schelling writes, "when we cease to be an object for ourselves, whenever the intuitive Self, going back into itself, becomes identical with what it intuits" (I, 3, 88). This intellectual intuition, which can be produced only through freedom, permits us to gain access to what *is* "in the proper sense of the term," and with respect to which "all the rest is but *appearance*." Spinoza's error consisted, as we know, in objectifying this intuition of the absolute in himself. He did not recognize that through this intuition, which is like the tangential point of the finite Ego and the absolute Ego, the absolute became identical to him. He believed, to the contrary, that it was he who was becoming identical to the absolute, and he accepted, in accordance with this presupposition, the idea of self-destruction. In doing so, he fell victim to a general illusion, in any case an illusion held in common by all *Schwärmer* and nearly impossible to uproot: the illusion that consists in surreptitiously putting one's Ego in the place of the absolute in order to make acceptable to oneself precisely the idea of one's own disappearance, one's own annihilation in the absolute object.

One might ask oneself, returning now to tragedy, whether the tragic hero does not proceed to a substitution of the same order when he voluntarily accepts to take onto himself without reserve crimes imposed by destiny and, struggling nonetheless against the inexorable, to be frightfully punished for what comes properly speaking from *Fatum* itself. By identifying thus with what is fated, by refusing to allow certain of his actions to be dissociated from himself, that is, by boldly laying claim to the ultimate and unforeseeable consequences of these actions, the tragic hero, because he means to speak always on his own behalf, loses and gains in one stroke the absoluteness of his freedom.

Just as a *Schwärmer* would have had difficulty being satisfied with the idea of his own disappearance into the abyss of the divine if he had not always already put his own Ego in the place of God, the tragic hero has been able to suffer his punishment only by condemning himself and by inflicting upon himself, as Oedipus did, the most terrible of punishments (blindness, exile, wandering in the midst of the unthinkable).

To be sure, as Schelling strongly underscores:

> In this intellectual state which Spinoza described in accordance with the testimony of his self-intuition, all conflict within us is supposed to disappear, all struggle, even the most noble, the struggle of morality, is supposed to end, and all the contradictions that sense and reason inevitably create between morality and happiness are supposed to be resolved. (I, 3, 91)

Of course, tragic drama does not involve exactly the same thing. Indeed, the situation is, if you will, exactly the inverse: only in absolute dissonance, at the heart of the most unbearable dissymmetry between happiness and merit, can the hero—painfully exposed to the blows of fate, but refusing them all the more resolutely any passive stance—rediscover, that is, reconquer—even if most often at the price of his loss or complete self-forfeiture—the *harmonia aphanes* evoked by Heraclitus's Fragment 54. In nearly the same epoch, in the Homburg essays, and in particular in his study "On the Difference of Poetic Modes," Hölderlin sought to conjugate, under the title of the "harmonically opposed," on the one hand, the *Fühlbarkeit des Ganzen* ("the capacity of the whole to be felt" or "the feelability of the whole") and, on the other hand, the secession of one "part" which, preyed upon by the "excess of in-tensity" (*Übermass der Innigkeit) or the "excess of uni-city" (Übermass der Einigkeit*), excessively individualizes itself. Such a separation cannot however disturb or dislocate the harmonic integrity of the whole, for it is solely due to a separation of this sort—the absolute laceration of which the hero is the victim—that the whole can return upon itself, accede to its highest, most comprehensive uni-totality, and give way to the "infinite cohesion or context" (*unendlicher Zusammenhang*), where parts and whole can be felt with an equal vivacity. But again in order for this to take place, the part must suffer, endure unity (*Einigkeit*); properly tragic *pathos* is always that of *Vereinzelung*, isolation, solitude, and concentration upon oneself to the point of the most extreme dissidence.[13]

One could thus risk the thesis that for Schelling tragic illusion—for in tragedy too it is certainly a matter of illusion—would be the inverse, the symmetrical negation of the Spinozist illusion: tragedy also would consist in the objectivation of an intellectual intuition.

To be sure, one will have to wait for the *System of Transcendental Idealism* to see Schelling define in these terms—without explicit reference to tragedy—the work of art and the specific intuition that corresponds to it: "This universally recognized and absolutely undeniable objectivity of the intellectual intuition is art itself. The aesthetic intuition, in fact, is precisely the intellectual intuition become objective."[14] Nothing however forbids us to think that in the course of the analysis of Greek tragedy, in the last of the *Letters* of 1795, this idea already came to light which could not be retained in the context of the *Letters*: the idea that beyond the apparently unsurpassable alternative of dogmatism or criticism, tragedy was or had been able to represent—and precisely solely in the space of re-presentation—an attempted aesthetic conciliation of the two diametrically opposed imperatives—the imperative of dogmatism: "Annihilate yourself! Behave in a purely and simply passive manner vis-à-vis absolute causality!" and the imperative of criticism: "Be!"[15]

Thus, this first interpretation of the tragic phenomenon already points—precisely by way of the aesthetic sphere, and thanks to an aesthetic version of the intellectual intuition—in the direction of the philosophy of identity. A first landmark, a first stone will have been thereby placed to be built upon later in a reconstructive or retrospective mode.

And in fact, some years later, in the *Lectures on the Philosophy of Art*, Schelling will reassert his earlier interpretation, and in nearly the same words. But of course, it is to this "nearly" that we shall have to pay particularly close attention.

In the *Lectures* of Jena and Würzburg, Schelling sketches out his interpretation of tragedy and the tragic in the frame of an analytic of the sublime. The point ought to be emphasized, for Schelling here parts company with Kant,[16], who had illustrated his definition of the sublime (mathematical and dynamic) only with examples taken from the natural sphere. In contrast, Schiller—whom Schelling follows closely here—although he too seeks to discover the ultimate foundation of the natural sublime, seeks further to discover the similarities and differences between the natural sublime and its historical counterpart.

Schelling's analysis of the sublime presupposes the determination of at least two concepts which I shall have to present very quickly here: the concept of genius (already at the center of the study of art and its production in the *System of Transcendental Idealism*) and the concept of poetry.

Schelling instructs us in §63 that one can call genius "the eternal concept of man in God," insofar as it is permissible to consider the genius as "the immediate cause of his productions." To be sure, it is man who effectively produces, but man apprehended as that which, within him, is more than himself, man apprehended in his concept such as he is present in God himself. In other words, the genius can be seen as "the divine immanent in man"—the divine which is inherent in man or inhabits[17] man—and which constitutes a kind of "fragment of the absoluteness of God."

The second concept we have to confront before proceeding to Schelling's analytic of the sublime is more difficult and surprising in various respects. Schelling opposes in fact "poetry," in the strict sense, to "art" (or better: to what he calls *die Kunst der Kunst*, the essence of art, that which, in art, is properly art or artistic). As for poetry, it represents "the real side of genius"; it is at the basis of the "information" or "uniformation"—"esemplasis," if one follows Coleridge's[18] lead—of the infinite in the finite. To this staging or imaging of the infinite responds, on the ideal side, the uniformation of the finite in the infinite, the principle of which is art.

One will note that in the definition of the two latter—complementary rather than antagonistic—concepts, the schema of *mimesis* seems to have no place. Schelling takes equal care to cut short all allegorical interpretation of the relations between the finite and the infinite: insofar as the infinite has been incorporated into the finite to the point of no longer being distinct from it (*Ineinsbildung*), the finite becomes truly independent, "consistent" (*etwas für sich Bestehendes*): it attains the status of Being/Essence (*Wesen*) in itself. And as such, it is what "no longer merely means something else," what no longer points or refers to anything exterior to itself. One must recall that in the background of this absolutization of the work, apprehended in its essentiality, there stands K. P. Moritz's truly inaugural essay "On the Formative Imitation of the Beautiful."[19] "It is the absolute itself," Schelling concludes, "which gives an independent life to the ideas of things present within it, by informing them eternally into finitude [*Endlichkeit*]."

It is in terms of these two different types of possible unity—the infinite incorporated into the finite, and the finite incorporated into the infinite—that Schelling distinguishes between *sublimity* and *beauty*: "The first unity, that which consists in the uniformation (*Einbildung*) of *the infinite into the finite*, finds its privileged expression in the work of art as sublimity; the second, that which consists in *the uniformation of the finite into the infinite*, as beauty." An object or action will thus be qualified as sublime when they are susceptible, precisely as finite beings, of taking the infinite into themselves; when they are properly, and in spite of their finitude, *capable of infinitude*, and this in such a manner that the infinite proceeds from and in the finite, that the infinite presents itself there in its difference (or differentiation), its pure alterity.

Having recalled these principal distinctions, we can leave aside the details of Schelling's analytic of the beautiful, in order to follow him in his study of the sublime, which begins in turn with a preliminary distinction: the sublime proceeds either from nature or from *Gesinnung*—which we can translate as *ethos* ("character").

In his analysis of the sublime—as I have pointed out—Schelling often depends rather heavily on Schiller, and in particular on the essay of 1793, "Über das Erhabene," published first in 1801. One cannot insist too strongly, however, on the capital importance of the beginning of this tradition in Kant, principally for all that concerns the connection between the problematic of the sublime and the question of the *destiny of man*.

> Therefore the feeling of the sublime in nature is respect for our own destiny, which, by a certain subreption, we attribute to an object of nature (conversion of respect for the idea of humanity in our own subject into respect for the object). This makes intuitively evident the superiority of the rational determination of our cognitive faculties to the greatest faculty of sensibility. (§27, 96; 96)

From Schiller, Schelling borrows what one can call his predetermination of the sublime. Freely paraphrasing Schiller,[20] Schelling indicates that the sublime of nature appears to us first of all wherever a sensible object is "offered" to us (*dargeboten*) which exceeds our "power of apprehension" (*Fassungskraft*) because it is incommensurable with this power. In other words, we experience sublimity when "our force [*Kraft*], insofar as we are living beings, is opposed to a natural power [*Macht*] in comparison with which [*gegen welche*] our force disappears into its own nothingness." That which, in nature, appears as the "incommensurable" (Schelling had said *Übermacht* in the *Letters*) not only causes our capacity of apprehension to fail but also manifests the comparative emptiness of our power insofar as we are merely and first of all living beings.

But this is only the first aspect—call it the negative aspect—of the feeling of the sublime that natural phenomena awaken in us. Schelling continues:

> The intuition of the sublime truly appears only when sensible intuition proves to be inadequate to the greatness of the sensible object, and now [as in a second phase which we distinguish abstractly] the true infinite stands forth [*hervortritt*], for which the former merely sensible infinite becomes the symbol....The sublime...is a subjection which betrays [in other words, lets appear, gives to be seen—if it were here a question of the view or vision] the infinite by means of the true infinite.

The sensible infinite—that which reveals itself to us at first as the incommensurable—is thus in reality only the mask of the true infinite which, as such, remains unseizable. Through the sublime, the infinite reveals itself in its double visage. It is actually more a matter here of transfiguration or 'transverberation' than of disguise or dissimulation. In fact, the sensible infinite hides nothing but rather translates or betrays what one must always decipher obliquely. For "there can be no more complete intuition of the infinite than where the symbol in which it is intuited hypocritically lays a finite claim to infinitude [*in seiner Endlichkeit die Unendlichkeit heuchelt*]" (I, 5, 462). Or again, to formulate differently this central thesis: there is properly speaking no absolute intuition or intuition of the absolute. Certainly, the absolute gives itself, offers itself to us—its essence consists in this gift itself—but always in the shadow or mirror of the sensible and, in reality, of the finite. The spectator who contemplates "that which, beyond him, is always relatively great," discovers therein, by means of the feeling of the sublime, "the mirror in which he glimpses [*erblickt*] the absolutely great, the infinite in and for itself" (I, 5, 463). Schelling is freely quoting Schiller here again, but modifying Schiller's text in an extremely important way, as Dieter Jähnig has perspicaciously underscored.[21] Whereas Schiller indicated in effect that in the experience of the sublime the relatively great becomes the mirror in which the spectator "glimpses the absolutely great in itself" [*in ihm selbst*], Schelling erases this reference to the subject which, since Kant, has been inscribed in the very definition of the sublime: it is the infinite "in and for itself" (*an und für sich selbst*) that appears in the contemplation of the sublime which Schiller had already called—but without drawing all the consequences—*absolute Contemplation.* Such a contemplation induces an "elevation of freedom" (*Erhebung der Freiheit*) which, delivered of all positive or negative interest in the object (fear, anxiety, desire, will to appropriation), attains to the "superior intuition" of the nonobjective and nonobjectifiable and thus attains at one stroke a glimpse of the coming to pass of the absolute. This "superior intuition" (*höhere Anschauung*) Schelling also calls an "aesthetic intuition" (I, 5, 463).

One can thus, it seems to me, follow D. Jähnig when he notes that what radically separates Schelling's analysis from its Kantian-Schillerian point of departure is that for Schelling the sublime intuition does not relativize merely objectivity (the greatness that reveals itself to be simply relative, even if it at first gave itself to be incommensurable) but also the subjectivity of the very intuiting subject, to the extent that Schelling is concerned with the absolute *in and for itself*. It is, in any case, always freedom that emerges victorious from the experience of the sublime, but from Schelling's perspective, human freedom thus exalted offers something like the first fruits of absolute freedom.

One can see further from this example the importance of the function of objectivation or, better, the veritative, "epiphanic" function of the work of art, once the sublime has ceased to belong essentially and above all to the domain of nature and of great natural manifestations: the starry sky, the storm, the unleashed ocean—these are the privileged examples on which Kant's interpretation rested. The study of the sublime—as opposed to the study of beauty—marks for Schelling no return to the subject, to the subjectivity of the subject who judges aesthetically, even in those passages where the analysis is explicitly concerned with the effect produced on the spectator.[22] If in fact, as the *System* of 1800 instructs, beauty and sublimity both rest on the same initial contradiction (*Widerspruch*), which is suddenly transformed into an "unexpected harmony," what properly characterizes the sublime is uniquely the *site* or the *place* within which this process of the reconciliation, the harmonic resolution of contradiction—the "intuiting subject" itself—comes to pass. This point is particularly important, especially when one thinks of the tragic work as exemplification of sublimity. The spectator—that is, the "intuiting subject" (I, 3, 620–21), which is here concretely the "public"—in fact, immediately finds itself implicated in the work itself and its achievement. The public participates (i.e., it actually takes part) in the "representation" or the "execution" of the work, which fully exists only through a complex process in which staging, effectuation, play, and so on, are necessarily also involved.

The intuition of the sublime remains necessarily an "aesthetic" or sensible "intuition" for another reason: as we have just seen, the absolutely infinite—in and for itself—does not offer itself directly but only through the mediation of the symbol or the mirror of the sensible (the relatively great). Schelling clearly recognizes that "This intuition of the sublime is in spite of its relation and its affinity with the ideal and the ethical, an aesthetic intuition, to use here for once this term" (I, 5, 463). Doubtless this strangely concessive formulation ought to give one pause. It raises the question of whether this remark is the mere restatement of the thesis from the *System of Transcendental Idealism* which posited that "the aesthetic intuition is nothing but the transcendental [intellectual] intuition." But let us leave the question open and pursue our examination of Schelling's analysis as it unfolds within the horizon of identity. To be sure, the infinite dominates unconditionally, reigns as sole lord, but nonetheless, it can "unfold its reign as lord only to the extent that it is intuited in a sensible infinitude which, as sensible, is always also a finitude" (I, 5, 463). Schelling can thus conclude, by invoking the concept of *poetry* he has already elaborated,[23] and by keeping in view the idea of human destiny: "To intuit the true infinite in the infinite of nature—this is the *poetry* which man is in a position to practice universally; for it is the intuiting one himself for whom the relatively great in nature becomes sublime as he takes it for a symbol of the absolutely great." We can omit consideration here of Schelling's analysis of the relation, and finally the identity, between beauty and sublimity (§66), since their opposition is simply quantitative rather than qualitative, to the extent that the beautiful and the sublime both constitute "a differentiated unification of the infinite with the finite." What it is instead important to emphasize, however, is the continuity of this determination with the determination in the *System* of 1800, where beauty was already defined as "finite presentation [*Darstellung*] of the infinite" (I, 3, 620). And it was precisely this deictic (expositional or demonstrative) function which, in the *System*, justified the privileged role of art for any philosophical enterprise. If philosophy has had to—and still has to—turn resolutely to the work of art and to what this work contains, it is because in the work the consciousness of the absolute comes to light, or better: because in the work the absolute *comes to pass*. The work is in its ground an *event*, the *absolute* event.

In the *Lectures* on the philosophy of art, Schelling paradoxically does not refer—as he did at the end of the *System* of 1800—to the "product of art" (*Kunstprodukt*) as "product" in order to define the essence and character of art but rather to the idea of chaos,[24] which serves as the transition from the sublime of nature to the sublime of art and to the sublime of the pinnacle of art: tragedy. "Nature," Schelling in fact remarks, "is sublime not merely with regard to its greatness, which is inaccessible to our faculty of apprehension, or to its power, which is invincible to our physical force, but also in a general way as chaos, or as Schiller also puts it, as the disorder [*Verwirrung*] of its phenomena in general." Schelling, who refers here explicitly to Schiller (I, 5, 463), might just as well have referred to Kant, who in the third *Critique* himself evoked chaotic nature as what eminently arouses in us the idea of the sublime: "But in what we are accustomed to call sublime there is nothing at all that leads to particular objective principles and forms of nature corresponding to them; so far from it that, for the most part, nature excites the ideas of the sublime in its chaos or in its wildest and most irregular disorder and desolation, provided size and might are perceived" (§23, 86; 84).

Schelling thus places the intuition of chaos itself—as *Grundan-schauung*—at the foundation of the intuition of the absolute: the absolute offers itself to us intuitively—*in nature as in history*—only in the deformed form of the chaotic. In fact, he goes so far as to say: "the intimate essence of the absolute, in which all reposes as unity and where the unity is all, is originary chaos itself." What presents itself initially as pure disorder or inextricable confusion reveals in reality, when it is a matter of the absolute itself in its irreducible nonobjectivity, the identity of form and "formlessness" (*Formlosigkeit*).

But this explanation of the idea of the sublime in terms of the fundamental intuition of chaos itself has decisive importance principally because this explanation renders comprehensible the nature and specificity of the second—and doubtless the most elevated—figure of the sublime: the sublime of *Gesinnung*. Here too, Schelling depends on Schiller, who had remarked in his essay "On the Sublime": the one who, in the face of the world as it is, wishes that all were organized in accordance with a wise economy (a domestic economy so to speak), has no hope of seeing his desire satisfied except in another existence; but inversely, "if he renounces willingly [*gutwillig*] the claim to submit the chaos of phenomena, rebellious against all law, to the unity of a knowledge, he thereby gains on another side more than all that he has lost" (614–15; 146). The intuition of the sublime at the very heart of the most chaotic arises thus from an economy more complicated than that to which the vulgar understanding and vulgar knowledge have accustomed us. This economy is a new economy in which gain does not simply equal loss but reveals itself to be without any common measure with the latter. It is this economic perspective—and it alone—which opens access to universal history in its extreme sublimity. Schiller writes: "Considered from this angle, universal history is for me a sublime object" (615; 147).

But what new insight does the consideration of "universal history" (*Weltgeschichte*) provide with respect to the general problematic of the sublime? Nothing less than this: the upheaval or insurrection of freedom in its struggle against natural forces. Nature and History, rigorously articulated, comprise the theater in which freedom can come into play and inaugurate its unfolding. Schiller clarifies: "The world, as historical object, is fundamentally nothing other than the conflict of natural forces [*Naturkräfte*] among themselves and with human freedom; it belongs to history to introduce us to the issue of this combat." But once freedom has directly come on stage, the spectacle offered us is incomparably more interesting—and of course it is the interest of reason that is here engaged—than all that the natural sublime had to offer, even as symbol of the infinite. In a sense, freedom, in its radical historicity, constitutes a permanent factor of disorder and disequilibrium; it engenders contradictions, foments conflicts, and can even lead to sufferings the translation of which is only too real, only too painfully tangible. However, "it procures us"—at least if we regard it with a "noble heart"—"a spectacle infinitely more interesting than that of tranquility and order deprived of freedom" (615; 147).

Indeed, Schiller goes one step further, assigning to history or, if one prefers, to the philosophical consideration of *Weltgeschichte*, an utterly specific mode of intelligibility which is supposed to put an end even to the illusory pretentions of reason when reason wishes to make the world coincide with its own practical imperatives:

> If one approaches history only in the expectation of light and knowledge, to what disappointment does one not expose oneself? All the well-intentioned attempts of philosophy to harmonize what the moral world requires with what the world effectively produces in reality are refuted by the lessons of experience....But what a difference, when one renounces explanation of these events, and when one regulates one's judgment in terms of this incomprehensibility [*Unbegreiflichkeit*] which properly belongs to them!

From the perspective of a "philosophical" consideration of history, Schiller formulates here as neatly as one could wish something like the matrix of the new interpretation of tragedy Schelling will expose: concerning universal history, renouncing explanation or ethical instruction does not, of course, mean renouncing reason itself. To the contrary, to adopt in one's judgments the point of view of *inconceivability* is to make the *identity* emerge that obtains between the phenomenal confusion, the disorder of the world as it is, and a rationality of a different order. To the one who is capable of elevating himself or herself to the *höhere Anschauung* evoked above, this rationality reveals the secret identity of the absolute and chaos.

Schelling will consequently have no difficulty whatsoever in transposing Schiller's lesson from the level of history to that of tragedy (*mythos*—"history," "narrative," or "intrigue"). He tells us that it is in fact "the intuition of chaos which induces the passage to the knowledge of the absolute." The understanding can decide to *take the inconceivable as its principle*, and that means—in the very terms of Schiller—"to adopt in one's judgments the point of view of inconceivability." This is, as Schelling clarifies further, "the first step leading to philosophy, or at least to the *aesthetic intuition of the world*." And in this latter formulation, one must understand by "world" both nature and *Weltgeschichte* or, in general, the *drama* in which freedom comes on stage. In order to attain this intellectual intuition of the world, in the most general sense, common sense or the understanding must radically overturn their habitual perspectives: the method of the understanding, always in quest of a new "condition," has as its ultimate goal the deduction of phenomena from each other. But here each phenomenon or "natural phenomenon" (*Natur-erscheinung*) affirms itself as totally autonomous, independent of all others. The phenomenon to which the aesthetic intuition opens itself is initially free of all fetters, a stranger to all laws, and characterized above all by its absoluteness. *Ungebundenheit, Gesetzlosigkeit, Unabhängigkeit, Absolutheit*—these are the traits that keep the vulgar understanding definitively at bay. This understanding thus has no way out other than by "recognizing the world as the true symbol [*Sinnbild*] of reason—in which all is unconditioned—and of the absolute—in which all is free and without constraint" (I, 5, 466).

From the sublime of (universal) history to the sublime of *Gesinnung*, which will take us back to tragedy, it is easy to proceed, for as Schelling strongly emphasizes: "the one in whom the sublime of *Gesinnung* is manifest can serve at the same time as a symbol for all of history." If, considered as a whole, and thus in its already chaotic figure, nature obeys rules and laws which are loose enough to preserve in themselves at least an "appearance" (*Schein*) of anarchy or independence with respect to general laws, opening thus a first glimpse of the aesthetic intuition, the world of history appears, in turn, disconnected once and for all from any "conformity to law" (*Gesetz-mäßigkeit*).

How can the chaos thus raised to its highest pitch reveal itself to be in a primordial identity with pure, serene, absolute rationality? With that rationality which, far from drowning all things in a lifeless nondifferentiation, grants to all of this Being-there its disconnectedness and its proper divinity?[25] Through tragedy, exemplarily, wherein the most opposed and conflictual extremes—freedom *and* necessity—are reconciled. It falls in fact to tragedy to manifest majestically the "historical" sublime of character, of "ethos" (*Gesinnung*), by showing the definitive victory of the *moralische Gesinnung*.

In the attempted a priori deduction of the poetic genres that the *Philosophy of Art* exposes in its "specific part" (*Besonderer Theil*), Schelling reaffirms the privilege of the tragic poem over the other genres (epic and lyric), a privilege essentially linked to the sublimity of the tragic poem. The tragic poem, for all that it is a drama (*Drama*), does not simply represent the synthesis of epic and lyric, but constitutes "the highest manifestation of art." As we have seen, drama is the *essential* phenomenon of art (I, 5, 690). Why? Because only the dramatic synthesis can shed light on and elevate to its highest power the fundamental conflict or antagonism between the infinite and the finite. This antagonism is expressed on the level of art, as we've seen, through the irreducible opposition between necessity and freedom.[26] In lyric poetry, the conflict and its resolution take place in the subject itself: hence, it is a matter of a *subjective* reconciliation of the antagonism between these two principles. In epic poetry, the accord between necessity and freedom is in a sense anterior to all differentiation: it manifests itself through the success of the undertaking, even if thus a place is left for chance. Necessity never shows itself here in the inexorable figure of destiny. Only in the tragic process can freedom and necessity emerge *as such*. But in order to emerge as such, the one and the other must appear at the end of the process in their equality and equilibrium. Thus, what is staged and exposed in the tragic is a combat in which irreducible and equally powerful adversaries confront one another. The combat must precisely present to the view *the equlibrium between freedom and necessity*. However, as Schelling emphasizes, "there is not true combat, if the possibility of winning does not exist on both sides." But is such a possibility conceivable when one knows in advance that each of the protagonists is profoundly invincible?

On the one hand, there is no question of defeating necessity, for a necessity one could beat would thereby cease to be necessary. On the other hand, there is also no question of defeating freedom, for it belongs to its essence to be invincible—at least if it wishes to remain free! In the face of this untenable alternative, there is no way out other than by reaffirming the contradiction in its pure state: both freedom and necessity must emerge from the combat as at once vanquished and victorious, in other words, as equals. This is what Schelling loudly declares:

> Such is doubtless the highest manifestation [*Erscheinung*] of art: that freedom should be elevated to equality with necessity, and that necessity in turn, without losing any of its absoluteness, should appear the equal of freedom; only through such a relation [*Verhältnis*] does this true and absolute indifference become objective which is in the absolute and does not rest on its simultaneity [*zugleichsein*] but on its equality [*gleichsein*]. (I, 5, 690)

Proceeding deductively, Schelling poses the question of the possibility-conditions of this *Verhältnis*, this strange relation of "equalization" where necessity wins without freedom succumbing and where, in turn, freedom can win without necessity being simply defeated. The answer leaves no room for doubt: only human nature—or better, the individuals who heroically represent human nature—can furnish the conditions of possibility of this singular game of he-who-wins-loses.

> It is only in human nature that the conditions can be found under which it is possible that necessity should win without freedom succumbing, and inversely that freedom should be victorious without interrupting the course [*Gang*] of necessity. The same person who succumbs to necessity can elevate himself anew above the latter by virtue of his *Gesinnung* ["spiritual disposition," "force of character," or "generosity"] so that the one and the other (necessity and freedom), at once vanquished and victorious, manifest themselves in their supreme indifference.

It is human nature, then, that constitutes the unique "means" (*Mittel*)—instrument, medium—of "presentation" (*Darstellung*) of this complex relation of mutual belonging.

Thus, Schelling takes up again, and nearly word for word (I, 5, 696–97), the interpretation of *Oedipus Rex* he had sketched some years earlier in the *Letters*, but this interpretation has nonetheless radically altered its sense, precisely as a function of this "framing" on which I have insisted at some length: the analytic of the sublime, the specific sublimity of *Gesinnung*, and the fundamental intuition of the absolute as chaos.

That which, in the *Letters*, was clearly situated *within the limits of art* and could appear necessary to the complete elucidation of human destiny, now fulfills a decisive function with regard to the absolute itself: the tragic poem has become a poem of identity or identification: freedom and necessity, in fact, identify themselves and each other in it [*s'y identifient en effet, et cela dans tous les sens du terme*]. They unveil their true identity and recognize themselves each for itself and the one through the other, the one in and across the other, while they render apparent or transparent the supreme identity, the indifference in which they finally come together and are reconciled.

Doubtless, a more speculative—"speculative" in the proper sense—interpretation of tragedy has never been proposed. But such an interpretation manifests equally at what point the philosophy of so-called identity can find its ultimate completion in a philosophy of art in which intellectual intuition and aesthetic intuition approach each other to the point of coinciding: a philosophy of art the cornerstone of which remains the concept of *Darstellung*, the final avatar of Platonic-Aristotelian mimesis. This exposition, this staging culminates, in turn, in the (necessarily tragic) presentation of the nonpresentable, of the absolute "itself," such as it offers itself to us, through the experience of the sublime, as chaos and/or as drama.

Chapter 8

❀

ON A TOWER OF BABEL
IN A PAINTING BY POUSSIN

Louis Marin

Hence can be explained what Savary remarks, in his *Lettres sur l'Egypte*, that we must keep from going very near the Pyramids just as much as we keep from going too far from them, in order to get the full emotional effect of their size. For if we are too far away, the parts to be apprehended (the stones lying one over the other) are only obscurely represented, and the representation of them produces no effect upon the aesthetic judgment of the subject. But if we are very near, the eye requires some time to complete the apprehension of the tiers from the bottom up to the apex, and then the first tiers are always partly forgotten before the imagination has taken in the last, and so the comprehension of them is never complete. The same thing may sufficiently explain the bewilderment or, as it were, perplexity which it is said seizes the spectator on his first entrance into St. Peter's in Rome. For there is here a feeling of the inadequacy of his imagination for presenting the ideas of the whole, wherein the imagination reaches its maximum, and, in striving to surpass it, sinks back into itself, but is thereby displaced into a moving satisfaction. (*CJ*, §26, 91; 90–91)

In the background of a painting by Poussin, *Landscape with Pyramus and Thisbe*, today at the Frankfurt Museum, one finds a strange edifice.[1] It is situated on a plain surrounded by a circle of mountains, which the gaze of the spectator discovers between a hill surmounted by a castle on the left and

177

buildings and monuments of a large city on the right. This edifice is illumi-
nated by the light of a sun absent from the painting, but which one divines to
the west, bronzing with its rays the incidental details of the terrain in the background. If one examines it closely, one notices that the edifice is rather
strange: compared to the castle and the city, it seems ruined. One can discern,
on two stories, an arcade with seven arches and, attached to this arcade, a
multi-leveled structure rising obliquely up to some remains of a wall: a hesita-
tion between vestige or ruin, and incompletion or interruption. Scanning
Poussin's *œuvre*, the spectator finds without difficulty castles, farms, towers,
dwellings, temples, and tombs, but no other example of the edifice at the back
of this painting: at most a drawing which the master may have executed, a
view of the Roman coliseum.[2]

The *Landscape with Pyramus and Thisbe*, painted in 1651 for Cassiano
del Pozzo, is itself relatively uncommon: it represents a storm. This seems at
least to be the "subject" of the painting, judging by what the gaze confronts:
two flashes of diffuse lightning cut across a sky of ink, a lightning-bolt strikes a
tree in the background, a furious wind, blowing from left to right, stirs trees
and bushes. Poussin himself confirms that the "subject" of the painting is
indeed a storm when he writes about it to Jacques Stella: "I have attempted to
represent a storm on earth, imitating as best I could the effect of an impetuous
wind." Pursuing the description of his picture, he inscribes in this attempt to
represent the tempest, in the background, a lion's attack on shepherds and
their flocks in flight, and finishes his letter by naming the two figures of the
foreground. In the final analysis, it is their names that give the work its name:
"And in the front of the picture, one sees Pyramus stretched out dead upon
the ground and next to him Thisbe abandoned to her sadness."[3]

Thus, a tempest on the earth, this doubled stroke of lightning, this wind,
and these swirling clouds of dust, but also the lion's attack, and Thisbe's abandonment to her sadness at discovering—dead—the body of her beloved:
meteorological, animal, and human tempests; level by level, the atmospheric
movements and their effects are consonant with those of instinct and those of
passion: nature, animal, man. But with the latter, (hi)story (*storia*) enters the
scene—at the front of the picture. It is figured by these two separated lovers
whom only death can re-unite. At the back of the picture—outside of the tempest but perhaps also as the tempest's cultural emblem—a vast edifice, ruined
or interrupted, is at once the document—the archive—and the monument of
this (hi)story.

However, the subject of the tempest has its own history within the history of the art of painting and representation which marks the myth of its origin and, as it were, its transcendental limit.[4] In book 35 of his *Natural History*,
Pliny tells us that Apelles—who is for modern artists, as is well known, the
originary hero of mimesis (along with Zeuxis and Parrhasios), despite the fact
that the works of these originary heroes can only be "seen" in the form of writ-

ten descriptions—that Apelles succeeded in representing what cannot be represented: flashes and bolts of lightning, thunder, in a word, the—*nonrepresentable*[5]—tempest. This renders comprehensible the master's humility when he states to Stella both his intention to paint a tempest and the distance mimesis takes from itself when it reaches its limit: "I have *attempted* to represent...imitating *as best I could*."

In "the front of the picture, one sees Pyramus...dead...and Thisbe abandoned to her sadness"—in the front of the picture, but in the last sentence of its description,[6] i.e., at once as its *fullest measure* and as its *supplement*,[7] comes the literary reference, the names of the actors of a story in its *dénouement*, the name of the picture: Pyramus and Thisbe. A story told by Ovid in his *Metamorphoses*:[8] two lovers, whom the mutual hatred of their families separates to the point where they can communicate only through the chink of a wall, which prevents them from seeing each other, decide to flee from the town in order to meet, at night, near the tomb and the spring indicated by a mulberry tree with fruits the color of snow. Thisbe arrives first, but she sees a lion, its jaws bloody from the carnage that it has just made of a flock of sheep. She runs to hide in a nearby grotto, but while fleeing, she drops her veil, which the beast tears to pieces and covers with blood. Pyramus arrives, discovers the bloody veil: Thisbe is dead, he thinks. He kills himself. Thisbe, the danger having passed, leaves her hideout to find the body of her beloved at the base of the mulberry tree where they were to have met. She kills herself. The blood of the two young people mingles finally in death and stains red the roots of the tree: its white berries turn black.

Rereading Ovid in terms of Poussin's letter, or rather rereading Poussin's painting in terms of this rereading, one realizes that the tomb[9] is the tomb of Ninus and that the town from which the lovers flee is the town of Semiramis, Babylon. In an instant, passing from the foreground to the extreme background, one discovers that the *colosseo*, the colossal edifice which had been so intriguing, is the ruin of the long-since interrupted construction of the tower of Babel.[10] Thus, in the—nonrepresentable—representation of a tempest on earth, several stories—the story of an original fulfillment of representation in painting and the story of an original fulfillment of languages, but also a story of love and death and a story of a metamorphosis—intermingle and intersect.

A word on the metamorphosis: it concerns the unhappy lovers only indirectly, commemorates only their disastrous destiny, and their mingled blood is merely an instrument. By means of them, the white fruit of the mulberry tree has become black. This metamorphosis does however directly concern the painter; it is the allegory of a genesis of colors between two contraries, white—the universal color of light, the absolute medium of visibility, the synthesis of the totality of mixed colors—and black—the noncolor of night and nonvisibility. But the passage from light to the night, from white to black can only take place as mediated by the color of blood, the united blood of Pyramus and Thisbe, red of death's violence, one of the three cardinal colors. The painting thus tells also this story of color in general by telling the story of Pyramus and Thisbe, but as an inverted genesis, a palingenesis,[11] that of the absorption of light into the night by means of blood, the story, if you will, of the destruction of painting and its vision[12] by the representation of the tempest as the nonrepresentable par excellence. It is this story that will be told in its way by the story of Pyramus and Thisbe, on the edges of Babylon, and in the foreground of a painting the background of which presents to the view the enigma of a ruined, interrupted tower, a tower the name of which—Babel— will be superimposed upon the image of the Roman Coliseum.

Thus, the threads of multiple stories are interwoven here: the pictorial mimesis of the tempest, the Ovidian metamorphosis of white into black, oriental Babylon and ancient Rome, the dramatic pastoral of the shepherds attacked by the lion, and the passionate tragedy of the lovers. These stories have in common that they all tell at once the origin and the end, the commencement and the termination, the foundation and the possibility, united and separated at their limits: the origin of representation and its end in the nonrepresentable instance of the natural storm; the origin and the end of all color, white and its negation in black; the beginning of loves and their end in death; the foundation and the possibility of the project of all architecture where the ruin is a design and the trace a monument, Orient and Occident mixed and separated forever. Of all these stories, all of which for Poussin basically tell the same story, the spectator, in accordance with his or her vision or meditative contemplation, can choose—in the diverse parts of the painting or on its diverse levels—the emblems, allegories, and symbols that reciprocally respond to, emblematize, allegorize, and symbolize one another.[13]

Thus, the three storms—the meteorological, animal, and human— express one another reciprocally, or better, they represent each other so completely in their direct or inverted correspondences that there occurs in the work a presentation of the nonrepresentable. Thus, the blasted tree perpendicular to the body of the dead Pyramus; thus, the glow from the lightning-bolt which figuratively strikes Thisbe with its arrow and illuminates her with its instantaneous brilliance; thus the black of the grotto and the spring, the obscurities of the stormy sky, the blinding whites of the sheets of lightning over the town and over the protagonists of the drama, and the reds of the shepherds' coats, of the cavalier galloping on his horse, or of the bloody reflexions the master places here and there as effects of the lightning; thus the tragedy in the fifth act of its dénouement in the foreground, the dramatic pastoral in the middle ground, and the Lucretian cosmic poem at the base of the sky.

The painting encloses within itself, then, a grand emblematization of pictorial mimesis—the theory of light and color, genres of painting (landscape, pastoral, and history), cultural history (ancient and modern, oriental and occidental), and the history of human passions the signs of which recount in painting the history of humanity (love, violence, and death). The entirety of this grand symbolic "system" turns, however, around another symbol: the central, immobile, unaltered lake, the calm surface of which reflects imperturbably the appearances of the things and living beings preyed upon by all these tempests, symbolizing the divine eye of the painter—or spectator—who regards apathically from his place of contemplation, *una tota simul*, like a god, "the prodigious efforts of nature," as Félibien says of another of the Master's storm-paintings—the animal power of instincts, the pitiful emotional errors of humanity.[14] Thus, in the background, the castle and its high tower in the midst of the storm, which the setting sun illuminates, and the town with its monuments from which the tomb of Ninus detaches itself, and between the two, in the painting, but further away still in the space it represents as also in the history it evokes, the tower of Babel from the Old Testament joined to the image of the Coliseum of ancient Rome. The meditative, immobile spectator—in the place of the painter, in the place of the Stoics' God, in his own place of contemplation—can thus situate now on the level of "enunciation" [*énonciation*], now on the level of "utterance" [*énoncé*], the self-representation of the structure of the painting in its "represented" terms: *suave terrae magna....* [*sic*–J.L.] Where does one stop within such representations, where is one to situate the law of the whole of what the painting presents to the gaze?[15] Babel, a tower, a strange edifice in the background of this painting by Poussin.

We shall have to abandon for a moment Poussin's miniscule and colossal tower of Babel in order to (re)construct it in accordance with a textual architecture that combines various components—Genesis, a treatise by Dante, and Hegel's *Aesthetics*—in order to extend across time an arch or an ark of theology, philosophy, theory, and history. This arch or ark has remained unbroken throughout the tradition from the Church Fathers, Augustin or Ambrose, from Philo of Alexandria or Flavius Josephus to medieval thought and to Dante, from the Renaissance and classical age theoreticians of art and architecture to the philosophers of the Enlightenment and the Romantic thinkers.

And in the beginning, as is only fitting, we should consult Genesis:

> Now the whole earth had one language and few words. And as men migrated from the east, they found a plain in the land of Shinar and settled there. And they said to one another, "Come, let us make bricks, and burn them thoroughly." And they had brick for stone, and bitumen for mortar. They they said, "Come, let us build ourselves a city, and a tower with its top in the heavens, and let us make a name for ourselves, lest we be scattered abroad upon the face of the whole earth." And the Lord came down to see the

city and the tower, which the sons of men had built. And the Lord said, "Behold, they are one people, and they have all one language; and this is only the beginning of what they will do; and nothing that they propose to do will now be impossible for them. Come, let us go down, and there confuse their language, that they may not understand one another's speech." So the Lord scattered them abroad from there over the face of all the earth, and they left off building the city. Therefore its name was called Babel, because there the Lord confused the language of all the earth; and from there the Lord scattered them abroad over the face of all the earth. (11:1–9; 7)[16]

The story that involves the tower of Babel is thus the story of an end and a beginning or of an origin which ends in order that a beginning should be also an origin: "Now the whole earth had one language and few words…there the Lord confused the language of all the earth." At the origin, one language and one speech, and with the end of this unity, within it, the confusion of languages and speech, their multiplicity and dispersion: "So the Lord scattered them abroad from there over the face of all the earth." This story is the story of a limit; it is itself at the limit of a double limit: at the origin, there is a unique and universal language, but there are also unique acts of speech: the speakers repeat the same. This unity and identity annul all story in the very story which is told of them, or rather they install story only at the very moment when this unity and identity are lost. At the origin the earth is not merely language and monologue, but tautology: a single language.

By the same token, the speech-acts [*paroles*] of this language resolve themselves into or exhaust themselves in the repetition of one single Name, that which Adam uttered and never stopped uttering—if one is to believe Dante—at his creation: "*Quid autem prius vox primi loquentis sonaverit?* What did the voice of the first one to speak intone? I do not hesitate to assert that it is manifest for every man of healthy mind that it was precisely the word, God, that is, *El* whether in the way of a question or in the way of an answer."[17] Adam communicates nothing, and takes pleasure in making his voice resound in the pronunciation of a name that contains all names, all creatures, in the joyous effusion of the monosyllable *El*: a cry of ecstasy, the pure sonority of speech and its tonality formed as voice. In the cry of Adamic ecstasy where, in a unique Name, all names and all articulations of language are virtually present, Dante hears the storm of Nature rumbling in the alterations of the moving air:

> Therefore since the air is made to undergo such great distur-
> bances by the ordinance of that lower nature which is the minis-
> ter and workmanship of God, that it causes the thunder to peal,
> the lightning to flash, the water to drop, and scatters the snow

and hurls down the hail, shall it not be moved to utter certain words rendered distinct by him who has distinguished greater things? (I, IV, 13)

The entire language of humanity is one vocal storm articulating the one sound; the entire convulsion of nature is a language of air, sounding and intoning through alterations of the one substance: the double resonance of a single voice, that of God in creative speech: "Let there be light and there was light,"[18] wherein Longinus, the Augustan rhetor, and Boileau, at the apogee of the classical century, hear the sublime. To be sure, Adam speaks, but the words and sentences he articulates will be forever formed of the unique sound, anterior to all names, the voice that does not speak but gives to be spoken as it withdraws into the universal cry. The one language is the storm which presents the nonrepresentable cry, the end of all language as its origin in the unnamable name. The universal deluge is the language of created nature which presents the nonrepresentable origin as its end. "So the Lord said, 'I will blot out man whom I have created from the face of the ground, man and beast and creeping things and birds of the air, for I am sorry that I have made them'" (Genesis 6:7; 4).

And this death sentence applies to all humans, animals, beasts, and birds *except* for one couple of each species who will go—as we know—with Noah and his family into the ark to keep life alive under the protection of humanity. The architecture of this ark is God, and Noah, its attentive worker:

Make yourself an ark of gopher wood; make rooms in the ark, and cover it inside and out with pitch. This is how you are to make it: the length of the ark three hundred cubits, its breadth fifty cubits, and its height thirty cubits. Make a roof for the ark, and finish it to a cubit above; and set the door of the ark in its side; make it with lower, second, and third decks. (Genesis 6:14–16; 5).

Divine speech is the *archē* of all architecture: the plan of the edifice is revealed, coming from on high, in an epiphany of transcendence that finds a material, takes on a form, encloses itself within an exact limit.[19] The sublimity of the ark takes place along this limit which appears in the form of a construction only insofar as it obeys Yahweh's commandment, responds through its architectural end to the end of Nature, the destruction of all creatures. Adam's cry of ecstasy, the universal storm of the deluge, the architecture of the ark; the sound at the border of the articulation of language, the air stirred for the effacement of all created flesh, the *archē* of architecture: a tri-unitary sublimity, tri-unitary presentation of the nonrepresentable origin-end, the first and last name that the first man—the most ancient ancestor, without father or mother—uttered, the sound he made resound, *El.*

One reads in the first pages of Hegel's *The Spirit of Christianity and Its Fate* a reflexion on "the impression made on men's hearts by the flood": "a deep distraction and it must have caused the most prodigious disbelief in nature. Formerly friendly or tranquil, nature now abandoned the equipoise of her elements, now requited the faith the human race had in her with the most destructive, invincible, irresistible hostility; in her fury she spared nothing; she made none of the distinctions which love might have made but poured savage destruction over everything."[20] Two great figures take on this effect of the storm, two great figures of the domination of Nature: Noah, who secured his safety with regard to the hostile power by submitting it, as well as himself, to a more powerful instance, God, who promised him to put the elements in his service and to keep them within their bounds, and Nimrod, who secured his safety by dominating Nature on his own, as a "rash man and one boasting in the strength of his arm." And Hegel, following the text here of Flavius Josephus's *Antiquities of the Jews*, adds:

> In the event of God's having a mind to overwhelm the world with a flood again, he threatened to neglect no means and no power to make an adequate resistance to Him. For he had resolved to build a tower which was to be far higher than the waves and streams could ever rise and in this way to avenge the downfall of his forefathers. He persuaded men that they had acquired all good things for themselves by their own courage and strength; and in this way he altered everything and in a short time founded a despotic tyranny. (374–75; 184)

In his commentary, the young Hegel notes: "He united men after they had become mistrustful, estranged from one another, and now ready to scatter. But the unity he gave them was not a reversion to a cheerful social life in which they trusted nature and one another; he kept them together, indeed, but by force" (375; 184). Noah's ark versus Nimrod's tower; divine architecture versus human architecture; the name of Yahweh at the origin of Adam's language versus the construction by men of their proper name: "Let us make a name for ourselves, lest we be scattered abroad upon the face of the whole earth." An independent tower, a proper name, works of the community which realizes itself through them.

In his old age, Hegel takes up again in the *Aesthetics* this idea from his youth:

> What is the sacred? Goethe asks. And he answers immediately: it is what unites souls. One can say, letting this definition serve as one's point of departure, that the sacred, as the goal of this union and this union itself, constitutes the first content of independent

architecture. We have the most familiar example of this in the legend of the tower of Babel....All men work here in common and it is this community that constitutes at once the goal and the content of the work. This union which they wanted to create...was supposed to mark the dissolution of a purely patriarchal association [that of Noah and his sons after the flood, bowed forever beneath the Law of the transcendent Name] and the construction which was supposed to rise up to the clouds was to have meant precisely the objectification of this dissolution and the realization of a greater union.[21]

An immense collective task, the rapprochement of all peoples:

> In order to realize this incommensurable work...to make all lands submit to a kind of architectonic transformation. If they dispensed with tasks which are required in our times by ethics, customs, and the legal organization of the State, it was solely in order to create among themselves a tie which was to have been indissoluble....But the same tradition adds that after having come together in a single center in order to realize this work of union, the peoples separated again, to follow each its own path. (14, 276; 2, 638)

Thus, the tower expresses the sacred, the bond uniting humanity, but the construction of this bond is at the same time its destruction; an interrupted edifice, a community that comes together only at the moment of its dispersion: both sublime precisely in this. "The sublime in general is an effort to express the infinite, an effort which in the world of phenomena finds no object which would lend itself to representation...inaccessible, inexpressible by all finite expression...the substantial unity which opposes itself to the totality of the phenomenal world," without any possible form in the external world, a-symbolic. "But if this inherent unity is to be brought before our vision, this is only possible if, as substance, it is also grasped as the creative power of all things, in which it therefore has its revelation and appearance and to which it thus has a positive relation" (13, 467–68; 1, 363). Thus, the universal tempest; thus, the plan of the architectural ark come from on high.

> But at the same time this essentially expresses the fact of substance's elevation above individual phenomena as such...with the logical result that...the substance is purified from everything apparent and particular and therefore from what fades away in it and is inadequate to it. This outward shaping which is itself annihilated in turn by what it reveals [*auslegt*], so that the revelation of

the content is at the same time a supersession of the revelation, is
the sublime. (13, 468; 1, 363)

At this point in his *Aesthetics*, Hegel finds a precise example of this negative or
annihilating celebration of the Power and Glory of the one God in Hebrew
poetry: "It cancels the positive immanence of the Absolute in its created phenomena and puts the *one* substance explicitly apart as the Lord of the world in
contrast to whom there stands the entirety of his creatures, and these, in comparison with God, are posited as the inherently powerless and perishable" (13,
469; 1, 364).

To Hebrew sacred poetry, one must add the tower Nimrod had built,
although Hegel situates them in two different places in his *Aesthetics*: one can
do so because the erection of the tower is intimately bound up with language,
the epideixis of discourse: it is a celebration of God, repeating without end
even if in a singular fashion the Name of God, all the Names of God, that is,
his infinite perfections. Or to follow in this point the Rabbinic tradition, the
tower celebrates the Name of God by constructing an idol of it, that is, the
proper Name of the community which edi-fies the Name in its universal
immanence: the community which—in accordance with a process that always
animates representation—takes the place of, substitutes itself for, *represents*
the Name of the Other in its unique transcendence.

Each member of the community, according to Flavius Josephus (and
this motif was taken up again in the Renaissance), wrote its name on each of
the stones of the Tower. Once baked, the stones became the homogeneous
material of construction. Language and architecture are inextricably intertwined by two inexorably coupled and inverted movements.

In his meditation on Babel, Dante evokes the "memorable" storm, the
remarkable catastrophe of language in connection with the astonishing enterprise of the construction of the Tower, a division of speech in connection with
the division of architectural work:

> For almost the whole human race had come together to the work
> of wickedness. Some were giving orders, some were acting as
> architects, some were building the walls, some were adjusting the
> masonry with rules, some were laying on the mortar with trowels,
> some were quarrying stone, some were engaged in bringing it by
> sea, some by land, and different companies were engaged in vari-
> ous other occupations, when they were struck by such confusion
> from heaven, that all those who were attending to the work, using
> one and the same language, left off the work on being estranged
> by many different languages and never again came together in the
> same intercourse. (I, VII, 19)

And the Lord came down to see the city and the tower, which the sons of men had built. And the Lord said, "Behold, they are one people, and they have all one language; and this is only the beginning of what they will do; and nothing that they propose to do will now be impossible for them. Come, let us go down, and there confuse their language, that they may not understand one another's speech. (Genesis 11:5–7; 7)

And Dante continues:

For the same language remained to those alone who were engaged in the same kind of work; for instance, one language remained to all the architects, another to those rolling down blocks of stone, another to those preparing the stone; and so it happened to each group of workers. And the human race was accordingly then divided into as many different languages as there were different branches of work; and the higher the branch of work the men were engaged in, the ruder and more barbarous was the language they afterwards spoke. (I, VII, 19–20)

The catastrophe of language is measured exactly by the ana-strophe of the tower. The wall of sense separating the society of speakers is built of the cut and piled stones of the wall of the tower that unites the community of workers. The architectural articulation of the tower, which is supposed to make of it a great organized body, can be put into effect only through the articulations of particular, specialized languages, the languages of technologies and arts, which by their very articulation disarticulate the originary unnamable Name, the name cried out in Edenic ecstasy with all the names of creation, because humanity wanted to make of this Name their proper name, because they wanted to appropriate it for themselves, to appropriate it to their immanence, to construct its representation. The community of this representation would have been its autonomous and independent subject: the noncommunication of languages on the site of the tower and the town is nothing other than the presentation of the noncommunicable instance of the other Name, and if the mutual translation of languages will attempt to surmount their mutual radical estrangement, will attempt to break down the forever disjointed wall of sense, trans-lation will remain an infinite, interminable task, forever opaque, as the interrupted edi-fication of the tower on the plain of Shinear testifies, the head, summit, or *archi-tectum* of which was supposed to have occupied the infinite and formless—sublime—place of the clouds.

Dante will make the storm of languages resound in the hollows of hell: "strange tongues, horrible language, words of pain, tones of anger, voices loud and hoarse, and with these the sound of hands, made a tumult which is

whirling always through that air forever dark, as sand eddies in a whirlwind."[22]
In this storm we encounter a second flood of which an interrupted and colossal tower will be the trace on the plain, the sublime Tower of Nimrod. Dante
and Virgil discover him, between the two last circles of hell, among the giants
ranged about Lucifer's pit: Nimrod, the first earthly potentate and tyrant, the
figure of the totalitarian absolute of the politician, planted like his tower up to
the waist in the soil. "'Raphel may amech zabi almi,' began the savage mouth
to cry, for which no sweeter psalms were fit." The speech of the unique tyrant,
untranslatable and incommunicable, a cry which, in hell, is like the nocturnal
echo of the Adamic cry in the light of Eden, the "negative" presentation of the
unnamable Name he wanted to appropriate for himself in having its representation constructed.[23]

> My Leader towards him: "Stupid soul, keep to thy horn and vent
> thyself with that when rage or other passion takes thee."…Then
> he said to me: "He is his own accuser. This is Nimrod, through
> whose wicked device the world is not of one sole speech. Let us
> leave him there and not talk in vain, for every language is to him
> as his to others, which is known to none." (XXXI, 67–81, 385–87)

Through the confusion of the unique language, "*the people unique unto
themselves*" becomes *the peoples each unique for the others.* But to accompany
Dante just one more moment in his account of Babel, not the entire human
race was gathered around the iniquitous work: *almost* all participated. The
totality, from the beginning, involves a remainder. On the site of Babel there
were those who preserved the vague memory of the sound that contained all
others, the guardians of the henceforth inarticulable Name:

> But those to whom the hallowed language remained were neither
> present, nor countenanced the work; but utterly hating it, they
> mocked the folly of those engaged in it. But these, a small minor-
> ity, were of the seed of Shem (as I conjecture), who was the third
> son of Noah; and from them sprang the people of Israel, who
> made use of the most ancient language until their dispersion. (I,
> VII, 20)

Sublime by virtue of its very withdrawal or retreat, this language is a "form of
language…created by God together with the first soul (I, VI, 16). It is the
unique and singular articulation of the Name. "With [the Hebrews] alone did
it remain after the confusion, in order that our Redeemer (who was, as to his
humanity, to spring from them) might use, not the language of confusion, but
of grace" (I, VI, 17).

Thus, from the origin, there has been an infinitesimal division, a secret
limit, just as Noah was the sole just one on the eve of the universal flood, at the

moment when the natural elements were entering into the discord of the flood: a marginal distance on the border of the whole, through which the undeniable intervention of Transcendence manifests itself, the blank of the nonrepresentable, which is the incommensurable memory. It is this unattainable measure that Dante seeks in *De Vulgari Eloquentia* through all the cities of Italy, in order to found the sublimity of the illustrious vernacular the odor of which he senses everywhere without ever being able to see the panther itself: "we say that in every kind of things, there must be one thing by which all the things of that kind may be compared and weighed, and which we may take as the measure of all the others" (I, XVI, 54). Thus, for example, one uses the concept of *unity* in order to compare numbers. So "also in colours all are measured by white, for they are said to be more or less visible according as they approach or recede from it" (I, XVI, 54). How is one to discern this vernacular

> whose fragrance is in every town, but whose lair is in none. It may, however, be more perceptible in one than in another, just as the simplest of substances, which is God, is more perceptible in a man than in a brute...in fire than in earth. And the simplest quantity, which is unity, is more perceptible in an odd than in an even number; and the simplest colour, which is white, is more perceptible in orange than in green. Having therefore found what we are searching for, we declare the illustrious, cardinal, courtly, and curial vernacular language in Italy to be that which belongs to all the towns in Italy but does not appear to belong to any one of them, and by which all the municipal dialects of the Italians are measured, weighed, and compared. (I, XVI, 55–56)

The language of the poem, its voice, is thus to be found on the limit, the border, that is, the sublime of a Babel which is at once pre- and post-Babelian, transcendent and immanent, belonging to all of us and to no one—a voice white like the white of the mulberry's fruits of old, before the lovers' death, an incommensurable unit of measurement, the white of the nonrepresentable outline of beautiful form, which Poussin will seek in turn for painting in terms of the—at once contradictory and complementary—definitions of the musical mode and the sound of speech.[24]

The totalitarian city, the colossal tower will remain forever the ruin of lost unity and the project of the immanent totalization of this unity. As in the background of Poussin's painting, the Babel-Coliseum will rise almost indiscernibly in the distance upon a plain between the tower of a castle on a hill and the monuments and buildings of a town on the flanks of a mountain.

But perhaps by means of the emblem of this monument one can comprehend the inexplicable eruption of the storm in Ovid's story, which Poussin

presents to the spectator's gaze as to his own: the storm, figure of the nonrepresentable in the history of representation in painting, figures an excess which
does not transgress the limits of such representation but does indeed transgress the fulfillment of its mimetic measure: the storm figurally presents the
limits of this measure. "I have attempted to represent a tempest on earth, imitating as best I could the effect of an impetuous wind." Poussin's tempest figures in the painting of history what Babel figures in the painting of architecture
and language: the equivalence of ruin and project, confusion and dispersion.
The nonrepresentability of this equivalence is clear: it disperses all in an
instantaneous fragmentation; it mixes all in confusion and continuity, without
articulatory distance; it is the stroke of the absolute force of differentiation
which, in a word, neutralizes all differences:[25] as in the brilliance of the light-
ning-flash in relation to the solar milieu of light; as in the clap of thunder in
relation to noise, sound, and voice: light that blinds instead of rendering visible, noise that deafens instead of rendering audible. The presentation of the
tempest in the painted tableau is the permanent risk of its destruction which,
in its own way, Ovid's metamorphosis of white into black also allegorizes.

   Still, in the dramatization of painting into which he fashions the story of
Pyramus and Thisbe, Poussin puts into play, or *represents*, the tempestuous
figure's effects of dissemination and confusion, dispersion and condensation,
effects which the Tower-Coliseum in the extreme background of his painting
recall. He puts them into play twice, in the space and in the time of representation. One will recall that Ovid had situated the lovers' assignation outside of
the town of Babel, Babylon, by the tomb of Ninus, at the foot of the mulberry
tree with white berries, near the spring and the grotto. The master, however,
disjoins and places at the two extremes of the representational scene the marks
of the single meetingplace of the young lovers: the tomb of Ninus rises on the
edge of the town in the background on the right, whereas the mulberry, the
spring, and the grotto are placed in the foreground to the left. Dissemination
of spatial signs, Babelian effects of the (nonrepresentable) tempest. One will
recall also that Pyramus kills himself because he discovers Thisbe's veil
smeared by the lion with the blood of the shepherds' flocks. Poussin, however,
chooses to represent Thisbe in the foreground abandoning herself to her sor-
rows as she discovers Pyramus dead, while at the same representational
moment, in the middle distance, the lion is in the process of attacking a white
horse the rider of which has been thrown to earth. In the representation, the
cause is contemporary with its most distant effect—a conjunction or rather a
condensation, of all the forces at work in the narrative—in a single represented moment, the very moment that summarizes them in their dramatic
development and their tragic dénouement.

   I see in Poussin's attempt to represent the nonrepresentable tempest—
by means of the story of an Ovidian metamorphosis and to the rhythm of the
confusion and dispersion of causes and effects, places and moments, to the

rhythm of the dissemination and condensation of significations and symbols—the archaic memory in classical modernity of an origin and end of all language [*du langage et des langues*], of architecture and its monuments, of society and culture, of history and narratives. The lake, that immobile mirror at the center of the picture, is the symbol of the presence of this memory in the painter's divine gaze; the Coliseum or tower of Babel in the background is its iconic monogram.

Afterword

❦

POSITING THE SUBLIME:
READING HEIDEGGER READING KANT

Jeffrey S. Librett

—for the Nonce[1]

All of the essays above respond, directly or indirectly, to the reading of the history of metaphysics broached by Heidegger around 1927 and elaborated in various directions by a broad number of thinkers up to our own "moment." Yet what does Heigegger's text say about or have to do with the sublime? Why Heidegger here, if it is a question of the sublime? Or why the sublime here, if it is a question of Heidegger? My way of focusing this question below depends on the following pragmatic considerations.

Five of the essays above concern the sublime in Kant. Two of the others (by Courtine and Marin) concern at least in part the sublime in the idealist aftermath of Kant. But none of them, except those by Escoubas, Lacoue-Labarthe, and Rogozinski, address in much explicit detail Heidegger's Kant-reading, and where even these do so, moreover, it is—except for the essay by Lacoue-Labarthe—most frequently to the early *Kant und das Problem der Metaphysik* that they refer. None, in any case, make reference to Heidegger's essay, "Kant's Thesis on Being" (1961).[2] I have therefore decided to provide in this Afterword a detailed examination of the latter essay. (The places where my own trajectory intersects those of the essays translated above will be indicated in footnotes.) This examination is intended: (1) to provide the reader with an explicit introduction to the relation between the Heideggerian thought of Being and the thought of the sublime (in the case of Kant), an introduction which is presupposed in a general way by all of the essays above, and (2) beyond this introductory function, to make some "positive" contribution to our understanding of the later Heidegger's Kant-reading, in particular to the way in which that reading alludes to, interacts with, at once inscribes itself within and outside of the Kantian sublime.

Approaching the question of the relation between Heidegger's thought of Being and Kant's thought of the sublime, as two forms of the thought of what exceeds representation, one finds one's path at once blocked and broken by a textual-conceptual curiosity: on the one hand, despite three published book-length studies on—and numerous essays and lectures which allude to—Kant,[3] Heidegger does not devote any major discussion to the Kantian sublime, or even more broadly to Kantian "aesthetics," and on the other hand, Heidegger frequently—and with a discretion bordering on the insidious—invokes key terms from the discourse of the sublime.[4] In particular, when he is arguing in "Kant's Thesis on Being" against the limitations of Kant's ontology, Heidegger shifts more or less surreptitiously into the register of the sublime at the precise moment when he begins to diverge from Kant and to point toward the necessity of his own way of thinking of Being. In what sense and for what reasons does Heidegger thus turn the Kantian sublime against the Kantian ontology within which this sublime operates?

The course of the argument in "Kant's thesis" dictates that, in order to answer this question, we begin with ontology, which becomes here the theme of position or positing. For Heidegger posits that Kant posits Being as position. The question—at once rhetorical and nonrhetorical—which we shall continuously pose with Heidegger is simply this: what is the position of that which is "beyond" position? My supposition—perhaps not quite a thesis—is that this position "beyond" position is the position of the sublime: the name of the sublime comprises and calls for the disruption *of* position as of its (always sententious) syntax, the syntax of the synthesis of sense as intelligible meaning with sense as meaningless sensuality. The sense of the sublime has, then, the sense of neither nonsensical sensuality nor super-sensuous sense, neither the pure moment nor the (purposive) concept, neither the time of thought nor the thought of time, but what one could call, for the nonce, a kind of nonce-sense: the nonce-sense of the nonce announced anon. In order to expose this supposition, I shall: (I) retrace in some technical detail Heidegger's description of Kant's theory of position, (II) examine how Heidegger positions himself with respect to this theory, (III) sketch how Heidegger inscribes his own "position" in terms of the sublime, and (IV) attempt to measure this inscription of the sublime against some of the details of the Kantian sublime "itself."

I.
Heidegger on the Limit of Pure Kant

Heidegger's essay, "Kants These über das Sein," argues then that for Kant Being is position, in the sense of positing, *Setzung, thesein.* Kant posits Being as positing. In Kant's position of or on Being, further, reflexion is always

implicated: Kant's position is the position of position, the reflexion of position back upon itself and hence also the (double) position of reflexion.[5] For
Heidegger, however, both the notion of position and the notion of reflexion
by means or in terms of which Kant contextualizes position belong to the
metaphysical tradition of the forgetfulness of Being, i.e., they are incapable of
allowing for a thought of Being which would not make of Being the mere criterion of beings. The question we shall ask, again, is how does Heidegger position himself with respect to position and its reflexions, or how can he place
himself in some sense outside of position or placing, how can he reflect upon
reflexion in some nonreflexive mode? But let me summarize in some detail the
course of Heidegger's account of Kant here, before pursuing some kind of
answer to these questions by going into the complexities of how Heidegger
frames his account of Kant's ontology with the determination of the relation
between its "object" and itself as a discourse "on" this "object."

The passage on which Heidegger centers his argument comes from
Kant's famous demonstration of the impossibility of the ontological proof of
the existence of God in the first *Critique*:

> 'Being' is obviously not a real predicate; that is, it is not a concept
> of something which could be added to the concept of a thing. It is
> merely the positing of a thing, or of certain determinations, as
> existing in themselves [*oder gewisser Bestimmungen an sich selbst*].
> (A 598/B 626)

Kant's view of Being as nonpredicable is for Heidegger legible only against the
background of the question that inaugurates Western metaphysics: what is the
being? This question is ambiguous, or has a double interpretation, for it asks
on the one hand: what is that which exists in general? and on the other hand:
what is that which exists most of all, what is the highest existent thing? Within
scholastic metaphysics, this double question is answered under the headings
of, on the one hand, *metaphysica generalis*, as general ontology, and, on the
other hand, theology, which along with cosmology and psychology makes up
the tripartite structure of the *metaphysica specialis*. Heidegger argues, here as
repeatedly elsewhere,[6] that these two interpretations of the question of the
existent/being share a common point of departure in the determination of the
Being of the being as grounding, ground, foundation. Thus, the Being of that
which is in general grounds the Being of that which is in specific, insofar as
Being in general constitutes the starting point for any consideration of its specific determinations; yet the highest being also fulfills the function of a
ground, albeit in a different sense, namely, as that which allows everything else
to come into Being, in other words, as creator. When Kant denies Being the
status of a real predicate, then, in the context of the negation of any ontological proof of the existence of God, he is displacing onto-theological meta-

physics on the site of its specifically theological moment. Defining Being as position, he refuses the notion of Being as a characteristic of a thing, and thus refuses the reduction of it to an ontic status, but he continues to adhere to the interpretation of Being as grounding. Positing in Kant is still the positing of a ground, positing as grounding. As for Heidegger, his entire interrogation of Kant's ontology will attempt to ask how and in what sense one can think the "ground" of this grounding, how one could occupy a position different from Kant's, which would place itself outside of the position of positing, or which would place itself on the ground of some interpretation of Being other than the interpretation of Being as grounding. In the opening remarks of "Kant's Thesis," he "poses" this question as follows:

> ob und inwieweit das heutige Denken schon befugt ist, eine Auseinandersetzung mit der These Kants zu wagen, d.h. zu fragen, worin Kants These über das Sein gründe, in welchem Sinne sie eine Begründung zulasse, auf welche Weise sie erörtert werden könne. (442)

> whether and to what extent today's thought is competent to risk an encounter with Kant's thesis, i.e., to ask wherein Kant's thesis on Being is grounded, in what sense it allows of a grounding, and in what manner it can be situated.

We shall return to the question of the status of Heidegger's *Erörterung* ("situation") of Kant's thesis below, after having traced the path Heidegger takes to the *Ort* of this thesis. Having attempted to "position" Kant within the context of the metaphysics Kant is in the process of displacing, Heidegger begins his commentary on Kant's *These*.

The first phase of Heidegger's commentary focusses—and he is thus still in 1961 militating against the epistemologizing neo-Kantian reading which would see in Kant's critical trilogy the definitive burial of all ontology—on the two "positive" senses Being takes beyond the negation of its sense as a real predicate, i.e., as what would comprise an additional characteristic of the thing. On the one hand, there is the logical use of the copula, for the unification of given representations, and on the other hand, there is what Heidegger calls the ontic use of the "is" to add the object to its concept, to determine the object as existing. (We shall return to this question of the "use" of the copula below (III).) The difference between these two functions of the copula is the difference between the determination of *what* something would be—its possible essence—if it were in addition posited as existing, and the determination *that* it is, the positing of its actual existence. These two functions of the copula mediate between subject and predicate, on the one hand, and subject and object, on the other. Kant distinguishes between these two types of position as relative and absolute position, respectively. They comprise the two fundamental dimensions of the traditional determination of Being, applicable in turn to both the being as the being-in-general and the being as the highest being.

According to Heidegger, the full import and ramifications of the distinction between these two modes of position only become clear when one takes into account the difference between its precritical and critical versions. Whereas in the precritical phase, the distinction between relative and absolute position is conceived in terms merely of the operation of the understanding, in the critical phase it is conceived in terms of the operation of the faculties of knowledge in general, including the receptive faculties addressed to the sensuous manifold by which the understanding must be *affected* in order to have knowledge of objects at all. That is, in Kant's critical phase, ontic position has become the "position of an affection" (451), the position that supplements the givenness of what is susceptible of being posited. (Again, we shall return below (III) to the question of how one adds to the given its givenness, or of how to take giving.) With this move, Kant has begun to think more clearly the *finitude* of the understanding, to distance himself from the rationalist metaphysics he had inherited from the Leibniz-Wolff school. The ground of the link between subject and predicate is no longer merely the logical copula. Rather, in order to be able to function as the ground of the (relative) proposition, the subject of the proposition must become an object of possible knowledge for the a priori syn-thesizing activity of a subject-ego. The ultimate ground of the proposition is now no longer in the proposition itself but in the synthetic unity of apperception, as the "highest point" of all use of the understanding, or as the essence of the understanding itself. This "highest point" is what Heidegger characterizes, in his *Erörterung* of Kant's thesis, as the *Ort* from which Kant thinks that he can determine the Being of beings. In the critical phase, logical and ontic theses have been reduced to the syn-thesis[7] of the understanding, as that which provides the ground of their possibility.

Kant's critical interpretation of the positing activity of the understanding exceeds his precritical interpretation not only insofar as the critical interpretation takes into account the dependence of knowledge of experience on the sensuously given, but further insofar as it consequently includes a specifically *reflexive* dimension. This dimension becomes most clearly manifest in connection with Kant's differentiation of his ontology of positing into the principles—or fundamental posits [*Grundsätze*]—of the pure understanding, which comprise the rules for the application of concepts to intuitions. Discussing only the fourth set of principles, the postulates of empirical thought, in which Kant submits the concepts of possibility, reality, and necessity to a transcendental analysis, Heidegger asserts that these principles comprise an explication of the determinations of Being, a set of ontological predicates that determine not the what nor the that but the *how* of Being in the sense of the *how* of the *relation* between *subject and object.* The modalities are ontological—as opposed to logical or ontic—predicates, because they do not merely posit logically or existentially, relatively or absolutely, but they interpret and determine such acts of position, that is, they characterize the relations between the posited and the faculties of knowledge involved in such positing. Thus, Kant defines the possible as "that which agrees [*übereinkommt*] with the formal conditions of experience, that is, the conditions of intuition and of concepts"; the "actual" [*wirklich*] as "that which is bound up with [*zusammenhängt*] the material conditions of experience, that is, with sensation"; and the necessary as "that which in its connection [*Zusammenhang*] with the actual is determined in accordance with universal conditions of experience"(248; 239).[8] By determining ontic position as the syn-thesis or composition of an affection, Kant has made it possible to envisage the necessary part played by reflexion therein. For ontic position always involves the differentiation of modalities. In turn, one must determine in what relation representations stand to the faculties of knowledge—sensuality or intellectuality—in order to justify the attribution of their modalities. And the determination of such relations is the business of reflexion.

When finally Kant appends to the discussion of the principles of the understanding a discussion of the "Amphiboly of the Concepts of Reflexion," he is taking what is for Heidegger his last step in the examination of the sense of Being. Very briefly, this step—which Heidegger characterizes as the sketching in of the lines in the *Ortsnetz* of the *Ort* of the receptive-positional understanding, to which we will return below—involves reflecting on the reflexion on representations involved in acts of positional judgment, i.e., in the application of the principles of the understanding.

> All judgments,…and indeed all comparisons, require *reflexion*, i.e., distinction of the cognitive faculty to which the given concepts belong. The act by which I hold together the comparison of representations with the cognitive faculty to which it belongs, and by means of which I distinguish whether it is as belonging to the pure understanding or to sensible intuition that they are to be compared with each other, I call *transcendental reflexion*. (286; 276–77)

For Kant, the concepts which guide the comparison of (conceptual) representations—identity and difference, agreement and opposition, inner and outer, and determinable and determination (matter and form)—suffice for such comparison within the context of a *formal* logic. But these concepts can be applied within a *transcendental* logic only after it has been decided what status the given representations have with respect to the faculties of knowledge. "The right determining of the relation *depends* on the answer to the question, in which faculty of knowledge they belong together subjectively—in the sensibility or the understanding" (286; 277; emphasis added—J.L.) The word *amphi-*

boly, or "ambiguity," in Kant's section-title refers, then, to the confusion of pure objects of the understanding with appearances, noumena with phenomena, which occurs when transcendental reflexion is elided or insufficiently carried out.

II.
Heidegger within the Limits of Pure Kant

Now—to return to the question we announced at the outset—once he has thus sketched out Kant's position on Being, what position does Heidegger take with respect to the former position? How does he delimit it, and how does he characterize his own act of delimitation? As Heidegger had argued in the earlier *Kant und das Problem der Metaphysik* that Kant shied away from the privilege he intially granted to the transcendental imagination as ontological faculty[9] in the first deduction, so he argues in the later essay that Kant fails to think through the consequences of transcendental reflexion.[10] Having marked the reflexion of reflexion in the "Amphiboly" as the limit—the *Ortsnetz* of the *Ort*—of Kant's thought on Being, Heidegger remarks that Kant's solution to the ambiguity of representations—are they phenomena or noumena?—by means of transcendental reflexion itself involves an ambiguity which Kant fails to glimpse. In order to characterize this ambiguity, and drawing on his previous analyses of the motif of the unity of Being and thinking since Parmenides,[11] Heidegger first suggests that Kant translates this unity into the unity of position and reflexion. Being reduces to the positive act of an understanding in the process of reflecting upon itself. Since one cannot posit, or attribute existence (as determined by modality), except on condition of reflecting on the relations between representations and one's own faculties of knowledge, reflexion is always already included within the activity of positing, but this activity also always requires a controlling movement of reflexion upon that reflexion. For Heidegger, Kant has failed to distinguish adequately between these two movements, or aspects of reflexion, or rather he has failed to realize the way in which they are *at once distinct and intertwined.* This intertwinement entails that neither reflexion nor the reflexion of reflexion ever quite punctually arrives as such, each being incessantly de-layed by the other, with the consequence that position is always only in the process of taking (and therefore taking away its) place.

In order to clarify the misunderstanding to which the notion of a simple opposition between position and reflexion in Kant's thought would lead, Heidegger characterizes the difference between the reflexion of position, the reflexion which "is" or gives or carries out position, and the reflexion of reflexion, as follows: reflexion on the first level proposes the horizon—the

limit—within which positedness, that is, objectivity, can be glimpsed. Reflexion on the second level functions, he asserts, as the "procedure" (*Verfahren*),
instrument, and "organon" (*Organon*) through which the Being which is
glimpsed within the horizon of positedness is "interpreted" (*ausgelegt*). Thus
we have the positing—the opening up—of a horizon, and then an interpretation of the modality of what appears within (and as) that horizon. But the
horizon, the limit, is here (still to be) posited anew in each "moment" of its
reflexive interpretation.

Position is the position of reflexion, and reflexion is always the reflexion
of position. The posited "object" of an interpretive reflexion, the horizontal
ground or delimited figure with respect to which interpretive reflexion would
orient itself, is always displaced and replaced anew in the reflexion which has
always not yet established its position. From the attempt in Kant to overcome
the confusion of objects of the pure understanding with appearances given
intuitively, we have moved to the attempt in Heidegger to argue for the
inevitability of the confusion of reflexion as positing with reflexion as interpretive de-positing or "ex-position" (*aus-legen*). How is it then that Heidegger
will propose his own position? What limit will Heidegger have thus drawn
around the Kantian problematic and how will this limit be interpreted so as to
comprise the frame of a mediation between Kant and Heidegger, object and
subject respectively here?

Heidegger introduces his answer to Kant toward the end of his essay as
follows:

> Wie aber nun, wenn wir Sein im Sinne des anfänglichen griechis-
> chen Denkens vernehmen als sich lichtend-währende Anwesen-
> heit des Je-Weiligen, nicht nur und nicht erst als Gesetztheit in
> der Setzung durch den Verstand? Kann für dieses anfänglich
> geprägte Sein das vorstellende Denken den Horizont bilden?
> Offenbar nicht, wenn anders die sich lichtend-währende Anwe-
> senheit verschieden ist von der Gesetztheit, mag auch diese Geset-
> ztheit mit jener Anwesenheit verwandt bleiben, weil Gesetztheit
> ihre Wesensherkunft der Anwesenheit verdankt. (472)

> But now what if we think/hear [*vernehmen*] Being in the sense of
> original Greek thinking as *sich lichtend-währende Anwesenheit des
> Je-Weiligen*, not only and not first of all as positedness in the
> positing of the understanding? Can representational thinking
> constitute the horizon for this originally imprinted Being? Evi-
> dently not, insofar as the *sich lichtend-währende Anwesenheit* is
> different from positedness, even if this positedness remains
> related to that *Anwesenheit*, because positedness owes its essential
> origin to that *Anwesenheit*.

In this extremely dense passage, in which almost every word would call for commentary, Heidegger suggests that *das vorstellende Denken* ("representational" or "pro-positional thinking") cannot constitute or image-forth or "inform" (*bilden*) the horizon or limit within which the thought of *Sein* as *sich lichtend-währende Anwesenheit des Je-Weiligen* would occur. Heidegger thereby apparently begins to position himself "outside" the space of position. But he does so only insofar as he also insists that the thinking of position and of the outside would only misconstrue that which is "outside" of it by thinking of it precisely *as* outside, by spatially representing it. Hence, to the degree that we do not simply do away with representational thinking, it will be necessary to think of Heidegger as being every bit as much inside Kant as outside Kant, every bit as much precisely where Kant is as elsewhere. In this sense, Heidegger simply repeats Kant's thesis on Being, proposes himself *no other thesis*, says nothing else or other. When Heidegger suggests here that "positedness" owes its *Wesensherkunft* to *Anwesenheit*, then, he is not suggesting that positedness simply derives from a temporally prior or epistemologically more original ground. Rather, if the "essence" of "positedness" comes from—has its *Herkunft* in—"presence" (*Anwesenheit*), it comes from a "presence" which has never yet arrived as such, from a "presence" still up ahead, coming on—*anwesend*—in the interpretive de-positing of its position.

But what, then, would be the meaning of Heidegger's own "position": *sich lichtend-währende Anwesenheit des Je-Weiligen*? One can translate it—with relative precision and in its proper near-unreadability—as the "self-clearing-enduring-(un)veiling presence of whatever whiles along and away without reason or ground as of the while itself."[12] The language of grounding conflated or confused with the language of the passage of time—the word *weil* as "because" and as "while"—appears here as a quasi name for the being (*des Je-Weiligen*), alluding to the necessary impossibility of the incessant effacement of the ontological difference. The being thereby appears as the self-(un)grounding Being of its own arbitrariness (*jeweilig* = "for the time being," "momentary," "for the nonce"). In *sich lichtend-währende Anwesenheit*, the "truth" (*Wahrheit, während*) of Being as *aletheia* "appears" as the (un)veiling of a moment without moment, or a momentousness without moment, the (un)veiling of the nonce which is always still the not-yet of the nonce, *l'annonce* of the (translative) nonce, the anon.

If Heidegger knows, then, that he can place himself neither simply outside nor simply inside of Kant's discourse, and if he here gestures in part toward being outside of it despite the claims that the outside/inside polarity would be properly of no relevance, how does he elsewhere inscribe himself inside Kant's discourse? More generally, how does he elsewhere negotiate the double line of the border between his determination of Kant's text and the text of this determination, such that one can no longer quite say who is who and therefore also against whom Heidegger is polemicizing—himself or Kant?—when he marks the limitations of the discourse of transcendental philosophy?

1.   Let us return to certain indications thus far elided. To begin with, and as only becomes readable toward the end of "Kants These," Heidegger has written at the outset that what he wishes to pursue is *eine einfache Über-legung*(273), a simple reflexion," concerning Being in Kant.[13] And he has gone on, again toward the beginning of the essay, to refer to his "encounter" with Kant through the use of a term which he frequently uses or mentions but which in this "context" takes on with particular clarity its double sense of position and reflexive ex-position: *Auseinandersetzung* (442).[14] Translated literally, the term means, "positing out of one another" or "positing out of itself" and suggests an interpenetration of the parties involved in the encounter which would not be a fusion but rather a kind of mutual disarticulation or dismemberment. Thus, Heidegger characterizes the discourse he would enable as, on the one hand, a variant of *Setzung* and, on the other, a *Setzung* that is no longer perhaps simply determinant or formative but one that would result in a kind of deformation, formlessness, or materiality. That is, it would result in a "return" to that Being which, as he writes at the end of the essay, has "allowed itself to be determined" as *Setzung* and thus would be nominally on the side of the *material* in the Kantian sense of das *Bestimmbare*.[15]

Further, Heidegger asserts at the outset of this essay that he means to enable this *Auseinandersetzung*—this *Setzung* which is at once (or for the nonce) no longer a *Setzung* but a kind of *Aussetzen der Setzung*, a cessation and ex-posure of positing—by juxtaposing certain texts from Kant which "reciprocally illuminate one another" and thus allow "what cannot be immediately said to shine forth" (die geeigneten Texte so einander gegenüberzustellen, daß sie sich wechselweise erhellen und dadurch jenes, was nicht unmittelbar ausgesagt werden kann, doch zum Vorschein kommt [441–2]). This passage calls for at least two remarks.

First of all, what is to appear nonimmediately here is not so much the immediate as rather mediation,[16] for appearing is mediation and mediacy, appearance is always still coming into the appearance to come—*Anwesenheit des Je-Weiligen*. For example, what "shines forth" from Heidegger's treatment of Kant's thesis is that this thesis presents itself only "episodically" (465), always mediated and in pieces. While counterbalanced by the form of the argument as the apparently linear narrative of the fate of one thought in Kant, the dismemberment of Kant's corpus as of his own which Heidegger operates, allows, or occasions in this essay nonetheless shows this one thought, this one position, to be deposited in several subpositions. It thus shows this thought to be temporalized as always again de-posited, reflected upon as the reflexion that returns to its point of departure only in the mode of nonreturn, i.e., as the self-positing that is precisely *not* in the position to reach back to the self it henceforth will have been.

But there is more matter for reflexion in Heidegger's characterization of his method here. For Heidegger's description of how he means to establish the possibility of this *Auseinandersetzung* with Kant is secondly also a (displaced) example of its realization. It adds itself as partial performance to that of which it speaks. That is, when Heidegger speaks of letting the fragments of Kant's corpus reciprocally illuminate (*wechselweise erhellen*) each other, the reciprocality of this illumination itself alludes to or inscribes itself within Kant's concept of reflexion, in particular as unfolded in the *Critique of Judgment,* where *Wechselwirkung* ("reciprocal effectuation") is the principle that governs the relation between understanding and imagination, or reason and imagination, in the judgments of beauty and sublimity, respectively. Through the reciprocal illumination or effectuation of these reciprocalities, Heidegger implies: (1) that his montage of Kant-quotations is perhaps more "aesthetic" object than philosophical essay and (2) that what is going on in "aesthetic" experience as Kant characterizes it is perhaps more a matter of an experience of the "history" of Being than something like the disinterested contemplation of art for art's sake. By making the fragments of Kant's text—the different versions and formulations of his ontology—stand in for the imagination and understanding/reason, Heidegger implies that the *Erkenntnisvermögen* have been displaced by or re-interpreted as fragments of text, which would always be composed of the elements of sensuality and the super-sensuous, or rather which would always consist essentially of some other and third (dis)figural-schematic possibility. In the place of *Erkenntnisvermögen* Heidegger inserts textual fragments, con-texts "lighting" each other up, where the *erhellen* alludes to the play of the *Lichtung* of Being. But do we know for certain that the *Erkenntnisvermögen* in Kant were not already fragments of text?

2. Having seen how Heidegger both takes his distance from Kantian reflexive position and places that taking-of-distance within the frame of such position, we are perhaps in a position to return to a call put on hold above: Heidegger's characterization of the reflexion of reflexion as the *Ortsnetz* of the *Ort* of the synthetically propositional understanding. Although Heidegger is apparently literalizing it to mean, "the net of the place" or "the network around the place," otherwise *Ortsnetz* merely means a telephone network[17] which connects either several towns or places, *Örter,* or the different telephones *within* a given town or place. The *Ortsnetz* is thus either the context *around* the place or the text *within* the place; it is undecidably—depending on the context of its use—the outside context or the inner space, extra-topical or intra-topical. Accordingly, when Heidegger speaks of the reflexion on the reflexion introduced in the "Amphiboly" as the *Ortsnetz,* he varies his formulations among those which suggest that the *Ortsnetz* is outside of the *Ort* and those which suggest that it is within the "*Ort*":

> das Ortsnetz ist noch nicht sichtbar, d.h. dasjenige, von woher
> Sein als Position, d.h. diese selbst ihrerseits eigens bestimmt wird
> (465). Wir müssen uns auch hier mit einem Hinweis begnügen,

204   Jeffrey S. Librett

der nur zeigen soll, inwiefern Kant in diesem "Anhang" die Linien im *Ortsnetz des Ortes* zeichnet, an den das Sein als Position gehört....Achtet nun die Reflexion auf diejenigen Zustände und Verhältnisse des Vorstellens, dadurch überhaupt die Umgrenzung des Seins des Seienden möglich wird, dann ist die Reflexion auf das *Ortsnetz im Ort* des Seins eine transzendentale Reflexion. (465–66; emphasis added—J.L.)

the telephone network is not yet visible, i.e that from which Being as position, i.e., position itself in turn is properly determined....We must content ourselves here too with an indication which is only meant to show to what extent in this "Appendix" Kant has traced out the lines in the *telephone network of the place* at which Being as position belongs....If now reflexion attends to those states and relations of representation through which in general the delimitation of the Being of the being becomes possible, then the reflexion on *the telephone network in the place* of Being is a transcendental reflexion.

What is the status of this apositional *Ortsnetz* of position? In his characterization of the *Ortsnetz*, Heidegger underlines Kant's remark that the difference between matter and form, as the difference between the determinable and the determination, has a certain privilege within the set of four oppositions which comprise the concepts of reflexion, coming prior even to any determination of the difference between inside and outside. If the space of reflexion as *Ortsnetz* "contains" the concepts of determination and determinability—the "Unterschied von Materie und Form...gehört in das Ortsnetz für den Ort des Seins als Position"(467)—but these concepts are prior to the determination of any space of containment, then reflexion is contained by what it contains. Insofar as it is constituted by the play of this—itself not yet constituted—difference between form and matter, then, the modality of the *Ortsnetz*—reflexive position in or as its inevitable postponement—would be situated *between* form and matter, determination and the determinable, possibility and reality, essence and existence. The modal status of the reflexion on reflexion, the question of the *how*—as opposed to the *that* or *what* of Being—is itself inaccessible to the discourses of the *that* and *what*. The movement of reflexion as the formation of a form must always involve the self-externalization and materializing (but never yet materialized) deformation of that form. Reflexion as the reflexion of reflexion involves consequently the self-externalization of self-externalization, the deformation of deformation "itself." The *Ortsnetz*—the positional network or textual place—of positive reflexion is positively unsituable, positively ex-posed.

Which helps explain why the telephonic "metaphor" is apposite: the distance of the voice—the place of self-affection—on the telephone is the distance from a voice heard within by means of a prosthesis of the liminal ear. This voice approaches that ear, at the distance of an inside (or a materiality), from (a formal-delimiting) outside. The telephonic voice, no matter how mundane its tone and message, is always liminally ecstatic. The voice is always telephonic; the apparently absolute nearness of its self-affective proximity is always only proximitative.

To place a call, or to receive a call, on this telephonic network is as Heidegger knows a somewhat risky business. For Heidegger characterizes Kant's tracing of the lines of the textual-telephonic network of reflexive position further as the *Sicherung* of a *Sicherung,* the securing of a securing (466). But *Sicherung* also means a "fuse" or "circuit breaker" in the sense of what shuts down an electrical apparatus before its circuits get blown out by an overload of current. The reflexion on reflexion is hence figured here as the fuse of a fuse. Heidegger's apparent refusal of the fuse, however, acknowledges its own confusion with the fusion of the circuits from which it would escape, and by acknowledging this confusion attempts in a sense to escape from them, to shut metaphysical thinking down. The circuits of reflexion, then, are enacted and constated in Heidegger's text as blown out insofar as shut down. The circuit breaker is here itself what overloads, blows out, and confuses the circuits, the net result being a nonmeasurable overload of circuitous ramifications. Indeed, for example, the *Sicherung* is also the safety-catch on a rifle, to prevent it from shooting off inadvertently, to prevent the shot from coming too soon, i.e., here to prevent the noumenal phantasm of a signifier from becoming the phenomenal experience of a signified, or to prevent the extraneous connotation from entering the context in a counter-purposive manner. If the shot—i.e., the safety-catch—comes both too soon and too late in Kant—for the shot is reflexive position in its self-anticipatory postponement—then it does the same in Heidegger. It comes too soon, for example, to prevent Heidegger from shooting off his mouth about the limitations of Kantian reflexion, but also too late to prevent him from thereby precisely *shooting off his own mouth* along with Kant's own. Heidegger's text is indeed loaded (and overloaded) with mixed "metaphors" for its own lack of synthetic composure.

III.
The Calling of the Sublime

Thus, as a telephonic network of reflexive *Auseinandersetzung,* Heidegger's discourse inscribes itself into the border of what can no longer quite be characterized as Kant's position on Being, even if it also cannot be characterized as any other position. On the basis of the "comprehension" of this inscription, one can see perhaps somewhat more clearly than would otherwise be possible what is happening at the end of Heidegger's essay. Here, Heidegger multiply invokes certain key terms of the (Kantian) discourse of the sublime, but without attributing them to Kant and without referring to the sublime as such. And he invokes the sublime here in order to characterize what, in the absence of the considerations above, one would have been tempted to misconstrue as what Heidegger would conceive to be his *own* pure nonposition on Being distinct from and simply "beyond" the position of Kant. Specifically, Heidegger invokes here the motifs of *Würde* and of the measureless source of all measure.

1. To start with *Würde*: Extending the thought of *sich lichtend-währende Anwesenheit des Je-Weiligen* which we have begun to discuss above, Heidegger argues that, if thought (in relation to Being) or reflexion (in relation to position) is ambiguous, namely as the establishment of a horizon on which the object can appear and as the tool of the interpretation of this horizon, then the tradition of "logic" and "Logos" essentially reduce to this ambiguity. Heidegger goes on to argue that therefore logic must be rethought as this ambiguity in its *questionable* character or in its *worthiness of question and thought*.

> Wenn nun aber das Denken in seinem Bezug zum Sein zweideutig ist: als Horizontvorgabe und als Organon, bleibt dann nicht auch, was "Logik" heißt, nach der genannten Hinsicht zweideutig? Wird dann "die Logik" als Organon und als Horizont der Seinsauslegung nicht durchaus *fragwürdig*? Eine Besinnung, die nach dieser Richtung drängt, *wendet sich* nicht gegen die Logik, sondern *verwendet sich* für eine *zureichende* Bestimmung des LOGOS, d.h. desjenigen Sagens, darin das Sein sich zur Sprache bringt als *das Denkwürdige* des Denkens. Im unscheinbaren "ist" verbirgt sich alles *Denkwürdige des* Seins. (472, emphasis added, except for *das*—J.L.)

> But now if thinking in its relation to Being is ambiguous: as the pre-sentation of the horizon and as organon, does not what "logic" means also remain in this respect ambiguous? Does not "logic"—as organon and as horizon of the interpretation of Being—become thoroughly *questionable/worthy of question*? A thinking which pushes in this direction does not turn against logic, but *uses itself* for a sufficient determination of the LOGOS, i.e., of that speech in which Being brings itself to language as that which, in thought, is *worthy of thought*. In this inconspicuous/nonappearing "is" all of Being that is *worthy of thought* conceals itself.

What I want to emphasize here is first of all the way Heidegger calls upon the expressions *fragwürdig* and *denkwürdig*—worthy of question and worthy of thought—expressions that recur obsessively throughout Heidegger's text.[18] Why all this emphasis on the linkage of thought and interrogation with "worthiness" or "dignity" (*Würde*) and the converse?

The question is particularly worth asking in our present context, since Heidegger makes use of the term "dignity" or "worth" in his brief discussion of Kant's "doctrine of the beautiful" in his Nietzsche lectures. There he defends Kant against what he sees as Schopenhauer's and, subsequently, Nietzsche's misreadings of Kant's aesthetics of disinterest. This defense takes the form of the argument that Kant's aesthetics of disinterest is an aesthetics not of mere indifference but, to the contrary, of an engagement beyond all empirical or purely conceptual interestedness.[19] When we find something beautiful, for Heidegger's Kant, we let it "come before us purely as itself, in its own rank and dignity [*Würde*]" (129); "the beautiful is what we dignify [*würdigen*] and honor as the pre-image/model [*Vor-bild*] of our essence" (132); and "the beautiful is "what provides the measure [*Maßgebende*]" (134). Readers of Schiller will recognize here that the *Würde* echoing in the late Kant-essay and throughout Heidegger's works echoes also back from them into the title and theme of Schiller's essay, "Über Anmut und Würde" (On Grace and Dignity"). There, *Würde* refers precisely to the sublime sensibility. "The domination of the drives through moral force is *spiritual freedom,* and dignity is the name of its expression in appearance" (413). But without going into Schiller's determination of sublime dignity in any detail, suffice it to say that it is a derivative of Kant's,[20] and to say that it would be perhaps precipitous to think of Heidegger as simply adhering to a Schillerian reading of Kant. The point here is merely to note that Heidegger broaches the discourse of the sublime when he speaks of "logic" as *würdig* of question and thought, and consequently wherever he speaks of *das Fragwürdige* or *das Denkwürdige.*

2. As in the passages from the Nietzsche-lectures just quoted, at the conclusion of the Kant-essay Heidegger links the thought of *Würde* with the thought of *the gift of a measureless measure* in a way that cuts to the heart of the Kantian discourse of the sublime and which is therefore worth looking at here in some detail. That which is, Heidegger says, "most worthy of thought" (*das Denkwürdigste*) is a consequence or an aspect of the interpretation of the ontological difference: that Being "is" not, but that there is—"it gives" (*Es gibt*)—Being. Heidegger characterizes this gift, as the giving of what gives the measure, by means of a condensed commentary on Parmenides' speech of Being. Since Being is no being, when Parmenides writes *esti gar einai,* we cannot translate this as "Being is," but at best as "there is Being" (*es gibt Sein*), or as *Anwest nämlich Anwesen,* which one might in turn translate as "coming (nominally) comes," or "coming is coming." In an emphatic tone, then, Heidegger reduces logic to tautologic, the speaking of Being toward Being, or as he says in the "Letter on Humanism," *l'engagement par l'être pour l'être.* But what good is a speech that goes nowhere, that stutters in the endless repetition

of an apparently contentless circularity? Heidegger's answer in the Kant essay is that Parmenides' tautology is "die Tautologie im höchsten Sinne, die nicht nichts, sondern alles sagt: das anfänglich und künftighin für das Denken Maßgebende" ("tautology in the highest sense, which says not nothing but everything: what gives the measure for thought at the beginning and into the future" [472–73]). And this thought, Heidegger adds, as if by way of after-thought, has to be thought as *time*.

Thus, at the conclusion of Heidegger's essay, the speech of Being, as the speech of a time "beyond" the metaphysical horizon of objective positioning, comes to speak in terms of the sublime. This speech would be first of all a speech that says nothing as *everything*, as the totality of what is or rather as the nothing of that totality in the sense of its Being. Secondly, it would be a speech that provides the *measure* for thought. And these two notions imply one another: what provides the measure for everything else is itself beyond measure, and the totality of everything in or as its Being is the measureless, the infinite.

But—before turning to measure this passage against the Kantian analytic of the sublime itself—how is one to understand the way in which the "It" *gives* a measure here?[21] In other words, how is one to *take* the measure of what *gives* the measure, the unmeasurable measure itself, the measure as the giving of the measure?

What gives the measure here must also be what takes the measure, taking the measure away even as it gives the measure. For to receive is also always to measure, to place, to re-cognize, to find a position for what is measured. But the reception of the measure as a measurable measure would be a failure to receive it as the measure of all other measures. The reception of the measure as immeasurable will therefore amount to a certain nonreception. Its giving will amount to its withholding, to its taking as its being taken away.

Thus, the measures that one would have to take to take the measure (of what gives the measure) while preventing its being-measured would be measures for which "measure" is no longer quite the word. They would involve a "use" that is no longer simply an application to some goal or to some end, no longer meant to secure or shore up some position, but a radically determinable use of the radically indeterminate. How would one determine this determinable use?

Heidegger's allusion, in the passage quoted above on what is "worthy-of-thought," to the way in which thought *sich verwendet* is perhaps "useful" here, as it turns us in the direction of this "use" which would not be a "use":

A thinking which pushes in this direction does not turn against [*wendet sich nicht gegen*] logic, but uses itself [*verwendet sich*] for a sufficient [*zureichende*] determination of logos, i.e., of that speech in which Being brings itself to language as what, in thought, is worthy of thought.

To "use" (up) one's thought or oneself in this way would be to "turn oneself" (*sich wenden*) and yet also in a certain sense always to "mis-turn oneself" (*sich ver-wenden*) in a "turn" (*Wendung*) of language, which would be a detour, a de-turning or mis-turning, a dis-torsion, a mistranslation. The thinking of Being, then, would distort itself as its language. To distort language would be to turn it away from its measuring instrumental-representational function. But at the same time, it would be to turn language back toward that function, and this for two reasons. First, because to operate against the purposive-evaluative-positional is still to *operate*, to work for the work against the work. But secondly, because to submit to the language of the work and its position is *to use up, to give away*, the position of opposition to positional measurement.

This rather strange structure of the (non)receptive "use" of the gift of Being can be illustrated once more in the case of Heidegger's determination here of the "end" of this "use," of what it serves. Namely, Heidegger proposes the "use" of thought "for" a "sufficient" determination of the *logos*, of the speech of Being. But how is one to read this reference to a "sufficient" determination of *logos* as the speech of Being? The term *sufficient* alludes obviously to "sufficient" reason, to the "sufficient" ground of a discourse on Being as grounding. Yet how could a discourse which would still provide a sufficiency of ground exceed the space of the power of the principle of sufficient reason on the ungrounded character of which Heidegger has elsewhere insisted at some length? Is Heidegger simply being unrigorous here? It would seem more probable that the use, the expenditure of the subject on a "sufficient" determination here performs itself in the *disappearance—into the discourse of grounding*—of a discourse which would exceed or escape grounding. Giving itself up to the discourse of self-grounding is the only way in which the discourse of non–self-grounding can attempt to renounce grounding itself.

Before taking up Kant's "own" discourse on the sublime (un)measure, let me illustrate this structure once more, with respect to the closing lines of "Kant's Thesis." Heidegger's closing apparent condemnation of the limits of the Parmenidean motif, as a version of which he has been reading a Kantian position, is deeply and elusively ambiguous: "The title of the metaphysical determination of the Being of the being, 'Being and Thinking,' does not suffice [*reicht nicht zu*] even to pose [*stellen*] the question of Being, never mind [*geschweige denn*] to find an answer" (473). While it would seem that Heidegger is saying here that the discourse of 'Being and Thinking' cannot reach into the space of his "own" question, it is at least also the case that to suffice *to pose* a question is to provide by anticipation for a sufficient grounding of its answer. That is, it is not at all clear that the question of Being can be *posed* even if and precisely when and where it is *posed and positioned*. This suggests in turn that the failure to pose the question amounts to a certain kind of success in allowing the question to be somehow other than posed. In this respect too, then, the (external) immanence of Heidegger's discourse to its object would perhaps allow for the sublimely immeasurable success of its failure to oppose that discourse with anything of its own. It is not surprising then that Heidegger closes by calling Kant's thesis a "pinnacle" (*Gipfel*) from which the "view" (*Blick*), the domain of the view, reaches back to the determination of Being as *hypokeimenon* and forward to the speculative-dialectical interpretation of Being as absolute concept (in Hegel). The pinnacle—the sublime cliché par excellence—has the last word on Kant, which is to say that the disappearance of the attempt to find a new position into the cliché of positional self-protection is the way in which that attempt succeeds in giving itself up to the wasting of itself and the refusal of such protection.

IV.
The Calling Back of the Gift of the Measure: Kant's Sublime

The question we now have to pose is: how does Heidegger's thought of the (sublime) taking of the measure measure up to Kant's analysis of the sublime?

Since the sublime occurs within the space of "reflexive judgment," it may be useful to delay consideration of (un)measure in Kant's sublime for the time of a brief comparative characterization of reflexion in the third and first *Critiques*. Reflexion in the third *Critique* is neither logical predication, i.e., logical position, nor the determination of a concept by an intuition, i.e., ontic position as the addition of the thing to the concept. Rather, reflexion here consists in merely departing from the intuition in search of its concept. This search must remain without end, because when it ends, the given—or rather the always not yet given—intuition will have been determined:

> The force of judgment in general is the capacity to think the particular as contained beneath the general. If the general (the rule, the principle, the law) is given, the force of judgment is determinate, which subsumes the particular beneath it (even when, as transcendental force of judgment, it provides [in the form of the principles of the understanding] the conditions in accordance with which alone one can subsume anything under that generality). But if the particular is given, for which the force of judgment should find the general, the force of judgment is reflexive. (87;15)

Reflexive judgment, then, is in a relation of supplementarity to determinate judgment, the one completing the other in order to replace it. Reflexion is a kind of syncopation[22] in the rhythm of determination, an incessant interruption of the figurations of the schematic imagination. It is itself neither determination nor simply (de)terminable: neither intuitive (*anschaulich*) nor conceptual per se, neither quite its object nor quite something other than its object, it is no *Seiendes* at all, and cannot be known theoretically nor brought to the standstill of a unidimensional essence. It can therefore be "experienced" in Kant's text only in terms of either "the feeling of life" (115;38) or "life itself," that is, either the aesthetic or the teleological, the subjective or objective modes of its play, which account for the main division of the *Critique of Judgment*, and the second of which I ignore here.

On the one hand, then, the interpretation of reflexion in the third *Critique* makes retrospectively clear that if reflexion in the first *Critique* operated in the *service* of the determination of whether or not given representations belong to sensibility or conceptuality, there too reflexion nonetheless *preceded* this determination. Reflexion takes place in the space of the uncertainty of not yet having determined the relations of given representations to the faculties of knowledge. Indeed, in "aesthetic judgment," the harmonious *agreement* of understanding/reason and imagination is also the *uncertainty* as to whether the representation that occasions this agreement belongs to the one faculty or the other.

But on the other hand, as is suggested by the supplementary relation between reflexion and determination I've just outlined, reflexion is in the third *Critique* too—despite its "disinterested character"—not without some involvement with position, with the positing of the existence of the object. This involvement of reflexion with position is made manifest (unless it is constituted) in a way that at least English readers of Kant would have little occasion to remark: by the German word for "reflexion." As we shall see in a moment, this constitutive manifestation has implications for the Kantian "sublime."

One can perhaps best introduce the proximity to "position" of the German signifier for "reflexion" by reference to the way in which Kant expresses, at the outset of the third *Critique*, the structure of "disinterest," as the essential quality of aesthetic reflexion. "Disinterest"—as the indifference to the existence of the object, the turn away from a discourse regulated by the determinations of the Being of beings—is determined here as a kind of interruption of *Legen* ("laying"), which is one version of positioning:

> The pleasure [*Wohlgefallen*] which we combine with the representation of the existence of an object is called 'interest'....Now when the question is if a thing is beautiful [and the same goes for the sublime] we do not want to know whether anything depends or can depend on the existence of the thing [*ob uns oder irgend jemand, an der Existenz der Sache irgend etwas gelegen sei, oder auch nur gelegen sein könne*], either for myself or for anyone else, but how we judge it by mere observation [*Betrachtung*] (intuition or reflexion)....We cannot better elucidate this proposition, which is of an extreme importance [almost "sublimity": *von*

vorzüglicher Erheblichkeit], than by opposing the pure disinterested pleasure in the judgment of taste to that which is bound up
with interest. (116–7; 38–9)

What J. H. Bernard translates here as "whether anything depends or can
depend on the existence of a thing" is put in terms of an idiom in German that
operates with the verb *legen,* one of the variants of the thought of *ponere*
("position"). To be sure, *ob uns...etwas an der Existenz gelegen sei* means
"whether for us anything depends on the existence," but one would translate
it literally as "whether for us something were layed on the existence," in the
sense of "whether anything lay in the existence which could be an opportunity
of which we might make profitable use," for if something *kommt mir gelegen,*
then it is for me an "opportunity" (*eine Gelegenheit*). The verb *legen* is at play
then as that from which reflexion would always operate a kind of departure
and of which it would always operate a kind of partition.

"Reflexion" departs from and partitions *legen* for the simple reason that
it is: *Über-legung,* over-laying, some more and other than position within
position, whose position "beyond" position bespeaks itself silently, i.e., does
not pose itself in thematic explicitness, in the name the German language
"gives" it and in the play of variants on this thereby disarticulated name in
Kant's text. That is to say, in Heidegger's (telephonic) context within the context of Kant, or in the text of Heidegger *overlaying* itself on the text of Kant.
Reflexion does not lay down or posit the law for an intuition or action, nor
does it connect a posited law, a concept with an intuition. Rather, as *sich selbst,
subjektiv, Gegenstand, sowohl als Gesetz* ("for itself, subjectively, object as well
as law") (219; 130), it incessantly imposes and deposes itself, "is" always
already the not yet of the law to be layed over the law.

For this reason Kant can write, in the preface to the third *Critique,* that
the aesthetic judgment is in the "embarrassment of not having any principle"
(*Verlegenheit wegen eines Prinzips*) (76; 5) or as Bernard renders it, "perplexity
about a principle." It is indeed the task of the *Critique* to analyze and establish
the legitimate limits of the self-application of this "perplexity" (*Verlegenheit*),
which evokes the participial *verlegt,* meaning "lost," "misplaced," or "displaced," and so has the sense of the *Verlegung des Legens* ("loss or misplace-
ment of placement"). But since "critique" is in Kant always "self-critique," the
turn of the faculty upon itself to delimit its legitimate scope, the result of the
third *Critique* is precisely the "perplexity of perplexity" (*die Verlegenheit der
Verlegenheit*).

These considerations on a certain dispersal of the signifier for "reflexion" in Kant put us perhaps in a "position" to glimpse a sense—often overread or overlooked—in which sublimity has a privileged relation to reflexion.[23] Such a privileged relation is indicated explicitly, even if indirectly, by
Kant's characterization of the (non)position of the subject of sublimity:

namely, *Überlegenheit*—which is almost but not quite *Überlegtheit*, or reflect-edness, deliberation, circumspectness. Translated correctly as "superiority" by Bernard, but literally something like "overlayedness," *Überlegenheit* consti-tutes in Kant-Heidegger's text a variant of *Überlegung*, overlays itself upon *Überlegung* and lays it out—*legt die Überlegung aus*—even while laying over and playing dead, as it were, in the discreetness of its general failure to be remarked. As respect for our "calling" (*Bestimmung*), the sublime makes "as it were [*gleichsam*, omitted by Bernard] intuitable the superiority [*die Über-legenheit*] of the rational calling of our cognitive capacities [*Erkenntnisvermö-gen*] to the greatest capacity of our sensibility" (180; 96). And:

> Power [*Macht*] is that which is superior to great hindrances [*großen Hindernissen überlegen*]. It is called dominion/violence [*Gewalt*] when it is superior to [*überlegen*] the resistance of that which itself possesses power. Nature, considered in an aesthetical judgment as power that has no dominion over us, is dynamically sublime [*dynamisch-erhaben*]./If nature is to be judged by us as dynamically sublime, it must be represented as exciting fear....For in aesthetical judgments (without the aid of concepts) superiority to [*die Überlegenheit über*] hindrances can only be judged accord-ing to the greatness of the resistance. (184; 99–100)

Finally, for example:

> In our mind we find a superiority over nature even in its immea-surability [*eine Überlegenheit über die Natur selbst in ihrer Uner-messlichkeit*]. And so also the irresistibility of its power...discloses to us a faculty of judging independently of and a superiority over [*Überlegenheit über*] nature. (185–6, §101–2)
>
> The surprise...is not real fear, but only the attempt, to be supe-rior to nature within and without [*der Natur in uns selbst, mithin auch der außer uns...überlegen zu sein*]. (195; 109)

Superiority, then, is the ec-static superiority of reflexion—as superimposition, superposition, or translation—over the position it both exceeds and occupies. Sublimity is the superiority to itself of what is de-posited because super-posed beyond or over the Being of both positedness and positing, objectivity and subjectivity in the sense of the first two *Critiques*. Sublimity overlays itself and lays itself over as Being "beyond" the Being of position.

But how exactly does the overlaying relate to the immeasurability of that which is its occasion, the subreption of its essential calling? How does Kant take the call of the measureless measure? I shall briefly try to sketch this with respect to the mathematical sublime.

The sublime is for Kant the absolutely great, the incommensurably great, hence that which can be measured only by the standard of itself. Since all empirical objects—all beings—are measurable in terms of or are comparable to some spatial units, the sublime object cannot be an object outside of us. The sublime "proper" must, concludes Kant, be something—some nothing—within us, which he calls the "use"[24] which the judgment makes of certain representations. Despite the fact that this "use" is determined as a reflexive use, it must nonetheless be situated, like reflexion "itself," in a sense "beyond" reflexion, since it is a "use" of the incomparable, whereas all reflexion is supposed to undertake the comparison of representations. *Überlegung* goes out "beyond" itself, or recedes into itself (as into the telephonic network of its calling). How does this reflexive "use" of "use" occur, or what measures are taken with the taking of measures here?

Now, all measurement is for Kant ultimately "aesthetic," i.e., it ultimately depends on the measurement "by mere intuition (by the measurement of the eye)" of a "fundamental measure" (*Grundmaß*, "measure of the ground," "ground of measure," or "measure as ground") (173; 89) in terms of which all other quantities would be measured. Hence, the estimation of sublime magnitude will be a matter of aesthetic measurement, not logical measurement, which proceeds through the concepts of number as manipulated by the understanding. Because it must involve the encounter with an excessive, immeasurable measure, the estimation of *sublime* magnitude will involve the *failure* to seize the dimensions of an object within one perceptual act of the receptive-presentational imagination as faculty of *Darstellung*. This failure comprises the subjective counter-purposiveness of the sublime and comes to pass as follows.

The activity of the imagination in the formation of images, or improper fundamental measures (for the "proper [*eigentliche*] unchangeable fundamental measure of nature is its absolute whole" [178; 94]), consists in both apprehension and comprehension. The temporal dimensions of these two functions are, as Kant specifies, linear successivity in time, and momentary simultaneity in time. What Kant calls the "maximum" of the imagination is reached when, in the attempted perception of extraordinarily large objects of "raw nature," the imagination—which is to receive spontaneously the impression of the sensuously given as a "moment" in time—can no longer comprehend, synthesize, or com-pose, what it apprehends, what it takes in bit by bit in each previous sub-moment. When imaginary comprehension fails to totalize apprehension, diachronicity can no longer be synchronized, metonymy can no longer be metaphorized: the present is shattered, or is recognized as always already shattered: the punctual frame of pro-positionality points to its proper dispersal. Kant characterizes this "moment" of the failure of imagination to attain the totality of the image—i.e., this "moment" of the collapse of that faculty which, for the Heidegger of the Kant-book, was the ontological faculty par excellence—as the displacement or "dis-position" (*Versetzung*), the position on the edge of position of the mood of the subject: "where the imagination reaches its maximum, and, in the effort to extend it, sinks back into itself, but is thereby displaced [*versetzt*] into a moving pleasure" (174; 91).[25]

But how does this "moving pleasure" (*rührendes Wohlgefallen*) or subjective purposiveness emerge out of the counter-purposive collapse of sensuous sense? Through the failure of the subject to synthesize the object in one image, the object—which otherwise would constitute a fundamental measure, or a unity in terms of which the imagination could, in combination with the understanding, measure other things—comes to have the sense of an infinite fundamental measure, and therefore of the infinite as fundamental measure of all things.

> But now the mind listens to the voice of reason which, for every given magnitude—even for those that can never be entirely apprehended, although (in sensible representation) they are judged as entirely given—requires [*fordert*] totality, hence comprehension in one intuition, and [imaginal] presentation [*Darstellung*] for all of these members of a progressively increasing numerical series. It does not even exempt the infinite (space and past time) from this requirement [*Forderung*] but rather it renders it unavoidable to think the infinite (in the judgment of common reason) as entirely given (in accordance with its totality). (176–77; 93)

The desire of *imagination* to present in a momentary image this measure which is immeasurable and counter-purposive for our sensuous imagination is thus *already*, in the "moment" of its paradoxical emergence out of its impossibility, the desire of *reason* to present the infinite itself, or that which evades presentation as such. But how is this *"already"* to be understood? Kant describes this paradoxical emergence of the sublime emergency in terms of a metaphorical passage from the sensible to the super-sensible versions of the immeasurable. What the imagination cannot grasp is (aesthetically-subjectively) incomparable by virtue of its noncomprehension: one can indeed only with difficulty compare what one cannot comprehend. But what is (conceptually-objectively or "properly") incomparable is the infinite conceived as given in intuition (i.e., the pyramids or St. Peter's Cathedral are not actually, objectively infinite).

> that magnitude of a natural object on which the imagination fruitlessly spends its whole faculty of comprehension must carry our concept of nature to a super-sensible substrate (which lies at its basis and also at the basis of our faculty of thought) [*muß...den Begriff der Natur auf ein übersinnliches Substrat...führen*]. (94; 178)

Through the metaphorical confusion of the subjectively incomparable with the objectively incomparable, the subject of the sublime discovers itself suddenly demanding the totalization of the moment as the totalization of the infinite. But the metaphorical passage—*führen...auf*—is particularly persuasive here only because reason is inscribed from the start in imagination: the function of *Zusammenfassung* ("comprehension") is already the demand for totality: "the mind listens to the voice of reason which, for every given magnitude...requires totality" (176–77; 93). The quasi phenomenal experience of the sublime is only dependent, even in the case of objects as impressive as the pyramids, on being close enough to see the parts and far enough away to be able to (begin to fail to) take in the whole. This experience is therefore possible with respect to every perceptual experience and at every minute, as the discovery of the impossibility of the totalization of the minute itself, however minute. The moment is always above all the *duty* of the moment, the "ought" of the "there ought to be" a moment. The subjective purposiveness of the failure of imagination consists in this discovery that "we" are not merely beings of sense, in the opening up of a position which, involved in the constitution of sensuous "comprehension" as its demand, finds itself nonetheless outside of the space of what simply is, on the border of *Seiendes* as its constitutive interruption.

If the demand of this "ought," then, is finally what Kant calls the properly sublime, in what sense can we understand this demand to be the demand of the super-sensible? As a *Forderung* or *Anspruch* (172; 88), it posits a law, calls for the constitution of the "moment" as what *ought* to be brought about. This (practical) position is not a knowledge, but a "desire" of reason—reason is for Kant the faculty of desire—a desire of the sensuous presentation of the super-sensuous. But if reason is a "super-sensuous" faculty, this only means here that it is on the border—or rather is the border, posits the border, posits as the border—between sensuous givenness, or receptivity, and whatever would be not sensuous but the (spontaneously posited or "discursive") sense or meaning above the ("intuitive") senses. We "are" this "super-sensuous" border only insofar as we divide ourselves from ourselves there, are "above" and "below" at once or by turns. That is, "we" who "have" such a "faculty" of super-sensuous or absolutely spontaneous position are not simply identifiable with this position, are not simply *in* the position of this position.

The desire of reason is indeed for Kant our calling, the call we receive and the one we try to put through, the one we take and the one we give. But this calling is only our calling to the extent that we are precisely *not* adequate to it, that we *cannot* identify ourselves with it, that it is in an important—indeed a "momentously" important—sense *not* our own. We have this calling only insofar as in a certain sense—a nonce-sense—we do *not* have it. Or again, in the idiom of *Being and Time*, we are our Being only insofar as we still *have* to be it. Kant emphasizes this nonadequation when he states that the "respect" we feel for the sublime is "the feeling of our incapacity to attain to an idea *which is a law [Gesetz] for us*" (180; 96). Insofar as we are incapable of attaining our own law (*Gesetz* or *Setzung*) we are exiled from (the theoretical knowledge of) our own positional calling. The only proof for Kant that we belong at all to the law, to the meaning of the law as to the law of meaning, is that we know ourselves to be excluded from its experience. Strictly speaking, we listen more *for* it than *to* it, as may well be marginally indicated by Kant's use of the phrase *hört...auf die Stimme der Vernunft* instead of simply *hört...die Stimme der Vernunft*. The "aesthetic" experience of the position of positing as our own unknowable (non)position is an experience that takes the (formless) form of *respect* as a mode of objectless desire. The sublime—almost nothing at all— would take place somewhere (i.e., nowhere) between sensuality and its sense, which does not mean as the figure of super-sensuous sense *in* the sensual[26] but rather its nonce-sensical disfiguration. The sublime is not; there is no such "thing" as the sublime. But still, the giving and taking of the sublime occurs— always only for the nonce—as its nonce-sense.

Accordingly, Kant determines the "moment" or the "nonce" of this nonce-sense once as a *sequence* of two feelings, the one negative, the other positive, so to speak, and once as a quasi simultaneous *alternation* between negative and positive feelings. The indirect pleasure of the sublime is the "momentary inhibition [*augenblicklichen Hemmung*] of the life forces, and immediately thereafter an all the stronger outpouring of them" (165; 83). This mininarrative of the moment of the sublime not only divides it into two, but also speaks of the first moment in terms of an inhibition of life, that is, again, of an inhibition of the moment, assuming that life is the continuing presentation of the moment. Some moments later in his text, Kant "compares" the quality of (properly incomparable) sublime pleasure to "a convulsion [*Erschütterung*], i.e...a quickly alternating [*schnellwechselnden*] repulsion from, and attraction toward, the same object" (181; 97), a dying and a vivification almost at once, a dialectics at a standstill. From the description of a linear sequence, then, we move to the description of a circularity or simultaneous repetition of opposed tendencies. Between the two descriptions and within each, the moment, the nonce, is broken or multiplied to several nonces at (n)once. The nonce-sense of the sublime is a nonnonce, always the anon of the nonce.

How, then, finally, would one take the measure of the distance between the giving/taking of the measureless measure in Heidegger and the giving/taking of the measureless measure in Kant? What gives the measure in Heidegger is, as we have seen above, indissociable from the textual network—the *Ortsnetz*—of reflexive position. The corresponding "context" in Kant would be perhaps most "fittingly" situated in the determination of taste as a network of dispositional displacements between—and not within—any given subject. For if what provides the measureless measure in the Kantian sublime is finally the reflexive activity of judgment, then judgment is in turn always the judgment *of the other* as delayed and as overlayed upon the judgment of the one who would take that measure. That is, the "displacement" (*Versetzung*) into "aesthetic" pleasure is a displacement into displacement "itself" with sociopolitical implications we can only briefly point to in conclusion here. As Kant writes in the section on *sensus communis*—and it is in this version of the *Mittelglied*, and not in the synthetic unity of apperception per se, that the ground of the ground in Kant is perhaps "ultimately" to be located[27]—the maxim of the reflexive judgment as of the extended "mode of thought" (*Denkungsart*) is *an der Stelle jedes andern denken* ("to think in the place of every other" [226; 136]). One can do this when he "posits himself beyond the subjective private conditions of judgment [*sich über die subjektiven Privatbedingungen des Urteils,...wegsetzt*], by which so many others are confined, and reflects upon his own judgment from a universal standpoint (which he can only determine by placing himself at the standpoint of others [*daß er sich in den Standpunkt anderer versetzt*])" (227; 137). The universal standpoint which is to be adopted in reflexion takes its stand, despite appearances, precisely nowhere at all, or at least it takes no position in the sense of a place from which positing of existence could be carried out by a subjectivity reflexively enclosed upon itself. Not only is reflexion disinterested and hence non, dis-, or over-positive, but insofar as it means thinking in the place of every other it means thinking in the place of every other thinking in the place of every other....It follows that to be in the place of the other is to be where he or she is not, for he or she is elsewhere, in the place of every other. To think in the place of the other is each time then to think in the place of a singular nothingness or absent place which is filled by a heterogeneous plurality—a dispositional network—of the others in turn. Again, such thought, which calls upon Kant to call it reflexion, does not involve merely the positional activity of a self-affecting subject, but the dispositional and displaced active-passivity of a neither subjective nor objective overlaying, montage, or collage of positions. It characterizes Kantian *Mitsein* or community as the Kantian equivalent of the principle of sufficient reason. Not "everything must have a reason," but "think in the place of every other"—which also means, "nothing yet has its reason," or "reason is the reason of the other"—is the fundamental quasi imperative, the ultra-ethics of the Kantian critical trilogy, its principle of hope.[28] It marginally exceeds the thought of the Being of beings to which the Leibnizian principle of sufficient reason still more unequivocally adheres, for it does not enunciate a criterion for what counts as an existent, but rather the syncopated rhythm of an interruption of criteria and of the positions over which criteria claim to dispose.

It is within the anonymous network of this telephonic common (nonce)sense, then, that Heidegger's reading of sublime position would measure itself against and communicate with Kant's reading of the sublime as the collapse of imagination into the demand of reason for totality. Kant returns Heidegger's call there, or overlays the text of that call upon his own, reads it back, and recalls it for reading.

In his essay, "LOGOS," Heidegger reads *legein* as *Legen* ("laying") and writes that *Legen ist Lesen* ("laying is reading") (201).[29] In these terms, Heidegger's and Kant's positions on (sublime) Being can be said to overlay, to read over, and in all possible senses to overread each other.[30] Such overreading constitutes the obligation to which the essays above, it seems to me, each in its singular manner, attempt to respond.

CONTRIBUTORS

❁

Jean-François **Courtine** is Professor of Philosophy at the University of Paris (X) and the Director of the Husserl Archives in Paris. He has translated Schelling's works into French and has written widely on German idealism and phenomenology, including two recent books on Schelling and Heidegger.

Michel **Deguy** is a poet and essayist. He is the Editor in Chief of *Po&sie*, and has been serving as President of the Collège internationale de philosophie since 1989. His numerous books include *Poèmes de la presque'île* (1962), *Figurations* (1969), and *Poèmes 1960–1970* (1973).

Éliane **Escoubas** is a former President of the Collège internationale de philosophie and teaches at the University of Toulouse. She is the author of, among other texts, *Imago Mundi: Topologie de l'art* (1986).

Philippe **Lacoue-Labarthe** teaches at the University of Human Sciences in Strasbourg and at the University of California, Berkeley. His many books and essays include *Typography: Mimesis, Philosophy, Politics* (1989), and *Heidegger, Art and Politics: the fiction of the political* (1990).

Jeffrey S. **Librett** is assistant professor of German in the Department of Modern Languages and Literatures at Loyola University Chicago. He has translated numerous critical texts from German and French into English and has published articles on Paul de Man, Kant, Schiller, Schlegel, and Heidegger.

Jean-François **Lyotard** taught for many years at the University of Paris (VIII) and is a visiting professor at the University of California at Irvine. His many books include *The Postmodern Condition* (1984), *The Differend* (1988), *Just Gaming* (with Jean-Loup Thébaud), and *Heidegger and "the jews"* (1990).

Louis **Marin** taught at the École des Hautes Études en Sciences Sociales. He wrote numerous books and articles, including *La critique du discours: sur la 'Logique de Port-Royal' et les 'Pensees' de Pascal* (1975), and *Le portrait du roi* (1981).

Jean-Luc **Nancy** teaches at the University of Human Sciences of Strasbourg, France, and at the University of California, Berkeley. His numerous books and articles include *The Literary Absolute* (with Philippe Lacoue-Labarthe, 1988), *The Inoperative Community* (1991), and *L'expérience de la liberté* (1988).

Jacob **Rogozinski** teaches at the University of Paris (VIII) and has been since 1986 Director of Programs at the Collège internationale de philosophie. He has published articles on Heidegger (in *Research in Phenomenology*), Lyotard (in *L'esprit créateur*), Marx, Deleuze, Sartre, and others, and is presently completing a book on the question of the law in Kant.

NOTES

❀

Notes for Chapter 1

1. Arthur Rimbaud, *Complete Works, Selected Letters*, ed. and trans. Wallace Fowlie (Chicago: University of Chicago Press, 1966), 215.

2. Ernst Robert Curtius, *European Literature and the Latin Middle Ages*, trans. Willard R. Trask (Princeton, N.J.: Princeton University Press, 1953).

3. One could, playing a bit, propose "On Height" [*sur la hauteur*].

4. For example: "Because of this all the ages and all of human life, which is not seized by the mindlessness of grudging envy, brings and awards the victory prize to them [Homer, Demosthenes, and Plato], and even now protects it from being removed, and is likely to keep them thus," Longinus, *On the Sublime*, trans. and with commentary by James A. Arieti and John M. Crossett (New York: Mellen Press, 1985), XXXVI, 2; 182. What remains for the moderns—we are at the beginning of the Christian era—is to struggle, despite the necessity of defeat, for a "defeat without dishonor" (XIII, 5; 84) in this age of imitation (μίμησίς τε καὶ ζήλωσις, XIII, 2; 79) measured by its distance from the *Pythian* origin, from the *divine exhalation* and from the *Homeric* beginning, which was followed by the age of the greatness of the Ancients (τῶν ἀρχαίων μεγαλοφυίας) ("Stesichorus, Archilocus, and Plato, more than all the others, have drawn on the Homeric source," XIII, 3; 82), down to "ourselves" and our "inferior times" (τὸ ἡττᾶσθαι). Chapter, section, and page references (the latter from the English language edition) are given hereafter parenthetically in text. The edition used by Deguy is: *Du sublime*, trans. Henri Lebègue (Paris: Éditions des Belles Lettres, 1965).

5. Homer is the one who knew how to measure "the leap of the [divine] steeds by a cosmic distance" (IX, 5; 55).

6. Deguy notes here that where the translation is by Lebègue, he will mark it "H.L." and that, elsewhere, the translations are his own. I have attempted, where Deguy makes a point of retranslating Longinus, to follow the sense of Deguy's versions, while still referring to the page in the English edition where the corresponding passage is to be found. The (polemical) play between his versions and those of Lebègue is nonetheless necessarily largely effaced in my own translation. Let the following general comment suffice, which Deguy inserts at this point:

Is not the *Traité du sublime*—relayed by Boileau across innumerable citations, across the resumption of the question in the eighteenth century by Burke, Kant, and many other aestheticians—accessible to us precisely in the bilingual edition published by Belles Lettres with a translation by M. Lebègue? The question of translation poses itself here: what is astonishing is that the tone of Lebègue's translation is much closer to Boileau than to us, i.e., to our archeological need.

The difficulty with the sublime is redoubled for us in this respect: the entire use of French here—lexicon, locutions, turns of phrase, general tone, and stereophonics of translation, beginning with the title itself, Περὶ Ὕψους, the translation of which as *sublime* loses sight of *the high*, which is precisely what is at stake in the sublime avatars of sublimity—is obsolete. It casts the text not back into its own distance from us today but back into our own seventeenth century. The *sublime* and the *academic* have become confused, in a Boileauesque manner, and have thereby become marginalized in mere "aesthetic theories." What we read in H. Lebègue's text is distant from the *sublime*; it displaces the sublime into the catastrophe of its collusion with "the old style," as one of Beckett's figures says, like a stereotypical painting with its *trompe-l'œil*, its obligatory motifs, its more and more recognizable because expected "figures"...

Doubtless it would be appropriate to restore, by retranslation, Longinus's book to the stature of its object, the ηυπσοσ, "the high," to which it ought to relate itself other than in an awkward pose, wearing stiff collars, or wearing the varnish of *haute-époque* furniture, "the sublime." And if nontranslatability is a clichéd mark of the *sublime* (the Bible, Dante), it would be fitting to reestablish the distance between the text and its translation.

7. To provide their complete inventory would be easy enough, in a tedious sort of way for, of course, the *Letter* consists in large part of quotations: a long series of combats, rapes, dangers, tortures, carnages, incests, deaths, shipwrecks, disasters, murders, and other torments.

8. The Marcel Proust of the *temps retrouvé* would offer Longinus pages of examples of the modern sublime, Marcel Proust, *A la recherche du temps perdu*, vol. 14 and 15, *Le temps retrouvé* (Paris: Gallimard, 1927); English: *Rembrance of Things Past*, vol. 3: *Time Regained*, trans. C. K. Scott Moncrieff, Terrence Kilmartin, and Andreas Mayor (New York: Random House, 1981).

9. Whereby we can glimpse one aspect of the "comical," which is to miss the exit?

10. Beethoven's famous adagio of opus 106 (cf. *Po&sie* 9).

11. Whence the examples of the *sublime*: inundation, the deluge, corresponding to the differences and the heterogeneities that preceded and remain *remarkable for one more moment* in the overwhelmed memory that attends the flood and in the dispersed vestiges (floating debris) of the drowning, before all is swept under by a homogeneity without remainder which thenceforth contains nothing of the sublime. And the same logic would apply to the image of volcanic fire.

12. In the tradition of Gorgias, *Encomium of Helen*, ed. and trans. D. M. McDowell (Bristol, U.K.: Bristol Classical Press, 1982), 23–27: "Speech exercises great power: that which is itself almost nothing at all and which is utterly invisible attains to

divine works...the power of discourse has the same relation to the disposition of souls as the disposition of drugs to the nature of bodies."

13. The essence of metonymy: *pars* pro *toto*.

14. Which is not a reason for the analyst (critic, rhetorician, or aesthetician) not to study them to reveal their subtle play! But Pseudo-Longinus's lesson, the question of figures and rhetoric, seems still so little understood that every minute one can read things like the following, from *Le Monde* (18 February 1983); V. Alexakis writes with respect to Georges Simenon: "He has banished from his work all literary artifice"!

15. "In this one figure the oath (which I term apostrophe) he made divinities of his ancestors, and stirred us to swear as if they were divinities" (XVI, 2; 100–102).

16. The Greek words here are ἐπικουρία and πανουργεῖν.

17. Reminder of Jean Cohen: "There are no figures in the *Discours de la méthode.*"

18. The sublime in *morals?* Isn't this in general the gesture of renunciation, the figure of "privation" (simplification, ascesis, etc.)?

19. "The silence of Ajax in the *Nekuia* is great and more sublime than any speech" (IX, 2; 53).

Notes for Chapter 2

1. It is in fashion in Paris and among the theoreticians, who often refer to it in recent years (Marin, Derrida, Lyotard, Deleuze, Deguy), as well as in Los Angeles and among the artists, as for example one of the them entitled a recent exposition and performance, "The Sublime" (Michael Kelley, April 1984). One finds further evidence of this fashion in Berlin (Hamacher), Rome, and Tokyo. (Not to speak of the use of the word *sublime* in the most current everyday speech) As for the texts, they are numerous and dispersed. Let it suffice to indicate their authors here, my indebtedness to whose works it would be impossible to convey adequately. But I do not intend to add to theirs one more interpretation of the sublime. I attempt rather to come to terms with what it is that they share and that the epoch shares in this fashion: that offers us all up to a thought of the sublime.

2. This perhaps excessively concise formula adopts the general perspective of Samuel Monk's classical study *The Sublime: A Study of Critical Theories in Eighteenth-Century England* (Ann Arbor: University of Michigan Press, 1960) which has been reconsidered with respect to France by T. Litman in *Le sublime en France* (1971) from both a historical and an aesthetical-conceptual perspective. My contribution is neither historical nor aesthetical.

3. I must not omit to mention at least once the name of Nietzsche, who thought, in one sense or several, something of the sublime, even if he hardly thematized it as such.

4. Walter Benjamin, *Gesammelte Schriften*, vol. I: 1, (Frankfurt am Main: Suhrkamp, 1980), 196.

5. Martin Heidegger, "Der Ursprung des Kunstwerkes," *Holzwege* (Frankfurt am Main: Vittorio Klostermann, 1980), 42; "The Origin of the Work of Art," *Poetry, Language, Thought*, trans. Albert Hofstadter (New York: Harper and Row, 1971), 56.

6. Theodor W. Adorno, *Ästhetische Theorie* (Frankfurt am Main: Suhrkamp, 1973), 292; *Aesthetic Theory*, trans. C. Lenhart, ed. Gretel Adorno and Rolf Tiedmann (London: Routledge and Kegan Paul, 1984), 280.

7. Georges Bataille, *Œuvres*, vol 7 (Paris: Gallimard, 1970).

8. Maurice Blanchot, "La littérature et le droit à la mort," *La part du feu* (Paris: Gallimard, 1949), 294; "Literature and the Right to Death," in *The Gaze of Orpheus*, trans. Lydia Davis, ed. P. Adams Sitney, with a preface by Geoffrey Hartman (Barrytown, N.Y.: Station Hill, 1981), 22.

9. This means at once that these two modes of thought are opposed to each other and that the thought of the sublime doubtless infiltrates and secretly disquiets the thought of the end of art. But I will not attempt to show this here. In turn, where Hegel explicitly speaks of the sublime, he does not bring anything of the thought of the sublime to bear (cf. Paul de Man, "Hegel on the Sublime" in *Displacement: Derrida and After*, ed. Mark Krupnick [Bloomington: Indiana University Press, 1983], 139–53).

10. See *Critique de la faculté de juger*, trans. A. Philonenko (Paris: Vrin, 1986), §§23–29, 84–114; *Critique of Judgment*, trans. J. H. Bernard (New York: Hafner, 1951), 82–120, for most of the allusions to Kant's text which follow.

11. The word can be found, for example, in the *Critique of Judgment*, §22, 80; 78.

12. "In the aesthetic evaluation of grandeur, the concept of number ought to be kept at a distance or transformed."

13. In this sense all of that which in Kant still derives from a classical theory of analogy and the symbol does not belong to the deep logic of which I am speaking here.

14. The latter formula is Lyotard's, cf. *Le différend* (Paris: Minuit, 1983), 118–19; *The Differend: Phrases in Dispute*, trans. Georges Van Den Abbeele (Minneapolis: University of Minnesota Press, 1988), 77–78. The former formula is Derrida's, "Le parergon," in *La vérité en peinture* (Paris: Flammarion, 1978); *The Truth in Painting*, trans. Geoff Bennington and Ian McLeod (Chicago: University of Chicago Press, 1987), 131–32. They are certainly not wrong, and they comment rigorously, together or the one against the other, upon the text of Kant. I do not attempt to discuss them here, preferring to take a different course—along the edge of presentation, but at a distance, and because presentation itself distances itself from itself. The political function of the sublime in Lyotard would call for a different discussion, which I shall undertake elsewhere.

15. Kant does not fail to indicate an aesthetic direction combining the two motifs: a sublime genre distinct from all others, and the determination of this genre as

a kind of total work of art. He in fact evokes the possibility of a "presentation of the sublime" in the fine arts in terms of the "combination of the fine arts in one single product" and he indicates then three forms: *verse tragedy,* the *didactic poem,* and the *oratorio.* There would, of course, be much to say about this. I shall content myself here with noting that it is not quite the same thing as Wagner's *Gesamtkunstwerk.* More particularly, Kant's three forms seem to turn around *poetry* as the mode of presentation of destiny, thought, and prayer, respectively, and it does not seem to be above all a matter of a "total" presentation.

16. One ought to analyze the relations between Kant's *Bestrebung* and Freud's *Vorlust,* that is, this "preliminary pleasure," the paradox of which consists in its tension and which occupies an important place in Freud's theory of the beautiful and of art.

17. I prefer on this point the first edition.

18. Hegel provides a kind of figure of this feeling by way of the other in his discussion of the infant in the womb of its mother. Cf. Jean-Luc Nancy, "Identité et tremblement," in *Hypnoses* (Paris: Galilée, 1984), 13–47.

19. I am choosing to ignore here the *economy* of sacrifice, which is quite visible in Kant's text where the imagination acquires "an extension and power greater than that which it has lost." I do not pretend that the offering is simply "pure loss." But at the heart of the economy (of presence, art, thought), it [*ça*] offers itself *also, there is* also offering, neither lost nor gained.

20. Gilles Deleuze, *Cinéma,* vol. 1, *L'image-mouvement* (Paris: Éditions de Minuit, 1983), 69, *Cinema,* vol. I, *The Movement-Image,* trans. Hugh Tomlinson and Barbara Habberjam (Minneapolis: University of Minnesota Press, 1986), 46.

21. I suspend here an analysis I pursue in *L'expérience de la liberté* (Paris: Galilée, 1988).

22. *Darbieten* or *Darbietung* ("offering") would be the word to substitute on the register of the sublime for *Darstellung* ("presentation"). But it is in each case a matter of the *dar,* of a sensible "here" or "here it is."

23. Cf. note 15 above.

24. It is remarkable that another Biblical commandment—the *Fiat lux* of Genesis—had been already a privileged example of the sublime for Longinus and for his classical commentators. From the one example to the other as from the one commandment to the other, one can appreciate the continuity and the rupture.

25. Cf. Jean-Luc Nancy, *Le discours de la syncope: I. Logodaedalus* (Paris: Flammarion, 1976).

Notes for Chapter 3

1. This text figures in a study of Kant in *Imago Mundi—Topologie de l'Art* (Paris: Galilée, 1986).

2. I will use here the abbrevations *CJ* for the *Critique of Judgment* and *CPR* for the *Critique of Pure Reason*.

3. Cf. Jacques Derrida, "Le parergon" in *La vérité en peinture* (Paris: Aubier-Flammarion, 1978); *The Truth in Painting*, trans. Geoff Bennington and Ian McLeod (Chicago: University of Chicago Press, 1987), and "Economimesis," in *Mimesis des articulations* (Paris: Aubier-Flammarion, 1975); "Economimesis," trans. R. Klein, *Diacritics* 11 (1981): 3–25.

4. In the introduction to the *CJ* (23; 10), Kant distinguishes between four sites of the inscription of concepts: *Feld* ("field"), *Boden* ("territory"), *Gebiet* ("domain"), and *Aufenthalt* ("domicile," in Philonenko's translation).

5. In the sense of the *aei* of which Heidegger speaks in "Ce qu'est et comment se détermine la physis," trans. François Fédier, in *Questions*, vol. 2 (Paris: Éditions Gallimard, 1968), 222, "On the Being and Conception of ΦΥΣΙΣ in Aristotle's Physics B,1," trans. Thomas J. Sheehan, *Man and World* 9 (1976): 244–45: "That which each time awaits itself in its proper place....In the *aei* that which in view is the arresting oneself, remaining, being belated—and in the truth in the sense of the entry into presence."

6. The process of stating is an apophantics.

7. The aspect is not the subjective face of things but the entry into presence.

8. Doubtless also in the greatest possible proximity to Cezanne when he speaks of the "imposing simplicity of nature."

9. Which inscribes itself in the term itself in the *Er-* of *Erhabenes*, whereby the passage to the limit is indicated.

Notes for Chapter 4

1. See in particular Jacques Derrida, "Economimesis," in *Mimesis désarticulations* (Paris: Aubier-Flammarion, 1975).

2. *Marges de la philosophie* (Paris: Minuit, 1972); *Margins of Philosophy*, trans. Alan Bass (Chicago: University of Chicago Press, 1982).

3. See "The Sublime Offering" by Jean-Luc Nancy in this volume.

4. Martin Heidegger, *Nietzsche*, vol. 1, (Pfullingen, Germany: Neske, 1961), 93–94; *Nietzsche*, vol. 1, *The Will to Power as Art*, trans. David Farrell Krell (San Francisco: Harper & Row, 1979), 79. Page numbers cited below parenthetically in the text, first the German, then the English edition.

5. Cf. "Der Ursprung des Kunstwerkes," in *Holzwege* (Frankfurt am Main: Vittorio Klostermann, 1950); "The Origin of the Work of Art," in *Poetry, Language, Thought*, trans. Albert Hofstadter (New York: Harper & Row, 1975). Page numbers for quotations from this text cited below parenthetically in the text, first the German, then the English edition.

6. Elsewhere, Heidegger's own proposal or project goes in this direction. For example: "Actually it cannot be denied that the interpretation of being as idea results from the basic experience of being as φύσις. It is, as we say, a necessary consequence of the essence of being as emerging *Scheinen* ("seeming," "appearing," "radiance"). And herein there is no departure, not to mention a falling-off, from the beginning. No, that is true. But if the essential *consequence* is exalted to the level of the essence itself and takes the place of the essence, what then? Then we have a falling-off, which must in turn produce strange consequences. And that is what happened. The crux of the matter is not that physis should have been characterized as idea but that the idea should have become the sole and decisive interpretation of being," *Introduction to Metaphysics*, trans. Ralph Manheim (New Haven, Conn.: Yale University Press, 1959), 182. The German edition is *Gesamtausgabe, vol. 40: Einführung in die Metaphysik* (Frankfurt am Main: Vittorio Klostermann, 1935), 191. Page numbers given below parenthetically, first of the German, then of the English edition.

7. Cf. Jean-Marie Pontevia, *Tout a peut-être commencé par la beauté* (Bordeaux: William Blake, 1985), 14–19.

8. In "The Origin of the Work of Art," this concerns essentially both "the imagination as faculty of the soul" (to derive the essence of the *Lichtung* from it does not by any means allow one to think the *Lichtung* with "a sufficient import" [58–59; 72–73]) and the beautiful defined simply as an object of pleasure (see "Epilogue," 67; 81). Jacques Derrida remarks in "Parergon" (*La vérité en peinture* [Paris: Flammarion, 1978], 42, 54; *The Truth in Painting*, trans. Geoff Bennington and Ian McLeod [Chicago: University of Chicago Press, 1987], 35, 46), the proximity of this Heideggerian reservation to the Hegelian reservation: for Hegel as for Heidegger the third *Critique* remains a "theory of subjectivity and judgment."

9. The two succeeding moments, Wagner and Nietzsche, are evidently comprehended within this closure.

10. The same text, in its first version, considers as most essential the fourth moment of the six Heidegger re-counts in the course on Nietzsche as the fundamental moments of the history of aesthetics.

11. Heidegger himself accepts the cathedral at Bamberg and in all probability also Dürer ("The Origin of the Work of Art," 26; 41 and 63; 77).

12. Heidegger's treatment of Wagner is overwhelming. In 1936, the sense of such a condemnation could escape no one. Despite everything, Wagner's enterprise is recognized in its principle, that is, in its "desire to safeguard the essentiality of art in existence": beyond its merely summary aspect, the total work of art has the merit of attempting to be "a celebration of the community of the people; religion itself." What saves Wagner, in other words, is his *artistico*-political project. What condemns him is that this project is merely *aesthetico*-political (by which trait it justly presides over the NationalSocialist project itself). Between Hegel (religion) and postromanticism (the "community" [*Gemeinschaft*] of the people), the path is as narrow as possible.

13. Cf. 56–57; 69. I allude here to the elaboration upon the opening-clearing trait (*Riß*) by means of which the work can be defined in a sense as the *archi-inscription*

of struggle (discord or *différend*) between earth and world (φύσις and τέχνη, cryptophilia and unveiling, reserve and clearing), which is the struggle truth *is*, an elaboration in which the (Aristotelian) concept of μίμησις is re-elaborated from top to bottom and in which Heidegger attempts to attain a determination of "figure" or "stature" (*Gestalt*) anterior to the eidetic grasp of the being as such. That the word *Gestalt* cannot be avoided and that the work is in this context expressly conceived in terms of *Ge-Stell* (which twenty years later will be the word for the essence of technology) indicate with sufficient precision the precariousness of this elaboration (which says nothing whatsoever about a possible eidetic overdetermination of the thematics of trait and trace).

14. And no longer comprehended, in accordance with its initial greatness, as *knowing*. After having once again recited the decline of this initial comprehension, Heidegger notes in passing, "it suffices to know that the distinction between matter and form emanates from the domain of the fabrication of the tool, that this distinction did not originally belong to the domain of art in the strict sense…but was applied to it retroactively." The eidetic determination of the being is contemporaneous with the interpretation of τέχνη as labor.

This probably explains that Heidegger's entire effort after the *Rektoratsrede* (that is, after the Nietzschean engagement of fundamental ontology in the aesthetico-political project of Nazism) is applied to removing τέχνη from the domain of *Einbilden*, from the formation and the imagination by which Heidegger thinks, from *Sein und Zeit* on, the transcendence of *Dasein* as *Weltbildung*: formation (imagination) of the world. In this sense, to paraphrase one of his formulae, the *Riß* (the archi-trait) of "The Origin of the Work of Art" is the negative, in the photographic sense, of the *Bild* of "Vom Wesen des Grundes." What is solicited there, in a difficult way, is the Kantian schematism, that is, the transcendental imagination conceived as τέχνη. Hence, the attempt in "The Origin of the Work of Art" to relate the essence of τέχνη to "language, myth, and poetry" (*Sprache, Sage, Dichtung*). The essence of art is *Dichtung* because *Dichtung* attests that art is not simply the imagination of the being but rather its revelation, which is something else altogether.

15. This is demonstrated perfectly by Éliane Escoubas in "Kant or the Simplicity of the Sublime" in this volume.

16. Above all, this does not mean that there is no Kantian aesthetics. I am forced here—by way of exception—to oppose Nancy's argument, who writes, in "The Sublime Offering" in this volume: "It is aesthetics, as a regional philosophical discipline, that is refused in the thought of art seized by the sublime. Kant is the first to do justice to the aesthetic at the heart of what one can call a 'first philosophy,' but he is also, and for this very reason, the first to suppress aesthetics as a part or domain of philosophy. As is well known, there is no Kantian aesthetics. And there is not, after Kant, any thought of art (or of the beautiful) which does not refuse aesthetics and which does not interrogate in art something other than art." I am not sure, first of all, that after Kant there is no thought of art "which does not refuse the aesthetic and which does not interrogate in art something other than art." Schiller and Hegel, for example, don't even for an instant refuse the aesthetic, and even the counter-aesthetics of Nietzsche that is, virile aesthetics (aesthetics from the viewpoint of the creator) remains by defin-

ition an aesthetics. This means that to "interrogate in art something other than art" is not perhaps a sufficient criterion: the more Hegel grants art the function of the presentation of truth (the Idea, the Spirit, the Absolute, and so on), the more he affirms the autotelic character of art, and the more he consecrates aesthetics to the grasping of art in its essence. The movement is doubtless equivocal if, through the very logic of the essence, art is thus explicitly apprehended only in its end (telos and completion). But this is also for Hegel the condition of the possibility of all aesthetics. I do not thereby contest that "it is aesthetics, as a regional philosophical discipline, which is refused in the thought of art seized by the sublime." I contest this indeed all the less as, concerning Hegel, one can only with difficulty speak of a "thought of art seized by the sublime." But I do think that these matters are not quite so simple. For Kant, in any case, such a refusal, if it takes place, is internal to aesthetics itself. Certainly, Kant's gesture, invoking Baumgarten's word for a first philosophy, is not at all indifferent—if only through its contrast with Hegel's weak gesture of resigning himself, in the absence of a better term and in view of its dominant usage, to call the science or philosophy of art an "Aesthetics." But if Kant's gesture is not indifferent, it is not indifferent precisely with regard to the earthquake it provokes in first philosophy: in ontology. With regard to the object of the first part of the *Critique of Judgment*, however, it is indifferent: a theory of the judgment of taste is just what one calls in the eighteenth century an aesthetics. The title (the name) does not change at all the matter at hand (the concept). In addition, the Analytic of the Beautiful, like that of the sublime, unfolds in the *name* of the "Analytic of the faculty of aesthetic judgment," and thus in the name of the "Critique of the faculty of aesthetic judgment," and they are not for no reason a theory of pleasure taken in the beautiful object or in the affect (emotion) of the sublime. There is indeed a Kantian aesthetics, systematic and complete. In sum, I would not speak of a "refusal" of aesthetics but of a collapse of aesthetics: the sublime disrupts the aesthetic, breaks up its very ground. And I would add: the fact that the aesthetic collapses at the touch of the sublime *in this sense* does not apply to the sublime in general: an entire thought of the sublime, of the excess of the beautiful, accommodates itself easily to the aesthetic (exemplarily, Burke).

17. In the tradition, for example, of Burke, "the terrible" (*das Schreckliche*) is a word for the sublime. This is perhaps because Vasari, not knowing how to characterize Michelangelo's great statuary, the *Moses* in particular, uses this word (aesthetically) as one says for the first time.

18. Georg Wilhelm Friedrich Hegel, *Theorie Werkausgabe*, vol. 13: *Vorlesungen über die Ästhetik*, ed. Eva Moldenhauer and Karl Markus Michel (Frankfurt am Main: Suhrkamp, 1970), 82; *Aesthetics: Lectures on Fine Art*, trans. T. M. Knox, vol. 1 (Oxford: Oxford University Press, 1975), 55.

19. Georg Wilhelm Friedrich Hegel, *Theorie Werkausgabe*, vol. 17: *Vorlesungen über die Philosophie der Religion*, ed. Eva Moldenhauer and Karl Markus Michel (Frankfurt am Main: Suhrkamp, 1970), 63–64; *Lectures on the Philosophy of Religion*, vol. 2, *Determinate Religion*, ed. Peter C. Hodgson, trans. R. F. Brown, P. C. Hodgson, and J. M. Strauss, with the assistance of H. S. Harris (Berkeley: University of California Press, 1987), 134–37.

20. For example when Hegel condenses his interpretation of the (sublime) relation that Genesis installs between God and His creation into this formula: "God strong in the weak" (64; 136).

21. Jean-Joseph Goux, "Moïse, Freud, la prescription iconoclaste," in *Les Iconoclastes* (Paris: Seuil, 1973); *Symbolic Economies: After Marx and Freud*, trans. Jennifer Curtiss Gage (Ithaca, N.Y.: Cornell University Press, 1990), 134–50.

22. Friedrich Schiller, "Uber Anmut und Wurde," *Werke*, vol. 2 (Munich: Karl Hansen, 1966), 391–92; "On Grace and Dignity," *Complete Works*, vol. 8 (New York: Collier, 1902), 187–88.

23. Sigmund Freud, "Der Moses des Michelangelo," *Studienausgabe*, vol. 10, ed. Alexander Mitscherlich, Angela Richards, and James Strachey (Frankfurt am Main: Fischer, 1969), 217. English in *Character and Culture*, ed. Philip Rieff (New York: Macmillan, 1963), 103. Page numbers are given below parenthetically, first in German then English.

24. This description is inspired by Winckelmann's analysis of *Laocoon*, which Schiller had quoted in "Über das Pathetische" (432; 159). For reasons that have to do with the problematic and internal economy of "Über Anmut und Würde," Schiller does not present this description as the description of a work of art. However, Schiller does allude in a note to the essays, "Über das Pathetische" and "Vom Erhabenen."

25. Longinus, *On the Sublime*, trans. with commentary by James A. Arieti and John M. Crossett (New York: Mellen, 1985). The French edition used by Lacoue-Labarthe is: *Du sublime*, ed. and trans. Henri Lebègue (Paris: Les Belles Lettres, 1965) *On the Sublime*, XXXV: "astonishing [for man] is always the paradox [τὸ παρ-άδοξον]." Chapter, section, and page references (the latter from the English edition) given hereafter parenthetically in text).

26. It seems to me that this is the second exemplary case of what happens to the figure of Moses when it enters the realm of art under the surveillance of the aesthetic discourse. Manifestly, a failure occurs. But perhaps Schönberg's struggle against the "form of opera" is sublime in its turn. The film version by Straub indeed suggests as much, insofar as it integrates the libretto for the third act—which, in contrast to the first two acts, had been written independently of the music—in the form of a merely spoken dialogue. This immense breakdown, which occurs in one of the rare scenes, if not the unique scene, of a modern tragedy, retrospectively casts a new light on the rest of the work. The work begins to oscillate between (sacred) oratorio and tragedy, that is, the (philosophical) didactic poem, which are Kant's three modes (*Critique of Judgment*, §52) of "sublime presentation," "insofar as" such a presentation "belongs to the fine arts." I will attempt to speak of this again elsewhere.

27. And in fact the entire speculative epoch understands it as such.

28. I permit myself to refer the reader to my essay, "Le dernier philosophe," in *L'imitation des modernes* (Paris: Galilée, 1986).

29. *Theorie Werkausgabe*, vol. 12: *Vorlesungen über die Philosophie der Geschichte*, ed. Eva Moldenhauer and Karl Markus Michel (Frankfurt am Main:

Suhrkamp, 1970), 272; *The Philosophy of History*, trans. J. Sibree (New York: Dover, 1956), 220.

30. We know that in the following editions of this text, Heidegger explicitly remarked this *Geschehnis* as *Ereignis*.

31. "Das Geheure ist im Grunde nicht geheuer."

32. Edmund Burke, *On the Sublime and Beautiful* (New York: Collier, 1909), 114.

33. "Das seiende Sein," *Einführung in Die Metaphysik* (Tubingen: Max Niemeyer, 1966), 27; *Introduction to Metaphysics*, trans. Ralph Manheim (New Haven, Conn.: Yale University Press, 1959), 35.

34. This is the proper effect of contamination which the thought of the sublime entails, as has been revealed by Neil Hertz, "A Reading of Longinus," *The End of the Line: Essays on Psychoanalysis and the Sublime* (New York: Columbia University Press, 1985), 1–20; originally published as "Lecture de Longin." *Poétique* 15 (1978); and Michel Deguy, "The Discourse of Exaltation (Megalogoreuein): Contribution to a Rereading of Pseudo-Longinus," in this volume. Sublime poetry, says Michel Deguy, "does what it says."

35. Only Michel Deguy, to my knowledge, has done justice to the thought of Longinus by listening attentively to the Greek. It is he, in fact, who opened up the path I am following here.

36. A bit further on (VIII, 1), concerning the five sources of the sublime, Longinus uses the same logic: the five sources, he explains, "presuppose as their common foundation orational talent, without which there is nothing at all." More precisely, there is a προϋποκείμενον, which is the δύναμις in speaking, the "faculty" (*Kraft*, in Kant's sense) or the power of speaking. And that is the gift. This is the reason why, thereafter, it is necessary to distinguish among the various sources between those that come from φύσις (the disposition to elevated thought and the disposition to vehement and enthusiastic pathos) and those that come from τέχνη (the "fashioning of figures" [σχήματα] "noble diction" [φράσις] and "arrangement" [σύνθεσις] "with a view to the dignity and elevation of the style"). Longinus's thought is moreover so unwavering on this point that, much later (XXXIX, 1 and 3), the principal element of σύνθεσις ("harmony") conceived in accordance with the model of musical harmony as a harmony of language, or of the arrangement of words, is said to be innate to humans (which explains, in turn, the power of its effects: it moves the soul).

37. Aristotle, *La poétique*, trans. Roselyne Dupont-Roc and Jean Lallot (Paris: Seuil, 1980), 43; *Poetics*, trans. James Hutton (New York: Norton, 1982), 47.

38. I share here without reservation Emmanuel Martineau's conclusion in his essay "Mimèsis dans la 'Poétique': pour une solution phénoménologique," *La revue de métaphysique et de morale* (1975). See also the essays concerning art in *La Provenance des espèces* (Paris: P.U.F., 1982). I ought to indicate, moreover, that—apart from the reading of "The Origin of the Work of Art" and Jean Beaufret's "*Phusis et technē*" (in *Aletheia*,

no. 1–2)—my point of access to the text of the *Poetics* was the same sentence from the *Introduction to Metaphysics* which Martineau cites *in fine*: "Thus τεχην provides the basic trait of δεινον, the violent; for violence [*Gewalt-tätigkeit*] is the use of power [*Gewalt-brauchen*] against the overpowering [*Überwältigende*]: through knowledge it wrests being from concealment into the manifest as the essent" (169; 160).

39. I permit myself again to refer the reader to *L'imitation des modernes* (Paris: Galilée, 1986).

40. Demosthenes is moreover placed under the sign of Phoebus Apollo: "But all of a sudden, as if animated by a divine breath, and so to speak possessed by the spirit of Phoebus, he offers his sermon in the name of the heroes of Greece" (XVI, 2).

41. Walter Benjamin, "Goethes Wahlverwandschaften," *Gesammelte Schriften*, vol. I, 1, ed. Rolf Tiedemann and Hermann Schweppenhäuser, with Theodor Adorno and Gershom Scholem (Frankfurt am Main: Suhrkamp, 1980), 194–97 (translation mine, J.L.).

Notes for Chapter 5

1. Jean-François Lyotard, "Sensus Communis," *Paragraph: The Journal of the Modern Critical Theory Group* 11 (1988): 1–23.

2. Philippe Lacoue-Labarthe, *La fiction du politique: Heidegger, l'art et la politique* (Paris: Christian Bourgeois, 1987); *Heidegger, Art and Politics: The Fiction of the Political*, trans. Chris Turner (Oxford, U.K.: Blackwell, 1990).

3. See Jacob Rogozinski, "The Gift of the World," in this volume.

Notes for Chapter 6

1. This text came directly out of the work done during the course of Jean-François Lyotard's seminar on *The Question of the Sublime* in 1985–86 at the Collège International de Philosophie. It is equally indebted to Jean-Luc Nancy's "The Sublime Offering" and to the other studies published in the "permanent tribune consecrated to the sublime" of the review, *Po&sie*. (At the moment of finishing this text, I have just become aware of the last piece in this dossier, Philippe Lacoue-Labarthe's "The Sublime Truth," *Po&sie* 38 (1986): 83–116, which elucidates in great depth, if in a somewhat different "light," several of the motifs I have addressed here.)

2. Cf. the extraordinary book by O. Chedin, *Sur l'esthétique de Kant* (Paris: Vrin, 1982), 172–75, as well as Lyotard, "Sensus Communis," in *Paragraph: The Journal of the Modern Critical Theory Group* 11 (March 1988): 1–23.

3. The hypothesis of the "chaotic aggregate" is evoked and held at a distance throughout the "First Introduction," *Première introduction à la critique de la faculté de juger*, trans. L. Gillermit (Paris: Vrin, 1982), 28–29, 39–40, 80, etc.; *Critique of Judg-*

ment: Including the First Introduction, trans. Werner S. Pluhar, with a foreword by Mary J. Gregor (Indianapolis: Hackett, 1987), 397–98, 405, 437, passim. On the hypothesis of a "step-mother nature," cf. *Critique of Practical Reason* (159; 152). As in the passage of the first *Critique* on "cinnabar," it is a matter of limit hypotheses, where Kant places the entirety of his thought in question, designating a point of the impossible which he immediately revokes or pushes away. Cf. also in the *Essay on Radical Evil* the insupportable eventuality of an absolute or "diabolical" evil. The sub-limited has to do with the impossibility of this limit.

4. Monstrous horror is, in the strict sense, unpresentable. In turn, sublimity is for Kant "nearly too big for all presentation." But, as Derrida remarked, it thus becomes impossible—or *nearly impossible?*—to fix the limit, to "delimit the trait of the *almost too*." Cf. "Parergon" in *La vérité en peinture* (Paris: Flammarion, 1978), 143–44; *The Truth in Painting*, trans. Geoff Bennington and Ian McLeod (Chicago: University of Chicago Press, 1987), 125–26. This effect of the limit or of the threshold is doubtless what demarcates Kant's thought of the sublime from the Heideggerian motif of the *Ungeheuer*: the Kantian sublime is not monstrous "e-normity"—it holds itself on its border, is appointed as its guard.

5. Immanuel Kant, "D'un ton grand seigneur adopté naguère en philosophie," in *Première introduction à la critique de la facultè de juger*, trans. L. Gillermit (Paris: Vrin, 1982), 108. This text has been analyzed by Derrida in *D'un ton apocalyptigue adopté naguère en philosophie* (Paris: Galilée, 1983); "Of an Apocalyptic Tone Recently Adopted in Philosophy," *Oxford Literary Review* 6 (2): 3–37. On the "proliferation" of veiled Isis at the end of the eighteenth century, one can profitably read *La quête d'Isis* by J. Baltrusaitis (Paris: Perrin, 1967).

6. Cf. Heidegger, *Kant et le problème de la métaphysique*, trans. Alphonse de Waelhens and Walter Biemel (Paris: Gallimard, 1954), 247, passim; *Kant and the Problem of Metaphysics*, 4th ed., trans. Richard Taft (Bloomington: Indiana University Press, 1990), 131–32, passim.

7. Martin Heidegger, *Interprétation phénoménologique de la* Critique de la raison pure (Paris: Gallimard, 1982), 157, 324.

8. The concept of a "transcendental violence" appears in an already old text by Derrida, "Violence et métaphysique," *L'écriture et la différance* (Paris: Seuil, 1967); "Violence and Metaphysics," in *Writing and Difference*, trans. Alan Bass (Chicago: University of Chicago Press, 1978), which affirmed that "the present, the presence of the present, and the present of presence, are all originally and forever violent" (195; 133). One will find no reelaboration of this concept in the subsequent works of Derrida.

9. Martin Heidegger, *Kant et le probleme de la métaphysique*, trans. Alphonse de Waelhens and Walter Biemel (Paris: Gallimard, 1953), 156; *Kant and the Problem of Metaphysics*, 4th ed., trans. Richard Taft (Bloomington: Indiana University Press, 1990), 67.

10. Cf. the still insufficiently elaborated "pre-critical" notation, of the *Observations on the Feelings of the Beautiful and the Sublime*, trans. John T. Goldhwait (Berkeley: University of California Press, 1960), 49–50: "A long duration is sublime. If it belongs to

the past, it is noble. If one situated it in an infinite future, it is frightening....Haller inspires a sweet fear when he represents future eternity, a solid admiration when he describes past eternity." Thirty years later, in the little text "On the End of All Things," Kant returns to this abyss of the future eternity: "This thought makes one shudder...it exercises however a kind of fascination....It is of formidable sublimity." This temporal dimension of the sublime is strangely absent from the *Critique of Judgment.*

11. I preserve here the interrogative mode. If the Kantian analytic of the sublime seems to place in question anew, and in part, Heidegger's Kant-interpretation—that of the "first" Heidegger, essentially of the Kant-book of 1929—can one conclude that it excedes also the thought of the "second" Heidegger, and notably in his conception of the truth as *aletheia*? For the moment, I prefer to reserve my response. (On this point, it is difficult for me to share the determination that leads Lacoue-Labarthe to privilege the sublime veiling of Isis to the detriment of the "negative" sublime of Moses and the Jewish law. But this decision—still too Hegelian?—would call for long analyses.)

12. Cf. in the "Transcendental Dialectic," the critique of the paralogisms of rational psychology, notably the "paralogism of personality" (*CPR*, 293–97; 341–44). On this question, I permit myself to point to my own "A l'appel de l'étranger: sur Kant et la question du sujet" forthcoming in *Critique.*

13. I have to take my distance here from the orientation followed by Jean-Luc Nancy in "The Sublime Offering," in this volume. According to him, "It is not exactly a matter of the infinite in the unlimitation on which the feeling of the sublime touches," and "the infinite does not exhaust the Being of the unlimited, it does not offer, as it were, its true moment."

14. Immanuel Kant, *La Dissertation de 1770,* trans. Paul Mony (Paris: Vrin, 1976), 57, *Kant's Inaugural Dissertation of 1770,* trans. William J. Eckoff (New York: n.p., 1894), reprinted (New York: AMS, 1970), 60. References given parenthetically below for D1770, forst French, then English editions.

15. Cf. G. Granel, *L'équivoque ontologique de la pensée kantienne* (Paris: Gallimard, 1970), 87–94. Cf. also G. Lebrun, *Kant et la fin de la métaphysique* (Paris: Plon, 1970), which refers to the occurrences of this other thought of the infinite in the entirety of Kant's works; see notably his analysis of the sublime, 420–26.

16. On this question, one can consult, despite its insufficiencies, M. Clavel, *La Critique de Kant* (Paris: Flammarion, 1980), 203, 245, passim.

17. Immanuel Kant, "Du premier fondement de la différence des régions dans l'espace (1768)," in *Quelques opuscules précritiques,* trans. S. Zac (Paris: Vrin, 1970), 98; "Concerning the Ultimate Foundation of the Differentiation of Regions in Space (1768)," in *Selected Pre-Critical Writings and Correspondence with Beck,* trans. G. B. Kerferd and D. E. Walford (Manchester: Manchester University Press; New York: Barnes and Noble, 1968), 43. We will have to return to this question of the body and the flesh in Kant.

18. Immanuel Kant, *Anthropologie d'un point de vue pragmatique,* trans. Michel

Foucault (Paris: Vrin, 1979), §16, 37; *Anthropology from a Pragmatic Point of View*, trans. Mary J. Gregor (The Hague: Nijhoff, 1974), 33.

19. Martin Heidegger, *Nietzsche*, vol. 3, *La volonté de puissance en tant que connaisance*, trans. Pierre Klossowski (Paris: Gallimard, 1971), 439; *Nietzsche*, vol. 3, *The Will to Power as Knowledge and Metaphysics*, trans. Joan Stambaugh, David Farrell Krell, and Frank A. Capuzzi, ed. David Farrell Krell (San Francisco: Harper and Row, 1987), 80.

20. Martin Heidegger, *Interprétation phénoménologique de la* Critique de la raison pure (Paris: Gallimard, 1982), 137.

21. "To grasp the One, and All in One, in an ideal act....Form for itself constitutes in this case the Being of the thing. Form makes up here all of the object. *Forma dat esse rei.*" Immanuel Kant, *Gesammelte Schriften*, vol. 21 (Berlin: de Gruyter, 1936), 91–92; *Opus Postumum*, trans. J. Gibelin (Paris: Vrin, 1950), 36–37.

22. Immanuel Kant, *Opus Postumum*, trans. J. Gibelin (Paris: Vrin, 1950), 163. The conception of the "passage" that dominates these last writings of Kant prolongs, in a certain sense, the project of the *Critique of Judgment*, but in a profoundly modified problematic.

23. But just what sort of community is this? Is it not forcing things a bit to pass from "logical" community (*Inbegriff*) to ontological community, or rather "transcendental" community (*Urgemeinschaft*)—conceived as the "chorus of monads" or the carnal agreement of the world? Have we sufficiently taken into account the Kantian concept of common sense, as the "indeterminate accord of our faculties a priori," which would permit a better articulation of these two acceptations or modes of community? In the hopes of returning to this question, let us point here again to Lyotard's study of "Sensus communis," as well as to the recent work of Jean-Luc Nancy on *La communauté désœuvrée* (Paris: Galilée, 1986).

Notes for Chapter 7

1. Peter Szondi, *Versuch über das Tragische* (Frankfurt am Main: Suhrkamp, 1964), 13. Reprinted in *Schriften I*, ed. J. Bollack, et al. (Frankfurt am Main: Suhrkamp, 1978); *On Textual Understanding and Other Essays*, trans. Harvey Mendelsohn (Minneapolis: University of Minnesota Press, 1986), 44. Page numbers cited below parenthetically in the text, first the German, then the English edition.

2. F. W. J. Schelling, *Sämmtliche Werke*, ed. K. F. A. Schelling (Stuttgart: Cotta, 1856–61), I, 3, 96ff. The French edition cited by Courtine is *Premiers écrits (1794–95)*, trans. Jean-François Courtine (Paris: P.U.F., 1987). Page references to German edition given parenthetically in text below.

3. "Art is the sole true and eternal organon and at the same time document of philosophy, which testifies ever and ceaselessly to that which philosophy cannot present externally....Art is for the philosopher the highest thing, because it as it were

opens to him the holy of holies" (I, 3, 627–28). Further: "Art is the sole and eternal revelation and the miracle which, even if it had only existed once, would have to convince us of the absolute reality of that highest thing" (I, 3, 618).

4. Schelling has directly in mind Professors J. F. Flatt, F. G. Süskind, G. C. Storr, and G. C. Rapp, of the Tübinger *Stift*. See also Schelling's letter to Hegel in Schelling, *Briefe und Dokumente*, ed. H. Fuhrmans, 1:56. On the intellectual situation in Tübingen, see also Fuhrmans 1:9–54.

5. Cf. also the preface to *Vom Ich* (I, 2, 77–78): "Give man consciousness of what he is and he will soon learn to become what he ought to be. Give him *theoretical* self-respect and *practical* self-respect will soon follow."

6. Cf. Hölderlin's letter to his brother from 2 June 1796, Friedrich Hölderlin, *Sämtliche Werke (Stuttgarter Hölderlin-Ausgabe)*, ed. Friedrich Beissner, vol. VI, 2 (Stuttgart: Cotta, 1958), letter no. 121; *Essays and Letters of Theory*, ed. and trans. Thomas Pfau (Albany: SUNY Press, 1988), 135: "To be sure, we also frequently long to transcend from this intermediary state of life and death into the infinite being of the beautiful world, into the arms of eternally youthful nature from where we emerged." Cf. the poem "An die Natur" in *Sämtliche Gedichte*, ed. Detlev Lüders, vol. 1 (Bad Homburg: Athenäum, 1970), 142–43.

7. Cf. also the Preface to *Vom Ich* (I, 2, 77). For its part, the ninth letter already evoked the *Schrecknisse der Schwärmerei*.

8. Cf. in particular G. E. Lessing, "Hamburgische Dramaturgie," *Werke*, vol. 6 (Frankfurt am Main: Deutscher Klassiker, 1985; *Hamburg Dramaturgy*, trans. Helen Zimmern ([1890]; reprinted New York: Dover, 1962, and also the indispensable work by Max Kommerell, *Lessing und Aristoteles. Untersuchung über die Theorie der Tragödie*, 4th ed. (Frankfurt am Main: Vittorio Klostermann, 1970). Cf. also W. Schadewaldt, "Furcht und Mitleid?" in *Hellas und Hesperien* (Zürich and Stuttgart: n.p., 1960), 346–88.

9. Cf. Friedrich Hölderlin, "Die Bedeutung der Tragödien," *Sämtliche Werke*, IV, 1, 274; *Essays and Letters on Theory*, 89: "Die Bedeutung der Tragödien ist am leichtesten aus dem Paradoxon zu begreifen."

10. Aristotle, *Poétique*, trans. R. Dupont-Roc and J. Lallot (Paris: Seuil, 1980), chap. 13 and note 2, 238ff; *Poetics*, trans. James Hutton (New York: Norton, 1982), 57–58.

11. Friedrich Hölderlin, "Über den Unterschied der Dichtarten," in *Sämtliche Werke*, IV, 1, 266–67; *Essays and Letters on Theory*, 83. Cf. also Jean-François Courtine, "De la métaphore tragique," *Revue philosophique de Louvain* 18 (1983): 37–62.

12. It is not at all a matter here of the *intuitus originarius* rejected by Kant but of that which is for Schelling the condition of any determination of the pure ego. Schelling derives this notion from a fleeting indication in Fichte's *Recension des Aenesidemus* and explicitates it in his texts from *Vom Ich* (I, 2, 106–7).

13. Friedrich Hölderlin, "Über den Unterschied der Dichtarten," *Sämtliche Werke*, IV, 1, 268–69; *Essays and Letters on Theory*, 83–89.

14. "This objectivity of the intellectual intuition, which is generally recognized and indeed impossible to deny, is art itself. For the aesthetic intuition is precisely the intellectual intuition become objective. Only the artwork reflects back to me what in no other way can be reflected, that absolute Identity [*jenes absolut Identische*] which even in the ego has already divided itself; therefore that which the philosopher allows to divide itself in his first act of consciousness is streamed back toward him, through the miracle of art, out of its products—and in no other way is it accessible" (I, 3, 625).

15. It is perhaps a hypothesis of this kind which would make it possible for one to comprehend Hölderlin's remark in his letter to Niethammer of 24 February 1796 (no. 117): "Schelling, whom I encountered before my departure, is content to collaborate in your journal and to be introduced by you to the world of the learned. We did not agree about everything, but we did agree that the new ideas can be most clearly exposed in the form of letters. You ought to know that his new convictions have made him take a better path, before the worse had been pursued to its end." In the "New Letters on the Aesthetic Education of Man," announced in the same post, Hölderlin intended to oppose himself to Schelling's emphasis on *practice*: "I would like to find the principle which explains to me the divisions within which we think and exist, but which possesses also the power to overcome the opposition between subject and object, between our ego and the world, between reason and revelation—on the theoretical level, by means of the intellectual intuition, without recourse to our practical reason. We need the aesthetic sense in order to do that." Cf. also the letter to Schiller from 4 September 1795 (no. 104): "I am attempting to prove that…the unity of subject and object in an absolute ego…is possible without a doubt on the aesthetic level, in the intellectual intuition, but is possible on the theoretical level only by way of an infinite approximation."

16. Cf. also Hölderlin's letter to Neuffer of 10 October 1794 (no. 93).

17. Cf. the theme of *Gott in uns* abundantly orchestrated by Hölderlin.

18. Samuel Taylor Coleridge, *Biographia Literaria*, ed. George Watson (London: Dent; New York: Detton, 1956; reprint ed., 1967), chap. 10, 91ff.

19. Karl Philip Moritz, *Schriften zur Ästhetik und Poetik*, ed. H. J. Schrimpf (Tübingen: n.p., 1962). On Moritz, see Peter Szondi, *Studienausgabe der Vorlesungen*, vol. 2: *Poetik und Geschichtsphilosophie I*, ed. S. Metz and H. H. Hildebrandt (Frankfurt am Main: Suhrkamp, 1974), 82ff., and T. Todorov, *Théories du symbole* (Paris: n.p., 1977), 179ff.

20. Friedrich Schiller, "Über das Erhabene," *Werke*, vol. 2 (München: Karl Hansen, 1966), 610; "On the Sublime," *Complete Works*, vol. 8 (New York: Collier, 1902), 140–41.

21. D. Jähnig, "Schelling," *Die Kunst in der Philosophie*, vol. 2 (Pfullingen: n.p., 1969), 239.

22. Cf. *System des transzendentalen Idealismus* (I, 3, 620–21); *System of Transcendental Idealism (1800)*, trans. Peter Heath (Charlottesville, Va.: University Press of America, 1978), 225–26.

23. Cf. also Friedrich Schlegel, "Entretien sur la poésie," in *L'absolu littéraire. Théorie de la littérature du romantisme allemand,* ed. Philippe Lacoue-Labarthe, (Paris: Seuil, 1978), 289ff; *Dialogue on Poetry and Literary Aphorisms,* trans. Ernst Behler and Roman Struc (University Park: Pennsylvania State University, 1968).

24. On the proteus-like concept of chaos in Friedrich Schlegel, see X. Tilliette's richly documented note in *Schelling, une philosophe en devenir,* vol. 1, 430–32, note 51. Cf. also Franz Norbert Mennemeier, *Friedrich Schlegels Poesiebegriff* (Munich: n.p., 1971), 25ff.

25. Cf., for example, this magnificent declaration in the *Aphorismen zur Einleitung in die Naturphilosophie:* "What I can boast of? The one thing that was granted to me: that I have proclaimed the divinity of the individual, the possible identity of all knowledge without difference of object, and thus the infinity of philosophy" (I, 7, 143–44).

26. I, 5, 687–88. One does well to recall here what Hegel instructed at the threshold of his lectures on Aesthetics: "It was absolutely necessary [after the Kantian attempt to reunify freedom and necessity on the level of aesthetics] to conceive in a more all-encompassing fashion the unity such as it realizes itself between freedom and necessity, the universal and the particular, the rational and the sensible" (G. W. F. Hegel, *Vorlesungen über die Ästhetik,* in *Theorie Werkausgabe,* ed. Eva Moldenhauer and Karl Markus Michel, vol. 13 (Frankfurt am Main: Suhrkamp, 1970), 89; *Aesthetics,* trans. T. M. Knox (Oxford: Clarendon Press, 1975), 60–61.

Notes for Chapter 8

1. Cf. Anthony Blunt, *Nicholas Poussin* (New York: Bollingen Foundation, 1967), vol. 2, plate no. 187.

2. Cf. W. Friedlander and A. Blunt, *The Drawings of Nicolas Poussin* (London: Warburg Institute, 1963), vol. 4, no. G 21, pl. 235. An attentive study of both the picture in Frankfurt and the sketch tends to convince me that it is indeed at least partially a view of the Coliseum.

3. Cf. Nicolas Poussin, *Correspondance,* ed. C. Jouanny, Archives, vol. V, 424. Cf. Félibien, *Entretiens,* (1985): 408, and my study of this painting published in *Versus* 29 (May–August 1981): 59–75.

4. I use the term *transcendental* in the Kantian sense of a critique of knowledge with a view to its foundation, that is, to the rigorous establishment of the conditions of possibility or legitimacy of its statements. The storm is in a sense the figure—perhaps it would be better to say the metafigure—of the conditions of possibility and legitimacy of representation (in painting).

5. Pliny, *Natural History*, trans. H. Rackham, vol. 9 (Cambridge: Harvard University Press, 1938–63), XXXV, paragraph 96, page 333. Cf. J. Bialostocki, "Une idée de Léonard réalisée par Poussin," *Revue des arts* 4 (1954): 131ff.

6. That the storm is indeed the "subject" of Poussin's painting would be proven *e contrario* by the magnificent description provided by Giovan Pietro Bellori in his life of Poussin (*Le Vite dei pittori, scultori e architetti moderni*, 1672, (Turin: Einaudi, 1976) 472), which opens with the drama in the foreground: "Corre Tisbe con le braccia aperte sopra il cadavero dell'amato Piramo e forsennata precipita a morte, mentre la terra e'l cielo e tutte le cose spirano funesto errore" ("With her arms open wide Thisbe runs upon the corpse of her beloved Piramns and in a mad frenzy plunges to her death, while the earth and the heavens and all things exude deathly error"), and which, after the description of the storm, finishes with the lion's attack: "questo é il leone che ha cagionato la morte agl'infelici amanti" ("This is the lion that caused the death of the unfortunate lovers").

7. I use these two terms in the sense in which Derrida introduces them in *De la Grammatologie* (Paris: Minuit, 1967), 208; *Of Grammatology*, trans. Gayatri Chakravorty Spivak (Baltimore: Johns Hopkins Press, 1974), 144–45, with respect to writing: the proper names of the "narrative actors" of the *storia* are added to their painted representation, they are "a surplus, a plenitude enriching another plenitude, the *fullest measure* of presence," but they supplant, only 'add themselves to' in order to 'replace' as if "somewhere [in the painted representation] something can be filled up *of itself*, can accomplish itself, only by allowing itself to be filled through sign and proxy". Consider the two definitions of *comble* ("plenitude"): (1) (Latin *cumulus*, with the sense of *culmen*, "ridge" or "pinnacle"). In architecture, a ridge, coping, or crown of an edifice. Part of an edifice on which the roof immediately rests. Figuratively, a culminating point, the highest degree. (2) (Latin *cumulus*, "heap") that which is above an already full measure; figuratively, surfeit, abundance.

8. Ovid, *Metamorphoses*, trans. Mary M. Innes (Baltimore: Penguin, 1955), IV, l. 58–169.

9. The tomb of Ninus is the monument that the painter highlights pictorially by illuminating it among the edifices of the town which appear in the background and to the right. As Blunt has written (*Nicolas Poussin* [New York: Phaidon, 1967], 204ff.), we have here a strange building composed of a square base supporting a pyramid. "His model is a number of tombs near Jerusalem known to Poussin through engravings from *Il Devotissimo Viaggio di Gerusalemme*, by Giovanni Zuallardo, Rome 1587" (205, n. 76). One finds this tomb again in the *Moses Exposed* of Oxford's Ashmolean Museum and in Chantelou's *Order*. In the latter picture one can recognize the same architectural structure, but reversed, as that in *Pyramus and Thisbe*: the tomb is tied to another construction (a monumental pilaster in the *Order*, a palace in *Pyramus*) by a bridge. On the values of this articulation, see our study on the *Order* (forthcoming). It is worth noting that this articulation is not effective in the represented space and its figures but visually operative on the level of the representation, not without having complex symbolic and ideological effects and investments.

10. One will note here that the introduction of the names Pyramus and Thisbe (cf. note 6 above), permits the projection, onto the representational whole, of a network of proper names, that is, of terms designating singularities or individuals: herein too, we see the phenomenon of fulfillment and supplementation.

11. On the "direct" genesis of colors in Poussin, see the wonderful study by V. Bätschmann, *Dialektik der Malerei von Nicolas Poussin* (Munich: Prestel, 1982), 39ff. See in particular the central position of red (*rubeus*) between the two extremes of white (*albus*) and black (*niger*) in the diagrams of the colors by Franciscus Aguilonius, *Opticum Libri Sex* (Antwerp, 1613), Prop. XXXIX, 40, and of Athanasius Kircher, *Ars magna lucis et umbrae* (Rome: 1646), book 1, part 3, fol. 65, quoted and reproduced on page 43 of Bätschmann. Amongst the *analogia rerum* of the colors Kircher gives, one finds, for white, *lux pura, ignis, intellectus, Deus*; for black, *tenebrae, terra, ignorantia, planta*; and for red, *lux colorata, Aurorae medium, error, homo*.

12. If one begins with this relation white → red → black, one can perhaps better understand Poussin's famous comment with regard to Caravaggio: "This man has come into the world to destroy painting," although one should not forget that Poussin adds that Caravaggio was in possession of the entirety of the art of painting. Cf. my *Détruire la peinture* (Paris: Galilée, 1977), 177ff. in particular.

13. This reciprocal expression of the allegories and symbols is one of the meanings one can give to the "delectation" which Poussin considered as the goal of pictorial mimesis. Cf. Anthony Blunt, *Nicholas Poussin* (New York: Bollingen Foundation, 1967), 1:354–56.

14. I have developed this point in greater detail in my article in *Versus* (see note 3 above) with reference to the stoics' theory of time and representation—*phantasia*.

15. This point is, it seems to me, essential to an understanding of one key element in Poussin's aesthetics, the notion of variation of which the famous letter on the musical modes provides an analogy in the arts other than painting, the music of "our worthy, ancient Greeks" and the epic poetry of Virgil. Each of the levels of a painting is determined by its "modal" difference from the others: to speak only of genres, the first level is history painting; the second level, bucolic or pastoral painting; the third, landscape painting. Each of the levels would comprise an emblematic "figure," specific to its order, of the modal variation of this level with respect to the others of which the singular contemplation within the totality of the tableau—in a word, the comprehension—would have for effect the delectation of the soul in the "intellectual beauty of the allegory," to adopt Blunt's expression. These references to the musical modes and to the "sounds of the speech" of Virgil's poem are to be placed in direct relation with what we write below on Dante and the Bible.

16. Marin has used here the translation established on the basis of the Hebrew, and in accordance with the translation by E. Fleg, published in *Sémiotique et Bible* 10 (June 1978). Cf. in the same number "Rudiments d'analyse. La tour de Babel," 1–26. I [trans.] am citing the Revised Standard Version (New York: Nelson, 1952). Book, chapter, verse, and page references to this edition given in text. The French translation used by Marin differs from the English here in that it begins with something like: "And

all the earth was one tongue and one speech," thus emphasizing the unity of speech—as opposed to the "one language and few words" of the Revised Standard Edition. This nuance is important to Marin's commentary in the paragraph immediately following this quotation.

17. Dante, "The *De Vulgari Eloquentia*," trans. A. G. Ferrers Howell, in *The Latin Works of Dante* (London: Dent, 1940), I, IV, 12. Page references given below parenthetically in text. Cf. Roger Dragonetti, "Dante face à Nemrod. Babel mémoire et miroir de l'Éden?" in *Critique*, issue on "Le mythe de la langue universelle" 387–88 (August–September 1979): 690–706, to which the present essay owes much.

18. Boileau, preface in *Œuvres complètes, le Traité du sublime ou du merveilleux dans le discours, traduit du grec de Longin (1674)* (Paris: Pléiade, 1966), 338; Longinus, *On the Sublime*, trans. with commentary by James A. Arieti and John M. Crossett (New York: Mellen Press, 1985), VII, 353.

19. On the presence in the Renaissance, in conjunction with the reading of Vitruvius, of "revealed forms comprising three exemplary models for architects: Noah's ark, the tabernacle in the desert, and the Temple in Jerusalem," see J. Rykwert, *La maison d'Adam du paradis* (Paris: Seuil, 1976), chap. 6, "Raison antique et grâce chrétienne," particularly p. 142ff. Cf. also Félibien, book 1 of his *Recueil historique de la vie et des ouvrages des plus célèbres architectes* (1687): "It is also true that this people held architecture in particularly high esteem, doubtless because this art has something divine about it and because in the Holy Scriptures God was not merely called 'sovereign Architect of the Universe' but he himself wanted to instruct Noah upon how he should build the Ark. He prescribed also to Moses the manner in which he wanted his tabernacle to be built, infusing the workers who served the legislator with the gift of the knowledge and wisdom necessary to the execution of his orders. Finally, David and Solomon followed, in the construction of the City and Temple of Jerusalem, nothing other than the idea God gave them." The essential reference is Saint Augustine, *Works*, vol. 2, *The City of God*, trans. Marcus Dods (Edinburgh: Clark, 1872), book 15, chap. 26, p. 98, and "Contra Faustum," in *Sanctit Aureli Augustini De utilitate credendi* (Vindobonae: Tempsky, 1891), XII, 30, where the Church Father shows how the Ark was organized and ordered by God through Noah and how it signifies Christ and the Church—in all details of its construction—as well as man—in its specific proportions. Augustine is himself in turn picking up on an ancient tradition illustrated by Philo, *Quæstiones et Solutiones in Genesim*, trans. Charles Mericier (Paris: Cerf, 1979) 2:2, and above all Ambrose, "De Noe," in *Corpus Sciptorum Ecclesiasticorum Latinorum*, vol. 32, part 1, *Sancti Ambrosii Opera*, ed. C. Shenkl (Vindobonae: Tempsky, 1897), 411–97.

We could trace this "fundamental" tradition from Francesco Giorgio's *Harmonia Mundi*, I, 3, 3, 101, to the allusions to it in *Le Dicerie Sacre, la seconda sopra la Musica, parte prima*, 243, by Giovanbattista Marino, the Cavalier Marin, a text with which we know Poussin to have been familiar.

Finally, is it not the Ark that reappears with a typically classical sobriety in Antonie Arnauld and Pierre Nicole, *La Logique ou L'Art de penser*, ed. Pierre Clair and François Girbal (Paris: Presses Universitaires de France, 1965), part 1, chap. 4, 52–54; *The Art of Thinking*, trans. James Dickoff and Patricia James (Indianapolis: Bobbs-

Merrill, 1964), 45–47, the famous chapter on the ideas of things and the ideas of signs, in order to illustrate that category of signs where the sign is joined to the thing it signifies?

20. G. W. F. Hegel, *Der Geist des Christentums: Schriften 1796–1800*, ed. Werner Hamacher (Frankfurt: Ullstein, 1978), 373; "The Spirit of Christianity and Its Fate," *Early Theological Writings*, trans. T. M. Knox (Philadelphia: University of Pennsylvania, 1971), 182. Page references given below parenthetically in text.

21. G. W. F. Hegel, *Theorie Werkausgabe*, vol. 13–15, *Vorlesungen über die Ästhetik*, ed. Eva Moldenhauer and Karl Markus Michel (Frankfurt am Main: Suhrkamp, 1970), 14:276; *Aesthetics: Lectures on Fine Art*, trans. T. M. Knox (Oxford: Clarendon Press, 1975), 2:638. Volume and page references given below parenthetically in text, first in German, then in English.

22. Dante, *Inferno*, in *The Divine Comedy*, trans. John Sinclair (New York: Oxford University Press, 1977), III, l, 25–30, 47–47. Canto, line, and page references given below parenthetically in text.

23. This point seems to me to be essential, i.e., the passage from a universal unity founded upon the transcendent Name, the other Name, to a totalitarian absolute founded upon a proper name. This is one of the working hypotheses of my *Le portrait du roi* (Paris: Minuit, 1981), which has to do with the political and ethical sublime.

24. Cf. Nicolas Poussin, *Correspondance*, letter of 24 November 1647, 371ff.

25. Cf. Longinus and his first definition of the sublime: "sublimity, brought out at just the right moment, disperses all in its path, like lightning, and shows first of all the power of the orator in all of its density," Longinus, *On the Sublime*, trans. with commentary by James A. Arieti and John M. Crossett (New York: Mellen Press, 1985), §I, 3, 9.

Notes for Afterword

1. "Nonce: 1. *For the nonce*: a. For the particular purpose; on purpose; expressly. Often with infinitive or clause expressing the object or purpose. *Obs.* exc. *dial.*...b. In Middle English poetry (and later, more or less archaically) used as a metrical tag or stop-gap, with no special meaning; frequently riming with *bones* and *stones*...c. For the occasion; hence (in modern use), for the time being, temporarily...3. *For the very nonce*: for the express purpose. *At the very nonce*: at the very moment...4. attrib. *nonce-word*, the terms used in this Dictionary to describe a word which is apparently used only for the nonce (see vol. I, p. xx); similarly *nonce-use*, etc.," *Oxford English Dictionary*, 1971.

2. "Kants These über das Sein" in *Wegmarken* (Frankfurt am Main: Klostermann, 1978), 439–73; "Kant's Thesis on Being," trans. Ted E. Klein, Jr. and William E. Pohl, in *The Southwestern Journal of Philosophy*, 4.3 (1973): 7–33. Page references of

German text hereafter given parenthetically in text. Translations my own unless otherwise indicated.

3. Cf. *Phänomenologische Interpretation von Kants Kritik der reinen Vernunft*
(1927–28) (Frankfurt am Main: Klostermann, 1977); *Kant und das Problem der Metaphysik* (1929) (Frankfurt am Main: Klostermann, 1973); *Kant and the Problem of Metaphysics*, trans. Richard Taft (Bloomington: Indiana University Press, 1990); *Die Frage
nach dem Ding: zu Kants Lehre von den transzendentalen Grundsätzen* (1935–36)
(Tübingen: Niemeyer, 1962), in English: *What is a Thing?*, trans. W. B. Barton, Jr., and
Vera Deutsch (Chicago: Henry Regnery Company, 1967).

4. The essay by Lacoue-Labarthe exposes and pursues the implications of this
tension at some length.

5. For one of the crucial texts on position and reflexion in German romanticism
from Fichte on, see Walter Benjamin, "Der Begriff der Kunstkritik in der deutschen
Romantik," in *Gesammelte Schriften*, ed. Rolf Tiedemann and Hermann Schweppenhäuser, I.1 (Frankfurt am Main: Suhrkamp, 1980), 18–40. On position in its relation to
the sublime, see the analyses of Paul de Man, which speak indeed incessantly of position in connection with the performative function of language. Without going into
those analyses, I shall let the quotation of two relevant passages suffice here. On Baude-
laire's "Correspondences": "The problem is not so much centered on *phorein* as on
meta (trans...), for does "beyond" here mean a movement beyond some particular
place or does it mean a state that is beyond movement entirely? And how can
"beyond," which posits and names movement, ever take us away from what it posits?"
("Anthropomorphism and Trope in the Lyric" in *The Rhetoric of Romanticism* (New
York: Columbia University Press, 1984), 251; and on Hegel's sublime: "the spirit posits
itself as that which is unable to posit, and this declaration is either meaningless or
duplicitous...by moving from knowledge to position, all is changed. Position is all of a
piece, and moreover, unlike thought, it actually occurs," "Hegel on the Sublime," in
Displacement: Derrida and After, ed. Mark Krupnick (Bloomington: Indian University
Press, 1983), 148. The present essay could be regarded as a kind of reconstruction of
the "philosophical" discourse on position in Kant and Heidegger, and therefore as a
kind of background or propaedeutic to the reading of de Man, especially to a reading
of his perhaps excessively derisive attitude toward Heidegger.

6. On the question of the principle of sufficient reason, see in particular: "Vom
Wesen des Grundes"(1929), in *Wegmarken* (Frankfurt am Main: Klostermann, 1967),
and *Der Satz vom Grund* (Pfullingen, Germany: Neske, 1957).

7. The essay above by Michel Deguy on Longinus carries out an extraordinary
interpretation of the function of "synthesis" in Longinus's sublime, which would bear
comparison with the problem of synthesis and its failure (the failure of the schematizing imagination) in the Kantian sublime.

8. Page references to Kant given below parenthetically in text first for the German, then English editions, as indicated in "Note on the Translation" above.

9. Escoubas stays very close to this analysis, and extends it into the analytic of

the sublime, in "Kant, or the Simplicity of the Sublime." Rogozinski provides a remarkable reading of the problematic of time in the Kantian sublime, which cuts to some degree against the grain of Heidegger's Kant-book, in "The Gift of the World."

10. In order to measure the distance between the Kant-reading Heidegger offers here and the Kant-reading he offers in *Kant und das Problem der Metaphysik*, one has to determine the relation between transcendental reflexion and transcendental imagination. If for the earlier Kant-study the point was to emphasize that the transcendental imagination was the ground of the inner possibility of ontological knowledge, for the later Kant-study the point is to emphasize that the reflexion of reflexion is the furthest point of Kant's thought of Being. Minimally, what the two approaches have in common is that each instance or process—transcendental imagination and transcendental reflexion—involves the space between the concept and the intuition, between the intelligible and the sensible, and each thus marks the point at which some other remains to be thought.

11. Cf. "Moira (Parmenides, Fragment VIII, 34–41)," *Vorträge und Aufsätze* (Pfullingen, Germany: Neske, 1954), 223–48.

12. Klein and Pohl render this as "the self-illuminating–enduring presence of that which is for a while" (32).

13. In the "Amphiboly," Kant speaks of the reflexion of reflexion as a regard cast upon the *Zustand des Gemüts* (466), "the state of the soul." One way in which the motif of the *Gemüt* is retained and displaced throughout Heidegger's texts is through his rather strange use of the terms *vermuten, anmuten, Mut*, and variations on these. Cf. in particular the analysis of *das Anmutende* in "Aus einem Gespräch von der Sprache," *Unterwegs zur Sprache* (Frankfurt am Main: Klostermann, 1895), 133.

14. Indeed, Heidegger uses this term to refer also to Kant's relation to the tradition *he* inherits (440).

15. In the introduction to the *Kritik der Urteilskraft* Kant writes that the understanding leaves the notion of the "super-sensuous substratum" indeterminate, that the force of judgment gives the notion determinability, and that reason determines this notion through its practical law (108; 33). The determinable is determined as matter, and the determination as form, in the section on the "Amphiboly" in the first *Critique*.

16. This would confirm what Paul de Man argues about Heidegger's relation to philosophers, without deciding one way or the other his reading of Heidegger's relation to Hölderlin in "Heidegger's Exegeses of Hölderlin," in *Blindness and Insight* (Minneapolis: University of Minnesota Press, 1983), 246–66.

17. Cf. Heidegger's telephonic connections have recently been worked out in some detail in Avital Ronell, *The Telephone Book* (Lincoln: University of Nebraska Press, 1990). In the course of her brilliantly athetic considerations on the telephone as synecdoche for technology, Ronell does not call upon Heidegger's use of the word *Ortsnetz* in "Kant's Thesis." This use implicitly characterizes telephony as what is neither merely a technical product nor purely of the essence of technology as encountered in

thinking, but undecidably both. It "places" telephony, that is, on the border of *Ge-stell*, at the (non)site of its greatest endangerment. I indicate the connections of the telephonic *Ortsnetz* to the voice of conscience below, if somewhat obliquely or fleetingly, by discussing Heidegger's replacement of reflexion with the aporetic structure of the assumption of the (sublime gift of) measure, both in Heidegger and in Kant. Although I do not attempt here, as does Ronell, to address the psychoanalytic implications of the telephonic network of position, one might cast the net further, in order to catch the distant echo of the maternal super-ego (for Ronell, the Other summoned by the telephone) in the word *Netz* in *Ortsnetz*: "netzen" means to moisten or sprinkle, as for example with tears of mourning.

18. Within "Kant's Thesis," for example, it would be the *Sache* of the thinkers, "immer wieder das Sein als das Denkwürdige zu zeigen, und zwar so, daß dieses Denkwürdige als ein solches im Gesichtskreis der Menschen verbliebe"(440), and cf. 441 passim.

19. Lyotard's essay in this volume pursues the sense in which the sublime is allied with a certain kind of "interest," and explores the economic implications of the metaphor of "interest." Lacoue-Labarthe argues against Heidegger's "thesis" in the *Nietzsche* lectures regarding aesthetics, in order to propose that the eidetic determination of the being is not a necessary condition of its consideration in terms of *phainesthai*, and that in Kant's exemplification of the sublime through the veil of Isis something of this non-eidetic mode of appearing gives itself to be read. Page references to *Nietzsche*, vol. 1 (Pfullingen, Germany: Neske, 1961) are given in text; translations are my own.

20. I discuss the relations between the Kantian and Schillerian versions of the sublime in "Vom Spiegelbild zur Unterschrift: Paul de Mans Ideologiebegriff und Schillers Dramen," in *Ästhetik und Rhetorik: Lektüren zu Paul de Man*, ed. Karl Heinz Bohrer (Frankfurt am Main: Suhrkamp, 1993), forthcoming.

21. The contributions to this volume by Nancy and Rogozinski pursue the problematic of the "gift" in great detail. And in Heidegger, the most relevant text is perhaps: "...dichterisch wohnet der Mensch..." *Vorträge und Aufsätze* (Pfullingen, Germany: Neske, 1954), 181–98.

22. I am stealing this term from Jean-Luc Nancy, in particularly in *Le discours de la syncope. 1. Logodaedalus* (Paris: Flammarion, 1976).

23. In an extraordinary essay on the Kantian sublime, *Spacings—of Reason and Imagination in Texts of Kant, Fichte, Hegel* (Chicago: University of Chicago Press, 1987), John Sallis has read the Kantian "Critique of Aesthetic Judgment" as in "a position ever so close to the dissolution of every position" (85) and has tried to show— thinking now more in terms of Heidegger's Kant-book than in terms of his late Kant-essay—how in aesthetic judgment there is a "certain erosion of the structure of reflective judgment in its initial, cognitively related sense" (97), such that judgment tends to become "assimilated to imagination"(98). My reading of the "signifier" for reflexion here—*Überlegung* as "over-laying"—would essentially corroborate this view,

if from a slightly different (and slightly less visual or theoretical) angle, where it is less a matter of the image than of the letter.

24. Cf. *Kant und das Problem der Metaphysik*, where Heidegger argues that Kant's use of the term *Gebrauch* ("use") to refer to the way in which thinking relates to intuition compromises Kant's insight into the privilege of intuition over thought, which would be the mere servant of intuition (64).

25. Cf. Paul de Man, "Phenomenality and Materiality in Kant," in *The Textual Sublime: Deconstruction and its Differences*, ed. Hugh Silverman and Gary Aylesworth (Albany: State University of New York Press, 1990), 93–6. Cf. the inscription of this passage in the thought of the unlimitation of the limit in Nancy's essay in this volume.

26. Jean-François Courtine's essay traces the development of this nonKantian, *idealist* conception of the sublime, as a reconciliation of infinite with finite, through Schelling's career and in connection with Schelling's speculative theory of tragedy.

27. Cf. Jean-François Lyotard, "Sensus Communis," in *Paragraph: The Journal of the Modern Critical Theory Group* 11.1 (March 1988): 1–23, as well as the recent studies of the notion of community by Maurice Blanchot, *La communauté inavouable* (Paris: Minuit, 1983), and by Jean-Luc Nancy, *La communauté désœuvrée* (Paris: Christian Bourgeois, 1986): *The Inoperative Community* (Minneapolis: University of Minnesota Press, 1991), ed. Peter Connor, trans. Peter Connor, Lisa Garbus, Michael Holland, and Simona Sawhney. On Nancy's thought of community, see the essays collected in Miami Theory Collective, eds., *Community at Loose Ends* (Minneapolis: University of Minnesota Press, 1991). In this collection, which appeared subsequent to the (de)composition of the present essay, Jean-Luc Nancy ("Of Being-in-Common" [2]) imitates, as he puts it, Kant's thesis on Being: "In imitation of a statement of Kant's thesis on being, one could say: *Community is not a predicate of being or of existence. One changes nothing in the concept of existence by adding or subtracting communitary character. Community is simply the real position of existence.*" Just as Being qua position does not add anything to the concept of the thing whose Being is posited, so community does not add anything to the concept of Being. Nancy's point here is that community does not add anything to Being because Being is already communitary. Because existence is already position, community becomes for Nancy here "the position of position" (2). This means in turn for Nancy here the *exposition* of position. What is posited is not a unitary essence but mere existence. In position, existence displaces essence, such that essentiality is deposed or exposed: "Existence is the essence, if you like, but insofar as it is posited. In the positing, essence is offered or given. That is, essence is exposed to being, or to existing, outside of being as a simple subsistence, or as an immanence" (3). This exposition of the in-common is, I believe, already communicated by Kant himself—imitating Nancy imitating himself, as it were—in the section of the third *Critique* on sensus communis. The essay by Marin in this volume discusses a Babelian sublimity which would bear "comparison" with the faculty of taste as sensus communis in Kant.

28. In *Kant und das Problem der Metaphysik*, Heidegger inscribes Kant's three questions: what can I know? what should I do? and what may I hope for? into the *meta-*

physica specialis of cosmology, psychology, and theology, respectively. This inscription would call for a long analysis, which would have to consider, for example, whether or not the second *Critique* simply articulates a psychology, and further whether the question of hope is not itself "answered" by aesthetico-teleological reflexion, etc.

29. *Vorträge und Aufsätze* (Pfullingen, Germany: Neske, 1978).

30. Thanks to John Llewelyn, Ned Lukacher, and Herman Rapaport for reading over and responding to the manuscript of this essay in its penultimate form.

INDEX

❀